The Scope
of the
Fantastic—
Theory, Technique,
Major Authors

Selected Essays
from the
First International Conference
on the
Fantastic in Literature
and Film

Edited by ROBERT A. COLLINS
and HOWARD D. PEARCE

Contributions to the Study of Science Fiction and Fantasy, Number 10

GREENWOOD PRESS
Westport, Connecticut • London, England

Library of Congress Cataloging in Publication Data

International Conference on the Fantastic in Literature
  and Film (1st : 1980 : Florida Atlantic University)
  The scope of the fantastic—theory, technique, major
authors.

  (Contributions to the study of science fiction and
fantasy, ISSN 0193-6875 ; no. 10)
  Bibliography: p.
  Includes index.
  1. Fantastic literature—Congresses. 2. Fantasy in
literature—Congresses. 3. Fantasy—Congresses.
I. Collins, Robert A.   II. Pearce, Howard D.   III. Title.   IV. Series.
PN56.F34I57 1980   809.3'0876'09   84-538
ISBN 0-313-23447-7 (lib. bdg.)

Library of Congress Catalog Card Number: 84-538
ISBN: 0-313-23447-7 (vol. 1)
ISBN: 0-313-23448-5 (vol. 2)
ISBN: 0-313-22547-8 (set)
ISSN: 0193-6875

First published in 1985

Greenwood Press
A division of Congressional Information Service, Inc.
88 Post Road West, Westport, Connecticut 06881

Printed in the United States of America

10 9 8 7 6 5 4 3 2 1

Copyright Acknowledgments

  The editors and publisher are grateful for permission to reprint from the following sources.
  Vladimir Nabokov, *Pale Fire* (New York: G. P. Putnam's Sons, 1962). Copyright © 1962 by
G. P. Putnam's Sons.
  Vladimir Nabokov, *Pale Fire* (London: George Weidenfeld & Nicholson Ltd., 1962).
  Edgar Allan Poe, "Berenice," in *The Complete Poems and Stories of Edgar Allan Poe*, ed.
Arthur Hobson Quinn and Edward H. O'Neill (New York: Alfred A. Knopf, Inc., 1946).
  Reprinted by permission of Farrar, Straus and Giroux, Inc. "Bone Bubbles" from *City Life* by
Donald Barthelme. Copyright © 1968, 1969, 1970 by Donald Barthelme.
  Donald Barthelme, "Bone Bubbles," from *City Life* (London: Jonathan Cape, Ltd., 1971).
Copyright © 1968, 1969, 1970 by Donald Barthelme.
  George MacDonald, *Phantastes* and *Lilith*, ed. C. S. Lewis (Grand Rapids, Mich.: Eerdmans,
1964).
  Edward Taylor, "The Almighty," in *The Poems of Edward Taylor*, ed. Donald E. Stanford (New
Haven: Yale University Press, 1960).

To Margaret Gaines Swann, patron of the International Conference on the Fantastic and founder of The Thomas Burnett Swann Fund. Without her generous support, the occasion for these studies could not have occurred. Lovers of the fantastic everywhere owe her a measure of gratitude.

Contents

TECHNIQUES OF THE FANTASTIC

AUTHOR STUDIES

Preface

Reality is traditionally a protean concept—every age restructures it, and the image of the resulting change in philosophical climate probably appears first in literature and its allied arts. *Realism*, the literary technique that has accompanied the dominance of physical science as a model for the real, has continued to lose ground since midcentury. Convinced that a shift in philosophical climate was well established, we issued, in late 1979, a call for papers to be read at the First International Conference on the Fantastic in Literature and Film. The consequences were astonishing: more than three hundred papers arrived in the space of a few months; two hundred were accepted for presentation. A selection of the best of those presented is included here.

Our respondents took a variety of approaches, expressing a wide spectrum of viewpoints that we have mirrored as faithfully as possible in organizing this collection and the companion volume: *The Scope of the Fantastic—Culture, Biography, Themes, Children's Literature*. The foremost concern for many critics was establishing a firm understanding of the term *the fantastic*. The half-dozen available critical treatments of the fantastic as literary genre were found to differ radically, both in technique and in the philosophical bases for definition. A corollary problem was the uncertainty over the nature of the "real," since one area of wide agreement concerned the apparent polarity of real/fantastic judgments.

Among the dozen chapters in this volume included under the rubric "Theoretical Approaches," some demonstrate the inadequacy of present theory, and others suggest the antecedents, philosophical or historical, that supply a rationale for the fantastic. Several chapters attack the narrowness of the structuralist approach, and others attempt to transcend the subject/object dualism and to "open up" theoretical perspectives without abandoning forms. There is a recurring reluctance simply to accept inherited definitions, generic distinctions, and concepts of world order. But such refusal invites the criticism that one contradicts oneself, writing sanely that all is insanity. For the reader, one major point of interest in this group of chapters may be observing the critics trying to move toward uncertainty and relativeness without falling into the void of meaninglessness and chaos.

Another area of inquiry that drew enthusiastic response concerned the techniques or strategies pursued by the authors of "fantastic" texts. Here the structural analysis of Tzvetan Todorov appeared to be the most widely adopted starting point, so much so that applications of his criteria to a text soon began to draw impatient boos or groans from audiences. Thus only the most thoughtful examples of such an approach are included in this series.

The authors to whom our respondents turned for fantastic texts were surprisingly varied, ranging from classical Greek to the postmodern and from recognized genre figures to those whose reputations seem nearly synonymous with scientific rationalism. As guest of honor at the conference, Nobel laureate Isaac Bashevis Singer inspired a number of critical essays on his work, the best of which is included here.

The surprisingly wide range of scholarly response to conference themes suggests that a general reexamination of contemporary criticism may soon be in order. Although *the fantastic* has yet to be defined in a generally satisfactory way, the perspectives supplied in this volume suggest the range of problems involved in such a definition. Meanwhile, the appeal of what may be called the "technique" is pervasive in almost all modern literatures (the authors studied include French, English, German, Spanish, Polish, American, Ukrainian, and Hebraic figures). The authors in this volume explore the literary significance of the cultural matrix; of the artists' responses to events in their own lives; and of mythic, archetypal, and psychological paradigms in relation to the fantastic. This collection and that contained in the companion volume reflect a first serious effort to explore the twentieth century's "reality crisis" through its effect on the arts, but it may be only a beginning.

We want to express our appreciation for the support and effort of the many persons who participated in this endeavor. We especially want to thank Professors Ernest Weiser, Allen Greer, William Coyle, Mary Sloane, and Jan Hokenson for their editorial assistance. For their dedicated technical support we thank Ann Hitt, Joy Schwab, and Phyllis Surbaugh.

*The Scope
of the
Fantastic—
Theory, Technique,
Major Authors*

Introduction—The Appeal of the Fantastic: Old Worlds for New

Eric S. Rabkin

> Fantasy creates an illusion of newness, of the source of human terror, and
> shows it—even if only subliminally—to be the old world of our
> prehistory, of our youthful development, of our culture's myths, or at
> least of other narratives. The psychological fantasies of fantasy may
> concern knowledge, or sex, or death, but they always give us the
> experience of control.

What makes fantasy and the fantastic so popular today? "For the past three
years," observed a recent article in *The American Bookseller*, "there has been
at least one, and often as many as three, major works of science fiction or fantasy
among the books on the national bestseller lists."[1] From the viewpoint of the
marketplace *Children of Dune*, *The Silmarillion*, *Lucifer's Hammer*, *The White
Dragon*, and *Gnomes* seem literature of a kind—and a newly significant kind at
that. In answer to my inquiry Marya Dalrymple, managing director of special
sales at Harry N. Abrams, was kind enough to confirm that *Gnomes* has become
the all-time bestselling book "of its type"—if *type* is defined as "non-fic-
tion...large-format, illustrated...expensive."[2] We cannot escape the escapism
of *Star Wars* or *Alien* or *Star Trek*. Many people believe that something new is
going on here. Why? Fantasies are wonders of childhood. We all had them,
possessed them, cherished them, created them. Fantasy was child's play. Fantastic literature and film are entertainments of adulthood—or perhaps wonders
adulterated. We buy them. Something is not quite right, but we're trying.

Our first corrective to marketplace myopia must be the recognition of the
universality of fantasy. To the literate Thomas Burnett Swann fantasy flows with
"that great stream of writing which includes...the *Odyssey*, *The Marble Faun*,
and *The Wind in the Willows*."[3] He could well have added fairy tales, gothic

romances, and space opera. From the ancient myths that Ernst Cassirer thought coeval with our very language to the writings of far-flung tomorrows, fantasy pervades human culture, that is, fantasy pervades humanity. In the introduction to the Penguin edition of *Tales from the Thousand and One Nights* (1973), N. J. Dawood suggested that the story of "Aladdin and the Enchanted Lamp" has been "presented to so many generations all over the world that it can perhaps be rightly described as the most renowned story invented by man."[4] We can begin to investigate this new phenomenon of fantasy by examining the old folk tale of the Orient.

Aladdin, you will remember, "was a headstrong and incorrigible good-for-nothing," so much so that "his father, grieving over the perverseness of his son, fell into an illness and died."[5] Soon an evil Moorish magician, claiming to be Aladdin's uncle, singles him out to retrieve a battered lamp from an underground treasure hoard. Aladdin cannot quite climb back out, weighted down as he is with gems he thinks are fruits, but when the impostor refuses to hoist him up without first receiving the lamp, Aladdin disobeys, and in retaliation the magician seals the ground above the boy. At that moment Aladdin recognizes the falseness of the magician's claims, a recognition that is the beginning of Aladdin's education. As it is written, "whoever possessed the lamp acquired beauty, wealth, and all knowledge." Aladdin escapes the cell by accidentally activating the jinnee in the ring the magician had given him for protection and in the course of the story comes to recognize the worth of the lamp itself, of the fruits that are gems, of the love of a beautiful woman, and of the "Sultan of China" as a worthy father-in-law and lord. He becomes married and respected. But the magician, learning of his success, comes stealing back again in disguise to capture the lamp. In the famous compressed phrase of the Andrew Lang edition (1898), he roams the streets offering "New lamps for old!" Such an exchange, clearly, is fantastic; the apparent fool trails behind him a jeering crowd. Aladdin's wife, who "knew nothing of the lamp or its magic powers," gives away her husband's prize possession, because she "merely wished to see what manner of whim it was that drove the Moor to change old things for new." By the use of the jinnee of the lamp the Moor removes Aladdin's palace and wife to a secret place, but Aladdin again accidentally activates the jinnee of his ring who in turn transports Aladdin to the neighborhood of his wife, where, by use of her wiles and a sleeping drug, Aladdin is able to behead the magician and return with increased fame to China. For good measure the Moor's younger brother, another magician, tries to revenge his brother's death, but Aladdin dispatches him as well and lives happily, finally succeeding the Sultan.

What shall we make of this tale? At the thematic level the story concerns knowledge. The lamp, an ancient symbol for knowledge, lights Aladdin's mind, but because he has kept it hidden from his wife, it has not enlightened her. Hence she is taken in and believes, with the crowd, that the new must be better than the old. We share Aladdin's knowledge, however, recognizing that the old lamp is really the new one, the miraculous and unique lamp just brought to light from underground, the first lamp of its age able to give its possessor command over all objects of desire. We may even feel that the invention of the tale itself constitutes the newness here, the invention of the lamp being the tale's great contribution to our common culture. In a sense that is true. The truly new lamp is the old one, the lamp unearthed and containing ancient powers.

At the psychological level this story concerns family relations. Aladdin is so untrainable a lad that in effect he kills his father, the primal, illegitimate Oedipal crime. In Sophocles this leads to tragic knowledge, and Oedipus puts out the lamps of his eyes, but in this folk tale the crime leads to the entrance of the Moor, the false uncle whom it is legitimate for Aladdin to kill. The lamp, giving its possessor virtual omnipotence, indulges the most infantile fantasy, what Freud called the "omnipotence of thought." In this tale the crime ultimately leads Aladdin to care for his mother, take a bride, legitimately kill both the Moor and the Moor's brother, and succeed the Sultan as father of all people. Here the ancient Oedipal guilt is transformed into a success story of knowledge. David Grossvogel noted that "it is difficult to talk of a first reading of *Oedipus* while it is difficult to talk of anything but a first reading of a detective story."[6] The same is true of Aladdin—we all know this old story, yet we take it as new. The evil magician offers new lamps for old, but we know better. In appreciating the tale of Aladdin and in enjoying fantastic literature, we take old lamps for new.

In the third stanza of "The Raven" (1845) Edgar Allan Poe wrote that "the silken sad uncertain rustling of each purple curtain / Thrilled me—filled me with fantastic terrors never felt before." The notion that these terrors had never been felt before revives the usual idea that the fantastic concerns the fundamentally new. The *American Heritage Dictionary* defines *fantasy* as "*unrestrained* imagination," but Stephen Prickett recorded Horace Walpole's sad observation that there is "so little fancy, so little variety, and so little novelty in writings in which the imagination is fettered by no rules, and by no obligation of speaking truth."[7] W. R. Irwin defined *narrative fantasy* as "the persuasive establishment and development of an impossibility," a process that gives his book the title *The Game of the Impossible*.[8] But games function only by virtue of their rules, rules agreed upon by all participants before the games begin. When the rules are absent we have Alice's Caucus Race, a perfectly "persuasive" invention in a Wonderland in which irregularity itself becomes the rule. The evidence of Aladdin is that imagination is fettered by human needs, and a fantasy becomes persuasive only when it entices us to accept old worlds for new.

Anne McCaffrey's *White Dragon* (1978) is in part an Oedipal story and in part a pleasing indulgence in both personal and cultural atavism. The hero Jaxom's "return to his birthplace had the same inexorable quality of his decision to rescue the egg."[9] In this somewhat medievalized world of nearly tamed mythical beasts, the wisest character, Robinton, notes "that imagination relied on memory—without one, the other was impossible."[10] Fantasy is restrained by the past. The memory that Oedipus relies on is in part the cultural freight we all take on with our language, but in part it is a common experience of child development: we all reach a point at which the protective power of the parent seems an unwarranted restraint while still recognizing that the protective power of the parent has been a necessary factor in our survival. The parent could easily have killed us but did not; how can we then wish to kill the parent, or even throw off that yoke, without feeling guilt? The dragon that St. George kills is a literary figment made to be killed, to allow the expression of what we all feel but all feel we must hide. The dragon, according to the Freudians, is a phallic beast, and perhaps it is, indicating yet another common source of the human memories that restrain imagination and channel it. In *The Dragons of Eden* (1977) Carl Sagan suggested that the extraordinary frequency of dreams about snakes may recall our arboreal past: "it is easy to wonder whether the dream world does not point directly as well as indirectly to the ancient hostility between reptiles and mammals."[11] At another point Sagan considered the frequent reveries of flight reported by daydreamers in trees and saw there, too, a vestige of our arboreal, brachiating pasts. Anne McCaffrey's dragons are winged, the intelligent bearers of nearly coequal men. Perhaps in taming the prehistoric snake by making it the vehicle of our prehistoric dream of flight McCaffrey has used the memory before memory to shape our oldest world into a new.

The memory of myth arises out of our past to lend substance—and restraint— to our fantasies, not only the myths of kings but the fables of beasts and the dreams of the garden. These mythologies can themselves be changed but changed as pasts. When Hesiod substantiated his own Iron Age, he pointed to the vanished Golden Age long past. Twentieth-century writers, following on the nineteenth-century exfoliation of Norse myth, have peopled the bookstores with Conans and Elrics. The line of artists who created their own usable pasts extends through H. P. Lovecraft and William Butler Yeats to William Blake and beyond. Some new worlds depend on the prior making of the old. But in all cases the mythic past is alive in the present reading. I. B. Singer's "Esther Kreindel the Second" spoke with the mannerisms of her dead namesake, so "it was like listening to a corpse speak."[12] Poe's "Ligeia" (1838) possesses the mere body of the Lady Rowena Trevanion. The most common fantasy of our Christian world is resurrection, the old taken for new. When Swann set his *Day of the Minotaur* (1966) on ancient Crete, he fashioned a Crete recalling our own fallen age of technology: "The bronze robot Talos, guardian of the coast, lay rusting beside the great Green Sea, and no one remembered how to repair him."[13] The new arises from the resurrection of old knowledge. As Swann wrote, "I don't think of myself as escaping into a past of Fauns and Tritons and Ant-boys, but rather of fetching such creatures and their forests into the present."[14] The fantasies of the present are the revivals of the fantasies of the past, although sometimes the past may be newly made.

An excellent example of the new past is Wil Huygen and Rien Poortvliet's *Gnomes* (1976), not so much a collection of stories as a natural history or perhaps a supernatural history. But each of the supernatural facts drawn into the delineation of the world of this book recalls something from a human past. Here are the first two paragraphs from the section called "The World of Smell":

Like animals, the gnome "sees" a great deal of the world through his nose. Even if he should become blind and deaf he would still be able to recognize his whereabouts and know what was happening about him in the forest; a familiar smell guides his every step.

Man no longer has this gift, though echoes of it still return in a spring breeze, the perfume of flowers, the scent of old farm villages, or a sudden smell of the sea, which somehow remind us of a happy youth, or of days gone by. City people use their noses only to take note of cruder smells such as smoke, perfume, food, kitchen smells, body odors.[15]

Clearly, the persuasiveness of this fantasy rests in our desire to make our own older selves new again. *Gnomes* presents an old world that we *want* to make as new, and so we do.

Marya Dalrymple observed that the "hand-written script also lends a certain intimacy" to *Gnomes*, an obvious atavistic indulgence. She further suggested, about both *Gnomes* and *Faeries*, that "extensive details...such as height, weight, habits, etc....intensify their reality, and consequently their escape value."[16] This observation strikes me as profoundly true and, in at least two ways, remarkable. First, it is remarkable in that the details concern creatures that, after all, do not exist. No accretion of supposed detail can add reality to the fictive. Second, even granted this reality, one normally thinks of the desire to escape as diametrically opposed to the reality principle. Yet Dalyrymple is correct, because these details are rhetorically akin to details in any ordinary natural history, thus allowing us to be persuaded into accepting them as appropriate background against which to revitalize the old world, grant it a reality, and create a place for us to escape to.

Ian Ballantine went even further:

Can it be entirely an accident that just when energy is becoming short, the two populations, Hobbits and Gnomes, that live in energy efficient houses that are partial [*sic*] or entirely underground, are the most popular titles in literature?

The interests of young people in commanding multiple skills, in building their own housing, in natural food and homeopathy are to be found in Gnomes.

Young people's concern about preserving nature is reflected in warnings in Faeries.

The extremists and myself, would say that Gnomes and Faeries are not escape. On the contrary they give an insight into life styles of the future.[17]

It may be true that these fantasies give insight into our future, but if that is so, it follows not from the fact of young people's interest so much as from the fact that adults who sense problems look for solutions they find congenial and handy. Energy was always in short supply for the Plains Indians, but they did not build underground homes. On the other hand, when threatened with exposure, humankind has always returned to dreams of caves—or of wombs. If our future

Earth comes to look like Middle Earth it will be because people who have grown up in the heritage of our culture have so shaped it.

In addition to natural history other sorts of details may help create or revive a usable past. In *An Atlas of Fantasy* (rev. ed., 1979) J. B. Post presented authoritative-looking maps for lands from Atlantis to Zothique with stops along the way in Hell, Narnia, Oz, Poictesme, Treasure Island, and Yoknapatawpha. Most of these maps have about their drawing styles a hint of the outmoded, relics of an old world to be brought into the present and taken for new. The fact that this trick works as well for high fantasy as it does for psychological novels, for religious allegory as for adolescent adventure, indicates the thoroughness with which fantasy pervades literature and suggests that the process of renewal we speak of here is much more important and widespread than we might guess if we confined ourselves to Andre Norton's Witchworld or Edgar Rice Burroughs's Barsoom.

Post noted in the preface to his revised edition that "the ever growing interest in fantasy has inspired most publishers to want maps in their major books if for no other reason than maps are now becoming fashionable, and because 'Tolkien has them.' "[18]

The fashion is not new at all, as Post's own collection makes clear; what is new is printing technology that makes it economical to indulge this fashion. This fashion itself is a code of conventions, a set of rules like "once upon a time" or "the game of the impossible" to lend "reality and, consequently, escape value" to fiction. Tolkien's own trilogy, whether read as an antiwar novel, an adventure story, or a religious quest, is obtrusively derivative from an old world of Old English and a Celtic past, an old world made new. Other authors can appropriate Tolkien's old world or his new one, either serving as well as the old worlds for their own new creations, as with Terry Brooks's *Sword of Shannara*. In going back suggestively to other works of literature, fantasy authors make other works into their own literary pasts, just as mapmakers make white space into safe territory.

The activity of mapmaking is a taming activity, a way of coping with the wildness of the world; metaphorically, the delineation of the relations of geography settles the uncertainties that we have about our bodies. The world of the map never dies and cannot in itself experience upheaval. The great activity of Robinson Crusoe, and all of Jules Verne's sons of Crusoe, is the making of maps, the drawing of lines across the world to make the present new world a derivative of an old world. One of the greatest of such makings of a map is Thomas More's *Utopia* (1516) in which the body of that far-off island is drawn and quartered into surpriseless and perfect regularity. But all true utopias, whether or not accompanied by a drawn map, are blueprints, lines, and boundaries to contain the unknowns of human life. For such a task the future is unfit, for in the future lies uncertainty. The past, however, is nicely stable, skewered on our memories, and looking different only according to our angle of thrust. For William Morris, for example, *News from Nowhere* (1890) came back from a future identical to his imagination of the fourteenth century. The obligatory guide through the blueprint landscape at one point recognizes the "pastness" of his ostensible future: " 'it is the child-like part of us that produces works of imagination. When we are children time passes so slow with us that we seem to have time for everything.' He sighed, and then smiled and said: 'At least let us rejoice that we have got back our childhood again. I drink to the days that are!' ' "[19] All utopias, like the lands of the tales of Araby and the hero stories of myth and the forests of Gnomes and the Terra Tolkiensis, persuade us by offering old worlds for new, and the atlas goes on.

Detective stories, for example, offer us the fantasy, as W. H. Auden noted, that hidden guilt will be revealed. These are worlds of justice clearly different from our own world, worlds that will exist not in the future but in the past, in an earlier, quiet time. Grossvogel is right in asserting that Agatha Christie's world "was never more than nostalgia and illusion...the bucolic dream of England," but he was wrong in saying we could not reread Christie's world.[20] We can—and we do—when we pick up the next novel. The penchant for series reflects the stability of an old world. There is the good old world of Hercule Poirot, the good old world of Nero Wolfe, and the good old world of Ellery Queen. Each case is, like the Moor's copper lamps, trivially new; each solved tale is, like the enchanted lamp, the old unearthed with its truly new powers, the powers to tame the uncertainty of the world, to map our way through the real unknown. Arthur Conan Doyle, known for his evocations of period London, knew this and so brought his own old worlds into each new one. "The Adventure of the Speckled Band," for example, begins with literary self-reference:

On glancing over my notes of the seventy odd cases in which I have during the last eight years studied the methods of my friend Sherlock Holmes, I find many tragic, some comic, a large number merely strange, but none commonplace; for, working as he did rather for the love of his art than for the acquirement of wealth, he refused to associate himself with any investigation which did not tend towards the unusual, and even the fantastic.[21]

The fantastic in the stories of Sherlock Holmes is always explained, and so the ostensibly new is revealed as part of the old and familiar. But in the reading we get the pleasure of taking the old for the new.

Series characters or settings abound in moderately fantastic fiction, ready-made old worlds of security masquerading in each manifestation as the excitingly new so that they can finally be felt as the comfortably old. This is true in Westerns, where the good guys win, and in romances, where love conquers all. This is obviously true in the worlds of comic books. Stan Lee, the odd genius behind *Marvel Comics*, wrote that in creating his returning character of Doctor Doom, he was "trying to dream up some soul-stirring, senses-staggering, super-sensational new villain to take the comicbook world by storm."[22] How did he confirm the existence of this new character?

it wasn't till the year 1964 that we really had time to do the kind of origin tale I felt Doc Doom deserved. I wanted a saga of epic proportions, one that would make the reader really understand what motivated him, what had turned him into a villain, what made him the tragic, tortured tyrant he was. I wanted the kind of story that would have made a perfect 1940's movie, with such old time actors as Basil Rathbone, Peter Lorre, and John Carradine.[23]

What his readers are to take as new is, in short, another version of the explicitly old, complete with creation myth—and take up Doctor Doom they did. *Marvel Comics*, with Spiderman and the Hulk, is one of the outstanding publishing successes of the last two decades.

The fantastic confusion of old and new, as with future utopias from the past and Aladdin's enchanted lamp, is common. Arthur Conan Doyle's *Lost World* (1912) has chapters each of which has its name used somewhere in the chapter itself. In chapter 8, we find an interesting error. The chapter is called "The Outlying Pickets of the New World" and refers to a temporary barrier to our characters' further exploration. Within the body of the chapter the narrator wonders to himself, "Are we really just at the edge of the unknown, encountering the outlying pickets of this lost world of which our leader speaks?"[24] The word *lost* of the text has become the word *new* in the title. The archetypal lost world is the Garden of Eden, and the archetypal new world is Paradise Regained. Both are mythic lands, existing in time out of time and hence in the same time, the old and the new conflated in an image of natural harmony. Here is Doyle's description of that new/lost world, of "the fairyland beyond":

For a fairyland it was. . . .the thick vegetation met overhead, interlacing into a natural pergola, and through this tunnel of verdure in a golden twilight flowed the green, pellucid river. . . .Clear as crystal, motionless as a sheet of glass, green as the edge of an iceberg, it stretched in front of us under its leafy archway. . . .It was a fitting avenue to a land of wonders. All sign of the Indians had passed away, but the animal life was more frequent and the tameness of the creatures showed that they knew nothing of the hunter. . . .monkeys. . .chattered at us as we passed. . . .Bird life was abundant. . .while beneath us the crystal water was alive with fish of every shape and colour.

For three days we made our way up this tunnel of hazy green sunshine.[25]

The colors are the primaries of fairyland, and the tamed environment and three-day passage to resurrection is Edenic, a modern version of the ancient story revealing its roots in vegetation myths. This is, however, science fiction, the most popular branch of fantastic literature today.

Elsewhere I have discussed the surprisingly deep relationship between science fiction and fairy tales, a relationship made apparent in myriad sleeping cities and lost civilizations and evil sorcerer/scientists and lurking witch/aliens.[26] But the most important element common to both science fiction and fairy tales is Eden, our new/lost garden of hope, the fantastic future dreamed up out of our past. Once we spot Eden in the background we recognize that these two major fantastic genres also offer us old worlds for new.

A rehearsal of all hidden Edens in science fiction would require a listing of perhaps half of all science fiction. For the present discussion of the ways we are enticed to take old worlds for new, three observations suffice. First, science fiction is not set resolutely in the future but often in the past; second, that past is most commonly Edenic; and third, even the most aggressively futuristic tales may seek their resolution in Edenic devices.

To think of science fiction as set in the future is frequently an error. The setting may appear to be the future, but, as we have noted with that branch of science fiction called "utopian fiction," the future is often only the past in costume. In other cases the time of science fiction may be the actual past, carried to our characters by time machine or through the discovery of lost lands. In yet other works the science fiction is set in a timeless time of myth or even in the conventional past of fairy tales themselves: the novel of *Star Wars* begins "Another galaxy, another time," and the movie begins "A long time ago in a galaxy far, far away."

The past of science fiction is most frequently Edenic. When H. G. Wells's Time Traveller arrives in A.D. 802,701, he finds "all the world a garden." Ursula Le Guin's *Word for World Is Forest* (1972) has creatures and forest in perfect accord. Ray Bradbury's Earthmen-turned-Martian at the end of the *Martian Chronicles* (1950) blow up the technology that separates them from the land. Arthur C. Clarke's characters in *The Fountains of Paradise* (1978) sensibly "turned away from the dreams of the past. . . and walked toward the reality of the future."[27] How is that future conceived?

If we could thaw out all that water and CO_2 ice, several things would happen. The atmospheric density would increase, until men could work in the open without spacesuits. At a later stage, the air might even be made breathable. There would be running water, small seas, and, above all, *vegetation*—the beginnings of a carefully planned biota. In a couple of centuries, Mars could be another Garden of Eden.[28]

This old world for a new world is created by what Olaf Stapledon called "the Aladdin's lamp of science."[29]

One of the most resolutely futuristic works of science fiction is Poul Anderson's *Tau Zero* (1970), an excellent novel of technical detail and character analysis that follows an isolated spaceship crew from lift-off in the near future to and through, at relativistic speeds, the final collapse of the universe. Although the book is set almost entirely on the hurtling craft, it opens and closes on planetary surfaces. On the eve of departure, about to lose the world, the hero and heroine, who will finally wind up together, stroll through the Stockholm pleasure park Millesgarden. Note how this fantasyland is given its own reality by bringing into its present some references from a number of mythic pasts:

But when the sun went down, the garden seemed abruptly to come still more alive. It was as if the dolphins were tumbling through their waters, Pegasus storming skyward, Folke Filbyter peering after his lost grandson while his horse stumbled in the ford, Orpheus listening, the young sisters embracing the resurrection—all unheard, because this was the single instant perceived, but the time in which these figures actually moved was no less real than the time which carried men.[30]

Having survived the harrowing journey through the furthest possible future, the hero and heroine are finally together.

On a hill that viewed wide across a beautiful valley, a man stood with his woman.
Here was not New Earth. That would have been too much to expect. The river far below them was tinted gold with tiny life, and ran through meadows whose many-fronded growth was blue. Trees looked as if they were feathered, in shades of the same color, and the wind set some kinds of blossoms in them to chiming. It bore scents which were like cinnamon, and iodine, and horses, and nothing for which men had a name....the air was warm; and humankind could thrive here.
...''We'll need to take from the past what's good and forget what was bad....''
...Steely-scaled, with a skirling along its wings, passed overhead one of those creatures called dragons....
Then he laughed, and made her laugh with him, and they were merely human.[31]

Here is Eden again, complete with dragons, the old world given for a new, in the crystal language of fairy tales.
Fairy tales, like science fictions, often rely on the story of the Garden to structure their consolation. ''Rapunzel,'' in the Lucy Crane translation of 1886, begins like this:

There once lived a man and his wife, who had long wished for a child, but in vain. Now there was at the back of their house a little window which overlooked a beautiful garden full of the finest vegetables and flowers; but there was a high wall all round it, and no one ventured into it, for it belonged to a witch of great might, and of whom all the world was afraid. One day that the wife was standing at the window and looking into the garden, she saw a bed filled with the finest rampion, and it looked so fresh and green that she began to wish for some.[32]

Her husband successfully steals some rampion one night but on the next night is caught. The witch wants to punish him, but he quickly mentions his wife's craving. ''Then the witch said, 'If it is all as you say you may have as much rampion as you like, on one condition—the child that will come into the world must be given to me.' ''[33] How does the witch know that there is a child to be born? More importantly, how does the reader know? Simply put, the reader must race backward mentally to validate this assumption, to pick up the convention of pregnancy cravings. The garden is obviously Edenic, and man and woman are excluded. The consequences of the Fall had been toil and childbirth and death, and here we have the husband's toil and the wife's impending childbirth.

Death will follow, unless redemption intervenes. The story of Rapunzel is a sexual story in which the heroine, named after the vegetable that is itself a phallic icon, is secreted in a tower that "had neither steps nor door, only a small window above." There she lets down her hair, and the witch comes to her by day while a prince comes to her by night, until he is found out and pushed from the tower, his eyes being punctured by the thorns below, reminding us of both Oedipus and Christ. The witch abandons Rapunzel in "a waste and desert place," and the prince blindly wanders the world. Years later he stumbles upon Rapunzel who weeps into his eyes and restores his sight; their penance done, they repair to take up their dominion with their twin children conceived in the tower, a boy and a girl. The knowledge of eros, which is the temptation to fall, has been expiated, and the final characters are the family twins, a perfect male/female relationship regained/created new in a world before sex.

Notice that this version of the Fall not only recalls conventional images from the Bible story but includes standard fairy-tale conventions as well, items such as unspoken knowledge and multiplication of plot elements. One significance of generic convention has already been discussed: the recollection in one text of other previous texts provides for the current narrative world the old worlds that it can make new. In a related way the repetition of plot events, the two trips to the witch's garden, the three days of journey, and the four treasure rooms in the underground hoard Aladdin visits all serve to highlight the "madeness" of the fictional world. As Claude Lévi-Strauss wrote, "the function of repetition is to render the structure of the myth apparent."[34] The obtrusion of structure offers a narrative map and provides the older framework on which the newer text is built. In detective tales that framework is within the genre as a whole, each example vivifying the old world again. With Nathaniel Hawthorne the repeated tableaux scenes of *The Scarlet Letter* (1850) and the tale of Maule's curse in *The House of Seven Gables* (1851) serve in sophisticated ways the function that triple repetition serves more simply in fairy tales. In some of today's most sophisticated literature the surface tale seems sometimes only an excuse for dressing out the complex hidden—and somehow permanent—structures about which the texts circle, as in the self-reflexive reveries of J. L. Borges and the impossible geometries of Alain Robbe-Grillet. As convention, repetition, and structure become more significant, surface content becomes less so; the trivial newness of the narrative world may be less if the vivid involvement with the skeleton of narrative is more.

Why is the fantastic so popular today? It is popular today for the same reasons it has always been popular, although today's surface manifestations are not those of a year or a century or a millenium ago. Fantasy creates an illusion of newness, of the source of human terror, and shows it—even if only subliminally—to be the old world with which we are familiar, the old world of our prehistory, or of our youthful development, of our culture's myths, or at least of other narratives. The psychological fantasies of fantasy may concern knowledge or sex or death, but they always give us the experience of control. The road from

Oedipus may not seem at first to run from the Brothers Grimm to Jules Verne
and thence to Borges, but the path is clearer seen by the light of Aladdin's lamp.
The tale itself is a device Scheherazade uses to captivate her Caliph, to keep
him from following his custom of taking his pleasure at night and beheading his
wife the next day. The tale of Aladdin, like all other tales she tells, keeps him
in suspense. For a thousand and one nights, each night a new story, each night
the same old story. As in our supposedly modern self-reflexive literature, structure takes on an independent interest for us. We watch fascinated as, by the tale
itself, Scheherazade controls her own world and in the telling creates perhaps
the greatest example of the thousand and one ways fantasy exchanges old worlds
for new.

NOTES

1. *The American Bookseller*, July 1979, 43.
2. Marya Dalrymple, letter to author, 6 August 1979.
3. Thomas Burnett Swann, quoted in Robert A. Collins, *Thomas Burnett Swann: A Brief Critical Biography* (Boca Raton, Fla.: The Swann Fund, 1979), 10.
4. N. J. Dawood, Introduction to *Tales from the Thousand and One Nights* (New York: Penguin, 1973), 12.
5. Ibid., 165.
6. David Grossvogel, *Mystery and Its Fictions* (Baltimore: Johns Hopkins University Press, 1979), 23.
7. Stephen Prickett, *Victorian Fantasy* (Bloomington, Ind., and London: Indiana University Press, 1979), 19.
8. W. R. Irwin, *The Game of the Impossible: A Rhetoric of Fantasy* (Urbana: University of Illinois Press, 1976), 9.
9. Anne McCaffrey, *The White Dragons* (New York: Del Rey/Ballantine, 1978), 405.
10. Ibid., 175.
11. Carl Sagan, *The Dragons of Eden* (New York: Random House, 1977), 137.
12. I. B. Singer, "Esther Kreindel the Second," in *Short Friday and Other Stories* (New York: New American Library, 1965), 68.
13. Thomas Burnett Swann, *The Day of the Minotaur* (New York: Ace Books, 1966), 3.
14. Collins, *Thomas Burnett Swann*, 1.
15. Wil Huygen and Rien Poortvliet, *Gnomes* (New York: Harry N. Abrams, 1976), n.p.
16. Dalrymple, letter to author.
17. Ian Ballantine, letter to author, 13 August 1979.
18. J. B. Post, *An Atlas of Fantasy*, rev. ed. (Baltimore: Mirage Press, 1979), vii.
19. William Morris, *News from Nowhere*, in *The Collected Works of William Morris* (New York: Russell & Russell, 1966), 16:102.
20. Grossvogel, *Mystery and Its Fictions*, 52, 43.
21. Arthur Conan Doyle, "The Adventures of the Speckled Band," in *The Annotated Sherlock Holmes* (New York: Clarkson N. Potter, 1967), 1:243.
22. Stan Lee, *Bring On the Bad Guys* (New York: Simon and Schuster, 1976), 13.

23. Ibid.

24. Arthur Conan Doyle, *The Lost World* (1912; reprint, London: Pan Books, 1977), 81.

25. Ibid., 76-77.

26. Eric S. Rabkin, "Fairy Tales and Science Fiction," in *Bridges to Science Fiction*, ed. George Slusser, George Guffey, and Mark Rose (Carbondale: Southern Illinois University Press, 1980), 78-90.

27. Arthur C. Clarke, *The Fountains of Paradise* (New York: Harcourt Brace Jovanovich, 1978), 174.

28. Ibid.

29. Olaf Stapledon, "Interplanetary Man," *Journal of the British Interplanetary Society* 7, no. 6 (November 1948): 215.

30. Poul Anderson, *Tau Zero* (New York: Berkley, 1970), 1.

31. Ibid., 186-188.

32. Jakob Grimm and Wilhelm Grimm, "Rapunzel," in *Household Stories of the Brothers Grimm*, trans. Lucy Crane (1886; reprint, New York: Dover, n.d.), 72.

33. Ibid., 73.

34. Claude Lévi-Strauss, *Structural Anthropology*, trans. Claire Jacobson and Brooke Grundfest (Garden City, N.Y.: Doubleday/Anchor, 1963), 1:226.

THEORETICAL APPROACHES

A dozen approaches to the tangled skein of theory are included here. All approach two mandatory themes: the problem of the genre—defining categorical boundaries; and the prevalence of dualistic structures, especially the real/fantastic polarity, from which several papers seek a retreat into a kind of monism. Thus Peter Cersowski found, historically, that Franz Kafka and J. L. Borges effected a revolution, overturning the natural/supernatural dualism of nineteenth-century criticism, and Jan Hokenson found Jean-Paul Sartre and Albert Camus turning to the irrational as "the human" within the chaos of existence.

The Copernican Revolution in the History of Fantastic Literature at the Beginning of the Twentieth Century

Peter Cersowsky

The works of Franz Kafka and J. L. Borges represent a transcendental
kind of fantastic that is fundamentally different from the spiritualistic type
solely described by Tzvetan Todorov.

One of the most provocative points in Tzvetan Todorov's highly provocative book on the fantastic is his exclusion of twentieth-century literature from the genre. To him the end of the nineteenth century also marks the end of the history of fantastic literature. This restriction is based on his definition of *the fantastic* as the "hesitation experienced by a person who knows only the laws of nature, confronting an apparently supernatural event."[1] Todorov's sole example to demonstrate that the fantastic is no longer valid in the twentieth century is Kafka's "Metamorphosis". According to Todorov, Gregor Samsa's transformation into an insect is regarded as a natural phenomenon by the characters involved in the story. So the tension between a natural and a supernatural perspective does not exist any more, as the theorist argues. Accordingly, the characters do not experience any "hesitation" about the true nature of the text.

The question poses itself whether Todorov's definition is indeed applicable historically and, if so, to what extent this would be the case. The most convincing aspect of his argument is his hinting at the fact that in or about 1900 something decisive happened to fantastic literature, a fact that seems all the more plausible since the turn of the century was a crucial turning point in all of the arts. So why should not fantastic literature be marked by this epochal change as well? Only a completely ahistorical, inflexible theory of the genre could be blind to this perspective. If there is such a historical break, could not the typical structure of fantastic literature be replaced by a kind of literature that can be labeled "fantastic" in spite of its different structure?

In trying to tackle these problems hypothetically I first want to focus on German literature, for the turn of the century in Germany was accompanied by a decisive boom of fantastic texts. Marianne Wünsch's statement that "potentially all literature of that age is fantastic literature" may be exaggerated; yet it points towards a significant trend.[2] A recent bibliography by Jens Malte Fischer supplementing his article on "German Fantastic Literature between Decadence and Fascism" lists 167 titles, although it does not attempt to be complete.[3] A survey of these texts reveals that Todorov's conception of the fantastic would apply to them, for they are normally based on the dualistic structure of a natural and a supernatural level of experience.

This is the case with one of the most representative authors, Gustav Meyrink. His most famous novel, *The Golem*, presents the natural world of the Prague ghetto in authentic details and includes autobiographical experiences of the author.[4] But there is a supernatural counterworld revealing a spiritual dimension. It is constituted by the conception of a "world beyond" and other theories of occultism pertaining to the title figure. A similar dualism characterizes all other novels by Meyrink. In *The Green Face* the natural level is represented by the city of Amsterdam, and the supernatural crystallizes in the myth of the Eternal Jew.[5] The setting of *Walpurgisnight* once again is Prague transcended by spiritual elements.[6] *The White Dominican* combines the elements of a realistic *Bildungsroman* with religious transcendence in the Christian sense.[7] Meyrink's most complex piece of fiction, *The Angel from the Western Window*, provides an ingenious identification of a contemporary protagonist with the Elizabethan age.[8] Both he and his Elizabethan ancestor are under the spell of a spiritual dimension governed by "The Black Isais."

The occultistic or spiritualistic novel flourished during those decades apart from Meyrink's ground-breaking works. Georg Korf's *Other Side of the World*, for instance, bears the subtitle "Metaphysical Novel."[9] A citizen of the modern world, who is an employee in "one of the largest patent offices in Berlin," is taken on a journey through "the world beyond" by a messenger of this sphere (p. 1). "I hope you will realize that the disposition of your soul and your spiritual individuality do not necessarily belong to the material sphere," he explains (p. 62).

Similarly, the dualistic conception is illustrated by Karl Hans Strobl's novel *Revolution Beyond*.[10] Strobl wrote about a revolt by the underdogs of the spiritual sphere who have destroyed the order "that separates and differentiates the sensuous from the non-sensuous and who are about to oppress mankind" (p. 152).

Often the elements of the spiritual world take on allegorical significance. An example of this category can be seen in Strobl's novel *Ghosts in the Swamp*.[11] It is about the city of Vienna contaminated by tuberculosis and isolated through quarantine. The natural background is transcended by the city's becoming an allegorical realm of birth and death in general. These powers are embodied in an American, who is a man of progress and who is trying to bring about the reconstruction, the rebirth, of the death-infected city. Besides, there is the character Schembera, who works for the sake of destruction.

Meyrink's *Angel from the Western Window* contains a definition that is as simple as it is convincing: "What is meant by a 'ghost' is usually a dead person who has come back, or part of it."[12] Accordingly, all characters that live their lives of immortality in the spiritual sphere, whence they intrude upon the material world, are to be considered as ghosts.

The element of "hesitation" in Todorov's sense is evoked by a large number of the texts listed by Fischer. *The Golem* raises the question whether the spiritual experiences of the protagonist are not merely a dream of the narrator's, who falls asleep in the bed of a Prague hotel at the beginning of the novel and awakes at the end. Similarly, the motto of *Ghosts in the Swamp*, a quotation from the text itself, runs: "Perhaps all of us here... and all these events are nothing but the dream of some dying brain."[13] The same applies to Meyrink's *Angel from the Western Window*: what appears as immortality in the eyes of the protagonist is rationalized by a newspaper report. Phantoms are regarded as "hallucinations" or "jokes of sportive carnivalists" (p. 520). The hero of Hanns Heinz Ewers's novel *The Sorcerer's Apprentice*, a text that shows an outbreak of religious hysterics beyond the borderline of the natural in an isolated alpine village, is uncertain too: "Was all that merely a wild dream? Had he never left this road in order to descend into the magic valley of Scodra?"[14] Similarly, the narrator of Alexander Moritz Frey's story "The Uninhabited House," which deals with supernatural phenomena in an old house, feels "as if I had dreamed everything— or as if I were still dreaming. Then again I felt convinced by the reality of my experiences. But this conviction did not prevail, it vanished and was once more replaced by the belief in the dream."[15]

The texts mentioned so far can be said to represent the normal type of fantastic literature at the beginning of the twentieth century. In spite of their publication dates they actually exemplify a continuance of the earlier structure of the genre as it is grasped by Todorov's definition.

In 1910 Franz Kafka, whose works were all written during the same quarter of a century that brought forth such an immense quantity of fantastic literature, wrote a short story with the title "Unhappiness". In it he adopted the ghost motif with which he must have been familiar, for instance, through Meyrink's early tales. The central character is visited in his room by a "spectre." Significantly, however, there are no hints at all in Kafka's text that his spectre is a messenger from some spiritual world, a ghost representing eternal, immaterial life. Instead, it seems to be a completely integrated part of the protagonist's own world. Although the latter is, in fact, excited because of the ghost's intrusion, he is not surprised at all. He even has expected it. The spectre itself is characterized as a child, an element that would be entirely incompatible with Meyrink's or Strobl's spectres. It does not behave differently from a normal visitor, talking to the protagonist in a conversational tone. Yet this does not imply that the ghost has become part of a factual, natural world. Instead, its existence is entirely determined by the perspective of the protagonist. As a first-person narrative the whole text is written from his point of view. So there is the element of unified perspective that was described as the characteristic trait of Kafka's writings by Friedrich Beissner.[16] This is indicated not only by the fact that the ghost has been awaited by the protagonist, but in addition, the latter mentions that "your nature is mine, and as my nature prompts me to treat you kindly, you must not behave differently either."[17] The ghost obviously has appeared as a result of the hero's "unhappiness," which is described as "unbearable" while he is alone (p. 44); it seems to disappear as soon as its host is getting "tired" of it (p. 48).

Certainly, the authenticity of the ghost's existence is not questioned as it would be in the normal type of fantastic literature. But this does not at all imply that the reader is not uncertain about the visitor's true nature. At first sight the text may suggest an allegorical view of the child as an incarnation of the protagonist's "unhappiness." But then its being a child would hardly be compatible with this meaning, for the child motif in Kafka is usually related to the opposite idea, namely, happiness.[18] Still, we may try to insist on an allegorical reading. The child might be regarded as a counterfigure, an incarnation of happiness, appearing to distract the protagonist's melancholy. But what about its being described as a "spectre" then? Again, this is a motif that is never associated with unhappiness elsewhere in Kafka. So why did the ghost come to see the protagonist? What becomes of it when the confrontation is over? What about the strange conversation with one of the narrator's neighbors in which they refer to the ghost? What are the female ghosts like that are mentioned here? Can ghosts be, in fact, "fed,"as it is said (Kafka, "Unhappiness," p. 49)? There are questions upon questions raised by the text.

There is no longer a tension between the natural and the supernatural in Kafka's "Unhappiness", for the represented world is constituted wholly in the conception of the protagonist. Nevertheless, this does not bring about the end of "hesitation." Instead, there is even much more uncertainty than in the normal type of fantastic literature. Whereas in this type the reader's doubts were confined to two possibilities of grasping a text, "Unhappiness" opens a virtually unlimited range of divergent aspects.

In spite of the different subject matter, the structure of "Unhappiness" is identical with that of the "The Metamorphosis". There, too, the unity of point of view replaces the tension between the natural and the supernatural. Again, the story is seen through the eyes of the protagonist, Gregor Samsa. Significantly, the famous beginning does not say that one morning he *was* transformed into a gigantic vermin but that he "found himself...transformed"[19]. Accordingly, there is no "hesitation" in Todorov's sense either. Instead, Gregor once and for all clarifies that "it was no dream" (Kafka, "Metamorphosis," p. 71). Gregor is not even surprised at his transformation. Thus far Todorov is right.

But whereas he elsewhere mentioned the "implied reader" as a constituting element of the fantastic who, also, is to experience the uncertainty, he entirely neglected the reader's position when talking about "The Metamorphosis". As with "Unhappiness" the reader of this text is not at all free of uncertainty. Nothing could be a better proof than the vast quantity of critical appreciations of "The Metamorphosis", most of them differing widely. One of the most certain things we may say about this tale is that the problem regarding the nature and the function of Gregor's transformation has not been completely solved so far. We still are extremely uncertain about it, an experience that is structurally motivated by the one-dimensional perspective of the text.

We know that Kafka disliked Gustave Meyrink's writing because of its similes.[20] Similes can become a means to establish a transempirical dimension of meaning. This is exactly what happens in Meyrink, where the transempirical takes on the shape of the spiritualistic. So when Kafka objected to Meyrink's metaphors, he ultimately opposed his spiritualistic way of writing, which seems plausible if we consider the different structure of his own texts.

This structure also corresponds to Kafka's personal view of reality. A fragment says that "the real events can... never be reached by our feelings.... They are dream-like fictions, solely confined to ourselves". [21] There is no natural reality at all, and there cannot be any supernatural dimension either. Instead, "All is fantasy," for everything is constituted through the perspective of an individual.[22] I cannot see why the kind of literature illustrating these views should not be labeled "fantastic," the more so since it evokes not less, but much more, uncertainty than the normal type of fantastic literature.

The application of the label "fantastic literature" to Kafka can also be philosophically rooted: I am thinking of Arthur Schopenhauer's "Essay on Ghost-Seeing and on Phenomena Connected with It." Kafka had a copy of this text in his library. In any case he undoubtedly came in touch with Schopenhauer's ideas through his friendship with Max Brod, who was a great admirer of this philosopher during his early years. Schopenhauer's "Essay" is the attempt to replace the "spiritualistic" theory of ghosts by something new. Spiritualism, according to Schopenhauer, says "that man is made of two substances that differ fundamentally, a material one, the body, and an immaterial one, the so-called soul. After their separation in death the latter... influences the bodies and their senses... though it is immaterial." [23] This is the conception illustrated by the normal type of fantastic literature at the beginning of our century. It is, however, replaced by an "idealistic" or "transcendental" conception in Schopenhauer's treatise. This conception is based on the assumption that a spectral vision is also a component of the world structured by the individual perception, an assumption that, as we know, adopts Immanuel Kant's theory of subjectivity. Schopenhauer stated in his "Essay" that according to this conception, the ghost "would neither be more nor less ideal than the physical perception, which, as we know, is necessarily based on idealism" (p. 251). So the only thing that "a ghost-seer who knows his business well... would affirm, is the mere presence of an image in his perceptive intellect" (p. 249). When Schopenhauer stressed that the "primary cause" of a spectral appearance lies "within ourselves," the affinity of this point to the structure of Kafka's "Unhappiness" is not to be overlooked (p. 298). The cognitional axiom of Schopenhauer's concept, namely, Kant's theory that the basis of any experience lies in human subjectivity, is called the "Copernican revolution" in the history of philosophy. Similarly, the significant difference between Kafka and the normal type of fantastic literature can be characterized as the Copernican revolution in the history of our genre.

The relevance of Kafka's transcendental structure as a central characteristic of twentieth-century fantastic literature is indicated, for instance, by Jorge Luis Borges, who is intimately familiar with Kafka's works. Borges wrote a story under the title "Tlön, Uqubar, Orbis Tertius," which ostensibly appeared in an *Anthology of Fantastic Literature* in 1940.[24] What is it that can be called "fantastic" in this text? The subject matter does not have anything to do with ghosts anymore. "Uqubar" is the name of a country that is described in a certain edition of an encyclopedia. This is the only source from which we learn about its existence. Tlön is also an "imaginative realm," namely, a planet. It is the subject matter of Uqubarian literature, which is "of a fantastic kind" throughout, and it is also described in an encyclopedia (p. 432). The name in yet another encyclopedia, the concise form of which is *Tlön*, is *Orbis Tertius*. The origin of all that is the decision of a secret society to invent a country, a fantastic world that is to be "rather compatible with the real one" (p. 442). "The world will be Tlön," it says (p. 443). The fictional world presented by Borges is a world that is identical with the preconceptions of it. The society's idea and the articles in the encyclopedias are not to be separated from reality. The world is structured precisely as it is conceived. It is nothing but "a succession of intellectual activities" (p. 436). Every detail of Tlön is determined by this structure: to find an object is the same as to "produce" it in one's mind. On the other hand, objects actually grow indistinct as soon as they are forgotten. A doorstep is no longer there, because the beggar does not transgress it any longer.

The cognitional basis of this world picture is explicitly named in Borges's text: it is the philosophy of idealism. Borges mentioned Schopenhauer, among others, who "presents a very similar concept in the first volume of *Parerga and Paralipomena*" (p. 438). This is the volume that also contains Schopenhauer's *Essay on Ghost-Seeing*. "The world as idea"—here is the basic assumption of Borges's text, too. Even though the subject matter is different, the transcendental structure that was first illustrated by Kafka is elaborated in "Tlön, Uqubar, Orbis Tertius" as well, as is the case with most other works by Borges.

Besides, the text evokes the reader's extreme uncertainty. As the traditional dualism between the natural and the supernatural is also given up in Borges, such uncertainty is no longer restricted either to two alternatives of reading. Instead, the tale is highly complex as a whole in its labyrinthine structuring of countries and names. The same applies to the cultural activities of the three countries (or articles). Their books always contain "the neat for and against of a doctrine. A book without any self-refutation counts as incomplete'' (p. 439). Books like these were also written by Kafka. His endless chains of contradictory ideas cause the same effect of uncertainty amounting to utter confusion. As with Kafka, the confusion evoked by Borges is rooted in the all-pervasive subjective conception too.

These traits should not leave any doubt that Borges's tale is indeed a piece of fantastic literature. Together with Kafka's path-breaking works it represents a transcendental kind of the fantastic that is fundamentally different from the solely spiritualistic type described by Todorov. Both Borges and Kafka show that Todorov's point concerning the end of fantastic literature in the course of the twentieth century is wrong.

NOTES

1. Tzvetan Todorov, *The Fantastic: A Structural Approach to a Literary Genre*, trans. Richard Howard (Ithaca, N.Y.: Cornell University Press, 1975), 25.

2. Marianne Wünsch, "Auf der Suche nach der verlorenen Wirklichkeit: Zur Logik einer fantastischen Welt," appendix in *Der Engel vom westlichen Fenster*, by Gustav Meyrink (Munich: Langen Muller, 1975), 544. With the exception of Todorov's book, English translations appearing in the text are mine.

3. Jens Malte Fischer, "Deutschsprachige Phantastik zwischen Décadence und Faschismus," *Phaicon 3: Almanach der phantastischen Literatur*, ed. Rein A. Zondergeld (Frankfurt: Suhrkamp, 1978), 93-130.

4. Gustav Meyrink, *Der Golem* (Leipzig: Kurt Wolff, 1915).

5. Gustav Meyrink, *Das grüne Gesicht* (Leipzig: Kurt Wolff, 1916).

6. Gustav Meyrink, *Walpurgisnacht* (Leipzig: Kurt Wolff, 1917).

7. Gustav Meyrink, *Der weisse Dominikaner* (Vienna: Rikola, 1921).

8. Gustav Meyrink, *Engel* (Leipzig: Carl Schunemann, 1927).

9. Georg Korf, *Die andere Seite der Welt* (Goslar: H. A. Weichmann, 1914). Further references appear in parentheses in the text.

10. Karl Hans Strobl, *Umsturz im Jenseits* (Munich: Rosl, 1920). Further references appear in parentheses in the text.

11. Karl Hans Strobl, *Gespenster im Sumpf* (Leipzig: Staackmann, 1920).

12. Gustav Meyrink, *Engel* (Munich: Langen Muller, 1975), 478. Futher references appear in parentheses in the text.

13. Strobl, *Gespenster*, 5.

14. Hanns Heinz Ewers, *Der Zauberlehrling oder die Teufelsjäger* (Munich: Muller, 1909), 472.

15. Alexander Moritz Frey, "Das unbewohnte Haus," in *Phantome* (Grünwald: Haus Lhotzky, 1925), 206.

16. Friedrich Beissner, "Kafkas Darstellung des 'traumhaften innern Lebens' '' (Bebenhausen: Rotsch, 1972).

17. Franz Kafka, *Erzählungen* (Frankfurt: Fischer; New York: Schocken, 1946), 48. Further references appear in parentheses in the text.

18. Cf., for instance, Kafka, *Erzählungen*, 280.

19. Franz Kafka, "The Metamorphosis," in *Erzählungen*, 71. Further references appear in parentheses in the text.

20. Max Brod, "Franz Kafka: Eine Biographie," in *Über Franz Kafka* (Frankfurt: Fischer, 1966), 46.

21. Franz Kafka, *Hochzeitsvorbereitungen aus dem Lande und andere Prosa aus dem Nachlass* (Frankfurt: Fischer; New York: Schocken, 1953), 281.

22. Franz Kafka, *Tagebücher, 1910-1923* (Frankfurt: Fischer; New York: Schocken, 1951), 546.

23. Arthur Schopenhauer, *Parerga und Paralipomena I*, Zurich ed., 10 vols., ed. A. Hubscher (Zurich: Diogenes, 1977), 7: 317. Further references appear in parentheses in the text.

24. Jorge Luis Borges, "Tlön, Uqubar, Orbis Tertius," in *Obras Completas*, ed. Carlos V. Frias (Buenos Aires: Emecé, 1974), 440. Further references appear in parentheses in the text.

The Fantastic in Contemporary Fiction

Richard Alan Schwartz

> The turn to the fantastic in literature represents in some ways a new
> method if not for imposing a sense of order on our chaotic world at least
> for turning the chaos into something positive and useful.

The world of the fantastic has become the world of much of our foremost
contemporary literature. Art is no longer Stendhal's mirror on the highway of
life, reflecting accurately and unbiasedly all that passes; rather, it has become a
fun-house glass, wildly distorting everything that appears in it and furthermore
reveling in the distortion. Associated with the fantastic quality of modern writing
are a sense of energy, vigor, and vitality and a celebration of the imagination
itself. Moreover, at least in the stories told by our finest writers, a real concern
for the human condition remains at the heart of the fiction. Why the sudden turn
from realism, and what is the role of the fantastic in contemporary literature?
Although we are approximately twenty to twenty-five years into the present
resurgence of fantastical literature, these questions still merit consideration.

John Barth once complained of God that he "wasn't too bad a novelist, except
he was a Realist."[1] The departure from realism that Barth's statement represents
can be viewed from at least two perspectives: literary history and the evolution
of certain existential sensibilities in the twentieth century. Barth, at least, views
realism as something of an aberration on literary history. In an interview with
John Enck he remarked, "What the hell, reality is a nice place to visit but you
wouldn't want to live there, and literature never did, very long."[2] Indeed, even
a casual glance at our literary past reveals a relative lack of interest in realism,
except during the past two hundred years or so. That fact in itself is not sufficient
grounds for abandoning what has in modern history become a significant and
fruitful literary tradition. But although reality itself may be infinite in its vari-

ations, the ways of representing it are perhaps exhaustible. Where can the realistic traditions of Richardsonian psychological introspection and Fieldingesque expansive social examination now evolve beyond the psychological portraits painted by Henry James, Fëdor Dostoevski, and Virginia Woolf and the social landscapes drawn by James Joyce, Émile Zola, and Leo Tolstoy? Perhaps other avenues of realism are available for exploration, but to the writer who would advance the repertoire of literary possibilities, a total disassociation from realism becomes another viable possibility. Moreover, in an era in which technological innovations and bizarre human occurrences contribute a sense of fantasy to our everyday reality, where the bounds of realism seem more elastic than firm, a rediscovery of the fantastic becomes all the more appropriate.

The twentieth century has brought forth other considerations in addition to a geometrically increasing technological potential. When W. H. Auden proclaimed in "For the Time Being" that "Nothing like It has happened before," he seemed to be referring to a sensibility unique to our time. The modern worldview is unpleasant. The notion of a God who cares actively about each individual has largely been replaced by a God who, if he exists at all, seems removed from our daily existence. Thus an Ernest Hemingway character recites the Lord's Prayer, "Our Nada who art in Nada." With the felt absence of God no absolute, external force exists to give meaning or shape to our existence, and so our *raisons d'être* become relative and internally focused. Moreover, truth has been revealed to be not merely elusive but ultimately unknowable: Werner Heisenberg's uncertainty principle has supplanted Isaac Newton's laws; probability theory has replaced causality.

Making sense out of and imposing order upon this bleak universal picture has been the primary task of modern literature. Turn-of-the-century naturalists sought to establish the fact of an indifferent universe; later writers simply accepted this fact as an axiom and sought solutions. Joyce and T. S. Eliot were foremost in turning to mythology and legend as a way to revitalize our links to the past and to all humankind and thereby afford us at least a feeling of continuity. William Faulkner and Joyce used their cultural heritages for similar effects. The art-for-art's-sake writers turned inwardly to art to chisel out an ordered world from the chaotic universe surrounding them. Existentialist writers sought to find meaning in commitment to action, to humankind, and to the fact of the void itself. These alternatives were successful, but none has proved universally "the answer." The turn to the fantastic in literature represents in some ways a new method if not for imposing a sense of order on our chaotic world at least for turning the chaos into something positive and useful.

The art-for-art's-sake movement is in some ways a logical predecessor to the art of the fantastic in that both schools celebrate artifice and imagination. Yet significant differences exist in the manner of those celebrations: the earlier school being more High Church, the later inclining toward Bacchanalia. Generally, more geared toward poetry than prose, more to lyricism than narrative, the art-for-art's-sake group seeks to stimulate our imagination through application of intricate form; moreover, some sense of the beautiful and the elevated appears to be its chief aesthetic goal. One complaint about this often solipsistic art movement, however, is that it produces a sterile beauty. Wallace Stevens pointed out in his "Anecdote of the Jar" that the jar he plants on the Tennessee hillside to furnish the rural wilds a sense of form and order does not "give of bird or bush, / Like nothing else in Tennessee."[3]

The literature of the fantastic, on the other hand, seeks to fill itself and its readers with a life force. We are made to marvel at and share the gusto with which Tyron Slothrop plays Rocket Man during the Malta conference, with which Henry Burlingame litters colonial Maryland with his identities, with which J. Henry Waugh becomes an entire cast of drunken baseball players, with which "Jes Grew" sweeps the nation and fills everyone's soul with rhythm and dance. Although carefully constructed novels, manifestly concerned with form, *Gravity's Rainbow*, *The Sot-Weed Factor*, *The Universal Baseball Association, Inc.*, and *Mumbo Jumbo* also explode outwardly into a celebration of activity. Even the nightmare world of John Hawkes is dynamic in its terror. Dr. Sear states in Barth's *Giles Goat-Boy* that "a certain kind of *spiritedness* was absolutely good. No matter what a person's other Answers are. It doesn't have anything to do with education . . . and it's the most valuable thing in the University. Something about Dean Taliped's [Oedipus's] energy even at the end."[4] Dr. Sear is expressing one of the major concerns not only of Barth but of all writers of the fantastic.

Contemporary writers mine the fantastic for this vitality as a way of combating the bleak aspects of our age. Black humor, which frequently uses elements of the fantastic, acknowledges the negative facts of our existence but, without seriously trying to effect a change in the facts themselves, generates vigor and energy from them. The vigor and energy become the reply to our absurd plight. *Catch-22*, for example, does not really seek to end war or petty politics within the military or bureaucratic red tape. Instead, it represents them in such a way that we are at once compelled to acknowledge their reality and are enabled to cope with them through laughter.

At the heart of fantastic literature, then, a discrepancy occurs between thematic assumptions and ideas, on the one hand, and our reading experience, on the other hand. This discrepancy is used to confront and cope with the problems of our age. One such problem is the inability to know anything for certain. Truth, in the sense of comprehensive understanding of what is or what was, is certainly beyond our grasp, and even our ability to ascertain the accuracy of basic facts is questionable. Einsteinian relativity brings home the unknowability of truth through its elimination of any absolute point of reference. All points of view are equally valid, and so truth must somehow be an amalgamation of viewpoints. The cubists' tendency to superimpose several perspectives of the same object atop one another reflects an understanding of this principle, as does, for example, Faulkner's use of multiple narrators in *The Sound and the Fury* and *As I Lay Dying*. But even those artistic attempts to reproduce truth have limitations, because each juxtaposition of viewpoints yields its own unique insight and effect, and no particular juxtaposition is more valid than any other. Writers of the fantastic have, in effect, given up the attempt to capture truth and have dwelt upon rendering for us the fact of its unknowability. To be always unsure of the nature of one's past and present can be despairingly disorienting, but our contemporary writers use that uncertainty as an occasion for celebration and, in essence, turn it against itself for our delight and our salvation from despondency and stagnation.

John Barth's *The Sot-Weed Factor* and Thomas Pynchon's *The Crying of Lot 49* are fine examples of how the fantastic can be used to deal with truth's uncertainty. The politics of colonial Maryland are depicted in *The Sot-Weed Factor* as a tangled mass of special interests. Each time we and Ebenezer come to believe we understand the realities of the situation, new evidence comes forth that compels us to reverse our conclusions. We are convinced for 480 pages that Baltimore represents goodness, and Coode its opposite, and then Burlingame reappears to show that Coode is the saint and Baltimore the devil.[5] By the book's end Burlingame convinces us that both leaders are scoundrels and that Governor Nicholson represents the path of righteousness. Furthermore, and more appropriate to the issue of the fantastic, by the story's conclusion we have witnessed Burlingame undergo so many incredible transformations that we are unsure even if Coode and Baltimore ever really existed or if they were instead Burlingame himself. Thus we end the story with virtually nothing tangible in our hands. Not only are we no wiser about American history than when we began reading, we are inclined to be skeptical of those truths we thought we knew. What we receive in return for our disillusionment, and what ultimately makes that disillusion not merely palatable but delightful, is the merriment of watching Barth's fantastical account of history, with its outrageous impostures, its bizarre coincidences, and its incredible twists and turns.

To carry over the point about truth's uncertainty from the fictitious world to our own experience, Barth employs a technique that I have labeled the "anti-tall-tale." Tall tales are, of course, devices of fantasy that begin by appearing credible and then, after the introduction of a fallacious element, build slowly, at first imperceptibly, until the audience, having accepted the premises, finds itself accepting the absurd conclusion. The anti-tall-tale works in the reverse manner. Instead of leading the audience to accept as fact something highly fictitious, the anti-tall-tale induces the listeners to accept as fictitious something that proves factual.

Barth uses John Smith's and Henry Burlingame's private journals in this anti-tall-tale way. The highly sexual account of Pocahontis, for example, is delightful precisely for its imaginative debunking of a revered historical figure. It appears to be a straightforward burlesque of the virtuous Indian maiden. We take it to be entirely fictive; yet ultimately, it proves closer to "the truth" than our traditional accounts. John Smith, for example, commented that he could have "done what he listed" with her and mentioned how she and her women came "naked out of the woods, onely covered behind and before with a few green leaves...singing and dauncing with most excellent ill variete, oft falling into their infernall passions.''[6] William Strachey, first secretary of Virginia, discussed in his 1615 *Historie of Travaile into Virginia Britannia* how Pocahontis enjoyed trying to ''turn on'' the male youth of Jamestown. He described her as a wanton girl who would ''get the boyes forth with her into the markett place, and make them wheele, falling on their hands, turning their heels upwards, whome she would follow and wheele so herself, naked as she was, all the fort over.''[7] The revelation that Barth's highly erotic account of Pocahontis is accurate at least in its tenor, or that Burlingame's wild legalistic manipulations in the final courtroom scene were actually those employed in Maryland's first murder trial, or even that a historical Ebenezer Cooke not only existed but also wrote a ''Sot-Weed Factor''—all events that appear in the novel—flabbergasts us, in much the same way tall tales do.[8] Moreover, it leaves us in a position of uncertainty about our own knowledge of what else is fact or fiction. If these bizarre occurrences prove basically factual, what then of the machinations of John Coode, the illicit lusts of Isaac Newton and Henry More, or even the existence of that incredible Sacred Eggplant aphrodisiac?

Thomas Pynchon employed versions of anti-tall-tales in *The Crying of Lot 49*. His almost encyclopedic knowledge allows him to bring forth obscure facts about history and science. Thurn and Taxis, for example, really ran the postal system for the Holy Roman Empire; other postal systems occasionally challenged them; the U.S. postal system actually enacted postal reform laws in the 1840s to drive out competition; Maxwell's Demon exists as a concept in modern physics; and so on. If these things are somehow ''true,'' then what of the Trystro, of the WASTE system, of cigarette filters made from bones of dead soldiers? The point is that Pynchon combined fact and fiction so that we are scarcely able to tell which is which. He used both to construct a plot that seems totally surreal, but the intrusions of ''truth'' into that surreal world cause us to question what is real and what is not. As with Barth, we are left with bemused uncertainty. A direct result of the fantastic elements—the game of Strip Botticelli, the performances of the Paranoids, the brilliant parody of revenge tragedy entitled *The Courrier's Tragedy*, the cartoon *Porky Pig and the Anarchists*, and so on—this bemusement turns the uncertainty into something positive, something we can cope with and even enjoy.

We have no dearth of writers of the fantastic. Donald Barthelme's character struggles up a glass mountain in New York City, using plumbers' friends as hand grips, seeking a symbol, only to be disappointed by discovering an enchanted princess in its stead. Robert Coover presented the Julius and Ethel Rosenberg execution as public entertainment that takes place beneath a gigantic neon sign on Times Square. Ishmael Reed reveals opposing conspiracies, dating from Moses, that lead to the emergence of jazz and its suppression (and, incidentally, to the Crusades and World War I). None of these writers tries to depict life as we live it, but all address fundamental needs in our twentieth-century existence. They all have essentially thrown up their hands at the task of their predecessors. They seek not to impose order on our existence but to face the disorder and uncertainty directly. At the same time, though, through their use of formal techniques and their employment of fantastic plots and devices, they generate from the very fact of our chaos and uncertainty a sustaining vitality. The vitality overcomes the despair and stagnation that otherwise would emanate naturally from our bleak circumstances and replaces them with a celebration of life.

NOTES

1. John Enck, "John Barth: An Interview," *Wisconsin Studies in Literature* 6 (Winter-Spring 1965): 8.

2. Ibid., 11.

3. Wallace Stevens, *Collected Poems* (New York: Alfred A. Knopf, 1974), 76.

4. John Barth, *Giles Goat-Boy* (New York: Doubleday, 1966), 691.

5. John Barth, *The Sot-Weed Factor* (New York: Bantam Books, 1969), 517-26.

6. The quotations from Smith and Strachey can be found in Philip Young, "The Mother of Us All: Pocahontis," in *Three Bags Full: Essays in American Fiction*, ed. Philip Young (New York: Harcourt Brace Jovanovich, 1967), 179-80.

7. Ibid., 180.

8. See David Morrell's account of Maryland's first murder trial in *John Barth: An Introduction* (University Park: Pennsylvania State University Press, 1976), 27.

Todorov and the Existentialists

Jan Hokenson

Critics of the fantastic are rightly beginning to question Todorov's rubrics
and his typology in general. A wider reading of Jean-Paul Sartre's
"*Aminadab*" and Albert Camus's "Hope and the Absurd in the Work of
Franz Kafka" would help formulate those questions more clearly.

Perhaps because French existentialism was so intently focused on the here and
now, decrying illusionism of all sorts, commentators on the fantastic often overlook Sartre and Camus's provocative critiques of the mode. That is unfortunate,
because the existentialists' observations mark, in France, both the end of a long
line of theorists who blithely assumed that *fantasy* meant an escape from reality
and the anticipation of, indeed the transition to, the typology of Tzvetan Todorov
in the 1960s. Todorov's study of *le fantastique* is a major contemporary text;
yet it is derived in great part from the earlier work of the existentialists.[1]

When Sartre and Camus were writing on the subject—Sartre in *Situations I*
and *II* (1947-48) and Camus in *Le Mythe de Sisyphe* (1942) and *L'Homme révolté*
(1951)—the accepted definition of the *fantastic* had not changed since the nineteenth century. The work of Gaston Deschamps and Hubert Matthey (in 1905
and 1915) reaffirmed old confusions: *le fantastique* designated a loose cluster
of the marvelous, the supernatural, the oneiric, the *féerique*, the gothic, even
the irrational, as modes of escape from quotidian reality, for both protagonist
and reader.[2]

Translations into French of Franz Kafka's novels and parables in the 1930s
prompted many of the finest minds of the 1930s and 1940s, years of war and
occupation, to reexamine fantasy as a mode while trying to fit Kafka into outworn
critical rubrics. Indeed, Sartre thought he had discerned that the very nature and
use of fantasy as a mode had significantly changed since Arthur Rimbaud, Edgar

Allan Poe, Lewis Carroll, Prosper Mérimée, and had begun developing into something different in the present century.

Sartre's most vigorous theoretical formulation of the fantastic occurs in his essay "*Aminadab*; or, The Fantastic Considered as a Language,"written in 1947.[3] In turn, *Aminadab* is the title of an abstruse, thoroughly Kafkaesque novel by the then young novelist Maurice Blanchot in 1942. Blanchot has since turned almost exclusively to literary criticism, being now one of France's most articulate interpreters of the "postmodern." Like many young writers of the 1940s, however, Blanchot began by fictionalizing the existentialist absurdity of the human condition through special Kafkaesque symbols of the nonreal and the maybe-real. His novels are of interest now mostly as literary history and as Sartre's pretext.

Sartre summarized the plot, stressing (not excessively) Kafkaesque features, and concluded that although Blanchot claimed he had not read Kafka before writing *Aminadab*, there is a resemblance in style: "I do not know how this conjunction came about. . . . What must the nature of the fantastic be in our time if it leads a French writer, convinced of the necessity of 'thinking French', to find himself, upon adopting fantasy as a mode of expression, on the same terrain as a writer of Central Europe?" (p. 57) The reader's first surprise, in Sartre's subsequent answer to himself, is that politics and the history of Central Europe since the time of Kafka do not enter into the discussion, which remains exclusively aesthetic and philosophical. The second surprise is the passionate intensity with which Sartre interrogated the meaning of the fantastic, which would seem to be antipathetic to his own concerns as a writer.

First, Sartre demolished the idea of the "extraordinary." To achieve the fantastic it is neither necessary nor sufficient to portray extraordinary things, because "the strangest event will enter into the order of the universe if it is alone in a world governed by laws. . . . You cannot impose limits on the fantastic; either it does not exist at all, or else it extends throughout the universe" (p. 57). This is Sartre's crucial point, at once esthetic and literary-historical. It is esthetic, because Sartre defined the *fantastic mode* as a closed system; and historical, because he found that *all* of Kafka's predecessors strove "to create a world that was not of this world," whether in the manner of Lewis Carroll's systematic application of mathematical principles to beget a universe or of Charles Nodier's attempt, recognizing that the writer is primarily a liar, to attain the absolute lie (p. 58).

The unstated existentialist principle here is that, so practiced, the fantastic is an evasion of the human responsibility to engage directly and unceasingly in the world around one and in nothing but *human* affairs. The fantastic thus joins mysticism, asceticism, religion, metaphysical systems, and all irresponsbile attempts to escape the human condition through illusionism or any extrahuman transcendence.

Sartre saw the modern age (post-World War I) as an age of *dis*illusion, and he believed modern fantasists were compelled by public events to return to the human. Now, to find a place within the humanism of our time, fantasists abandon fairies, genii, ghosts, and goblins as useless and outworn conventions and attempt to locate the fantastic in people: the natural person, the social person, "the man who removes his hat when a hearse goes by, who shaves near a window, who kneels in church, who marches in step behind a flag" (p. 60).

Each such action in this natural realm has reasons, is a clear means to a clear end. What is the fantasist to do with such ordered, reasoned material in his work? Sartre invented a scene in a café:

I sit down and order a cup of coffee. The waiter makes me repeat the order three times and repeats it himself to avoid any possibility of error. He dashes off and repeats my order to a second waiter, who notes it down in a little book and transmits it to a third waiter. Finally, a fourth waiter comes back, and putting an inkwell on my table, says, "There you are." "But," I say, "I ordered a cup of coffee." "That's right," he says, as he walks off (p. 61).

Sartre noted that if readers of such a tale think that the waiters are playing a joke or that they are involved in some collective psychosis, the writer has failed. But if readers have the impression that the writer is talking about a world in which these absurd manifestations appear as normal behavior, they find themselves plunged all at once into the heart of the fantastic.

None of *these* actions—in this ostensibly normal realm—has reasons, and one finds proliferating means but no ends. Sartre concluded that the fantastic is the revolt of means against ends: "either the object in question noisily asserts itself as a means...or it refers back to another means, and this one to still another, and so on *ad infinitum*," without our ever being able to discover the ultimate end, unless perhaps a glimpse of a blurred and composite image of contradictory ends (p. 61).

With some fine swipes at modern bureaucracy Sartre said that the individual in modern fantasy is an instrument, a means to no knowable end. Again Sartre made a historical distinction and even pinpointed its appearance in literary history, notably in the years between Kafka's writing of *The Trial* and *The Castle*. "The old technique," said Sartre, presented the hero as a familiar type of fellow (Sartre never admitted the generic existence of heroines); we could readily identify with him, he lent us his point of view, he was our sole way of access to the fantastic. Such a man was Joseph K., a perfectly normal fellow. Joseph K. sets off, by contrast, the strange character of the new world, as we share in his astonishment and follow him from discovery to discovery, seeing with him the fantastic *from the outside*, as spectacle, almost as dream images. Not so with the bizarre anonymous surveyor in *The Castle*; we know almost nothing except his incomprehensible obstinacy in remaining in a forbidden village, and that, to attain this end, he sacrifices everything, treating himself as a means, but we never know the value this end had for him and whether it was worth so much effort. Sartre found the same anonymity and attitudes in Blanchot's protagonists, and we have seen a proliferation of such heroes in fantastic literature since 1947, most especially in German and French. Sartre added that we are thus forced, by the very laws of the novel, "to assume a point of view which is not our own, to condemn without understanding and to contemplate without surprise that which amazes us" (p. 65).

The second unstated existentialist principle, covertly being argued here, is that the human condition is "fantastic": the natural realm, the real world of daily actions, is, when closely examined, as bereft of logic and order and reason as any imaginary "second world" invented by Nodier or Carroll. To escape excessive rationality, there is no need to escape *up* into ethereal phantasms; rather one need only look around oneself, attempt to track every object and action to its *ultimate* end in first causes or last causes, to find oneself "plunged all at once into the heart of the fantastic" (p. 61). In this natural realm one cannot discern, any more than in a Kafka or a Blanchot novel, a coherent teleology. (One of Sartre's points is that the invented "second world" of old fantasy was a coherent closed system, primarily because the reader's viewpoint was analogous to that of an angel looking down on human life.) Instead, one can see only means and no final ends. In this reality in which, without God, humans find themselves unable to explain their existence and therefore in this "absurd" condition, those humans conscious of their state find themselves plunged into irrationality. The merest hairbrush becomes an object without coherent sense or use, unless as a sinister menace to the civilized reasoning mind—to what Jean-Baptiste Baronian termed the opposite of the fantastic, *la raison raisonnant*, "the reasoning reason."[4]

In many ways Sartrean existentialism itself may be interpreted as an attempt to constitute a coherent system of ends, although only in the social, never the metaphysical, realm. The question of means and ends was the axe that split Sartre and Camus in the famous break of 1952. Sartre argued that toward humanity's goal of universal liberty from political oppression the individual must be treated as a means toward that future and must therefore on occasion be sacrificed in bloody revolution; Camus countered that in an absurd universe each individual is the only conceivable end, both as living creature and as participant in collective political action, and must therefore engage in lifelong political revolt against oppressive conditions but must never be sacrificed to an unknowable future—a sacrifice that would make of Sartre's Marxist teleology another religious altar.

The quarrel is pertinent to this discussion of the fantastic, because it was already brewing in the 1940s and it informs many of the theoretical formulations that Todorov drew upon for his very influential book. Todorov ended his *Introduction à la littérature fantastique* quoting the café anecdote from Sartre's essay and effectively presenting Sartre's conclusions as his own, without either suggesting or appreciating the polemical base from which Sartre was speaking.

In his essay Sartre was claiming Kafka—and the fantastic—for existentialism. In the sudden postwar euphoria of slackening censorship and instant trans-Atlantic fame, he wanted to emphasize that existentialist literature is the literature of the modern age and that the problems therein posed are not French but human, as Kafka affirmed. Sartre wanted to decry the illusionism of escapist fantasy and to point to the esthetic value of an *existentialist* fantastic, while covertly advancing its philosophical and social significance to the modern individual. But for Todorov, the literary theoretician, to adopt wholesale such a view of literary history—which almost wholly elides surrealism—is a dubious move that has led to some confusion.

Todorov's book is in two parts, the first two hundred fifty pages describing a typology and the last twenty-five pages refuting or vitiating the typology. Todorov ably distinguished the fantastic from the uncanny and the marvelous, arguing that the true fantastic is achieved only gradually—that is, through what Sartre called "the old technique" of hero identification—only to reverse himself in the final section, claiming that we now live in an age of the "generalized fantastic," the mundane Kafkaesque fantastic that Sartre described as extant not in imagined second worlds but in this our own; the *true fantastic* is then defined as *not* a gradual but an immediate plunge into the incomprehensible, without hero identification, and Todorov's readers are left wondering what he means. My purpose here, aside from the merely informational one of giving the existentialist viewpoint some exposure, is to refer some of the internal contradictions in Todorov's book to their source in Sartre's neglected essay.

To return to the 1940s, the *bête noire* of existentialists was illusionism, however defined and practiced, but most especially organized religion and analogous metaphysical systems that defer humankind's questions to an unknowable afterlife. Sartre roundly condemned such illusionism in his essay and lauded in Kafka the dramatization of humans in quest of truth, tantalized by possibility but never granted certainty nor therefore rest. He pointedly added that such a world cannot be called "absurd," "as M. Camus called it in *The Stranger*," because absurdity means the complete *absence* of ends. He insisted that the "absurd would be an oasis, a respite, and thus there is no place for it" (p. 62).

It is at this point, the "absurd," that Sartre and Camus parted company in their views of the fantastic. Both writers were dazzled by Kafka's achievement in restricting the fantastic to this world, both insisted that Kafka was the first artist (although Camus gave due credit to what he termed the "surrealist experiment") to find reality itself fantastic, and both writers believed that Kafka's *oeuvre* constitutes in itself a redefinition of the mode that must henceforth be understood to designate, perhaps to the exclusion of ghosts and goblins, gothic and oneiric, the everyday reality of every human being.

As all readers of Camus know, to him the "absurd" is the inexplicable birth and death of humankind on this planet, thus, imagistically, the "divorce" between the actor and the décor, between reasoning people and the inexplicable world they find themselves forced to inhabit. To Camus teleology is itself an absurdity, a horrendous farce politically perpetrated upon humankind for the purpose of profit, that is, power over the credulous. In his essay "Hope and the

Absurd in the Work of Franz Kafka'' (written for *The Myth of Sisyphus* but published only as an appendix to the postwar edition, because Nazi censors proscribed publication on any such subject as Kafka the Jew), Camus asserted that Kafka had dramatized the elemental conditions of human life, ephemeral political systems notwithstanding. To Joseph K. of *The Trial*, Camus said, life is constant questioning of fantastic circumstances, irrational and impossible but real. The reader understands, continued Camus, that there will be no answers, ever, to humankind's questions and that this condition of reasoning without the possibility of knowing is absurd or "fantastique."

The contrast with Sartre is clear. Whereas Sartre insisted that Kafka protagonists constantly seek a reasoned explanation for their travails and a consequent boon, Camus insisted that Kafka protagonists inhabit an inexplicable universe in which they suspect that their questions are ludicrous and that they are a mere pawn of unknowable forces. In some of his most violent prose Camus condemned, as he believed Kafka condemned, *hope* (the last ill out of Pandora's box) of ever finding reasons or ends. Camus therefore found Joseph K. of *The Trial* emblematic of the modern *individual* and the unknowable surveyor of *The Castle* representative of the absurd human *condition*.

Writing on Kafka five years earlier than Sartre, Camus never extended his observations into a critique of the fantastic as a mode. It is nevertheless strikingly apparent to readers of the Kafka appendix that Camus believed—as deeply and as sincerely as Sartre—that if humanity would see clearly, behind the many veils maintained by insane hope and sundry authorities, humankind would recognize—in terror—that we inhabit the realm of the fantastic; the realm of means without ends; the world of strangeness, of bizarre happenings, of objects without purpose, of messages without content, of letters without senders, of policies without signatories or people, of catastrophes without cause.

Todorov's blurred distinction between gradual and nongradual entry into the fantastic, between presence and absence of hero identification, can therefore be more clearly understood when viewed in its historical context as a restatement of the leading existentialists' interpretation of Kafka in the 1940s. Indeed, it is from Sartre's original juxtaposition of *The Trial* and *The Castle* specifically that Todorov derived his unexplained, often ungainly transition from "old" to "new" or "generalized" fantastic literature. By omitting in his quotation from the essay Sartre's eloquent contrast of Joseph K. with the anonymous surveyor, Todorov argued the existentialist case without the context, in imprecise and confusing terms; by ignoring the polemical bases of the essay as an apologia for existentialism, Todorov diffused the persuasiveness of his source and, in turn, risked some questionable implications about his own understanding of literary history.

For Sartre to deplore—continuously and overtly for forty years—the surrealists is one thing; he believed they were, despite their Marxist roots, silly utopians playing word games in escape from the harsh truths of conscious existence, that is, enemies of all he stood for esthetically and politically.[5] But when Todorov covertly adopted the same posture in an ostensibly impersonal typology, effectively excluding the achievements of the surrealists from serious consideration of the fantastic, original polemic comes down to us as mere bias. Critics of the mode are rightly beginning to question Todorov's rubrics and his typology in general. A wider reading of Sartre's essay and Camus's appendix would help formulate those questions more clearly.

Todorov and Sartre would agree: from the critical point of view there may indeed be two eras of the fantastic, one before and one after Sartre's existentialist interpretation of *The Castle*.

NOTES

1. Tzvetan Todorov, *Introduction à la littérature fantastique* (Paris: Seuil, 1970), translated by Richard Howard as *The Fantastic* (Cleveland: Case Western Reserve, 1973).

2. Gaston Deschamps, "La Littérature fantastique et terrible," *Je sais tout*, September 1905, 151-60; Hubert Matthey, *Essai sur le merveilleux dans la littérature française depuis 1800* (Lausanne: Payot, 1915).

3. Jean-Paul Sartre, "*Aminadab*: or, The Fantastic Considered as a Language," translated from *Situations I* by Annette Michelson in J-P Sartre, *Literary Essays* (New York: Philosophical Library, 1957). Further references appear in parentheses in the text.

4. Jean-Baptiste Baronian, *Panorama de la littérature fantastique de langue française* (Paris: Stock, 1978), 23-24.

5. See Dominick LaCapra, *A Preface to Sartre: A Critical Introduction to Sartre's Literary and Philosophical Writings* (Ithaca, N.Y.: Cornell University Press, 1978), 33, 84-85.

Todorov's Fantastic, Kayser's Grotesque, and West's *Miss Lonelyhearts*

Rebecca R. Butler

This single test case is not meant to be taken as sufficient grounds for discarding Todorov's thesis, nor was it intended to challenge any of the details of his description of the fantastic, but it is meant to place his analysis within a broader perspective.

In his theoretical study *The Fantastic: A Structural Approach to a Literary Genre*, Tzvetan Todorov put forward some provocative hypotheses toward a systematic definition of the *fantastic*. He hoped, if successful, to be able to identify and predict the progress of a work of fantastic fiction if given no more than a single element from the narrative, much the same way that a famous anthropologist, with a single bone, identifies a particular animal and reconstructs its entire skeleton.[1] As he pursued this ambitious undertaking Todorov became guilty of some awkward swings between the extremes of sweeping generalization and suffocating narrowness, and his seemingly absent-minded self-contradiction casts doubt occasionally on his credibility as a critic.[2] Despite some weaknesses in presentation, the specific conditions he established and the frequent illustrations he developed make an appealing, indeed, an exciting, case for his definition, which would, if useful, allow us to discuss with some precision the nature of a great many works whose effects and contents are now vaguely called "weird, improbable, bizarre, unearthly, extravagant, eerie, or peculiar," for lack of better terminology. However, Todorov eventually limited the arena of the fantastic so strenuously that he called into question the usefulness of that definition. In his view the fantastic occupies a period that lasted only from the late eighteenth to the late nineteenth century and no longer exists in the twentieth century. He attempted to support his point with a discussion of "The Metamorphosis," showing that Gregor Samsa, instead of continuously feeling some hesitation, confusion, or indecision about the unnatural change that has overtaken him, works to adapt to his new condition. "With Kafka," Todorov wrote, "we are thus confronted with a *generalized* fantastic which swallows up the entire world and the reader along with it" (p. 174). Apparently, in an attempt to rescue the term from that meaningless (especially in fiction) designation of everything that does not belong to the category of the real, Todorov has excluded too much from the province of the fantastic.

It seems unlikely that fantastic fiction ended abruptly with the tales of Guy de Maupassant. A twentieth-century novel that comes to mind as meeting Todorov's conditions for the fantastic is *Miss Lonelyhearts*, by Nathanael West.[3] Moreover, it illustrates a great many parallels between Todorov's description of the fantastic and the aesthetic category of the grotesque as discussed by Wolfgang Kayser in *The Grotesque in Art and Literature*. Such a comparison may provide some evidence that the fantastic operates on a wider stage than Todorov has claimed for it and not unquestionably as a separate genre.

In fantastic fiction as Todorov described it there occurs at least one event whose cause is uncertain; the reader as well as the character involved hesitates in understanding the situation as having a natural or a supernatural explanation. Because the fantastic exists only as long as this hesitation lasts, the doubt and indecision about the nature of the extraordinary circumstance lingers, ideally, even when the story is finished. If a natural solution to the ambiguity is offered (as in detective stories), the fiction belongs to the neighboring genre of the "uncanny." But if the explanation is definitely supernatural (as it may be in a ghost story), the other neighboring genre of the "marvelous" exercises dominion. Whatever themes or contents the fiction may include, this hesitation must occur for the reader if the story is to belong to Todorov's category of the fantastic. Beyond this requirement there are the more general effects of an intensity of feeling, usually some fear, horror, or suspense; an experience of limits or of the crossing of natural limits; the blurring of ordinary boundaries; a sense of the excessive; a perception of the uncanny, the mysterious. Perception actually becomes a theme of the fantastic, as do metamorphosis; the collapse of the boundaries between mind and matter and between the word and the thing it denotes; madness; multiple personalities; a fusion of human and inhuman; all kinds of distortions of time and space; the demonic, particularly sexual demonism; and sadism.

Miss Lonelyhearts seems to be a good test case for the fantastic, because never has a novelist more delicately avoided a resolution and retained the ambiguity of his fiction more scrupulously than in this "portrait of a priest of our time," created by West from saints' legends and psychological case histories. With masterful balance and deliberation West maneuvered his conscientious columnist through a nightmarish Depression-era New York City made peculiarly unbearable by his verbally sadistic feature editor Shrike and the shocking letters it is his job to answer for his newspaper's lonelyhearts column. Not only does Miss Lonelyhearts hesitate in interpreting the cause of some of his extraordinary experiences, he is uncertain about his own perceptions, about the possibility that he is suffering delusions, is going mad. Although Miss Lonelyhearts finally abandons his doubt, this uncertainty persists for the reader throughout the course of the narrative.

As the novel begins, Miss Lonelyhearts sits reading the morning's letters, one of which is from a sixteen-year-old girl born without a nose, who is considering the possibility that some supernatural causation is at work: "What did I do to deserve such a terrible bad fate?" she writes (p. 7). She wonders if she "did something in the other world" before she was born for which she is being punished (p. 7). The other letters are equally troubling. Miss Lonelyhearts, too, considers a spiritual solution: "Christ was the answer," he immediately thinks (p. 8). But he hesitates to accept that explanation, fearing that he will lose control, that he will become "sick" if he gives in to the supernatural. This character is peculiarly suited to the experience of the fantastic, because he takes symbols very seriously, we gradually learn, and even searches the sky for signs of superhuman agency. But there the besieged columnist sees "no angels, flaming crosses, olive-bearing doves, wheels within wheels" (p. 11). In fact, Miss Lonelyhearts tries to avoid the supernatural explanation, seeking normality in drink, in sex, in a retreat to country living. Nevertheless, his hesitation persists when he cannot escape what Todorov called "the brutal intrusion of mystery into the context of real life" (Todorov, *Fantastic*, p. 26). Miss Lonelyhearts becomes frighteningly aware that he cannot depend on a reliable order when one day "all the inanimate things over which he had tried to obtain control took the field against him" (West, *Miss Lonelyhearts*, p. 20). His ordinary possessions seem animated with a life of their own and finally drive him out onto the street, where "chaos was multiple." This is what Todorov described as the intense forcing of limits, the experience of the extreme, and a fusion or blurring of boundaries between ordinarily separate categories, here the animate and the inanimate. Again, while resting in the park, the distraught young man suddenly becomes aware that the shadow of a monument is moving forward across the ground in great jerks, "not as shadows usually lengthen" (p. 33). This uncanny sight sends him hurrying away, attempting to rationalize his strange experience. Of course, the letters themselves represent a distorted, nightmarish existence, and one of those letter writers, Mr. Doyle, illustrates, in his person, the blurring of boundaries and the failure of conventional order: "The cripple had a very strange face. His eyes failed to balance; his mouth was not under his nose; his forehead was square and bony; and his round chin was like a forehead in miniature. He looked like one of those composite photographs used by screen magazines in guessing contests" (p. 75).

In the face of such a repellent natural world, Miss Lonelyhearts turns gradually toward a supernatural source of order and meaning. Even though he fears that the mysterious power that stirs within him when he chants the name of Christ is actually hysteria, both his waking and his dream worlds attest that the risk is worthwhile. The physical world seems dead, "a world of doorknobs" (p. 17);

spring has come but no vegetation grows in the park, and in the country woods "there was nothing but death—rotten leaves, gray and white fungi, and over everything a funereal hush" (p. 62). In one of many revealing dreams, Miss Lonelyhearts sees himself as a magician who makes doorknobs flower, speak, and bleed. In another he finds himself, first in a pawnshop window, surrounded by discarded objects, then on a beach where this inanimate flotsam "yearns" and "strives" with a will of its own to undo the order imposed on it by humans. These dreams intensify rather than dispel the fantastic, because they are elaborations on the very ambiguity that occupies Miss Lonelyhearts's waking life.

When he returns to New York from the country, he looks out where crowds of people move through the street with a "dream-like violence" and sees "their broken hands and torn mouths." He wants to find some redemptive solution for them, knowing, he thinks to himself, that "dreams were once powerful," and "that he was capable of dreaming the Christ dream" (p. 64). Not at this point, or even when Miss Lonelyhearts rushes out to heal the crippled Doyle, is the reader invited to understand that this character is simply mad; on the contrary, his world and the people who inhabit it are so forbidding, so bizarre, so ominous, that Miss Lonelyhearts's desire to invoke a sacred dimension, while possibly a symptom of a disintegrating mind, responds to a universal need for a meaningful order. In fact, this turn of events answers to one of Todorov's themes of the fantastic, that of "madness viewed as, perhaps, a higher reason" (p. 40).

At last we reach what Todorov identified as the culminating scene of intense and ambiguous mystery. In the final chapter, "Miss Lonelyhearts Has a Religious Experience," not only does a peculiar metamorphosis take place, but the collapse of the separation between mind and matter seems complete. Miss Lonelyhearts now thinks of himself as "the rock," having internalized the notions of indestructibility, immovability, and calm. He has retreated to his room, where he "rides" his bed like a flying carpet, in search of vision. As he stares at the ivory Christ nailed to the wall, it begins to spin like a bright fly while the dead contents of the room rise to it like a fish to bait. Miss Lonelyhearts's heart becomes a rose, "and in his skull another rose bloomed" (p. 93). Gradually, he realizes that his heart is becoming one with God's, and finally, "his brain was likewise God's" (p. 94). At this enigmatic juncture the doorbell rings, and Miss Lonelyhearts uncannily knows that it is Doyle, sent by God, he believes, to prove his conversion. But instead of a miraculous healing, the would-be savior is inadvertently shot by the cripple.

With even so selective an illustration as this, it is clear that this novel meets the criteria established in Todorov's theory. It is certainly not a story that stays within the bounds of the uncanny, nor can it be called a tale of the marvelous. It pursues a hesitation between the natural and the supernatural as far as it can be followed. Yet once we turn to Kayser's wide-ranging analysis of the grotesque, completed in 1957, we may be less satisfied that we have been on the right track. For one thing, the language of Kayser and the language of Todorov are often identical: both wrote of the "uncanny," "distortion," "uncertainty," "confusion," and the "fusion" of ordinarily separate realms. For Todorov's term *hesitation* we read in Kayser "transitional moments"; both examined "metamorphosis," "madness," "dreams," "horror," and the "demonic." Kayser, in fact, used the term *fantastic grotesque* and made this one of two subdivisions of the aesthetic category of the grotesque.

The primary effect of the grotesque as Kayser explained it is a "sense that the natural order of things has been subverted."[4] Whether inanimate objects themselves or the character's reaction produces this perception, an alienation and estrangement from the world results. Ominous and sinister elements intrude into an otherwise realistic setting. There is a blurring of distinction between animate and inanimate realms; the laws of statics, symmetry, and proportion are invalid. The fusion of mutually incompatible worlds becomes a picture of our world, which is breaking apart.

To return to Miss Lonelyhearts, sitting at his desk, reading his morning's letters: In those letters Miss Lonelyhearts is catching disconcerting glimpses of what Kayser called the "sinister background of the brighter and rationally organized world" (Kayser, *Grotesque*, p. 21). The willful animation of the contents of his room, the unnatural movement of the shadow in the park, the hideously incongruous face of his correspondent, Mr. Doyle, are grotesque experiences, producing, as they do, the sense of surprise, confusion, and the ominous that accompanies Miss Lonelyhearts's growing conviction that the natural order of things is dissolving. Even so apparently small a thing as the failure of new vegetation to appear with the spring, when perceived in combination with these other disorienting events, contributes to Miss Lonelyhearts's anxiety that vitality and stability have abandoned the natural world, leaving behind a ghastly mixture of demonic things and monstrous people where there had been, he thought, logic, proportion, and meaning. West called his novel a "moral satire," and Kayser discussed the role that disillusionment such as Miss Lonelyhearts feels plays in the satiric grotesque, quoting from Goethe: "Looked at from the height of reason, life as a whole seems like a grave disease, and the world like a madhouse" (p. 60). Writers with satiric purposes use the grotesque not only to mock tradition and society's cherished ideals but to demolish complacent categories, to deprive the apparently meaningful of meaning, and to shake the reader's confident expectations about his world. Except for suicide, Miss Lonelyhearts has no practical advice to give his pathetic correspondents.

It is no wonder that Miss Lonelyhearts seeks meaning elsewhere when the natural world fails him. As Kayser explained, "We are so strongly affected and terrified because it is our world which ceases to be reliable, and we feel that we would be unable to live in this changed world. The grotesque instills fear of life rather than fear of death" (p. 185). That is a striking inversion and one that Todorov touched upon when he discussed the incompatibility that often exists between sex and religion in fantastic fiction, where the general rule is that "one world must die that the other may live" (p. 129). In grotesque literature the entire living world may seem to die, and in *Miss Lonelyhearts* it gives place to a macabre, a ghostly, or a monstrous world in which street crowds with broken hands and torn mouths move trancelike and violent in search of a sustaining dream from the marquee of a movie house or from a love-story magazine. In his dreams and in his chanting the name of Christ, Miss Lonelyhearts is clearly motivated by this fear of life. The desperate man attempts to invoke a transcendent order. His apparent madness is a theme, as already noted, found in both fantastic and grotesque art. Insanity, in Kayser's view, is the ultimate estrangement, self-estrangement; and "the encounter with madness," he continued, "is one of the basic experiences of the grotesque which life forces upon us" (p. 184). Whether Miss Lonelyhearts's belief that he experienced a mystical union with God is a delusion or whether it is genuine, the loss of identity that accompanies it undercuts the very foundations of personality, of human nature.

There is one last feature of the grotesque, as Kayser defined it, that must be matched with its counterpart from Todorov's thesis on the fantastic, and this is the inexplicability of the perceived fundamental dislocation. As Kayser concluded his investigation of a topic that he pursued through several centuries of European and American painting and literature, he emphasized that a crucial requirement of the grotesque is that it must, finally, point to no meaning. More exactly, the artist employing the grotesque must imply no cause, no source, no meaning-fulness, no purpose guiding and reconciling us to this subversion of the natural order of things; otherwise the grotesque vanishes. Neither physical disfigurement, nor the living dead, nor animation of the inanimate, nor religious visions, nor miracles may be explained or evaluated within the purview of the grotesque. What Kayser, looking into the incomprehensible heart of disorientation and dislocation, called "inexplicable" and "meaningless" answers to Todorov's condition of "indecision." The reader experiences that all-important "hesita-tion" or "indecision," as Todorov explained it, because he cannot be certain whether some peculiar circumstances have a supernatural or a natural explana-tion, and ideally, this indecision continues indefinitely. In that masterfully am-biguous conclusion to *Miss Lonelyhearts* we can watch Todorov's "indecision" and Kayser's "inexplicability" converge. When Miss Lonelyhearts, rushing down the stairs with arms outstretched, is shot by Doyle, the reader is being invited to view the story's denouement through bifocals, as it were, to entertain a doubled, a split, perspective, in other words, to hesitate indefinitely between two explanations, both having been made equally valid: (1) Miss Lonelyhearts dies a martyr, the mistaken victim of one he came to save; (2) Miss Lonelyhearts's ludicrous end is pathetically and grimly suited to the peculiarities of his religio-sexual pathology. The first meaning answers to a supernatural interpretation; the second, to a natural. There is a third meaning, that sheer random bad luck put the clumsy Doyle on the stairs when the overwrought columnist was ill with a raging fever. If the story is to exert its full power, all of these possible expla-nations, no single one of them, must be allowed. To assign any definite cause, meaning, or purpose would minimize the sense of an awesome and dreadful mystery that it is the goal of the writer to prolong. Once more we find Todorov and Kayser in agreement—whether this style, structure, or effect is called fantastic or grotesque—that in this kind of fiction the brutal intrusion of mystery is paramount, and that mystery must be deliberately preserved.

This single test case is not meant to be taken as sufficient grounds for discarding Todorov's thesis, nor is it intended to challenge any of the details of his description of the fantastic, but it is meant to place his analysis within a broader perspective. Indeed, some significant exceptions to his theory seem to have arisen. First, although it has been demonstrated how completely West's novel meets Todorov's major and minor criteria for the fantastic, this demonstration conflicts both with Todorov's conception of the fantastic as a genre existing within the bounds of the eighteenth and nineteenth centuries and with the prevailing critical views of *Miss Lonelyhearts*, all of which recognize the novel's irony, satire, and grim humor, and none of which considers the novel fantastic. Therefore, Todorov's expectation of picking up at random a thread in a narrative and from it identifying and reconstructing the whole, the way that the anthropologist he mentioned worked with a single bone, would seem doomed to disappointment.

In speculating why and how Todorov's theory may have been undermined, the failure may be located somewhere between two of the limiting conditions he set on this so-called genre: the specified historic period and the dichotomy of natural-supernatural that fields the important "hesitation" response. Perhaps because from the mid-eighteenth to the late nineteenth century the supernatural was gradually losing its unquestioned status as an actual reality, and coming to be understood as an imaginary realm, the "hesitation" that Todorov found is largely a function of that cultural shift, evidence of external influence rather than inherent to an aesthetic structure. What makes *Miss Lonelyhearts* seem to be an example of the fantastic, then, may be this issue of belief, of supernatural versus natural agency, which is the book's subject. Still another explanation for this novel's seeming to fit into a category otherwise unsuited to it lies in Eric Rabkin's more expansive analysis of the fantastic. The extremity of Miss Lonelyhearts's experience is chiefly satiric, and "satire," according to Rabkin in *The Fantastic in Literature*, "is inherently fantastic," because it depends upon the reversal of perspectives and is usually ironic in tone (pp. 145-46). Finally, the large territory of overlapping and duplicated terminology, themes, purposes, effects, motifs, and techniques that exists between Todorov's mapping of the fantastic and Kayser's study of the grotesque makes the usefulness of Todorov's definition all the more doubtful.

Perhaps it is unfair to compare one critic's very early work with the seasoned product of another, but the comparison here is instructive. While identifying clear and reasonable criteria, Kayser established a broad base for his subject, historically, geographically, in terms of artistic media, and he designated the grotesque an "aesthetic category." Todorov, in *The Fantastic*, radically limited the range and effect of the fantastic, which he called a genre, and regularly interspersed his explication with leading statements such as this: "Any description of a text, by the very fact that it is made by means of words, is a description of a genre'' (p. 7). Whereas Kayser recognized the relatedness of the fantastic and the grotesque modes and provided an appropriate category for their conjunction, which he named the fantastic grotesque, Todorov never mentioned the grotesque at all. Without a doubt, Todorov's theoretical approach is stimulating and therefore entirely worthwhile. Let the explorer in pursuit of the fantastic, however, follow it advisedly and not overlook the rich terrain of the twentieth century, even though it is not shown on Todorov's map.

NOTES

1. Tzvetan Todorov, *The Fantastic: A Structural Approach to a Literary Genre*, trans. Richard Howard (Cleveland: Case Western Reserve University Press, 1973), 13-14. Further references appear in parentheses in the text.

2. Eric Rabkin mentioned his differences with Todorov in *The Fantastic in Literature* (Princeton, N.J.: Princeton University Press, 1976), 118. Further references appear in parentheses in the text.

3. Nathanael West, *Miss Lonelyhearts* (New York: Avon Books, 1959). Futher references appear in parentheses in the text.

4. Wolfgang Kayser, *The Grotesque in Art and Literature*, trans. Ulrich Weisstein (1957; reprint, New York: McGraw-Hill, 1966), 21. Further references appear in parentheses in the text.

Poetics of the Uncanny: E. T. A. Hoffmann's "Sandman"

Shelley L. Frisch

The tale's narrators continually force an identification of their narratees
with the unnerving events of Nathanael's life, so that the narratees adopt
their own anxieties and fear of the uncanny.

Sigmund Freud defined the "uncanny" as "that class of the frightening which
leads back to what is known of old and long familiar."[1] He illustrated this
conception of the uncanny by analyzing E. T. A. Hoffmann's "Sandman,"
which comprises the first of Hoffmann's "Night Pieces," written in 1816.[2]
Hoffmann's "Sandman" explores the increasingly schizophrenic world of a
young man, Nathanael, who cannot shake his obsession with a childhood fairy
tale, and who reacts hysterically to a salesman who seems to be the Sandman
come to life. Readers share Nathanael's mounting distress and find themselves,
like Nathanael, ultimately incapable of distinguishing between the fantasy of
fairy tales and the reality stressed by other characters in the story.

The story begins in epistolary format. In a letter from Nathanael to his friend
Lothar, Nathanael reflects on his recent encounter with a barometer salesman/
optician, whom he identifies with the Sandman. From a flashback we learn that
when Nathanael was a boy, his father had associated with a dreadful alchemist
named Coppelius, and during the experiments the two conducted together, Nathanael's father died. On the evenings that Coppelius came to visit, Nathanael
was always sent to bed early, with the warning that the Sandman was coming.
Upon questioning his nurse Nathanael discovered that the Sandman plucks out
the eyes of children who do not obey their parents' orders to go to bed; he then
transports the eyes to the "half-moon" to feed his children. Curious to see the
dreaded Sandman for himself, Nathanael hides in the closet of his father's study

one night and is discovered by Coppelius, who attempts to harm the boy: but Nathanael is saved by the intervention of his father.

We then return to the present and to Nathanael's encounter with an Italian optician named Giuseppe Coppola, who exclaims in faulty German that he has eyes to sell. Nathanael draws back in terror, both at the similarity of the optician's name to the alchemist Coppelius's and to the mention of eyes as the product for sale. Memories of the Sandman come flooding back, and Nathanael reels in panic until he realizes that Coppola is selling spectacles and telescopes, not eyes. Still, he is struck by these uncanny similarities and remains haunted by the possibility of their identity.

Nathanael buys a telescope from Coppola and with its aid discovers a neighbor of whom he was hitherto unaware, a beautiful but strangely immobile woman named Olimpia. He pursues her, only to discover that she is an automaton, whose eyes have been implanted in her by Coppola. At this discovery Nathanael goes mad and falls into a long illness, during which he produces eerie, fantastic poetry. Upon recovering he returns to the "rational" world of his correspondent Lothar and his girlfriend Klara, who, he now believes, are right in dismissing the extraordinary events he has experienced. Nathanael is disappointed that they reject his poetic ventures but agrees that they are irrational. Finally, though, he spies Coppola/Coppelius once again, through his telescope, and jumps to his death from a tower.

This short summary provides the essentials of the material from which Freud drew in his essay to explain how events become uncanny. Freud noted that Nathanael's fear of losing his eyes represents a castration complex, akin to Oedipus' self-blinding when he discovers that he has killed his father and slept with his mother. Nathanael may harbor a secret wish to kill his father, Freud explained, and finds his wish fulfilled in the figure of the Sandman/Coppelius, the instrument of his father's death. Because he then wishes to repress that fulfilled wish, Nathanael buries the memory of the Sandman. When he encounters the optician Coppola and notices in him two uncanny resemblances (similarity of name and business of selling "eyes"), Nathanael succumbs to a temporary madness. The "un-" prefix of *uncanny*, Freud explained, denotes a confrontation with that which is familiar but until that moment successfully repressed. Repeated encounters with Coppola/Coppelius, in which the motif of eyes continues to play an important role, reinforce the feeling of the uncanny, in which repetition constitutes an important factor.

Freud isolated the Sandman as the focal point of interest in the story, thereby countering the view of other critics who attributed the presence of the uncanny to the mechanical doll Olimpia. Freud considered it irrelevant to debate the humanity of Olimpia, because establishing whether she is in fact living or a mere automaton does not address the *effect* of the uncanny on Nathanael. It is through his perceptions of the uncanny, maintained Freud, that we can best understand the meaning of the story. Freud concentrated in part on the biographical background of E. T. A. Hoffmann himself, whose father abandoned the family when Hoffmann was young, and on Freud's own case studies; both of these factors are said to bear out the verisimilitude of Nathanael's experiences.

Freud's dissection of Nathanael's psychoses illuminates the character of Nathanael and the relationship of Hoffmann to his main character. Freud followed Nathanael's increasing madness with a shrewd explication of how Nathanael's feelings of the uncanny escalate. He accurately noted the central role of the Sandman and the subsidiary role of Olimpia in unleashing long-repressed anxieties, which may be connected to an ambivalent feeling of Nathanael (and perhaps of Hoffmann) toward an inattentive father. Most important, Freud stressed that the uncanny involves something long familiar and yet unfamiliar, which by its reappearance at unexpected moments disconcerts an unwary victim.

Overall, however, Freud's interpretation of "The Sandman" fails as a literary interpretation of the fantastic. Freud admitted that the uncanny in literature differs from the uncanny in life; yet he treated the confusion of Nathanael, in which fantasy and reality intermingle, more as a case study of schizophrenia than as a work of literature. Freud even underscored the psychological "truth " of Nathanael's visions by describing similar personality disorders among his own patients. Freud once remarked to a friend that he was not fond of reading and commented: "I invented psychoanalysis because it had no literature."[3] He viewed the story through the perspective of the protagonist's neuroses and constantly judged its truth value. Freud thereby committed the error that Jonathan Culler called "premature foreclosure—the unseemly rush from word to world."[4]

It is within the German Romantic circle itself that we discover a more pertinent analysis of the literary creation of the uncanny. Ludwig Tieck's "Shakespeares Behandlung des Wunderbaren" of 1796 lays a theoretical foundation for the manner in which the illusion of the supernatural is created in the comedies and tragedies of Shakespeare.[5] Tieck's discussion of comedies treats the *Wunderbare* ("marvelous") in much the same manner as Tzvetan Todorov's recent *Fantastic: A Structural Approach to a Literary Genre*: the supernatural events described provoke no definitive reaction of anxiety in either the characters or in the implicit reader.[6] According to Tieck the supernatural world is moved so close to the reader (or viewer) that it becomes accepted as part of the fictional premise.[7] His examination of tragedies demonstrates how fear and anxiety can be induced in the reading or viewing audience by the use of particular fictional techniques.

The characteristics of the tragedies that compel the viewer both to accept and to be repelled by the supernatural are three, according to Tieck. First, the world of the supernatural is presented as distant and incomprehensible and is always subordinated to the "real" world; consequently, the passions and events concerning the major characters attract the attention of the viewer and are of more interest than the ghosts themselves. Thus we yearn to understand Hamlet's dilemma but care little for his father's apparition. Second, the supernatural must be prepared in some way. If the appearance of Hamlet's father's ghost were to open the play, Tieck explained, we would not have developed a necessary fear of him; instead, we would simply accept the ghost as part of the fictional framework. We must be convinced that it is both possible and frightening for him to appear, so as to share the characters' dismay when we must formally face him. Therefore, *Hamlet* opens not with the ghost himself but with the frightened sentries who ponder his reality. Third, a natural explanation of the supernatural increases our intellectual uncertainty and thus augments our suspense. In the case of Hamlet we can attribute his vision of the ghost in part to Hamlet's proclivity to melancholy and superstition.

All three of these characteristics accurately describe the evocation of the supernatural in Hoffmann's "Sandman." First, the "real" character Nathanael commands our attention far more than the Sandman Coppelius or the automaton Olimpia. The fantastic characters remain abstractions for us, but Nathanael's raptures and fears seem close and comprehensible. Second, the Sandman does not appear in the story until the reader has heard of the evil he can perpetrate and how great Nathanael's fear of him is, and so we are prepared to experience with the sympathetic character Nathanael the uncanny similarity he draws to the optician Coppola who sells "eyes." Finally, although we identify with Nathanael we have just enough reason to doubt the reliability of his perceptions that we cannot shake a nagging doubt about the actuality of the Sandman throughout much of the story.

Recent "reader-response" criticism has called for a renewed interest in this type of poetics. Like Tieck reader-response critics examine the means by which readers' reactions are encoded into texts. However, their analyses go further than those of Tieck by showing that the reader is *addressed* directly and indirectly within the text. Walker Gibson spoke of the "mock reader" in texts, Stanley Fish of the "informed reader," Gerald Prince of the "narratee," Walter J. Ong of the "fictionalized audience," Wolfgang Iser of the "implied reader," and Christine Brooke-Rose of the "encoded reader."[8] None of these "readers" is identical to the "real" reader who peruses a book in his living room. These *narratees* (to use Prince's apt term) are the fictional counterparts of "narrators": they exist within the fictional framework itself. Although the critical literature on Hoffmann has nowhere recognized the role that the narratee plays in his works, I will demonstrate that this role is crucial in creating the uncanny effects of "The Sandman."[9]

The story opens with a letter from Nathanael to his friend Lothar, which he begins by exclaiming: "*You* certainly must be disturbed" (Hoffmann, "The Sandman," p. 93). The exclamation sets the narrative tone for the tale as a whole. Second-person narration, addressed to a sympathetic narratee, appears not only in the introductory letters but in the subsequent interpretation of them by an additional narrator whose reliability is even more questionable than Nathanael's. The second narratee is told by this narrator that he has experienced similar encounters with the fantastic: "Have you, gentle reader, ever experienced anything that possessed your heart, your thoughts, and your senses to the exclusion of all else? Everything seethed and roiled within you; heated blood surged through your veins and inflamed your cheeks. Your gaze was peculiar, as if seeking forms in empty space invisible to other eyes, and speech dissolved into gloomy sighs" (p. 104). We, the "real" readers, are thus allied with the anxieties of Nathanael, with an equally nervous narrator who continually apologizes to us for needing to set down Nathanael's experiences in a story, and with two narratees in whom Nathanael and the narrator explicitly attempt to instill feelings of the uncanny. Our uncomfortable intimacy with all of these figures forces us to confront the fantastic along with them and heightens our personal horror of each appearance of the dreaded Sandman.

The narrator overtly states his intention to make his narratee, whom he calls the "gentle reader" and the "sympathetic reader," receptive to the supernatural occurrences of the story (pp. 104-5): "my dear reader, it was essential at the beginning to dispose you favorably towards the fantastic—which is no mean matter" (p. 105). He expresses the hope that his narratee will picture the characters as vividly as if he had seen them with his own eyes. Nathanael pleads for understanding and acceptance of the supernatural from his narratee Lothar.

The "real" reader is left with the question of whether he ought to accept the role assigned to both of these narratees and thereby declare its events uncanny. Christine Brooke-Rose's article "The Readerhood of Man" suggests that a text with an apparent overencoding of the reader gives rise to the truly ambiguous text:

The clearest type is the truly ambiguous text. . . . [It] *seems* to overdetermine one code, usually the hermeneutic, and even to overencode the reader, but in fact the overdetermination consists of repetitions and variations that give us little or no further information. The overdetermination functions, paradoxically, as underdetermination.[10]

Hoffmann's "Sandman" provides us with two narratees after whom we may model our own interpretation of events. The "real" reader thus becomes an overencoded reader, who is told repeatedly that he ought to accept the uncanny. That this text remains nonetheless fundamentally underdetermined is attested to in the ample critical literature on "The Sandman," which debates and redebates the question of the relative reliability of the narratees and the story's other characters.

In the end the "real" reader must dismiss as inconsequential any attempt to distinguish between "actual" supernatural events and "mere" products of Nathanael's and the narrator's imaginations. The production of uncanny effects in literary texts rests precisely on the intellectual uncertainty built into the text. Freud's study of the uncanny concentrates on removing stories from the literary sphere and ascertaining their degree of psychological truth. Tieck directed his attention to the manner in which responses to the supernatural events are incorporated structurally into a text and thereby addressed the specifically literary conventions that separate fact from fiction. In applying reader-response critical theory to Hoffmann's "Sandman," I hope to have demonstrated that the tale's narrators continually force an identification of their narratees with the unnerving events of Nathanael's life, so that the narratees adopt their own anxieties and fear of the uncanny. Remarks addressed in the second person to these narratees necessarily draw in the "real" reader as well. We become the "gentle" and "sympathetic" reader about whom the narrator exclaims: "Everything seethed and roiled within *you*" (Hoffmann, "The Sandman," p. 104).

NOTES

1. Sigmund Freud, "The Uncanny," in *The Standard Edition of the Complete Works of Sigmund Freud*, trans. and ed. James Strachey et al. (London: The Hogarth Press, 1955), 17: 220.

2. E. T. A. Hoffmann, "The Sandman," in *Tales of E. T. A. Hoffmann*, trans. and ed. Leonard J. Kent and Elizabeth C. Knight (Chicago and London: University of Chicago Press, 1969), 93-125. Further references appear in parentheses in the text.

3. Quoted in Neil Hertz, "Freud and the Sandman," in *Textual Strategies: Perspectives in Post-Structuralist Criticism*, ed. Josue Harari (Ithaca, N.Y.: Cornell University Press, 1979), 318.

4. Jonathan Culler, *Structuralist Poetics* (Ithaca, N.Y.: Cornell University Press, 1975), 130.

5. Ludwig Tieck, "Shakespeares Behandlung des Wunderbaren," in *German Essays*, ed. Max Dufner and Valentine C. Hubbs (New York: Macmillan, 1964), 4: 61-101.

6. Tzvetan Todorov, *The Fantastic: A Structural Approach to a Literary Genre* (Cleveland: Case Western Reserve Press, 1973), 53-57.

7. Tieck, "Shakespeares Behandlung des Wunderbaren," 65. Recent research on the fairy tale has led to similar conclusions about the presentation and reception of the supernatural in that genre. See especially Max Luthi, *Es War einmal*, 4th ed. (Gottingen and Zurich: Vandenhoeck & Ruprecht, 1973).

8. Walker Gibson, "Authors, Speakers, Readers, and Mock Readers," *College English* 11 (1950): 265-69; Stanley Fish, "Literature in the Reader: Affective Stylistics," *New Literary History* 2 (1970): 123-62; Gerald Prince, "Introduction to the Study of the Narratee," in *Reader-Response Criticism*, ed. Jane P. Tompkins (Baltimore: The Johns Hopkins University Press, 1980), 7-25; Walter J. Ong, "The Writer's Audience Is Always a Fiction," *PMLA* 90 (1975): 9-21; Wolfgang Iser, *The Implied Reader: Patterns of Communication in Prose Fiction from Bunyan to Beckett* (Baltimore: Johns Hopkins University Press, 1974); idem, *The Act of Reading: A Theory of Aesthetic Response* (Baltimore: Johns Hopkins University Press, 1978); Christine Brooke-Rose, "The Readerhood of Man," in *The Reader in the Text*, ed. Susan R. Suleiman and Inge Crosman (Princeton, N.J.: Princeton University Press, 1980), 120-48.

9. Most of the recent literature on the "Sandman" can be grouped according to the following six goals. 1. Analyzing the psyche of the main character Nathanael, generally with reference to Freud's "Uncanny" essay: Ilse Aichinger, "E. T. A. Hoffmann's Novelle 'Der Sandmann' und die Interpretation Sigmund Freuds," *Zeitschrift für deutsche Philologie* 95 (1976): 113-32; Hélène Cixous, "Fiction and Its Phantoms: A Reading of Freud's *Das Unheimliche*," *New Literary History* 7 (1976): 525-48; and Hertz, "Freud and the Sandman." 2. Describing the roles of peripheral characters in evoking the suspense of the tale: S. S. Prawer, "Hoffmann's Uncanny Guest: A Reading of *Der Sandmann*," *German Life and Letters* 18 (1965): 297-308; Allan J. McIntyre, "Romantic Transcend-

ence and the Robot in Heinrich von Kleist and E. T. A. Hoffmann," *German Review* 54 (1979): 29-34. 3. Uncovering implicit and explicit social criticism: Lienhard Wawrzyn, *Der Automaten-Mensch: E. T. A. Hoffmanns Erzahlung von Sandmann* (Berlin: Klaus Wagenback, 1977); Herbert Kraft, "E. T. A. Hoffmann: Geschichtlichkeit und Illusion," *Romantik: Ein literaturwissenschaftliches Studienbuch*, ed. Ernst Ribbat (Konigstein: Athenaum, 1979), 138-62. 4. Fixing the role of the narrator: Maria Tatar, "E. T. A. Hoffmann's 'Der Sandmann': Reflection and Romantic Irony," *MLN* 95 (1980): 585-608. 5. Ascertaining Hoffmann's attitudes toward the writing process as reenacted by the story's characters: Raimund Belgardt, "Der Kunstler und die Puppe: Zur Interpretation von Hoffmanns *Der Sandmann*," *German Quarterly* 42 (1969): 686-700; Ursula Mahlendorf, "E. T. A. Hoffmann's *The Sandman*: The Fictional Psycho-Biography of a Romantic Poet," *American Imago* 32 (1975): 217-39; Jean Delabroy, "L'Ombre de la theorie (A propos de *L'Homme au sable* de Hoffmann)," *Romantisme* 24 (1979): 29-41. 6. Exploring the natural or supernatural basis of the events related: Ernst Fedor Hoffmann, "Zu E. T. A. Hoffmanns 'Sandmann,' " *Monatshefte* 54 (1962): 244-52.

10. Brooke-Rose, "Readerhood of Man," 135.

Uncle Henry's Trousers; or, The Metaphysical Status of Other Worlds

Stephen Prickett

> We learn more about Uncle Henry if we view him from another world, but the patch on the seat of his trousers is meaningless if we do not start from this world. Reality, like patchwork, is relative.

A modern novelist, John Fowles, saw a deep-seated need of the English "to create imaginary worlds other than the world which is the case":[1]

This desire, or need, has always been strongly linked...with the notion of retreat, in both the religious and the military sense; of the secret place that is also the redoubt. And for me it is here that the Robin Hood—or greenwood—myth changes from merely symbolizing folk-aspiration in social terms to enshrining a dominant mental characteristic, an essential behavior, an archetypal *movement* (akin to certain major vowel-shifts in the language itself) of the English imagination. (pp. 288-89)

This idea is not original. George Santayana, for instance, said something similar in 1914 about the importance of his "inner atmosphere" to the Englishman.[2] I do not know if this particular quality is as foreign to Americans as both writers imply. What interests me is the imagery by which Fowles tried to convey his meaning. He described this "retreat" into a "secret place" in terms of "an archetypal movement akin to certain major vowel-shifts in the language itself" (p. 289). To illustrate this he cited the work of that quintessentially English (and totally untypical) landscape painter Samuel Palmer during his brief visionary period under the influence of William Blake at Shoreham in North Kent. Palmer's landscape is "a place outside the normal world, intensely private and enclosed, intensely green and fertile, numinous, haunted and haunting, dominated by a sense of magic that is also a sense of a mysterious yet profound parity in all existence'' (Fowles, *Daniel Martin*, p. 290). In broad terms, the ''movement'' Fowles referred to is the Romantic movement, but he was selecting one particular aspect of it. We are not talking of enthusiasm for the political and social ideals of the French Revolution or even of a dramatic change in attitudes to Nature but primarily of an inward shift in self-consciousness—a greater sense of individuality that is accompanied by a desire for mental *privacy* in what seems to be a new way.

For a significant minority the powers of language, and the parallel symbolic systems of the visual arts, begin to be exploited not for what they can communicate to others but for what they can create for the possessor. They are seen as providing an area of internal space, whether for escape or for renewal. This desire for a Xanadu may or may not be, as Fowles argued, a typically English preoccupation. It is certainly not a *majority* preoccupation in any society. What it is typical of (if anything) is a continuous *minority* tradition beginning in European literature with Plato, but that includes specific English works such as Andrew Marvell's *Garden* and Samuel Coleridge's *Kubla Khan*, where the external world is seen in terms of the inner life of the mind. Although it is related to that much broader group of loosely associated ideas that we refer to under the umbrella term of the pastoral convention it distinguishes itself by its explicitly *visionary* overtones. We are given to understand that this ''other world'' of the Romantics is not only special, secret, magical, and set apart from the mundane world but *more real*.

There is a long tradition of the creation of ''other worlds'' in English literature. We think of Edmund Spenser's *Faerie Queene*, Thomas More's *Utopia*, and even *Gulliver's Travels*. Yet the moment we have listed examples like these we can see a difference. These pre-Romantic other worlds bear a different relationship to this one. Traditionally, the creation of alternative worlds had been to flatter, moralize, or satirize aspects of this one. Dante, Spenser, Jonathan Swift, and John Bunyan were all allegorists, and they wrote for audiences trained in the reading of allegory. If we want to understand the antics of the Lilliputian Ministers, performing on the high wire, we need look no further than the politics of Queen Anne's reign—and then, perhaps, to the nature of political balancing acts in general. But with the other worlds of the Romantics we encounter a different and startling kind of claim: that the ''reality'' of these worlds is not an adjunct of this world but that the reality of *this* world is somehow dependent upon the reality of the other, fictional creation.

This claim is so odd that it is worth pausing to consider the kind of philosophical climate from which it sprang. For Blake, for instance, the power of the true artist lay not in imitation of life or natural forms but in ''Imagination'' or ''Vision,'' not confined to the knowledge supplied by the five senses. In the margin to William Wordsworth's *Poems* of 1815 he wrote, ''One Power alone makes a Poet: Imagination, the Divine Vision.'' In part Blake seems to have conceived of the poet's Imagination in terms of its power to perceive and explore the world of Platonic absolute forms, but it also had for him practical implications

that are un-Platonic. In his early work *There Is No Natural Religion*, dating
from about 1788, we find him arguing that *all* human knowledge, including that
of science itself, is ultimately dependent upon Imagination. "If it were not for
the Poetic or Prophetic character the Philosophic and Experimental would soon
be at the ratio of all things, and stand still, unable to do other than repeat the
same dull round over again."[3] According to Blake, because Nature is perceived
by the senses it is subject to the limitations of sense perception. It cannot, for
instance, by the very definitions of Lockean empirical science, point beyond
itself to anything greater. In other words, there is nothing cumulative or spec-
ulative about sense data. Touch, taste, and hearing would tell us nothing about
sight if we happened to be born blind. How much less, then, can Nature, the
creation of sense data, point toward the "Infinite," which, Blake insisted, lies
at the heart of an individual's religious experience? It is, on the contrary, the
"poetic" or "prophetic" function of the Imagination that mediates revelation
to humans, showing them that their perceptions are not finally limited by their
five senses.

Thus Blake emphatically rejected the dominant Baconian and Lockean theory
of knowledge that assumed that "facts" would somehow suggest their own
order. To him it was obvious that we cannot even define what we mean by a
fact without an initial hypothesis. Sense data demand a prior imaginative structure; our knowledge of the world depends ultimately on the preconceptions—
the ideas and values—that we bring to it. For these preconceptions we rely upon
the Imagination, which applies innate ideas to the external world.

The first thing we notice about this argument is that it sounds a good deal
more like Immanuel Kant than Plato. Kant, too, had argued for the existence
of innate ideas, operating through "Reason." Although he himself had insisted
that the ideas of Reason were regulative only—that is, without specific content—
subsequent German idealists such as Friedrich Schelling, Johann Fichte, and, in
England, Coleridge and Thomas Carlyle seem to have interpreted Kant to mean
that it was possible to perceive spiritual truths by direct mystical intuition. As
Carlyle put it with characteristic enthusiasm: "Not by logic or argument does it
work; yet surely and clearly may it be taught to work; and its domain lies in the
higher region whither logic and argument cannot reach; in that holier region
where Poetry and Virtue and Divinity abide, in whose presence Understanding
wavers and recoils, dazzled into utter darkness by that 'sea of light', at once the
fountain and the termination of true knowledge."[4]

So far as we know Blake was not directly in touch with contemporary trends
in German philosophy in the way that Coleridge and Carlyle were, but he *had*
had access to many of the same intellectual currents through Emanuel Swed-
enborg, who had also been a major influence on Kant. There are, it is true,
major differences between the "idealism" of Blake, Coleridge, and Carlyle.
But questions of influence or of similarity in detail are unimportant here. What
is significant is that we find appearing in the final years of the eighteenth and
the early years of the nineteenth centuries, in poets as different in outlook as

Blake and Coleridge, the well-grounded philosophic belief that the constructs of the Imagination are not merely logically prior to sense perception but are also more *real*. For John Locke and his fellow empiricists the primacy of the external everyday world had been so obvious that it was taken for granted. Fiction was a secondary imitation of this world. A number of the finest creative minds of the age had begun to invert that commonsense relationship and suggest that our common external world was actually less solid and substantial than the internal constructs of the individual mind. It is no accident that the visionary Samuel Palmer, whom Fowles took as his example, was a follower and disciple of one such thinker.

Yet Blake's claim for the visionary nature of poetry had other implications, no less important. In *A Vision of the Last Judgment* he linked this notion of the primacy of the mind directly with the human religious experience: "Vision or Imagination is a Representation of what Eternally Exists, Really & Unchangeably. Fable or Allegory is form'd by the daughters of Memory. Imagination is surrounded by the daughters of Inspiration. . . . The Hebrew Bible & the Gospel of Jesus are not Allegory, but Eternal Vision of Imagination of All that Exists" (Blake, *Complete Writings*, p. 604). This argument, stated thus, has two important corollaries, both of which Blake was fully aware of. The first is that by claiming the Scriptures as "Imagination" he was solving in his own way the problem of the status of biblical narrative. Although the work of German historical critics such as Gotthold Lessing and Johann Eichhorn was still largely unknown in England at the end of the eighteenth century, it was beginning to filter through in radical Unitarian circles in the 1790s, and a few British critics, such as Nathaniel Lardner, Thomas Belsham, and Alexander Geddes, were in touch with their German counterparts and working along parallel lines. For them the notion of the Bible as the infallibly dictated word of God, historically correct in every detail, was no longer acceptable. The concept of "history" itself was changing. The Bible was to be understood as the mythology of a primitive semitic people, encrusted with miracle and legend; a mixture of popular superstition and what Eichhorn delicately called "pious fraud." Blake's solution was to reject *both* the enlightenment radicalism of the historical critics and the rigid certainties of biblical literalists. Both groups had made the fundamental mistake of relegating the Scriptures to the "outer" world of sense and science and denied their "inward" reality. Debates over historical authenticity of miracles were beside the point—and simply played into the hands of the materialists. In Coleridge's words, "extremes meet": biblical literalism partook of the empiricist "single vision" as much as did the German higher criticism. Both led to atheism. For Blake, in contrast, the Bible was the supreme example of "Eternal Vision"—that "other world" of the Spirit.

From this conclusion came the second corollary. In *All Religions Are One* (1788) Blake's "Voice of one crying in the wilderness" proclaimed that "The Religions of all Nations are derived from each Nation's different reception of the Poetic Genius, which is everywhere call'd the Spirit of Prophecy" (Blake,

Complete Writings, p. 98). Two years later, in *The Marriage of Heaven and Hell*, he elaborated this close connection between poetic genius and prophecy into a scene where the prophets Isaiah and Ezekiel "dined" with him. Ezekiel explains how "we of Israel taught that the Poetic Genius (as you now call it) was the first principle and all the others merely derivative" (Blake, *Complete Writings*, p. 151).

This claim, that the poet is also a prophet and seer, is not isolated. Others, apparently less visionary, were prepared to make very similar assertions. In Book XII of the 1805 *Prelude*, for instance, Wordsworth described what he called the "genius of the Poet" to his friend Coleridge in the following terms:

> Forgive me if I say that I, who long
> Had harboured reverentially a thought
> That Poets, even as Prophets, each with each
> Connected in a mighty scheme of truth,
> Have each for his peculiar dower, a sense
> By which he is enabled to perceive
> Something unseen before.[5]

Similarly, Percy Bysshe Shelley in his "Defence of Poetry" supported his claim that "poets are the unacknowledged legislators of mankind" by reference to their traditional role "in the earlier epochs of the world" as "legislators or prophets."[6] He appealed, through Sir Philip Sidney, to classical Roman antecedents, but he could no less confidently have done as Bishop Percy did in his preface to the *Reliques of Ancient Poetry* and appealed to the Anglo-Saxon and Old Norse traditions. Behind this new confidence in their prophetic function that links Blake, Wordsworth, and Shelley is a common eighteenth-century source: Bishop Robert Lowth's *Sacred Poetry of the Hebrews*.

Lowth's lectures of 1741 had been first published in Latin in 1753 and finally achieved much wider circulation with the English translation of 1787. They had been one of the key influences on the great revival of biblical studies that was to accompany the dawn of the Romantic movement. By the end of the century the classical models that had so dominated the Augustan literary sensibility had been largely supplanted by Hebrew ones. Lowth was the first critic of modern times to demonstrate how Hebrew poetry, unlike European verse, depended not on rhyme and meter but on repetition and parallelism. More significantly for our purposes, he had gone on to argue, with a wealth of scholarly detail, that the poets and prophets of Israel were one and the same: "The prophetic office had a most strict connexion with the poetic art. They had one common name, one common origin, one common author, the Holy Spirit. Those in particular were called to the exercise of the prophetic office, who were previously conversant with the sacred poetry."[7] By the end of the eighteenth century the effects of such scholarship were to reinforce the new philosophical idealism from Germany to make a belief in the primary reality of the poet's vision if not a critical commonplace (it is argued too vehemently for that) at least a logically and historically tenable position. The normal, commonsense view of the relationship between "fact" and "fiction" could be, and was, inverted. By the time Fowles is speaking of—the time, say, of Palmer in the 1820s—the creation of "other worlds" no longer demanded simply a willing suspension of disbelief but acceptance as a symbolic statement of a higher reality.

This is a distinction that must be framed with some care. When, for instance, George MacDonald in the 1850s purported to describe to us in *Phantastes* Anodos's adventures in Fairyland, he was obviously not trying to persuade us that his narrative is *literally* true. We are left in no doubt at all that the narrative is a symbolic fiction. It is also clear that we are meant to accept those symbols as having a higher and more absolute metaphysical status than the symbols in a "realistic" novel or in a traditional allegory. When Christian, in *Pilgrim's Progress*, is seized by the Giant Despair and incarcerated in Doubting Castle, we are in no doubt what is going on allegorically. The physical event in the allegorical narrative immediately refers to a familiar mental state in our world. It mirrors that state, but it does not claim to possess any more profound reference. In contrast, when Anodos in *Phantastes* is seduced by the Willow and comforted by the Beech we seem to be encountering a different *kind* of event masquerading as allegory. It is evidently not sufficient to describe it as an allegory of seduction and subsequent guilt; it is almost as if he is suggesting that our experiences of guilt in this world are themselves also allegorical of a much more profound betrayal that lies behind both. MacDonald's other world is less concerned to reflect this than to point *through* it—in a way that is, in this sense, different from the allegory of Spenser or Bunyan.

The rejection of allegory is a common thread in Romantic aesthetics—and has often been commented upon. But what is less often observed is that the reason for that rejection is not primarily aesthetic so much as metaphysical. Coleridge had prefaced his *Ancient Mariner* with a quotation from Thomas Burnet:

I can easily believe that there are more invisible than visible beings in the universe. But of their families, degrees, connections, distinctions, and functions, who shall tell us? How do they act? Where are they to be found? About such matters the human mind has always circled without attaining knowledge. Yet I do not doubt that sometimes it is well for the soul to contemplate as in a picture the image of a larger and better world, lest the mind, habituated to the small concerns of daily life, limit itself too much and sink entirely into trivial thinking.[8]

The charge against allegory is, by now, familiar. By showing us merely the world we already know, it does not do justice to the depth, complexity, and mystery of the *real* universe. It is, in short, not *fantastic* enough to be true. This is a theme that was taken up by Charles Kingsley: "the whole universe is larger than the little corner of it that any man, even the greatest poet or philosopher, can see; and as much grander, and as much more beautiful, and as much more strange."[9] Allegory, simply as allegory, is, MacDonald wrote, "weariness." It succeeds only when it reveals to us more than we know already, when it presents us with not our own world, however reshaped, but with a larger, more multi-dimensioned view of existence. We need, said MacDonald, the "Fantastic Allegory." Hence Dante, the supreme allegorist, passed the test, for he was also much more than a mere allegorist. As Blake might have pointed out he left this world a different place, changed unpredictably simply by the existence of the *Divine Comedy.* What does not alter is the moral law. In *Lilith* Mr. Raven explains to the symbolically named Mr. Vane:

"There is in your house a door, one step through which carries me into a world very much another than this."
"A better?"
"Not throughout; but so much another that most of its physical, and many of its mental laws are different from those of this world. As for moral laws, they must everywhere be fundamentally the same."[10]

Mr. Raven had clearly read his Burnet.

By the end of *Lilith*, MacDonald's last book, this sense both of unknown richness and complexity of the physical universe (or universes) and of its fundamental moral continuity has been made even more explicit in the course of the narrative itself. The moral reality common to both this world and the other is death. Yet in the other world death is not experienced as an ending but as a beginning—a prelude to action. The biological fact of death as we know it here is displayed now as being only an expression of a much more important psychological and spiritual process of "letting go" in order to receive. Christ's epigram "He that would save his life must lose it" is the theme of the book. In it we are made to watch a process akin to the transformation scene in a pantomime, where what at first appears to be a totally opaque backdrop is slowly discovered to be no more than the finest of transparent gauze as the lights at the front of the stage are dimmed and those behind the screen turned up. By the end of *Lilith* the life that is to be achieved through death is so much more real to Vane than this life that it is *this* world that is experienced as the shadowy one—a theme that is taken up by C. S. Lewis in the chapter of the last of the Narnia stories entitled "Farewell to the Shadow Lands."

Since what is at issue here is the relationship of multiple worlds to each other, what we would expect is that it is the points of transition or intersection that are important. That, as we have seen, is exactly what we do find in these "adult fairy stories" of George MacDonald. Anodos's passage into Fairyland is well-known: "Not knowing what change might follow next, I thought it high time to get up; and, springing from the bed, my bare feet alighted upon a cool green sward; and although I dressed in all haste, I found myself completing my toilet under the boughs of a great tree" (MacDonald, *Phantastes* and *Lilith*, pp. 19-20).

The description of the bedroom "coming to life" must tap some kind of childhood fantasy in us all. But MacDonald is also giving us a clear lead into the status or "reality" of his other world. What with us is mere imitation—carving or decorative flower designs—there is "natural" and springing with life. The washbasin is now an active Blakean metaphor: "The cistern contains; the fountain overflows." The spring of water is literally a River of Life, transforming from imitation to reality everything it touches. Anodos's first action is to bathe himself in an act of baptism in this water of life: it is the morning of his twenty-first birthday—the first day of his legal manhood. The tree above him—the bed in which he has hitherto slept—may even be interpreted as his "family tree." For Anodos, however, this transformation has a no less important personal and "inner" meaning. We recall that the floral pattern of the carpet is his *own* design. What he designed as an imitation of Nature has now, in this other world of Fairyland, taken on a genuine life of its own. Imitative art has been turned into creative art. What we find in this whole passage, in short, is one of the most concretely realized examples of the new Romantic attitude toward the other worlds of the artist. The private, inner, secret, fictional world provides the "reality" from which this one draws its imitations.

This brings us to Uncle Henry—or, at least, his trousers. I allude to the 1933 Hollywood movie of *Alice*, which contains the last of these transitions that I want us to consider: through the looking-glass. Let me remind you of the exact context:

> In another moment Alice was through the glass, and had jumped lightly down into the Looking-glass room.... Then she began looking about, and noticed that what could be seen from the old room was quite common and uninteresting, but that all the rest was as different as possible. For instance, the pictures on the wall next the fire seemed to be all alive, and the very clock on the chimney-piece (you know you can only see the back of it in the Looking-glass) had got the face of a little old man, and grinned at her.[11]

Uncle Henry, you will recall, is one of those "pictures on the wall next the fire" that seem to be alive. His face stares with full Victorian pomposity into *this* world, but from the other side of the looking-glass we can see his rear view, and those trousers, so elegant from the front, turn out to have a large patch on the seat of them. Purists will doubtless object to the liberties of Hollywood, but this kind of detail is only what Sir John Tenniel added so successfully elsewhere, and the idea of making what Lewis Carroll (pseudonym for Charles L. Dodgson) vaguely called a "picture" into a photograph is a nice one in view of his own hobby of photography. Carroll had, moreover, described just such a gap between pretension and reality in his poem *Hiawatha's Photographing*.

Carroll's hidden and secret redoubts in the *Alice* books are almost certainly the best known of all nineteenth-century other worlds of fiction. In them the tradition he had inherited from the Romantics and from his friend MacDonald comes to full flower. Novalis, the German Romantic and mystic who was perhaps the greatest single influence on MacDonald, observed that life might become a dream. Carroll's dream in *Through the Looking-Glass* is, like its forerunners, one of a greater and fuller reality. As in *Phantastes* we notice at once that the world behind the mirror is one of more abundant *life*. The clock smiles, the flowers argue and sulk, chessmen dither and philosophize, and Uncle Henry in the photograph apologizes for his patched trousers. But as we read on we discover that this initial sense of a richer and more complicated world than our own is not part of a "higher" reality so much as an *inverted* one. The lateral inversion of the mirror image persists at every level. At its simplest it is what prevents Alice from walking in the direction she wants to go, out of the garden; at another level it involves the inversion of the normal laws of Nature—Alice must run in order to stand still, the White Queen inverts time, and screams before she pricks herself. Beneath these levels, however (and, as critics such as A. L. Taylor and Derek Hudson have ably demonstrated, there are many of them), lies the one of most immediate interest to us: an aesthetic inversion—that of the genre itself. Partly because Carroll is so often treated as being *sui generis* I have been at pains to demonstrate that there *is* behind him a tradition of "other worlds," and that *Through the Looking-Glass* shares with them certain metaphysical and aesthetic assumptions. Yet what he does is to *invert* that tradition. At its simplest we find it simply in specific parodies. As is well known, for instance, the White Knight's Song is intended as a parody of Wordsworth's *Resolution and Independence*. But even here there is a quality that should give us pause. Carroll had a keen ear for rhyme and phrase, and his parodies of Isaac Watts in *Alice in Wonderland* demonstrate how adept he was at imitating particular forms. Here, however, he is less interested in parodying the form of Wordsworth's poem, as its "hidden curriculum": the unstated assumptions of poet and leech gatherer that almost make the poem a study in noncommunication. The only phrase that the White Knight "hears" (although he retells every word) is the aged man's desire to drink his health, and that—to labor the obvious—is a misunderstanding, since he takes it as a compliment, when in fact it is a request for a tip!

Similarly, there are other sly inversions in the "hidden curriculum" of *Through the Looking-Glass*. Carroll, we know, had read *Phantastes*. Like MacDonald's book, *Alice in Wonderland* is a birthday book, set on May 4, 1862 (Alice Liddell's tenth birthday). *Through the Looking-Glass*, however, is set (as might be expected) on its direct calendar opposite: November 4. It is, in Carroll's own words, "an un-birthday present." But the total thematic parody is much more than a matter of such details—skillfully planted as they are. "Dream literature"— in which we must include *Phantastes*—although it may be about a higher *reality*, had nonetheless been about the dream of the protagonist. Tweedledum and Tweedledee convince Alice that since (they argue) the Red King is dreaming about her, her existence is dependent on her being the object of his dream. When she grows afraid they will wake him, they argue that she, as his dream unreality, cannot affect him.

"If I wasn't real," Alice said—half laughing through her tears, it all seemed so ridiculous—"I shouldn't be able to cry."

"I hope you don't suppose those are *real* tears?" Tweedledum interrupted in a tone of great contempt. (Dodgson, *Alice*, pp. 144-45)

Just as Tweedledum and Tweedledee are mirror images of each other, so Alice seems to have found *her* mirror image in the Red King (remember she is eventually going to be a White Queen). Most commentators on this passage are content with a passing reference to George Berkeley. Yet it is important—so much so that it forms the argument of the last chapter. It is, in a curious sense, the far end of the tradition we saw beginning with Blake and the idealists. The fictional protagonist dreams that she is no longer the dreamer. The logic is clear enough. If the "other" world is more real than this one it must follow that someone from this world entering the other is herself *unreal*. Alice is now denied reality by her *own* creations. I am told that in the Royal Air Force there was reputed to be a mythical bird, called the "Shitehawk," whose peculiar attribute was to fly in ever decreasing circles until it finally disappeared up in its own latter end. Similarly, for a fictional heroine to be accused of being what she undoubtedly is, a work of fiction, seems appropriate, if unconventional. The only thing that *is* real is the work of fiction: in this case, the Red King's (or is it Alice's?) dream.

This brings me to the point of my title: we learn more about Uncle Henry if we view him from another world, but the patch on the seat of his trousers is meaningless if we do not start from this world. Reality, like patchwork, is relative.

NOTES

1. John Fowles, *Daniel Martin* (New York: Signet Books, 1978), 288. Further references appear in parentheses in the text.

2. George Santayana, *Soliloquies in England* (Ann Arbor: University of Michigan Press, 1967), 30.

3. William Blake, *Complete Writings*, ed. Geoffrey Keynes (London: Oxford University Press, 1966), 97. Further references appear in parentheses in the text.

4. Thomas Carlyle, "The State of German Literature," in *Critical and Miscellaneous Essays* (London: Chapman and Hall, 1869), 1:96.

5. William Wordsworth, *The Poetical Works*, ed. Ernest de Selincourt (Oxford: Oxford University Press, 1950), lines 300-305.

6. Percy Bysshe Shelley, "A Defence of Poetry," in *English Romantic Poetry and Prose*, ed. Russell Noyes (New York: Oxford University Press, 1956), 1098.

7. Robert Lowth, *Lectures on the Sacred Poetry of the Hebrews*, trans. G. Gregory (London: Ogles, Duncan, and Cochran, 1816), 2:18.

8. Samuel Taylor Coleridge, *The Complete Poetical Works*, ed. Ernest H. Coleridge (Oxford: Clarendon Press, 1957), 1:186.

9. Charles Kingsley, *Madam How and Lady Why* (London: Macmillan, 1889), 112.

10. George MacDonald, *Phantastes* and *Lilith* (Grand Rapids, Mich.: Eerdmans, 1964), 227. Further references appear in parentheses in the text.

11. Charles L. Dodgson, *Alice in Wonderland and Through the Looking-Glass*, ed. Donald J. Gray (New York: Norton, 1971), 111-12. Further references appear in parentheses in the text.

Primitive, Newtonian, and Einsteinian Fantasies: Three Worldviews

James D. Ziegler

Although there are some glimmerings of the Einsteinian worldview on the horizon, we are still in the same relationship to the Einsteinian worldview as the illiterate European peasants were to the early Newtonian worldview.

Fantasy, as a genre of the creative imagination, can be described as a chimerical or fantastic notion, where "fantastic" connotes unrestrained extravagance in the creations of the imaginative faculty. Despite this definition, fantasy, like all other human activities, cannot be wholly unrestrained. Restraints are placed on humans not only by their biological, psychological, and social natures but by the *Weltanschauung* of their times. Thus *fantasy* must be redefined as an extravagance in the creations of the imaginative faculty within the constraints of human nature and of worldviews. I will leave to biologists, social scientists, theologians, and philosophers the problem of human nature and address the problem of restraints imposed on the creative faculty by the worldview current at the time in which fantasists create their works.

The dominant worldview before the seventeenth century is often referred to as "pre-Newtonian," a term that may also apply to peoples who have not yet accepted the Newtonian system of thought. Since such peoples may otherwise represent different cultural levels, despite basic similarities in worldview, the term *primitive* is more convenient to describe the pre-Newtonian *Weltanschauung*.

Several aspects of such a worldview stand out. There is no clear division between the divine and the human or between living and inert matter. The characteristic division is between good and evil, which are almost Manichaean in their expression. Fantasy's role in the primitive mind is primarily moral. Myths, fairy tales, folk stories, and anecdotal material reflect this view of the universe as basically a moral system. Good and evil are absolute and objective. Both fantasy and nonfantasy are attempts to answer holistic questions such as "What is Truth?" "What is good and just?" "What is life?" Whether one reads Plato or Aristophanes, these questions are implicit. Plato's account of Atlantis and Aristophanes's description of Cloudcuckooland each reflect their common preoccupation with eternal verities. Also implicit in the two accounts is a moral comparison with the "real" world. The two men, however, must locate their mythical land either in the past (Atlantis) or in space (Cloudcuckooland). The descriptions must have points of similarity to the experience of humans living in the present on Earth, and these similarities must be sufficiently a part of the general worldview so that readers can comprehend and accept the moral message being conveyed. Primitive fantasy, as analyzed through the structuralist approach of Claude Lévi-Strauss, displays a striking feature: the tales are always synchronous. Even tales laid in the past can be understood only in reference to the present. The primitive mind rejects the diachronous system.

The system of thought associated with the name of Sir Isaac Newton changed, and changes, people's worldview. No longer are they engaged in a holistic approach to the world. The type of questions they now ask are: "What happens when a rock falls from a height?" "How does the blood move through the body?" "How can I exploit a vein of silver ore without the miners drowning or suffocating?" When individuals like Galileo Galilei ask these questions, they are also rejecting the synchronous approach. They are examining discrete phenomena in an attempt to satisfy immediate objectives such as allaying curiosity, healing sickness, killing enemies efficiently, and amassing wealth. Although moral questions may emerge, the phenomena themselves are not moral. The examination of the phenomena can only occur serially, resulting in a diachronous activity. The seven decades separating Galileo's *Starry Messenger* from Newton's *Principia Mathematica* encompass the revolution.

Newton's great achievement was to point out that the examination of a small segment of the universe can produce a greater knowledge of the universe itself. This can be done because the universe is the same throughout. For the next two centuries explorations of nature and humans supported Newton's conclusion. The result was the development of a closed system operating by fixed rules that could be discovered by reason based on observation. Such discovery was made possible by the objectification and quantification of the observations. Observers approached a phenomenon as external to themselves with characteristics that could be described in numerical terms. Since relationships between numbers had been known since the time of Pythagoras, phenomena could now be quantified. Such phenomena would be value free in these terms, and reason could be applied to answer the nonholistic questions in the minds of the observers.

This methodology resulted in the triumph of science—not because science proved the truth of philosophical or theological systems, but because it solved the everyday problems facing humans. Although the seventeenth century witnessed modern scientific explorations in many fields, physics dominated. In succeeding years the methods of physics were applied to other areas of human knowledge. In the process human knowledge replicated physics, further legitimating science as the only valid worldview, one that was only limited by the people's use of their innate intelligence and the tools available at the time.

In nonscientific areas the Newtonian worldview also dominated. Art, music, and literature reflect this domination. The machine became the model. Individual works by artists, musicians, and writers had to be understood as machines that demonstrated at the same time their discrete individuality and their place in the universe. Fantasy shared in this. Charles Perrault took the primitive French folk stories and transformed them into Newtonian fairy tales. In *Beauty and the Beast* Beauty is the scientist, and the Beast is nature. Through understanding, fear and revulsion give way to love and partnership. The Fairy Godmother in Cinderella can be seen as the scientist delivering humankind into the Promised Land of a better life as personified by Prince Charming. The Wicked Stepmother represents ignorance and jealousy, which are overcome by the fitting of the glass slipper upon Cinderella's foot. The glass slipper can be understood as science, Cinderella's foot as humankind. When humans accept science, they are transformed, fear and jealousy are defeated, and they live happily ever after.

Fantasy's response to the changing *Weltanschauung* may also be seen in the comparison of Cyrano de Bergerac's account of a voyage to the moon with the story of the flight of Icarus. The myth of Icarus is explicitly a moral tale. In Cyrano's account, however, individuals leave Earth for another physical object in the universe. When they arrive, that object is identifiably similar to Earth and is inhabited by similar living creatures, with similar concerns. Icarus uses wings made of feathers held together by wax; Cyrano uses rockets and beef tallow. Icarus flies too close to the sun, the wax melts, and he falls to Earth. Cyrano returns to Earth by a demon taking him to hell, which requires a passage back to Earth. Cyrano solves the problem of his return by a method lifted from the primitive worldview.

From Cyrano de Bergerac to Jules Verne, fantasists have taken the latest discoveries of Newtonian science and put humans through fantastic adventures. In all cases, however, these adventures occur in the Newtonian universe. The picaresque stories of Gil Blas, the erotic fantasies of Casanova, the lies of Baron Munchausen, the tales about Till Eulenspiegel, Jonathan Swift's satire in the account of Gulliver's travels—all are Newtonian. Fantasists joined the other, less extravagant users of the imaginative faculty in turning away from the search for the good, the true, and the beautiful to portray the real, the material, within the continuum of time.

This might appear at first to be untrue. Although fantasists such as H. G. Wells, Jules Verne, and Edward Bellamy reflect the Newtonian system, others like Mary Shelley, Edgar Allan Poe, and Bram Stoker appear to violate it. In their fantasies the premise seems to be one of deliberate flight from the Newtonian worldview. A closer reading, however, demonstrates that humans' attempt to violate the Newtonian system in these works regularly leads to disaster. Dr.

Frankenstein creates a monster and is destroyed by it. Members of the Usher family attempt to survive without following the Newtonian principles and are killed off by the collapse of their house. Dracula would appear to be successful in transcending the Newtonian world; yet even he is destroyed by it in the end.

The fact that Dracula was written toward the end of the nineteenth century, and that it points to a non-Newtonian worldview, reflects what was happening in science. Scientists in the latter part of the nineteenth century were having increasing difficulties in reconciling their discoveries with Newtonian principles. Light, in particular, demonstrated properties of both matter and energy. The Newtonian system posited that matter and energy were discrete and different. The line between matter and energy became even more blurred with the work of Henri Bequerel and Wilhelm Roentgen, the discoverers of radio waves and X-rays. The development of quantum mechanics by Max Planck explained the phenomena but destroyed the barrier between matter and energy. By 1900 physicists were shifting from studying energy as an affective principle to a conception of energy as the basis of the universe.

The lack of adequate theoretical framework inhibited scientists in their attempts to explain phenomena such as radioactivity, electromagnetism, random particle activity, and osmosis. The laws of thermodynamics, which had enabled humankind to create the modern industrial society, were inadequate when applied to these phenomena. The foundations of the Newtonian system were developing cracks. The biggest crack was a growing realization that human understanding and control of nature required more than simply better observations and better tools. The seventeenth-century revolt against the then-prevailing assumption that events on Earth were punishments for sin, meliorated by God's grace, had led to the Newtonian system. It would appear that the next step would be a similar questioning of the Newtonian assumptions, with an almost infinite number of possible systems to replace the Newtonian system.

Perhaps this would have happened except for the publication of three papers by a Swiss patent office functionary in 1905-6. These papers, by Albert Einstein, although they did not have the breadth or simplicity of Newton's *Principia Mathematica*, did explain satisfactorily the discrepancies between scientific observations and the Newtonian system. In this way they are analogous to Galileo's *Starry Messenger*. Science, and humankind, then waited for the new Newton to synthesize all of the activities of scientists in the coming decades. Einstein, however, was to be the Newton of the new system, with the publication of *The General Theory of Relativity* in 1915. (The three earlier papers were published under the title *Special Theory of Relativity*.) Einstein was to spend the rest of his life in an attempt to achieve what the successors of Newton had done by developing a comprehensive system—in this case, the unified field theory. He failed, but the search is still going on, as indicated by the awarding of the Nobel Prize in physics for 1979 to men who have brought us closer to the formulation of the unified field theory. In the absence of the unified field theory Einstein's general theory of relativity expresses the contemporary worldview.

All of us are familiar with the word *relativity*. It has passed into discussions of, and inquiries into, all areas of human thought and endeavor. It has given rise to the "big-bang" theory of the universe, to situational ethics, to anarchy in the humanities. Unfortunately, most of those who use Einstein as the authority for their ideas have misused his theories. "Relativity," and its twin "uncertainty" (from Werner Heisenberg's principle), have been used to justify the rejection of absolutes, which in turn has led to the substitution of the subjective and ephemeral for the objective and eternal in nonscientific activity. Even in science the recent trend has been toward research in applied science rather than further exploration in Einsteinian problems. The present status of intellectual activity can best be summarized by statements such as this: "Since everything is relative and uncertain, whatever I express is as valid as anything else. The only criterion is the marketplace."

This approach might be acceptable if the marketplace were free. In ideas, as in goods, market research by pollsters has replaced the free exchange of intellectual endeavors. The statistician reigns supreme, and the result is presold formulas. These formulas dress up the Newtonian system in Einsteinian terminology. Whether it is *Star Trek*, *Star Wars*, or the latest horror flick, the Newtonian special effects demonstrate the only attempts at fantasy.

Apparently, we are aware that Einstein shattered the Newtonian worldview, but we are still unable to escape our bondage to Newton. We need some standard, and the statistician provides that standard. The computer has replaced the human brain in creating fantasy to such an extent that the brain is routinely referred to as a giant computer. But computers cannot escape the Newtonian universe, as HAL demonstrates in *2001: A Space Odyssey*. What makes HAL different is the reinjection of a primitive worldview into the Newtonian universe. In fact, much of twentieth-century fantasy appears to be the survival of the primitive worldview in the Newtonian system. This is part of the twentieth-century attempt to deal with evil, because the realities of our time are more fantastic than most of our fantasies. None of the Newtonian fantasists could imagine horrors such as World War I, Stalinism, Nazism, World War II, Viet Nam, Kampuchea, concentration camps, Gulags, modern urban terrorism, or nuclear bombs.

Only the last horror owes anything to Einstein. The others result from following Newtonian principles. But all of the horrors of the twentieth century pose a significant problem for fantasists. They have three solutions. First, they can trivialize or make banal the reality around them. This is the solution of most contemporary fantasists. Second, they can escape from the horrors of the present by creating their own world. One direction is indicated by Tolkien, another by Norman Rockwell. Third, they can illuminate the present by exaggerating its flaws and absurdities. Works such as *One Hundred Years of Solitude*, *The Yawning Heights*, and *Gravity's Rainbow* illustrate this solution. This third solution also reflects the Einsteinian worldview.

To support my contention, remember that both the primitive and Newtonian systems were closed systems. Einstein created an open system. To Einstein and to modern science the universe is not closed. It appears closed to the observer, but that is relative to the observer. Move the observer, and the system changes. Because energy and not mass is the basis of the universe, motion is the norm. Both the observer and the object observed are moving. The perception of the observer is determined by the relative rates of velocity involved. Another observer moving at a different velocity than the first observer would perceive the object differently. When this premise is combined with the concept of an open system, the result is uncertainty. Newtonians focused their attention upon moving particles of matter. These particles did not change as their velocities changed, because Newtonians ignored the most crucial element involved—time.

To Newton time was a constant, to be measured in the same way that mass, density, and volume are measured. To Einstein time is relative in the same way that mass, density, and volume are relative. Since mass, density, and volume change as their velocities change, time also changes—hence the popular term *fourth dimension*.

It is this use of time that differentiates most clearly the Newtonian and Einsteinian worldviews. In terms of fantasy it means that time ceases to be diachronous. Time, however, does not become synchronous, as in the primitive worldview. Instead, it becomes something defined by the moving relationships of particles of matter. This means that time in the Einsteinian universe is achronous. Matter and time are determined by velocity, which in turn is the result of energy. Einsteinian fantasists will then concern themselves with energy and will subordinate matter and time to their proper, secondary roles.

Will fantasy reflect the Einsteinian worldview? I see some evidence that this is happening. Marcel Proust, in *Remembrance of Things Past*, illustrated this to some extent; here is a work in which movement from object to object replaces movement on the continuum through time—a movement that is without velocity and is certainly not Newtonian. The surrealists, also, represent a trend toward the Einsteinian system. Although they approach reality from the standpoint of the subconscious, their work illustrates the distortions that occur when the observer is placed on a different plane than that of the Newtonian system.

In conclusion, although there are some glimmerings of the Einsteinian worldview on the horizon, successful (in monetary terms) fantasy still hews to the Newtonian worldview. It is the juxtaposition of the Newtonian and primitive views that appears to be the major alternative to straight Newtonian fantasy. We are still in the same relationship to the Einsteinian worldview as the illiterate European peasants were to the early Newtonian worldview. Before the Brothers Grimm cleaned up the German folk tales and turned them into children's stories, the forest and its creatures, including humans, were dangerous and bloody. Now that Walt Disney has completely sanitized them, the stage is set for the next breakthrough. This will come with the emergence of someone like Aristophanes or Rabelais, who can then be followed by a bowdlerizing anthologist. At present,

Luis Bunuel, J. L. Borges, Thomas Pynchon, and Grigori Zinoviev are pointing the way. To seize on the essence of Einsteinian fantasy, watch *Un Chien Andalou*, read *The Yawning Heights*, and then imagine a universe in which velocity is the determinant.

The Imaginary: Synthesis of Fantasy and Reality

William G. Plank

> If we admit that the existence of *fantasy* is as one term of the dialectic
> fantasy/reality, we must also admit that the existence of *reality* is as one
> term of the dialectic and that the two terms find their synthesis in the
> imagination that is the epistemological basis for perceptions, that
> apparatus that constructs the world as world, whether that world is the
> world of Newtonian science, the world of literature, or the world of
> dreams and fantasy.

The categorization of fantasy into the Newtonian and Einsteinian worldviews by James Ziegler in the previous chapter demonstrates that the human imagination works within a framework provided by the history of ideas. We begin to see that "pure imagination" or "pure fantasy" are improbable concepts, and that fantasy depends for its existence on the perception of an accepted reality. How then does fantasy exist and what are the conditions of its existence? It is, in fact, one term of a dialectic formed by the assumed concept of reality and again, as Ziegler suggested, reflects the same values and the same assumptions about the nature of reality as the prevailing physics.

There is little real difference between the premises of reality and fantasy, and the writings of fantasists are a reflection of their values and their perceptions of the world. The fantasies in the semiautobiographical novels of Louis-Ferdinand Céline are hallucinations caused by the narrator's purported brain damage during the war, and these hallucination fantasies are orchestrated into the novels to maintain or vary the feverish quality of his works in general. In *Death on the Installment Plan* the gigantic Customer walks down the streets of Paris, her skirts brushing the tops of the buildings:"She tripped over a bus stop shelter and smashed a building.... The elevator squirted out and gored her eye."[1] All of the people Louis had known "were running in the caverns underneath the Lady, in her drawers, through whole streets and neighborhoods, compressed inside her petticoats" (p. 92). But this scene is no more bizarre or fantastic than a man's trip, described in *Rigodon*, through a burning Hamburg with his wife, his cat, and a troop of retarded children. They both reflect the monstrosities of a world gone wrong, of humanity's abuse of humanity, and the general analysis of a world that becomes a teratology.

Fantasies are restatements of the real world, restructurings of the building blocks of accepted reality, just as Mary Shelley's Dr. Frankenstein used parts of real people to create a monster. But our monsters can become monsters only by participating in the human. Frankenstein's creation was a monster because he was human—so human that it is easy to see in him the romantic hero, grotesque outside, misunderstood, lonely, superior physically and intellectually, bent on revenging himself against a creator who created him apparently only to suffer— disappearing finally into the waste.

It is necessary to conclude from the foregoing that fantasy is not merely a literature of escape, but that it is an alternative form, a genre for treating general literary themes. We think of Jorge Luis Borges as producing some of the finest examples of the literature of fantasy. His story "The Library of Babel" depicts an infinite library wherein all is written down and where librarians wander endlessly searching and preserving. However, the story appears as a reasonable and transparent parable of humans' confrontation with a universe in which they seek meaning and expect to find the key to that meaning, where sectarian violence occasionally breaks out, where humans persevere in solitude and try to maintain hope. Such a model of the universe is not an unexpected creation for an autodidact whose omnivorous curiosity lends a kind of exotic interest to apparently unrelated and banal objects: That tone of fascination with the existence of objects in themselves (compare Borges's story "The Zahir"), separate from the rigid control of a general intellectual construct or a disciplined empirical order, is one of the major characteristics of Borges's work. That tone may easily be interpreted as the presence of the fantastic and may lead us to a definition of *fantasy* in Borges: the absence of a logical and empirical hierarchy or order of things and the concomitant interest in the behavior of things themselves rather than in perceived relations. Those perceived relations are, moreover, the subject matter of Western science. Any kind of literature that does not recognize the priority of those relations to the things themselves is bound to appear somewhat bizarre— and that lack of a hierarchy makes the world of objects a labyrinth (*Labyrinths* being one of Borges's titles) and a fantastic place. The literary tone of autodidacts reflects their worldview.

The problem with autodidacts is that they in some way escape our educational system, which organizes knowledge for our culture and defines what the valid branches of learning are—definitions that, moreover, usually reflect the needs of the power structure, whether that power structure needs military officers, technicians, businesspersons, or laborers on the assembly line. Their fantasies tend to disturb our priorities and to give equal time to things that do not support the status quo.

This dialectic of fantasy/reality applies to most works we call fantasy, whether by E. T. A. Hoffmann, Gérard de Nerval, or Arthur Rimbaud, or even in the surrealists, whose surrealism was a function of their perception of bourgeois reality. How then do we recognize fantasy and distinguish it in or from folk tales, fairy tales, tall tales, parables, epic exaggeration, or simply poetry? I propose that fantasy is to a degree a linguistic and textual phenomenon, that there is a language of fantasy, and that the author gives signals to readers that prepare them for the way they are to understand the text. This language of fantasy may be distinguished by things such as exotic vocabulary, variation in the sequencing of perceptions, the presence of the narrator as evident narrator or by the handling of shifters in the text, and the use of code phrases such as "once upon a time" or exergues from recognized fantasies such as *Alice in Wonderland*. Microanalysis of various texts would no doubt reveal the signals whereby each author announces the attitude the reader is expected to take. There is, then, in structuralist terms, a *signifiant*, a signifier or a set of signifiers for the *signifié*, that is fantasy.

When we read fantasy, we pick up the *signifiants* of the fantasy because of our years of reading; our culture has taught us and our authors to observe this literary contract. But there is one author who does not follow the rules, who does not observe the contract, who warps that original cozy understanding made between author and reader, an understanding that may be built into the very posture of author in relation to reader or of scriptor as compared to lector in structuralist terms. That author is Franz Kafka. His failure to observe that contract changes the relations between author and reader and between reader and text and makes of him a unique figure in the history of literature, an author whose work attains the signified (*signifié*) of fantasy without the culturally accepted and linguistically expected signifiers and signals. He thus creates a fantasy that is the equivalent of reality. This explains the uncanny grip that stories of his such as "In the Penal Colony" and "The Burrow" have on the reader.

If we admit that the existence of *fantasy* is as one term of the dialectic fantasy/reality, we must also admit that the existence of *reality* is as one term of the dialectic fantasy/reality and that the two terms find their synthesis in the imagination. *Imagination*, that is, the ability of the human mind to create images by means of which it explains the world to itself, is the epistemological basis for perceptions of reality. These images, produced by the image-creating cognitive apparatus, are the manner in which that apparatus constructs the world as world, whether that world is the world of Newtonian or Einsteinian science, the world of poetry and creative literature in general, or the world of dreams and fantasy. Perhaps we should replace the word *imaginary* with *imagic*, since imaginary has picked up a bad reputation somewhere for meaning nonexistent, false, invalid. *Imagic* could be more in line with the *imaginaire* in the psychology of Jacques Lacan, that activity whereby the self becomes a self in the Lacanian psychogenesis.

The fact is that after these images are generated they are validated or invalidated according to whether the intellectual politics being applied to them is scientific, literary, fantastic, fictional, primitive, philosophic, or something else. Such an effort to decide on the validity of images is probably partly responsible for the argument between realism and idealism, an argument that could be interpreted as being political.

If the dialectic of fantasy/reality is the mode of existence of both fantasy and reality, it bcomes increasingly difficult to distinguish one from the other, and terms such as *reality, fantasy, science fiction, primitive bricolage* (in Lévi-Strauss's discussion in *La Pensée sauvage*), *empirical science, theoretical physics,* and *philosophy* become nothing more than varieties of discourse validated by the prevailing value system of culture. It is very difficult to make any hard and fast rule about the difference between *bricolage* (that willy-nilly way that primitives have of making sense of their world, the "science of the concrete" as Lévi-Strauss called it), our scientific structures, and our science fiction. This is why we frequently find that science fiction preannouncs science itself and why scientists write science fiction themselves. Science itself we sometimes perceive as containing the exotic terms of fantasy, and the uneducated reader may not be able to distinguish between science and science fiction. One is led to wonder whether education is, in fact, education or whether it is cultural and linguistic conditioning. In the modern world science has taken on the aura of the exotic, with its specialized terminology, its incredible successes in physics, medicine, and space—in a word, modern science has developed a vocabulary, a style, a discourse, that was ready-made for application to fantasy. The language of science itself as we read it in the scientific journals is a fantasy: that scientific language makes a claim for bare objectivity, eschewing style, and in the bleakness of its prose makes the exaggerated claim to be the language in which truth unadorned is couched. As such it is one of the most visible of styles with the most unscientific of claims, that of being the vehicle of truth.

The mind's ability to create images is the basic epistemological behavior of the human mind: the assignment of truth or validity to these images is the role of a politics of the intellect, a politics that is certainly related to the technological, commercial, or magical power of a culture. Politics is the study of power, and it is the political, technological power of a culture that defines what is real and what is fantastic. Reality therefore becomes an exercise in politics, and the fantastic is the realm of the powerless and the disaffected. Power, whether military, political, academic, scientific, or something else, validates itself through its claim to being real, true, and right. Tyrants have a monopoly on reality, a reality maintained by the army, the courts, official science, the economic system, or the editors of professional journals. The literature of authority is the real literature, whether it is the classic possible of the French seventeenth century or official Soviet realism. It is therefore simply no accident that the greatest exercise in fantasy in history—surrealism—was also a revolutionary movement that struck at the roots of bourgeois authority and the bourgeois conception of reality.

Borges's fantasy, as I have suggested, is a dismantling of the Western hierarchy of organization by an autodidact. Céline was against everything but cats, some children, and female dancers whose art rescued the human body from its innate nastiness by elevating it to geometry. Kafka disturbs us deeply, because he was able to break that literary and political distinction we have created between fantasy and reality.

The worldview of fantasy is a nonempirical or pseudoempirical organization of the world paralleling the primitive approach to the world—it is a kind of *bricolage*. It may be argued that fantasy is not only an attempt to escape from an unacceptable cultural condition—a common and not very surprising assumption that may be made about all persons who create a world of their own—but that it also is a return to a kind of primitive epistemology. To the extent that Lévi-Strauss demonstrated the validity of this "primitive" "reasoning," we may see in fantasy a valid view of the world and a look into a primordial kind of world organization. Again, it is perfectly logical that cubism and surrealism, making revolutionary claims, should have been concerned with primitive art.

We now find ourselves in the position of having to assert either that science fiction is not fantasy or that science is fantasy. Science fiction, as Ziegler suggested, describes what could happen given the laws of a Newtonian universe and to a lesser extent given the view of an Einsteinian universe. After all, there is not very much difference between what does happen according to "natural law" and what *could* happen. Natural law becomes the basis of a new classicism. Seventeenth-century French classicists sought not what did happen but what could have happened according to their classic preconceptions. It is precisely the role of our science fiction to show what could happen according to our scientific and technological values and preconceptions. Science fiction therefore is the expression of the politics of science and technology just as surely as the tragedies of Jean Baptiste Racine and Pierre Corneille and the whole French classical doctrine were expressions of the triumph of the French monarchy. As such, science fiction is an expression of conservatism, of the technological status quo. As a valuing of the model of natural law it is the subjection of the imagination to that model of natural law; it is the framework in which the imagination is appropriated and coopted by the capitalist-industrial society. Science fiction is a bourgeois phenomenon, and *Star Wars* and *Star Trek* are simply realistic depictions of modern cultural values—when they are not expressions of a nostalgia for a nineteenth-century frontier adventure.

If we seek an absolute definition of *fantasy* we have to be content with the idea that fantasy is the author's claim to fantasy, to the announcement that he or she is writing fantasy. Ironically, *Star Wars* entertains and amuses us by emphasizing that there is a difference between fantasy and reality, while giving us a realistic view of our technological values. But Kafka frightens us by maintaining the identity of fantasy and reality in a literature that seems not to be fantasy at all but unquestioned accepting of the reality of a bad dream from which we have not yet awakened.

NOTES

1. Louis-Ferdinand Céline, *Death on the Installment Plan*, trans. Ralph Manheim (New York: New Directions, 1966), 91. Further references appear in parentheses in the text.

Consciousness, the Fantastic, and the Reading Process

Ralph Yarrow

How does the fantastic nudge, persuade, or bludgeon consciousness into changing its focus?

Le soleil se couchait. Les deux égarés entendirent quelques petits cris qui parassaient poussés par des femmes. Ils ne savaient si ces cris étaient de douleur ou de joie; mais ils se levèrent précisément avec cette inquiétude et cette alarme que tout inspire dans un pays inconnu. Ces clameurs partaient de deux filles toutes nues qui couraient légèrement au bord de la prairie, tandis que deux singes les suivaient en leur mordant les fesses.

Voltaire, *Candide, ou l'Optimisme*

[The sun was setting. The two wanderers heard a few little cries that seemed to be uttered by women. They did not know whether these were cries of pain or joy; but they rose to their feet precisely with the anxiety and the alarm that everything inspires in an unknown country. These cries came from two girls, stark naked, who were running lightly along the edge of the meadow, while two monkeys followed them and bit their buttocks.]

Most fantasy leads us into a world that seems unfamiliar. Like Candide we have difficulty in deciphering its language or judging its standards of behavior. We experience "precisely" a sense of unease and alarm; and like Alice we tend to react by indignantly invoking the norms we are familiar with. (She is scandalized by not being asked to tea or by the unconventional approach to dormice and teapots.) Similarly, Candide resorts to the standards he is familiar with and heroically shoots the nibbling monkeys, being unable to conceive that they could be the girls' lovers.

Candide, in fact, never catches up with the reality of the world (and eventually has to retire from it), because he consistently censors from his imagination anything potentially disturbing. But without some kind of disturbance you never learn anything. "Habit is a great deadener," said Samuel Beckett, paraphrasing Marcel Proust.[1] This is as true of reading (listening, viewing) as it is of social behavior. As long as we go on "reading" the same language we go on seeing the world in the same way. That fact is bad enough in any event but disastrous if our language gives us the kind of blinkered reality that Candide gets from Pangloss.

Candide's problem described above is presented precisely in terms of deciphering linguistic signs, although these signs are vocalized rather than written. Candide's disquiet stems from the unfamiliar and ambiguous quality of the sounds, and he soothes it by interpreting them according to his own habit. He does not want to allow ambiguity any lease of life and prefers to shoot first and ask questions afterwards.

In some cases this might look like sensible behavior, where danger threatens one's very existence. But here it is not Candide's life that is in danger but his set of moral values. In spite of everything that has happened to him he still believes in the existence and superiority of something called "human nature"; and he cannot take the attack made on this notion by the possibility that girls might prefer monkeys, or that the sexual behavior of humans and monkeys might not be all that different. Candide desperately clings to his (inherited/authorized) version and so *automatically* (using an automatic device, and without conscious intention) removes anything that threatens to establish a new interpretation. ("Off with their heads" yells the Queen of Hearts like a nineteenth-century Dalek when anything upsets her.)

The fantastic—unless and until we become blasé about it—is a threat or a challenge, a shock or a seduction. It takes us into "another world," beyond the looking-glass or the grave, removed in time or space, but a world that is a mirror image of, a revelation of, an analogy for, the everyday one. It is a chance to "use the imagination," which means sidestepping habitual frames of reference and seeing what else is there—a new perspective or a change in the functioning of consciousness.

Consciousness is an act, a process, but one that, unlike many processes, can be relatively easily reprogrammed. Since it is so basic to the way we live, we cannot afford to allow it to become autogenic. Otherwise its focus—our "mental set"—gets stuck. Since there are means of altering the focus—which makes consciousness an intentional, although not always fully deliberative, act—it is worth asking what the fantastic and the way it operates can show us about the nature and functioning of consciousness. How does the fantastic nudge, persuade, or bludgeon consciousness into changing focus?

In many ways it is clear that the fantastic is merely an exaggerated form of techniques common to much literature. It asks us to perform the same "suspension of disbelief" but more violently. The violence may be necessary, because, so often, habit has dulled the response to more subtle forms of persuasion—hence, perhaps, we have Edgar Allan Poe and the origins of gothic horror; certainly, Dada and surrealism. Perhaps it was relatively easy to fall into the habit of not asking too many questions about the realist novel, but we have even managed to do it about fantastic literature by "naturalizing" it into comfortable escapist fantasy: horror movies at midnight are not even a ritual any more; they are just boring.

So the techniques of fantastic literature—sudden removal into another sphere, confrontation with the grotesque or the absurd—may be an indication of a certain frustration with less flamboyant means, of a pressing desire for initiating a change in sensibility. Certainly, something like this statement from R. M. Rilke's symbolist novel *Die Aufzeichnungen des Malte Laurids Brigge*—a "novel" containing descriptions of the fantastic and the supernatural as though they were everyday events—would support this: "Is it possible that in spite of inventions and progress, in spite of culture, religion and worldly wisdom we have remained on the surface of life?...If in fact all of this is possible, if there's just a faint chance of it being possible—then surely, for the sake of everything that exists, something has got to happen."[2] Half a century later Eugène Ionesco put it like this:

As our knowledge becomes separated from life, our culture no longer contains ourselves (or only an insignificant part of ourselves)....So the problem becomes that of bringing our life back into contact with our culture, making it a living culture again. To achieve this, we shall first have to kill "the respect for what is written down in black and white"...to break up our language so that it can be put together again in order to reestablish contact with "the absolute"; it is imperative to push human beings again towards seeing themselves as they really are.[3]

What this means in terms of actual literary process, then, is making us "read" in a new way, extending our use and understanding of the possibilities of language, and extending ourselves and our world by reading. Many of the literary trends of the last hundred years have in fact been aiming by various means at the "breakup" of language and its stranglehold on reality. Disrespect for "what is written down in black and white" links writers like Laurence Sterne and Samuel Coleridge (more decorous in his terminology, perhaps, he wondered "whether the too great definiteness of Terms in any language may not consume too much of the vital and idea-creating force" [4]) with Arthur Rimbaud, Alfred Jarry, Antonin Artaud, and the surrealists on the one hand and James Joyce, Marcel Proust, Thomas Mann, and Günter Grass on the other hand. Despair at language—voiced elegantly by Hugo Hofmannsthal's Lord Chandos or vehemently by Beckett's narrator ("de la foutaise d'un bout à l'autre"[5])—nonetheless calls up an attempt, however ironic, to defeat it at its own game, to balance the destruction of fossilized discourse by monumental or gymnastic efforts to found a new one, which in turn requires similar agility from the reader.

In this process "nonsense" is a useful tool. Whether of the Edward Lear kind or Joyce's more daunting attempt—a sort of Irish Jabberwocky on an Esperanto base, perhaps—or the devices to inhibit linear reading practiced by writers of the French new novel, the result is the same: denial of expectations, implying a need to look in a different way and for something else. Refusal of conventional structure, plot, or "meaning"; the move away from realism toward emphatic fictionality—all act in this way, sometimes revealing the arbitrary nature of the world created by language, sometimes pointing to kinds of perception and expression that cannot be simplistically defined.

Changing language—breaking it up and reinventing it, as Beckett did in *Comment C'est*—is a practical technique for changing our vision of reality, since it is language that makes that reality comprehensible to us. So by changing language we change the focus of consciousness.

But how in fact are these changes in language perceived by us? Since they can only be perceived by virtue of consciousness, it is equally true to say that our ability to read in any particular way depends on the manner in which consciousness is functioning. So to change reading habits we have to change consciousness first. To explore this chicken-and-egg question further we need to look more closely at techniques of disrupting and redirecting the reading process.

Perhaps an initial, although simplified, distinction to make would be between more rationally oriented techniques and more subliminal kinds of persuasion. The former tend to occur more readily in the novel and in plays whose main focus is on language, and the latter are more obvious in the case of poetry and theatrical "language" of a less obviously verbal kind—structure, action, decor, and so on. The former have more the characteristics of the blunt instrument— a deliberate shock to logical expectations, a blocking of the normal channels of communication; the latter work in a more subtle way as incitements to see more in language or structure; they are attempts to put "sensibility...into a deeper, more subtle state of perception by assured means," as Artaud suggested.[6] These two kinds of technique, which are frequently found together, seem to be operating stages in the process of reorientation, something like the instructions to children for crossing the road—stop, look, listen, and then proceed. The first three are essential if you want to get a clear view of the situation and be able to assimilate any new factors. Candide misses out on these stages and just proceeds according to the habitual response.

The same is true of characters like the Smiths and the Martins in Ionesco's *La Cantatrice chauve*: they go on making remarks about potatoes or their numerous and indistinguishable acquaintances who all go by the name of Bobby Watson. They talk and act like automatons whose every response is conditioned merely by the conventional conversational trigger in the preceding sentence. They could—and, as the end of the play shows, would—go on forever without stopping or noticing anything strange: they are, as another Ionesco title puts it, "Victimes du devoir," where the duty is first linguistic. The repetition of formulae tends to replace perceptiveness by acceptance: people agree that everyone ought to be a rhinoceros or that there is nothing better than "pommes de terre au lard." (They even agree, in another context, that Godot will certainly come tomorrow, and so there is no need to attend to what is going on at present.)

Ionesco's principal characters are often striving to escape from deadly banality (deadly as the *"Tueur sans gages,"* or the condemnation to a life of automatic responses or animalistic reproductive behavior) to an imaginary world of freedom and beauty—the "cité radieuse," the lightness of flight in *Le Piéton de l'Air*. Their progress is blocked by the clogging weight of inert matter, and the increasing opposition of the living and the dead produces an escalation toward violent explosion characteristic of the structure of Ionesco's work.

But logic, and the logic of banality, is useful in its own destruction precisely because it provides a graded mechanism for moving along the road to the absurd or the fantastic. The more the Smiths talk about Bobby Watson, the more dead he becomes—two, three, and four years gone in successive speeches. He becomes "un véritable cadavre vivant" (like the one that grows on stage in *Amédée*), part of the dead weight of habitual banality that oppresses Ionesco's world. But the mathematical logic reveals the absurd futility of the characters' speech and behavior, just as rhetoric destroys itself and the whole edifice of language and thought in Lucky's speech in *Godot*, and what starts as *qua qua* ends up by implication as *caca*. So logic provides a means to undo itself and enable the reader/audience to move gradually toward a perspective that, although beyond conventional logic, has not abandoned logical processes. The imagination is able to comprehend successive stages of the fantastic or illogical aspects of reality by virtue of this opposition: the content (what we read) may be illogical, but the structure (that which determines the *way* we read) remains within our grasp. We might call this the progression toward transcendence, the movement toward escaping restrictive limits of thought and behavior, changing worlds, getting out of a mental set.

Something similar is happening in the "detective" format of Poe and, more recently, of Alain Robbe-Grillet. Rational possibilities of solution are increasingly blocked by impossibilities, until we finally have to accept that the murderer belongs to another species altogether (Poe's gymnastic gorilla in *The Murders in the Rue Morgue*) or is merely an ironic allegory for our own attempt to impose certainty on the text (Robbe-Grillet's *Les Gommes*, *Le Voyeur*, and *La Maison de rendez-vous*). Conventional logic is defeated and has to leap to another framework for us to grasp what is happening; in the same way the notions of math and grammar are punctiliously retained in the looking-glass world but used to serve purposes different from those to which Alice is accustomed. In Poe's "adventure" pieces (*A Descent into the Maelström* and *Narrative of A. Gordon Pym*) we are offered a travelog that is then transformed into a crescendo of fantasy in which we, like the protagonists, rapidly lose our bearings: but the framework still remains, offering just a hint of how to come to terms with the experience. In the majority of cases the technique for doing this is built into the structure of the work.

Figure 1. Structure in Ionesco

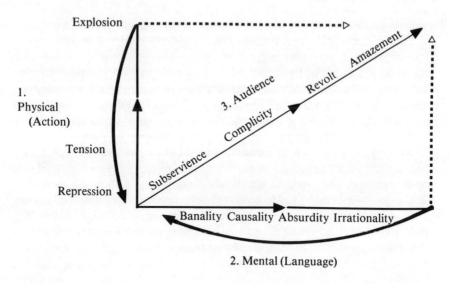

2. Mental (Language)

In some cases the functions may be reversed, for example, in Robbe-Grillet's *La Maison de rendez-vous*: the explanations of the murder offered are in themselves logical enough, but their sequence and number make them confusing and finally impossible. But the *opposition* between the functions remains the motive force for changing our understanding of what the novel is.

The structure of Ionesco's plays can be represented, simplistically, by a diagram (see figure 1). Axes 1 and 2 represent the pattern of experience for the characters, and axis 3 represents a possible synthesis in the experience of the audience. Whereas axes 1 and 2 are circular (situations recur, the characters do not learn), axis 3 is at least ideally open-ended. The dotted lines represent possibilities. The movement along the axes is itself affected by opposing forces—those tending toward acceptance and habit and those allowing imaginative freedom and openness. The structure is repeated many times, as, for example, the move from conversation to language games to nonsense to animal noises in *La Cantatrice chauve*, the enclosure of the old couple by physical objects and their final leap through the window in *Les Chaises*, and the use of erotic crescendo in *Jacques* and *La Leçon*.

The tension between opposing forces means that there are many actual or potential hiatuses in the course of development of a structural sequence. Language and behavior become so absurd and inflated that they call up their opposites. For the characters, trapped and puppetlike entities devoid of independent thought or action, this means that the breakdown of language is merely another way of confirming its banality, and the outbreak of mindless instinct confirms behaviorist conformity: the circle closes. The audience, however, may use their freedom to acquire a degree of balance: not totally involved in and subject to the language and behavior they are observing, they can by reference to other frameworks perceive it as abnormal and essentially *theatrical*. They have the chance at any moment to observe this technique, which Ionesco referred to as "théâtraliser la parole" (theatricalize the word) and which was intended to "donner au théâtre sa vrai mesure qui est dans la démesure" (show theater's true capacity, which is in the immeasurable).[7] Each shock conveyed by action or speech is a potential chance to perceive this theatrical quality and escape the domination suffered by the characters.

Ionesco's theater clearly denounces the reductive and destructive use of language. It does not merely demonstrate and ironize this, however; it also presents an extension of language: in the wit with which banality is inflated to absurdity, in the inventiveness of near nonsense that harbors all kinds of appropriate significance—the maid's fire-poem in *La Cantatrice chauve*, Roberte II's use of the word *chat* in *Jacques*. Everyday cliché is transformed into Ionesco's conscious *parole*. This is reinforced by the "theatrical language" of grotesque action, overwhelmingly massive presence of objects (chairs, corpses), bizarre occurrences (clocks striking 17), and horrible situations (bestiality, rape, murder).

All of these things are means to move us toward what Ionesco called his "feeling of amazement," which occurs at moments when, as it were "unintentionally, you put yourself completely outside everything."[8] This amazement, this sudden sense of being outside and yet involved, characterizes the theatrical experience produced by Ionesco's work: it is his version of catharsis. This moment of liberation from received systems is also a moment of realization that one can amend those systems: the possibilities and the limits of one's creative freedom are understood. Ionesco wrote that for him drama is a way to reestablish "ma joie d'exister ou mon étonnement d'être (my joy at existence or my astonishment at being)."[9]

For the characters in Beckett's *En Attendant Godot* existence is waiting. Most of the time it is awful, because what they are waiting for does not turn up. Vladimir and Estragon suffer from the same trouble as most Beckettian characters: they are under some inherent obligation to express themselves, but there is nothing to say and nothing to say it with. Already Vladimir and Estragon are further along the road than most of Ionesco's characters: habitual systems of language and behavior seem so inadequate that they can only engage in them as a conscious performance—a little gallop of their own around conventional triggers like the good old days or the problem of the crucified thieves or enjoying a performance by the grotesquely pompous rhetorician Pozzo and the *machine-à-penser* that reduces thought to rubble, Lucky.

It is "theatricalization," then, of the absurdity of ritual action and speech, of other people's words and behavior, and this realization is achieved by a stop-go technique that makes Vladimir and Estragon constantly hesitate on the brink of expression and lament their inadequacy to achieve it; it constantly brings the audience up short before the negation of expected structures of plot, character, and "meaning." Speech and action move in little spurts, and in between are numerous and carefully orchestrated pauses. The pauses, as has been frequently observed, become in a sense more eloquent than the nonsense that separates them: they articulate the waiting and the awful sense that what is to come is even more futile than what has just occurred. The anguish of "for God's sake say something" leads to the desperate forcing out of little constipated knots of waste material. It is in the pauses that Vladimir and Estragon realize the futility of the situation and communicate it to the audience: like the negation of expected structures, they offer a chance to perceive the deadliness of habit.

Endowed with a limited repertoire that inevitable physical decline renders gradually less available, Estragon and Vladimir nevertheless differ from Ionesco's automatons by virtue of their painful awareness (they are more like Ionesco's heroes, the Jacques or Bérengers who try to resist the pressures to conform). They are halfway to shaking off conventional personality attributes, and they can use this apparently negative situation, just as they can use the wordless gaps, to move outside recognizable social or linguistic systems. They never do move outside, however: they are always waiting for Godot. Perhaps the worst habit of all is our tendency to believe that things will be better tomorrow: it links us more firmly to expectations based on our own or someone else's yesterday. But if for Vladimir and Estragon *Godot* is a kind of enslavement, for us it could be a new theatrical experience. But it will be so only if the negations, the nonsense, the pauses, enable us not only to realize the banality of repetition but to discover at least the possibility of doing old things in new ways. Godot must be able to do anything, however fantastic.

It is this possibility that so many of Beckett's fictional narrators seek. They move toward physical nullity and mental emptiness, toward being a sort of living gap, in fact. They are in a hurry to rid themselves of their burden of words, which defines yesterday's self. The condition of being potential, of being prior to language, is what they seek to return to (Molloy seeking his mother, although not her presence so much as the space she occupied; the narrators of *Comment C'est* passing on the burden of speech to the next in the chain, becoming themselves merely the impetus to expression).

The inventiveness of structure and meaning that characterizes Beckett's work is clear in *Comment C'est*, where language becomes a mosaic of ambiguous possibility; Beckett's *parole* is charged at ever more frequent intervals with the means whereby its irreverence and richness are generated, and we are offered the chance to take part at least to some degree in the constant process of revision. The pause, even after each word, becomes a sign of methodological and ontological doubt—who goes where from here and how? But it is also by the same token the sign of a place of transformation, the location in consciousness of a new reading and writing.

These are examples of techniques to expose and explode banality by making it absurd, in a similar way to the questioning of any form of accepted conduct by its transposition into a fantastic situation. By a similar process they also lead to an appreciation of the fantastic in terms of insight, amazement, the chance of alternative perception and organization—they create the space for new possibilities.

Beckett and Ionesco are aware of the danger of crystallization that threatens language, which is why for Beckett structures have to be self-destructing. Anyone's *parole* can be authorized into orthodoxy, and we often live our lives as though they were someone's novel. So fantasy itself sometimes has to be exploded toward the fantastic, and this is the kind of demolition job Robbe-Grillet's novels and films undertake. Conventionalized fantasies (Hong Kong, New York) escalate into such obviously manipulated fictionality that we cannot escape realizing it. Fantasy as opiate (in *La Maison de rendez-vous*) implies subservience to cliché, mental set, or system: most of Robbe-Grillet's characters are victims of obsessions or are at the behest of organizations and routines, which are often the more powerful for being sinister, unacknowledged, or unrecognized. These are the fantasies that kill, and narrator and reader are repeatedly incited to act them out. But the process is pointed out to us—and so we are allowed to escape from it—by the numerous "replays" divided by breaks in the text. Sections move toward increasing degrees of obsession and fixity, with frequent scenes of murder and violent domination. But the narrative is organized around breaks between sections or "glissades" from one point of view to another within sections. These structural gaps allow us to experience the organization of the text and offer the possibility of alternatives. We have to read the text as a compositional process.

These examples suggest that a variety of techniques can propel us toward the possibility of "reading" the world in another way. Whether they employ shock tactics or more subtle persuasion, they end up by leaving us with the sense of a gap between the conventional, everyday, habitual, or expected and the situation in which we find ourselves. The impossible, absurd, or fantastic nature of this situation is realized as a kind of gasp or catching of the breath, as a loss of bearings or landmarks, an absence of form or sense.

It is this that impels a transition from consuming the language of conventional expectation to being prepared to use one's imagination to discover the resonance of the *parole* of the work. Since the "stop-go" process is repeated many times, readers are able to move step by step from the familiar to the fantastic, from the general to the particular imaginative use of language. They migrate from being "average readers" toward becoming the "ideal" or "implied" readers required by the text.

Each stage of this linguistic process, which necessarily results in a new reading of reality, a new focus of consciousness, seems to involve a moment of escape or transformation from one structure or meaning to another. In the case of poetry this expansion of significance clearly operates in terms of metaphor.

In this we also see one means—stop and go—by which reading is pushed toward expanding possibilities. Another way is that, in poetry particularly, we are asked to learn to "read" sound, rhythm, and so on as well, each word striking a resonance with others. This interaction between sound and sense was seen by Paul Valéry as the basis of the poetic process for writer and reader. The "charm" that induces an extension of awareness is perhaps due to a combination of aesthetic and intellectual satisfaction as we begin to see the wide range of associative and combinative possibilities of a word. We participate in the organization of language. Also, in becoming aware of some of the ways in which sense and sound interact, we may get a sense of how languages form themselves. At this mythical or universal level, individual and discrete perception is linked to a kind of collective consciousness, but it is a level where language has its full power, not the level of the commonplace. The "fantastic" aspect of language—its inexhaustible creative potential—is gained when restrictive codes have been transformed into new and specific imaginative usage. In taking part in this process one is becoming more "individual" (inventive) and less automatic. Consciousness is able both to focus precisely and to keep a very wide scan of possibilities in play. *Parole* and the universal or fully potential level of language lead into each other: highly precise individual use of language is found where there is a state of maximum alertness and receptivity to all possibilities.

This looks something like the condition Beckett's Murphy hoped for, as "a point in the ceaseless unconditioned generation and passing away of line."[10] The individual and localized focus is fused with the ability to be present where form comes into being: a combination of alertness and nonactivity, something like the state one can achieve by attentive but relaxed (receptive) reading, "outside" all systems, but perceiving the way they arise.

This is clearly a special condition of consciousness; indeed, we might say it is *the* condition—consciousness as the ability to perceive, that is, as the potential for perceptual acts, a condition we frequently overlook in everyday life but one that reading or listening can, by particular techniques, reveal to us at any moment. It is a condition that not only liberates us from habit but gives us the means to reorganize our world. It makes of fantasy, and the move toward the fantastic, a precise tool for the extension of awareness not of the unreal but of the full scope of reality.

NOTES

1. Samuel Beckett, *En Attendant Godot* (Paris: Minuit, 1952), 157. Citations from Beckett, Rilke, and Artaud are from foreign language texts; translations are my own.

2. R. M. Rilke, *Die Aufzeichnungen des Malte Laurids Brigge*, in *Sämtliche Werke* (Frankfurt: Insel, 1955-66), 6: 726-28.

3. Eugène Ionesco, "Ni un dieu, ni un démon," *Cahiers Renaud-Barrault* 22-23 (May 1958): 130-34.

4. Samuel T. Coleridge, *Anima Poetae* (London: Heinemann, 1895), 19.

5. Samuel Beckett, *Comment C'est* (Paris: Minuit, 1961), 174.

6. Antonin Artaud, *Le Théâtre et son Double* (Paris: Gallimard, 1964), 139.

7. Eugène Ionesco, *Notes et Contre-notes* (Paris: Mercure de France, 1962), 15.

8. C. Bonnefoy, *Conversations with Eugène Ionesco*, trans. Jan Dawson (London: Faber, 1970), 61.

9. Ionesco, *Notes*, 34.

10. Samuel Beckett, *Murphy* (New York: Evergreen, 1957), 112.

Dislocating the Fantastic: Can This Old Genre Be Mobilized?

Howard D. Pearce

> The fantastic produces a strain, or what might be called a "collision," of the real-ideal, material-spiritual, dimensions.

Ludwig Wittgenstein's analysis of language is at root an attempt to clarify and strengthen the case for intersubjectivity. In *On Certainty* he argued against the meaningfulness of entertaining the question "Am I dreaming?" that question being, from his point of view, unpragmatic.[1] It serves no purpose to say "I am dreaming," because if I were dreaming when I made the remark, I would be dreaming that the words "have any meaning." We already "know" where we are, when we use language about our world. In the language game we can use a term meaningfully because it makes sense in a given context. That context is established by what can be called, loosely, "usage." In our playing with the question of the fantastic, the criteria of intersubjectivity and openness may be served by pursuing in the term *fantastic* itself ramifications and resemblances. Being careful not to disqualify the idea or the word by denying all distinctions, we should observe what the word itself has been taken to mean and what images of the fantastic might be discovered as pertinent. "Definitions" of critical terms too often try to lift word and concept out of the moment to some abstracted level of finality, to designate *the* meaning by isolating generically. I can end only in tentativeness, because my discussion remains grounded in temporality; my talk about the fantastic is itself finite, possible, open to further hermeneutic negotiations.

The word *fantastic* comes from the Greek root *phanein*, "to show," as do *fancy* and *phantasm*, and all three terms have to do with the essential problematic relationship between the actual, material dimension and that of the supernatural, spiritual, or ideal. If *fantastic* usually refers to insubstantial, noncorporeal, or nonexistent objectivities, *phantasm* can refer inversely, as in Platonic thought, to the inferior material world. At the level of perception what "shows" is mere sense impression, and it is distorted, phantasmic. Scholastic and Renaissance uses allow both the material and immaterial dimensions as referent. Even when *fantastic* refers to the nonphysical dimension it may presume the objectivity to be real, as in the instance of a ghost. But the term does not concern only the supernatural realm in terms of ghosts, specters, and spirits. Tzvetan Todorov's term *supernatural* restricts the fantastic to that dimension, and it treats the supernatural in terms of simple belief or disbelief.[2]

Akin to *fancy*, *fantasy* may refer to activities or objects of the fancy, act or object being not "supernatural" in the limited sense but merely ideal, not actual. To fantasize in the common psychological sense is to engage in activities that are played out in the field of the mind but that could conceivably be played out in the flesh.

The fantastic might be considered in relation to other critical terms, an immediate relationship appearing when we recall Plato's distinction between the eikastic and fantastic imaginations. The *eikastic* level, the lowest dimension of knowledge for Plato, involves sensory experience of objectively real, although inferior, entities. Yet eikastic art would at least have the virtue of imitating actually existing things, even if that makes it thrice removed from reality. *Fantastic* art would involve figments and implies artists who cut themselves loose from ordinary experience, who assume a freedom to create that makes them, like Plato's Ion, suspect. Sir Philip Sidney condemned the fantastic imagination as tending to "infect the fancy with unworthy objects," as in painting it will "please an ill-pleased eye with wanton shows of better hidden matters."[3] Sidney is in a long tradition considering it morally and spiritually suspect, a view that is reinforced with the rise of scientific materialist thought and that culminates in Abraham Cowley's calling the imagination "*Phansie*," a "wild *Dame*."[4] Sidney in following that tradition accepted Plato's premise that inferior, "infectious" representations are psychologically contaminating—to see the "unworthy object" is to undergo conditioning that makes us reflectors of the low, the uncontrolled. Elsewhere Sidney argued, however, that when the poet is "freely ranging only within the zodiac of his own wit," he is empowered to make "things either better than nature bringeth forth, or, quite anew, forms such as never were in nature, as the Heroes, Demigods, Cyclopes, Chimeras, Furies, and such like" (p. 157). Restricting the term *fantastic* to immoral or infectious representations, Sidney nevertheless, in praising the generation of "forms such as never were in nature," approved the activity that, contrasted to the eikastic, suggests the actual-ideal distinction. The fantastic might then be thought to involve the production of nonexistent objects or actual objects presented in improbable relationships or combinations. But the term might begin to imply the distinction between perception and imagination rather than that between two kinds of imagination. That argument was carried on in the twentieth century by Jean-Paul Sartre and again opened up by Edward Casey and Mary Warnock in opposition to Sartre.[5]

If the fantastic might be thought to involve production of images not drawn from the perceived world, or combined in an unlikely manner, it might in addition be held up for comparison to the sublime-beautiful distinction. Although differing in many ways, theories such as those of Joseph Addison, Edmund Burke, and Immanuel Kant reveal that underlying concern. Their thought can be traced from Longinus to implicit expressions of the same issues, as in William Wordsworth's theory of the imagination.

Addison, following Longinus, reflected the subject-object dichotomy and the tacit assumption that connections between the dual worlds are possible. The sublime in Addison remains fundamentally a transcending impulse. The pleasures of the imagination involve our apprehension of the "great" as something toward which we incline, a larger "beyond" that carries us right away from ourselves: "Our Imagination loves to be filled with...any thing that is too big for its Capacity."[6] Hating restraint, we feel free when we stand before a spacious horizon, which is for us an image of liberty. The idea of freedom is thus projected in both directions, outward into the physical scene that affects us and inward into our own subjective nature. Greatness, or what has generally been called "the sublime," clearly for Addison involves our making connection with some objectivity that is not mere sense datum but gives us back something of our own subjectivity. It yields the very idea of freedom. It is, then, like the fantastic imagination, to be recognized as the inclination toward the subjective "beyond," the "out there" that gives back something of our ideal nature. Like the fantastic it brings us closer to being agents constituting a world, as opposed to being mere empirical recorders of it.

Similarly, in Edmund Burke's psychology the sublime imposes on us the idea of the ultimate "terror," death (Adams, *Critical Theory*, p. 310). Using the terms *great* and *sublime* interchangeably, Burke identified the beautiful as being near, familiar, comfortable. Beautiful objects are "small," "smooth," "light and delicate," founded "on pleasure," and "not...obscure" (p. 311). Beautiful objects would not be likely to stimulate thoughts of the problematical nature of reality, of the difficulty of knowing reality, of "interiors," or of "absences." The sublime, on the other hand, "founded on pain," is "vast," "rugged," and "dark and gloomy" (p. 311). It troubles as it stimulates thought. It places us in obscurity and generates a sense of needing to probe, extend, go beyond the immediate impression.

Even in Burke's empiricist psychology the sublime carries implications of that tendency to entertain some ideal otherness in our relations, to apprehend our context as more than pure physical relations. Thinking the condition of death and the remote sets us back from the pleasurable moment, requires our probing the unascertainable, the thought of the ideal that beckons us beyond ourselves. We are caused to try transcending the determined empirical flow, to rise toward some subjectivity that we hope will be more than, and correlative to, our private selves.

Kant, similarly, led us toward this other-than-self. The noumenal world, although subjectively constituted, involves universals toward which we aspire and whose forms we use regardless of the radical ideal-material split. In Kant's epistemology the sublime is functional in effecting—what is only extrapolatable in Burke—our transcendence of our state of dependency. Beauty may open us up to Nature's laws, but experiencing the sublime makes us aware of our own freedom.

Kant was developing in his elaborate way the distinction that Aristotle in the *Poetics* played upon between probability and wonder. Although "probability" is an absolute necessity in the fabric of art, Aristotle admitted "wonder" as an ingredient in poetry. Indeed, although he spoke of it obliquely, wonder is for Aristotle clearly as necessary to tragedy as is probability. The very effect of the tragic requires wonder (*thaumastos*—the "marvelous," suggesting "magic" or "miracle"[7]): "There is more of the marvelous" if events occur with both surprise and probability (Aristotle, *Poetics*, p. 18). Unstated here is the implication that increasing wonder is a desirable goal in tragedy. Wonder seems even to be an end, as affect, toward which probability is a means. Aristotle pursued the question of the marvelous in chapter 24 of the *Poetics*, confirming that the wonderful is essential to tragic pleasure but warning that it must not override the criterion of probability. Probability and wonder, then, point to the same dimensions that are implicit in the beautiful-sublime distinction and in those other relationships: between perception and imagination, the eikastic and the fantastic. Probability is like Kant's beautiful, which is a means of apprehending principles of order in Nature; wonder like the sublime moves us to a sense of something beyond. For Kant the beautiful object "brings with it a purposiveness," whereas the sublime "may appear. . .to violate purpose in respect to the judgment. . .and as it were to do violence to the imagination; and yet is judged to be only the more sublime" (Adams, *Critical Theory*, p. 391).

The primordial relationship between subject and object, self and world, produces conceptualizations such as the "supernatural." But that transcending impulse, in essence, is the need, before conceptualization and before verbalization, to go beyond our mere facticity, our mere existence, in time. The subjective being longs for, desires, being like itself and beyond itself. To be more than mechanics, we want what we know will always be at least to some extent absent, some other subjectivity, whether it be found in other beings like ourselves, in some immanent universality like Carl Jung's collective unconscious, or some divine being different in kind from ourselves. The gestalt of that subjectivity is always ideal, constituted, beyond the empirical flow of experience, always the "more." The Christian heaven and the Platonic world of ideas are thus constituted. So are the Aristotelean "wonder," something Aristotle was very cautious about, and the Longinusian "sublime," encountered with less caution by the theorist we call Longinus.

The metaphorical value of the transcending impulse is there most patently in Longinus's term usually translated "transport." Longinus makes a similar dichotomy in his opposing rhetoric to the sublime. Rhetoric involves discipline, learning, and craft—all accomplishments in which we can be trained. But the first two traits necessary for sublime art, "great conceptions" and "inspired passion," are "for the most part innate" (Adams, *Critical Theory*, p. 80). Like Kant's beautiful and Aristotle's probability, rhetoric for Longinus demonstrates law, order, regularity, and control: "our persuasions we can usually control" (p. 77). The sublime strikes the audience with "power and irresistible might." On this count Aristotle's "marvelous" can be seen as similar, but Kant's "sublime" produces not just that sense of power but in addition one's own reflection of it and thus a sense of freedom. Longinus does not see this dichotomy as merely opposed principles but as mutually supportive. The sublime strikes "our attention before the figures, whose art" it throws "into the shade," concealing the craft involved in producing them (p. 89).

Involved in Longinus's sublime are considerations of freedom, power, and control and the extremely difficult issue of mimesis. If the referent of art is not surface reality, the three-dimensional world reduced to two dimensions in Plato's translation of mimetic art into the mirror metaphor, we are still dealing with the problem of how the literary work relates to the subjective, ideal, interior, or absent reality. For Longinus that reality is "soul." Flute and harp may cause even the "ignorant" listener to imitate, to try to "conform himself to the melody" (p. 98). But these musical instruments work essentially at the eikastic level: "although in themselves they signify nothing at all," they "often cast a wonderful spell." "Signifying" is the higher, more human motive. Longinus is assuming the subjective dimension and the power of the sublime to strike it; and the superiority of humankind lies in the powers of its signifying tool, language. "In art the utmost exactitude is admired, grandeur in the works of nature; and . . . it is by nature that man is a being gifted with speech" (p. 97). Exactitude and grandeur, in art and nature respectively, involve still that pointing toward the real-ideal dimensions. In encompassing more, poetry is therefore superior to instrumental music, and to what poetry and the flute share as eikastic phenomena, poetry has added to it the power of the sublime. The flute deals in "spurious copies of persuasion," whereas poetry is a "genuine" activity of "human nature . . . being a harmony of that language which is implanted by nature in man and which appeals not to the hearing only but to the soul itself" (p. 98).

If the idea of the fantastic is entertained from this vantage, it remains a flexible and functional concept. As opposed to producing sharp and final delineations whereby we can place a work in categories like the fantastic, the uncanny, or the marvelous, it would reveal some quality or qualities in the tendency to deal with, extend toward, the ideal at the expense of the actual. The eikastic and the fantastic would not then be thought of as discrete categories but as inclinations. The impulse to transcend and the desire to encounter the unknown, the foreign, the strange, the wonderful, the fantastic, would involve negotiations toward the improbable, and those sought values would not be entities but objectives, "objectives" in the sense of both otherness and motive. As such an activity the fantastic would occur not *in* a subjectivity but in the very transactions possible in the confrontation of work by the reader. The strange, the wonderful, the marvelous, the absurd, all impinge on and escape whatever it is that may be called the "fantastic."

Perhaps beginning with the suspension of the subject-object dichotomy, placing the fantastic neither solidly in the objective nor ideally in the subjective, we might notice that we use the term *fantastic* in a restricted sense, in reference to literature, to suggest a quality. Longinus's sublime is not generically opposed to the regulating force of rhetoric; the two are mutual, interdependent. Similarly, the eikastic and the fantastic play upon and by means of one another. A realistic sort of art defines its limits by excursions toward the ideal, the improbable, the mysterious, the wonderful. Henry James's heroes and heroines are haunted, figuratively or literally, by the ideal, by potential forms that are what make the real dimension worth living in. Edgar Allan Poe's tales of the fantastic continually recall us to the conditions of probability, the *physis* from which flights of fantasy take off.

The fantastic-eikastic distinction shares with those other dichotomies—literal-metaphorical, rhetorical-sublime, objective-subjective, probable-wonderful—the meeting of the actual and the ideal, the natural and supernatural, and so on. But the fantastic differs from the metaphorical as the sublime differs from the rhetorical or the beautiful. For Longinus the rhetorical is an attenuating or amplification of an argument, description, narrative. The sublime may operate within the rhetorical context to strike a blow, to transform, to transport in one imperious swoop. The fantastic shares this quality with the sublime, although it ought to be thought of as a gestalt of effect, rather than, as Todorov has it, a moment in the reading process.

The quality of the fantastic might be referred to the subjectivity and named strain or intensity. Metaphor may be fantastic if it has this quality. Robert Frost's metaphors are less appropriately called fantastic than Wallace Stevens's; Robert Herrick's poems less so than Richard Crashaw's. Crashaw's "Flaming Heart" and Stevens's "Comedian as the Letter C" might be fantastic. We might refer the fantastic to the objectivity called "literature" and speak of a "collision" between the subjective and objective dimensions. But I am not sure that what I would think of as a fantastic work, John Barth's *Chimera*, essentially involves that actual-ideal confrontation. If we think in terms of probable-imaginative dimensions we might see such a tension. But, to quibble still with Todorov, we know beforehand that Franz Kafka's "Metamorphosis" is fantastic, and it is fantastic because the imagination and metaphor are under strain. There is often an element of audacity in the fantastic: for instance, in the Renaissance a "fantastic" could be a being capricious, extravagant, and odd. This quality would suggest how a work could be fantastic but not sublime. We might think deeply and darkly about Joseph Heller's Yosarian but not without a sense of the fantastic when we are experiencing his kind of madness. We could properly go, endowed with the play of the fantastic, to the works of Ken Kesey, Sylvia Plath, and

Flannery O'Connor—alert to the collisions of metaphors, events, characters, and so on that make those works fantastic.

A final example in this tentative theoretical discussion is Bernard Pomerance's recent play *The Elephant Man*.[8] I do not know that the play should be thought of as fantastic—all the more reason for restricting my observations to qualities and tendencies rather than trying to "fix" the play once and for all inside or outside the pale of the fantastic. I chose the play because it caught my imagination and because it reveals as well the underlying problem of the dualism on which I have developed my discussion; it produces—in dramatic technique consistent with the thematic premises—a strain, or what may be called a "collision," of the real-ideal, material-spiritual, dimensions.

Merrick, the elephant man, himself expresses the improbable transformation, the wonderful possibility that the material condition may not circumscribe an absolute natural condition. Grotesque of body, once a circus freak, and now a case study under observation in the hospital, he says, "Sometimes I think my head is so big because it is so full of dreams." Deprived of normal human relationships, Merrick has grown up as the helpless victim of adverse natural conditions. A monstrous subhuman creature, he has like an animal in a zoo served merely to satisfy curiosity seekers' sense of horror and their complacent belief in their own superiority. But his improbable translation of that grotesque condition into a sort of idealism becomes for others—doctor, actress, nobility—a transport. He becomes a mirror in which they see reflected their own nature, nature both material and spiritual, determined and free. His dreams are transcendent, translatable to others. The grotesque catches something of the sublime and in my tentative view might qualify as being fantastic. Such might be the argument if the fantastic can be thought to negotiate, to move us toward—as do the sublime and the wonderful—the free, the ideal, the absent, the wished for.

I have suggested that Merrick reveals in his own subjectivity a certain power of self-transformation. If he is the subjective pole of the metaphor, thinking of the objective pole raises the question of how this play treats the world, the nonself. The condition Merrick seems betrayed by is the world of circumstances—whether his condition is thought to be the result of genetic fault or disease—and in addition the world of history. We begin with historical facts: slides of the real Merrick, the Victorian moral overlay on a developing nineteenth-century medical science, the social conditions that allow exploitation and degradation of an unfortunate human being. But if Merrick is most fundamentally a victim he nevertheless gains a certain, although problematical, power beyond his own subjective being. Certainly, he has no power over those overwhelming social conditions. But he does gain a certain force in essentially two ways. I have already suggested that curiosity in others is converted by him into something akin to awe. Their lives are qualified by Merrick.

In addition, he becomes improbably an artist, capable of producing with his twisted body a model of St. Philip's Church (that image of humankind's highest aspiration toward the spiritual condition). As an artist Merrick can affect us not only as he does other characters in the play but also in opening us up to the idea of the artist and his art, like the church an image of aspiration, transcendence, and conversion, in this instance, of history into the dream. The absurd condition; the radical skepticism that can lead to despair; the possibility that life is illusion, that objective reality is meaningless, is transformed by the artist into an illusion of coherence and order that not only demonstrates the artist's control but also inspires an audience to "higher" illusions and the hope that dreams may not be *mere* illusion. Like the characters in the play the audience may come to admire the dream power in Merrick, that radiance that shines out of the carnival freak. The artist—builder of models—comes to represent a power that we stand before in a kind of awe, Aristotelean wonder. When Merrick dies (Act II, scene 20) we are aware of both the gross physical cause of his death, the huge head that could never be laid down even to sleep, and also the symbolic value of that head "so full of dreams." The scene is entitled "The Weight of Dreams."

Merrick translates for us his deformity, negative fate, into the pressure of dreams, the *largeness* that transcends the *grossness* of the physical. The grotesque victim and scapegoat has been transformed into a representative human being, through his improbable epiphany, through the unlikely revelation of the beautiful ideal in the repugnant actual. The show we the audience see is not a sideshow but the magic that leads from skulking curiosity, appropriate to the carnival, to a sense of what may be the *fantastic*—as the term subsumes the grotesque in the sublime, mutes showmanship in the mystery of the artist's power to move us, translates the actuality of historical fact into the ever-elusive, hoped-for "something more" that would have to be another kind of truth. When these antithetical forces are so reciprocally implicated that they produce the pressure of intense exchange, the atmosphere of collision, they may indeed be productive of the fantastic.

What I have tried to suggest is merely a beginning point for considering an imposing critical term. This activity, like the term itself, is ideal. It is a pursuit of meaning and understanding that is not actual in the positivist sense. But it is related to actuality. It cannot avoid the problem of mimesis, because it is itself grounded in reflective dimensions that are not simply either real or ideal, and it moves like all literature upon that interpenetrating, interdependent dimensionality that is not controlled by our either-or thinking. Pragmatically, if it does not mean something in relation to other theories and to imaginative literature itself, it is an empty exercise. I trust that it is an opening to possibilities rather than a generic closure, and I trust that it is not in itself too fantastic.

NOTES

1. Ludwig Wittgenstein, *On Certainty* (New York: Harper & Row, 1972), 49, 90.
2. Tzvetan Todorov, *The Fantastic: A Structural Approach to a Literary Genre*, trans. Richard Howard (Cleveland: Case Western Reserve University Press, 1973). Eric Rabkin,

The Fantastic in Literature (Princeton, N.J.: Princeton University Press, 1976), 118, did not disagree with Todorov's criterion of "the reader's hesitation" but did present a more open and complex discussion of the fantastic than Todorov's.

3. Philip Sidney, "An Apology for Poetry," in *Critical Theory Since Plato*, ed. Hazard Adams (New York: Harcourt Brace Jovanovich, 1971), 169. I cite Sidney and some other theorists from Adams's excellent and readily available text in that I feel no urgency in these instances to seek a more authoritative edition. Further references to Sidney's "Apology" and Adams's *Critical Theory* and to Burke, Kant, and Longinus appear in parentheses in the text.

4. Abraham Cowley, *Poems*, ed. A. R. Waller (Cambridge: Cambridge University Press, 1905), 295.

5. Warnock considered Sartre's view of the imagination in *Imagination* (Berkeley: University of California Press, 1976), 160-82; and Casey developed his theory of the imagination in *Imagining: A Phenomenological Study* (Bloomington: Indiana University Press, 1976).

6. Joseph Addison, *The Spectator*, no. 412 (London: George Routledge and Sons, n.d.), 594.

7. Aristotle, *Poetics*, translation by Leon Golden and commentary by O. B. Hardison, Jr. (Englewood Cliffs, N.J.: Prentice-Hall, 1968). Hardison considered the word etymologically on page 163. Further references to Golden's translation and Hardison's commentary appear in parentheses in the text.

8. In the spirit of tentativeness, my observations about the play rest on having seen a performance rather than on having studied a text; hence I cite no printed text.

The Literature of the Unknowable

John M. Lipski

The inherent cognitive limitations that lie at the foundations of modern science and, more generally, of all epistemological inquiry suggest the possibility of a literature of the *unknowable*, of the creation of a situation that by its very essence precludes the complete transference of knowledge to the reader.

Fiction and *fantasy*—these terms have often been used loosely, implying only a quantitative difference, an order of magnitude jump to the level of the "fantastic." In the realm of prose literature fantasy is fiction, but the converse is not always true. Surely, for example, no fictional character is more fantastic than the legendary Superman, whose feats transcend all bounds of probability and in some instances even of possibility. Mort Weisinger, writer of the Superman series, once received a letter from a group of MIT students informing him of Albert Einstein's verdict on Superman's extraordinary powers: "It is impossible for Superman to travel at 372,000 miles a second. According to my theory of relativity, nothing can exceed the velocity of light, which . . . is about 186,000 miles a second." Science fiction writer Isaac Asimov provided Weisinger with a ready reply: "Professor Einstein's statement is based on theory. Superman's speed is based on fact."[1] A lighthearted spoof, a humorous tip of the hat to one of history's greatest theorists, a defense of the realm of science fiction—Asimov's response is all of these things, and yet perhaps an even greater significance lurks behind these superficially banal words of a man whose writings have so often proved prophetic. During the twentieth century science has undergone several conceptual revolutions; the implications of these radical revisions extend far beyond the pale of the traditional scientific community to encompass virtually every human endeavor. It is ironic that "serious" fiction writers and their critics vehemently defend their right to interpret "reality" as they see fit while looking askance at their colleagues in "science fiction" for attempting to rewrite this reality in other fashions, often with considerable technological sophistication. The present remarks are not designed to defend the *raison d'être* of science fiction, which needs no defense in any case, but to explore briefly some of the implications of current scientific thought on other nuclei of literary creation.

How did Einstein "know" that Superman could never travel faster than light? How do astrophysicists "know" about the existence of black holes, unseen and unseeable cosmological entities that may nonetheless be described in incredible detail? How do they "know" of the reactions going on within stars or of the evolutionary cycles of galaxies, which may take billions of years to go through a single cycle? On the scale of the infinitely tiny, how does the quantum physicist "know" that the uncertainty principle holds or that subatomic particles undergo evolutionary patterns that the theory itself states may never be directly observed? In all such cases the hypotheses result from formal models derived from coarser observations; the resultant theory is then used to generate predictions beyond the scope of the original data. One may permit oneself the luxury of questioning the essential validity of such an approach and ask: but is there any inconsistency or fallacy in assuming, for example, that a theory based on the interaction of particles traveling at velocities less than the speed of light can say anything *at all* about particles that may travel at or greater than the speed of light? Moreover, if the theory does indeed predict the impossibility of exceeding the speed of light, any counterpredictions about what might or might not happen beyond this barrier are undemonstrable and in fact disallowed.[2] In this embarrassment of riches there is something of a paradox: such a theory appears to yield more than is put into it, and yet it reflexively restrains itself by holding out tantalizing possibilities that may never be directly perceived. We are assuming that our conceptual function, which dictates the scientific method (and all other forms of thought), is extendable past its own limits and also that, in the absence of crucially finite-dimensional arguments, it is extendable to infinite dimensional cases. We are in effect assuming extendibility of our conceptual functions (viewing the dimension of cognition as a function space) not only isomorphic to the postulates of formal logic but metrically equivalent as well, that is, in which the same values of truth and falsity would result from equivalently valued derivations.

Let us borrow a further idea from mathematics, which may turn out to be much more than a simple metaphor. A *manifold* is a means of approximating a space that is locally equivalent to some well-known space, such as normal Euclidean geometry, but that globally may exhibit no such equivalence. For example, the surface of a sphere is locally equivalent to two-dimensional space, hence the possibility of covering the surface of the globe with partially overlapping flat maps, but the sphere in its totality requires a three-dimensional representation. Carrying this notion over to the realm of metaphysics, the cognitive space in which extensions of hypotheses or more general thought processes are carried out is a manifold in that, locally, it approximates the extendible system that we think it to be, while globally, however, that is, in cases including "conceptual infinity," it may manifest some deviations from this regularity. If such is the case it might be a priori impossible to offer predictions that fall beyond the range of the input data. The difficulty lies in the apparent need to get "outside" in order to determine what the structure of cognition really is, vis-à-vis our own limited imagination (which is merely a product of the same cognition). It is impossible to use the normal mathematical recourse, which is embedding in a higher-dimensional space, for by definition such an enterprise removes us from the domain of human cognition. However, since all of our activities are confined to this same domain of cognition, it might be supposed that there is no fundamental harm in simply accepting as axiomatic the total extendibility of our cognitive functions; we may have our cake and eat it too, Superman and the theory of relativity.

Retreating from such easily achieved and trivial satisfaction, we may find it possible to determine at least some of the characteristics or limitations of the cognitive space, even given the essential impossibility of going "outside" to take one's bearings. A manifold may reveal its properties even when external travel is not allowed; for example, the curvature of the earth was determined and verified long before the advent of satellites made possible a direct visual representation of a complete sphere (flat-earth believers notwithstanding). Local perturbations in a manifold may in theory be perceived from observations made in or on the manifold itself, thus giving at least a modicum of insight into its global nature. In the case of our cognitive space, we then ask whether there have been any local perturbations that might qualify as pointers in the direction of a nonuniform and nonextendible structure. The answers to this question would be hotly debated, both in philosophy and in science, and at present I make absolutely no claim to rigor and precision in either area. Rather, I shall merely point out several areas that, at the current state of affairs, could be characterized as epistemological singularities, meaning, in other words, that knowledge runs aground at these points—the cognitive information sinks, so to speak. Such points of singularity imply that the theory, all theory, breaks down, and unexpected deviations may crop up that cannot be explained by any conceivable legerdemain.

The two greatest scientific breakthroughs of modern times are the theory of relativity and the theory of the quantum. Although addressing themselves to superficially different domains, the theories share much in common. As popularly conceived, *quantum* theory deals with the world of the atom and its constituents, and *relativity* is more frequently extended to cosmic dimensions and finds its most ready tests in astronomy. Nonetheless, when stripped of their pragmatic limits of application, both theories are profound epistemological statements. Each theory replaces earlier classical models, assumed to be valid everywhere and forever. Quantum theory represents the abandonment of the infinite divisibility of time and space and replaces it with the quantum as the minimal unit of discourse.[3] It had been known for some time previously that matter could be reduced to atoms and even subatomic particles, which might or might not be capable of further subdivision, but one still operated under the assumption that space and time themselves, although partitioned by these particles, were continuous variables and could be accurately described in the smallest units desired. The continuity of space is the basis for calculus and topology and their mathematical offspring; similarly, time was regarded as a linear continuum that could be partitioned into arbitrarily small units, asymptotically converging on the notion of the "instant." Quantum theory's uncertainty principle places a limit on the divisibility of space and time, stating in essence that there are definite (although in most applications negligible) limits to measurement, to the acquisition of knowledge. Beyond these limits, defined not only in absolute terms (for example, Planck's constant) but in terms of interactions among members of systems, space and time may no longer be said to "exist" in a unique fashion. Furthermore, this unsettling state of affairs is the result of the inevitable interaction, during any act of acquisition of knowledge, between the observer and the observed. From extensions of the theory one may further extrapolate that, at the subatomic level, space itself is not simply connected; for example, there is not a single uniquely specifiable universe but an infinite collection of eternally oscillating topological configurations.[4]

Relativity theory in its early form stated that the notions of simultaneity and successivity, regarded as intrinsic to the flow of the universe, were artifacts of the observation process, the framework in which the observations were taking place. The extension to general relativity states that the commonly accepted notions of space and time hold only locally, and the large-scale structure of the universe may be at once more complex and more indeterminate than ever suspected. Capturing the popular imagination have been "black holes," the ultimate in epistemological breakdown, representing the complete destruction and elimination of knowledge and all possibility of acquiring knowledge.[5] Although black holes have not yet been conclusively demonstrated, an elaborate theory has evolved to describe their properties, and it is believed that they will be discovered in due time.

Even the most rudimentary considerations show that there exist limits on the acquisition of knowledge, points at which the theory, a human cognitive creation, destroys itself, with no possible redemption arising from the ashes. Science, which etymologically means knowledge itself, and which has always stood for enlightenment, is the vehicle of its own destruction, since the very theories designed to enhance our knowledge have, to the contrary, shown that much currently accepted knowlege may be spurious, and the acquisition of "true" knowledge may be out of the question. Reeling from these revelations, many scientists were driven to extreme claims, for example, the total elimination of time and the notion of "becoming," the elimination of causality, even locally, the existence of several universes, and so on.[6] In the words of Werner Heisenberg, "quantum theory forcefully reminds us that natural science is made by man. This is not simply a symbolic representation of nature, but is part of the interplay between nature and man. What it describes is not nature as such, but nature as exposed to man's method of questioning. It makes Descartes' sharp separation between the world and the I impossible.''[7] Max Plank believed that there exists a "real world" but that "it lies beyond our senses, and as such cannot be apprehended at all: as the view of the physical world is perfected, it simultaneously recedes from the world of sense; this process is tantamount to an approach to the world of reality.''[8] A modern physicist has stated that the right order of concepts may not be the idea that "here is the universe, so what must humans be?" but "here are humans, so what must the universe be?"[9] Science is thrust into a new role not only of discovering the universe but in a very real sense of inventing it, creating it out of the human cognition. This not only is an extension of classical idealism but stems from modern views that certain scientific theories might simply be functions of the mechanisms of the human brain or that certain logical concepts might underlie the entirety of scientific discourse.[10]

Nor is the realm of the unknowable restricted to physics. Pure mathematics has its own questionable areas; for instance, there are (infinitely many) numbers whose structure can be explicitly and precisely specified but none of whose digits is, or can be, known. Even well-known numbers, such as *pi*, exhibit characteristics that are in theory inaccessible to empirical verification.[11] Similarly, general biological configurations, questions of form, and even the nature of life itself may be susceptible to unsurpassable epistemological limits.[12]

Under all of these views humans do not merely sit passively back as the universe evolves around them; they do not partake of a single unique "reality." Rather, humans, faced with the inherent indeterminacy, are at once the inventor and the recipient of the universe; their "reality" is a fluid, relative, and purely local concept that may not under any circumstances be arbitrarily generalized. This undercurrent of uncertainty and indeterminacy may give rise to feelings of anguish and bewilderment, but thinkers attuned to these ideas feel a tremendous sense of freedom from classical limitations. They are no longer restricted to global models of reality, which are extremely limiting, but are comparatively free to explore and even, when necessary, to invent local models not only compatible with their own experiences but consistent with any alternative vision of the universe that they might have.

The epistemological unchaining that results from considering cognition as only locally extendible may, at least in principle, be used to extrapolate an infinite variety of abnormal, bizarre, and ostensibly anomalous situations, configurations that, locally considered, do not at all match the world as we know it. Even given such comparative freedom, however, it is necessary to constrain the possibilities engendered by such an expanded cognition; one must normally establish at least a minimum of correlation between the novel configuration and the present state of the universe as we perceive it; a failure to do so creates a situation that most people would qualify as absurd or totally incomprehensible. It is equally clear that the restricting of cognitive operations only locally may be extended integrally to the domain of literature, where traditionally the fictional "reality" of the author has had to adhere to the same standards as those used in the sciences. Although all authors have the right to construct their own domains, from photographic realist and minimalist works to the most outlandish flights of imagination, the model of reality is required to be internally self-consistent and subject to a single, global set of axioms of some sort. Fact and fiction must be specified in the classical model, since only thus could readers sort out for themselves the threads that bind them, by the act of reading, to the world created by the author and embedded in the text. Even further restrictions have applied to the literary text, for the author is expected to indicate, by some means, the various streams that unite the characters and scenes in the work, the extent of knowledge shared by each personage, or attributable to each situation.

This is not to suggest that there have not been departures from the rigid framework of classical epistemology in literature, but such departures were couched in normally acceptable genres. For example, the "classic" surrealist text often completely does away with any clearly definable epistemological basis; such in fact is a defining tenet of surrealism, where the syntagmatic flow predominates, if not totally overpowers, the normal paradigmatic association. A variant form, the stream-of-consciousness narrative, carries this syntagmatic hegemony even to further levels, and readers are led to expect no further correlations than those made available by the immanence of the text they are reading; any attempt to establish paradigmatic order is violating the "rigid rules" of the genre. More generally, in many types of texts regarded as inherently "poetic," the use of inconsistent, contradictory, or merely chaotic signifiers is allowed, since the thrust of these texts is not toward the creation of a single cognitive structure but the presentation of a series of locally isolated images. In nearly all such texts it is possible, by subdividing the structure to a fine enough point, to arrive at a stage where each image is locally self-consistent.

Tzvetan Todorov's well-known definition of the *fantastic* stresses the dynamic element, the tension of ambiguity between a real but unlikely situation and a purely imaginary and impossible configuration.[13] Once the ambiguity is resolved the text passes into one of the above mentioned categories; thus the term *fantastic* refers not to a genre but to a state of (perhaps very tenuous) resonance between genres. In this definition Todorov came very close to articulating the type of cognitive nonextendibility that I have discussed in referring to the fantastic as an "evanescent genre." However, in the cases cited by Todorov, the true amplitude of the definition is not clearly visible. The authors discussed were firmly based in a classical view of the universe; whether their scenes were overtly supernatural or merely uncanny, they operated at all times with two well-defined states in mind, and the ambiguous tension that according to Todorov characterizes the fantastic is used as a literary gambit, a rhetorical device that is not meant to imply any philosophical disposition whatsoever. The authors are no more suggesting the duality of the universe than are the authors of serial thrillers, who leave their heroes apparently plunging to their doom, knowing full well that a complete (if only temporary) restoration to normality will occur in the succeeding episodes. The tension is created by the ambiguity that surrounds the act of reading, the fact that readers are not afforded sufficient information until some critical moment (or perhaps not at all) in order for them to arrive at an acceptable interpretation; however, implicit in nearly all such works of fantasy is the assumption that were such knowledge to be imparted, a full acceptance of the situation as described would ensue. Regardless of the deviation between the fantastic situations described and the phenomenological world as perceived by readers, the readers are reasonably certain that the world of fantasy operates through its own well-defined laws, and underlying the enjoyment of the fantastic is the titillating supposition that, at least in theory, it would be possible for readers to fully grasp the inner workings of the fantastic universe. That is, traditionally, literature that has been classified as fantastic, whether in the realm of science fiction, allegory, or some less easily defined category, deals with that which is unknown or unexperienced but that is, within its own internal self-constraints, knowable.

The inherent cognitive limitations mentioned above, which lie at the foundations of modern science and, more generally, of all epistemological inquiry, suggest the possibility of a literature of the *unknowable*, of the creation of a situation that by its very essence precludes the complete transference of knowledge to readers. The nonuniqueness of the universe, and the accepted possibility for information-sinks and spontaneous deviations from all known phenomena, may be logically reflected in literary texts, to create a structure that seals itself off from the cognitive sphere of readers. This may be done in very trivial ways, either by adopting the superficial imagery of modern scientific inquiry or by explicitly creating situations in which the paradoxes of science are woven in amidst other plot details, in the tradition of avant-garde science fiction.[14] It is also possible, however, to abandon all explicit reference to scientific epistemology and let the structure of the text itself, and the cognitive processes that it presupposes, be formed on the basis of the essential nonuniqueness and undecidability—to create a text, that is, of the unknowable, an inherently and intrinsically uncertain text.

These remarks may sound more programmatic than descriptive, a call to arms for a new form of liberated literature, and in a sense perhaps they are, since if literature is to evolve it must do so along pathways opened by more general aspects of human cognition. It is already possible to find works that demonstrate the nonregular extendibility of epistemological transfer, replete with singularities, indeterminacy, and simple unknowability. To describe even one such work in detail would make for a voluminous study that, in fact, remains a pressing need in contemporary literary studies. In briefly mentioning a few examples with which I am familiar, I make no claim about their superiority over others that might be proffered.

Among contemporary world literatures, two stand out as embodying a large number of epistemological innovations or at least departures from traditional molds, the literatures of France and Latin America. The latter literature, in particular, may be characterized by a strong reliance on inherent multiplicity and on the embrace of paradox and the refusal to force its texts into the strait-jackets of univocal interpretation.[15] Although most contemporary experimental Latin American novels use multiplicity in fact to form knowledge, since knowl-edge of multiplicity is knowledge gained, there are also works that may truly be considered to embody the unknowable. A prime example is the novel *Estudio Q* by the Mexican Vicente Leñero; ostensibly a novel about the filming of a soap opera about the filming of a soap opera, and so on, the novel's explicitly embedded levels open the possibility for an infinite number of embeddings, a series of mirror reflections inside mirror reflections whose only resolution comes at the asymptotal point of infinity, that is, beyond the human grasp. The reader is unable to sort out the levels of the text, not because the author is purposefully withholding information, but because such knowledge simply does not exist.

The Argentinian writer Ernesto Sábato, in his massive *Abaddón el extermi-nador*, placed himself and his previous novels as protagonists, and the text in effect describes its own creation. Sábato the author describes Sábato the character in the process of writing the novel itself, discussing his previous novels and sustaining discussions with characters from his earlier works, who come and go as though they were real personages. At no time is this ontological discrepancy explicitly revealed, but to make matters even more complicated, Sábato the author fills in the text with apparently realistic autobiographical details that purport to describe his genesis as writer. It turns out, however, that many of these details are pure fiction, and others are indeed truthful; thus the text of *Abaddón* oscillates between fiction and fact. Sábato the living author alternates with Sábato the hallucinating writer turned into a giant bat or the wonderstruck explorer experiencing mystical sites under the city of Buenos Aires. There is no possibility for experiencing any ontological priorities in the text, for the dis-tinction between fact and fiction, and between "realistic" fiction and fantasy, is placed in the realm of the unknowable. The novel, through its infinite reflex-ivity, its describing its own genesis at every step of the way, precludes a voyage outside it to an external perspective where this epistemological vacuum may be filled.

The Mexican writer Salvador Elizondo has, in his celebrated novel *Farabeuf*, exemplified another case of the fantastic as unknowable. *Farabeuf* condensed the events of more than half a century, an incident of Chinese torture occurring during the Boxer rebellion, which then, in the fashion of Alain Robbe-Grillet, becomes replayed incessantly and in infinite places throughout the pages of the novel. Time and space are destroyed and, more importantly, so is the possibility for any unique recovery. The reader, led by the Ariadne's thread of divination with the *I Ching*, simply must accept the impossibility of further resolution in the pursuit of the text.

Examples of the unknowable could be multiplied, in Latin American literature and elsewhere, but it is not the purpose of these remarks to offer either a bestiary or a taxonomy. The limits of human cognition, sensed most clearly in the academic pursuit of knowledge, return to haunt the literary creator, and with each step forward in the understanding of the universe we learn that we know less and less. In the literature of the unknowable, inherent indeterminacy and paradox reinforce the hypothesized cognitive nonextendibility not by destroying the double—or multiple—articulation of the text (since locally, it may be possible to extract a definite ontological configuration) but by placing the end of the epistemological rainbow in an ever-receding position impossible to reach. Only by stepping outside of the text's ontological realm, that is, outside our own limitations, could full knowledge be gained, knowledge that for mortals is impossible. By presenting only local approximations to an unknown and essentially unknowable global structure, one may entertain visions of a sort not hitherto dreamed possible, a world whose only bounds are those of the imagination itself, both creator of the text and captive in its implications.

NOTES

1. "Parade," *Detroit Free Press*, 23 Oct. 1977.

2. An extension of this theoretical limit, to include further aspects of the theory of relativity, is discussed in Robert Misner, Kip Thorne, and John A. Wheeler, *Gravitation* (San Francisco: Freeman, 1975), chap. 31.

3. Cf. Richard Schlegel, *Completeness in Science* (New York: Appleton-Century-Crofts, 1967), 235-36.

4. Most specifically, "quantum geometrodynamics." See John A. Wheeler, "From Relativity to Mutability," *The Physicists Conception of Nature*, ed. Jagdish Mehra (Dordrecht: Reidel, 1975), 202-47; and Misner, Thorne, and Wheeler, *Gravitation*, chap. 43.

5. Cf. John Taylor, *Black Holes* (Glasgow: Collins, 1973); Misner, Thorne, and Wheeler, *Gravitation*, chap. 33; Stephen Hawking and Gregory Ellis, *The Large Scale Structure of Space-Time* (Cambridge: Cambridge University Press, 1973), chaps. 8-10.

6. Cf. James Jeans, *Man and the Universe*, Sir Halley Steward Lecture, 1935.

7. Werner Heisenberg, *Physics and Philosophy* (New York: Harper & Row, 1968), 42.

8. Max Planck, *The Universe in the Light of Modern Physics*, trans. W. Johnston (New York: Norton, 1931), 15.

9. Arne Petersen, *Quantum Physics and the Philosophical Tradition* (Cambridge: MIT Press, 1968), 22.

10. Cf. Jacob Bronowski, "The Logic of the Mind," *American Scientist* 4 (1966): 1-14; and Misner, Thorne, and Wheeler, *Gravitation*, chap. 44.

11. Martin Gardner, "Mathematical Games," *Scientific American*, November 1979, 20-34.

12. René Thom, *Stabilité structurale et morphogénèse* (Reading, Mass.: Benjamin, 1972).

13. Tzvetan Todorov, *The Fantastic: A Structural Approach to a Literary Genre*, trans. Richard Howard (Ithaca, N.Y.: Cornell University Press, 1973), chap. 2.

14. Cf. Charles H. Waddington, *Behind Appearance* (Cambridge, Mass.: MIT Press, 1968).

15. John M. Lipski, *Narrative Multiplicity in the Modern Spanish-American Novel*, forthcoming, treats this aspect more extensively.

TECHNIQUES OF THE FANTASTIC

The following chapters examine the fantastic as a function of technique, either by applying existing typologies to specific works or by demonstrating how certain linguistic and structural patterns help to create "other worlds." Clarence Lindsay demonstrates Viktor Shklovsky's *ostranenie*, or "making strange the commonplace," and suggests that this technique may be the aesthetic origin and affective criterion of science fiction, and Carter Martin and Michael Collings demonstrate ways in which disjunctive language affects fantasy. Will McLendon and L. L. Dickson discuss the relationship of allegory to the fantastic, and Kathleen Glenn and A. B. Chanady apply Tzvetan Todorov's structural exegesis of the work of Julio Cortázar and Martín Gaite. Jules Zanger studies the allusive substructure of ideas behind the shocking surface structure of Edgar Allan Poe's "Berenice."

H. G. Wells, Viktor Shklovsky, and Paul de Man: The Subversion of Romanticism

Clarence Lindsay

> H. G. Wells's science fictions, like all art, were generated by formal
> requirements and solved formal problems. They appeared in order to
> repeat old conventions in new contexts or, in the case of *The Time
> Machine*, to invert the central convention through which the Romantic
> consciousness had expressed itself.

> [A] work of art is perceived against a background of, and by means of
> association with, other works of art. The form of the work of art is
> determined by the relation to other forms existing before it. *The material
> of a work of art is definitely played with a pedal, i.e. is separated out,*
> "voiced." Not only a parody, but also in general any work of art is
> created as a parallel and a contradiction to some kind of model. *A new
> form appears not in order to express a new content, but in order to
> replace an old form, which has already lost its artistic value.*
>
> Shklovsky, "Connection"

Shklovsky and other Russian formalists proposed a view of literature (and all
human activity for that matter) that attacked assumptions that even now dominate
critical thinking. For the formalists literature was independent of "reality."
Implicit in Shklovsky's work is the corollary theory that "reality," the material
of all fiction, is in fact simply the existing fictions and metaphors that have
become habitual and that are taken for reality. Such an understanding forces the
quotation marks that so often accompany the word "reality." Literature originates, according to Shklovsky, not in any need to reflect or to understand an
external reality but through a need to rescue the sensation of life that is constantly
being devoured by habitual knowledge. Art, said Shklovsky, is the crooked,
tortuous road where we are made to feel the stones. The crooked path is poetry;

the straight path, prose, the world of our deadened, habitual understandings. All literary devices aim at the same thing; their purpose is the recovery of strangeness (*ostranenie*), which has become in current critical language "defamiliarization."[1]

Shklovsky's emphasis on art's thirst for newness, for making strange, is especially appropriate to science fiction, which is a genre so often synonymous with strangeness. His understanding of literature is as a system in which forms take on meaning in relation to past forms.[2] This view is especially fitted for a genre that, as Darko Suvin said, promises us cognition and estrangement in its very name.[3] H. G. Wells used his science fiction to recover strangeness; by seeing Wells's science fictions in the general, formal context of romanticism, we can see how he was able to renew certain Romantic conventions and, more significantly, to subvert the principal convention through which the Romantic consciousness has expressed itself.

We should note the reclamation of a literary mode for which not only Wells but the entire genre of science fiction can claim either responsibility or credit. One of the techniques for making strange that Shklovsky mentioned is the repetition of an existing mode or formula in a new context. What science fiction has recovered, by repeating in new contexts (and, if the number of shelves devoted to science fiction at book stores is an indication, is still keeping fresh), is the adventure story and related corollary literary modes such as romance. Science fiction offered the opportunity to repeat the adventure story's conventions in startling contexts and to locate those extravagant moments of adventure in new landscapes. The Time Traveller's desperate search for his missing machine, which had been secreted away by the Morlocks, and his eerie, tenebrous struggles with those underground demons; Bedford's fierce battles with the moon men, his and Cavour's escape, their frantic search for their space ship as the deathly cold of the lunar night approaches; the protagonist of *The War of the Worlds* and his narrow escapes from the invading Martians, his imprisonment in a basement close by the Martian encampment, his fascinated witnessing of the Martians' drinking of human blood—these examples are the stock, familiar conventions of the adventure story given new life by the mere fact of their extraterrestrial and/or extravagant settings.

Wells not only makes an old form new by means of radically new contexts, but like all artists he has as his purpose the making strange of the commonplace, the defamiliarization of those aspects of life that have become imperceptible through familiarity. All art—Gertrude Stein's seemingly endless repetition of phrases and words, Mark Twain's absurd interruptions and wildly misplaced punchlines, Joseph Conrad's digressions and repetitions—seeks this breakdown of deadened, encrusted familiarity so that we can perceive experience painfully and bewilderingly afresh. One technique of Wells's that is common to science fiction is the extension and exaggeration of some facet of our experience into another setting. For example, the Time Traveller's discovery of the inverted class sytem of the Elois and the Morlocks in the year A.D. 802,701 (after making originally predictable errors based on his inherited assumptions) not only achieved its clear didactic purpose but awakened his readers to a new awareness of class that had been, perhaps, disguised by tradition and custom. But this device, although it serves to recover the sensation of life, still serves mainly a didactic purpose and is common to science fiction for that reason.

Another technique serves the pure aesthetic need described by Shklovsky, the need to recover the sensation of life. In Wells's science fiction the natural order is frequently violated, whether it is accomplished through time travel as in *The Time Machine*, space travel as in *The First Men in the Moon*, some external threat to the natural order as in *The War of the Worlds*, or some sort of Faustian tampering with the natural as in *The Island of Doctor Moreau*. The violation is always accompanied by the protagonists' discovery of the strange, awful majesty of what had been, before the violation, merely the commonplace. Bedford, about to leave for the moon and sensitive for the first time of the danger, of what exactly is at stake, discovers for the first time the strange beauty of the planet he is about to leave. When Bedford returns to Earth, images and scenes that he before would not have noticed now strike him as remarkably strange. "What strange men can have reared these vertical piles in such amplitude of space I do not know."[4] He is a Miranda awakening to a strange, if not necessarily brave, new world, a stranger in a strange land. The Time Traveller returns only a few hours after he has left, but his eight days in the future have altered utterly his sense of the present.

Such scenes are, in fact, curious twists of one of the standard Romantic conventions. The great Romantic writers William Wordsworth, Thomas Hardy, E. M. Forster, Virginia Woolf—poets and novelists—have depended in various ways on some version of the polarity of past and present. The past may intrude on the present as in Alfred Lord Tennyson's "death in life"; it may act both as poetic inspiration and at the same time as a synecdoche for an authentic self's relationship to experience as in Wordsworth; or it may be the source of patterns that we can impose on the chaos of the present, providing some sort of stability in a world of flux as in Woolf or Forster. In Wells's fiction the present, along with the accepted order of assumptions toward life, are instantly transformed into an irrecoverable past. His protagonists do not look back over the years and yearn for a distant and fading youth. Rather, through some sort of cataclysmic event (the invasion from outer space) or through some device (time travel), they are forced into a peculiar sort of nostalgia for the present. In Wells's fiction those science fiction devices replace the many traditional situations that stimulate the Romantic poet to reflect on past and present. Wells's Time Machine is Wordsworth's reflective vantage point above Tintern Abbey.

Another familiar Romantic theme is the celebration of the imagination's capacity for breaking barriers. The principal scientific devices in Wells's fiction, for example, the Time Machine and the space vehicle, are not so much instruments of technology as they are emblems of the imagination's power to transcend limits. The Time Traveller's audience, even as they are skeptical, are thrilled by the possibilities of unencumbered movement through time. Clearly, they and the Time Traveller represent a facet of Wells's eagerness, his surging, confident eagerness to allow the imagination full rein. When Cavour and Bedford find themselves on the moon's surface, they experience a thrilling release from the most basic of human limitations. They take gigantic leaps, frolicking like children in a strange lunar garden. But Wells, as other Romantic novelists have done, insisted on presenting the full curve of the Romantic experience, insisted on the despair and alienation that follow the breaking of bonds, the terror of the new. Cavour and Bedford's exuberant Romantic joy ends in a feeling of radical alienation:

I stared about me in the vain hope of recognising some knoll or shrub that had been near the sphere. But everywhere was a confusing sameness, everywhere the aspiring bushes, the distending fungi, the dwindling snow-banks, steadily and inevitably changed. The sun scorched and stung; the faintness of an unaccountable hunger mingled with our infinite perplexity. And even as we stood there, confused and lost amidst unprecedented things. (Wells, *First Men*, p. 59)

It is on these moments of awesome discovery that Wells spends some of his most intense lyrical imaginings. This disciple of imagination was at his best recording the dreadful loneliness of the successful imaginative leap. One of the most eerie scenes in literature is the haunting wail of the last Martian as his race's ambitious enterprise comes to its grotesque end.

These moments, as satisfying as they are, are repetitions of a standard Romantic discovery, admittedly made fresh by new contexts but still a recognizable, familiar convention of romanticism. But at least once in *The Time Machine* Wells achieved the creation of an entirely new form, a form that takes on its full meaning only when juxtaposed with the Romantic convention it displaced. The critical scene occurs after the Time Traveller escapes the Morlocks and, instead of returning to his present, turns the levers forward and journeys 30 million years into the future. The extraordinary power of this scene proceeds solely from the subversion of one of the heretofore unassailed dynamics of Romantic consciousness.

To understand the nature of that principle of Romantic consciousness and the full impact of Wells's complication of that principle, we need to consider a portion of Paul de Man's "Rhetoric of Temporality."[5] De Man began by tracing the gradual ascendancy of the term *symbol* as it begins to supplant in the latter half of the eighteenth century the more traditional rhetorical term *allegory*. The transformation of this key rhetorical concept from allegory to symbol is at the center of the conceptual tension of romanticism. From a traditional perspective allegory was seen as the fruit of the Age of Enlightenment and was consequently open to the charge of excessive rationality. Allegory and symbol, then, came quickly in the later eighteenth- and nineteenth-century critics' discourse to stand for nearly antithetical uses of language, symbol for art, allegory for nonart. The symbol—with the capacity to suggest the infinite through the particular and to imply a degree of organic intimacy between the mind of the perceiver and the experience being perceived (and thus transforming individual experience into general truths)—has come to be regarded as superior to allegory and moreover has come to be seen as the defining mode of romanticism. It is the appeal of the infinite, as De Man said, that makes up the main appeal of the symbol. Viewed through the symbol the "world is no longer seen as a configuration of entities that designate a plurality of distinct and isolated meanings, but as a configuration of symbols ultimately leading to a total, single and universal meaning" (p. 174). By emphasizing the mind of the observer as a synecdoche for the infinite, the elevation of the symbol is, according to De Man, actually a kind of ontological bad faith, because it disguises or even denies the self's temporal predicament.

Although critics have generally accepted the predominance of the symbol as the outstanding feature of Romantic diction, De Man brought that assumed predominance into question. He showed that in a number of instances allegorizing tendencies appear at critical moments in Romantic literature. Always, *allegory*, in the sense of recognition of the discontinuity of sign and meaning, thus a discontinuity of subject and object, reveals an "authentically temporal destiny." The symbol, with its organic dialectic between subject and object, humans and nature, is only a passing moment in romanticism's larger dialectic. The mystified self that sees itself immune to the impact of time comes to recognize the full impact of time. For De Man the authentic voice of romanticism emerges at this moment of recognition, when the illusions and mystification inherent in symbolic diction fall away and the self is made painfully aware of its predicament in time.

We have arrived at the point where De Man's conclusions have some bearing on a consideration of Wells's *Time Machine*. De Man suggested that this discovery of an authentically temporal destiny is a culminating moment in the Romantic experience. He identified as the authentic Romantic experience that moment when a human consciousness discovers its temporal confinement against or juxtaposed with patterns of nature that seem immune to time. He offered the following passages from the *Prelude* as instances of this immortality of nature:

> . . . these majestic floods—these shining cliffs
> The untransmuted shapes of many worlds,
> Cerulian's ether's pure inhabitants,
> These forests unapproachable by death,
> That shall endure as long as man endures. (p. 181)

or

> . . . The immeasurable height
> Of woods decaying, never to be decayed.
> The stationary blast of waterfalls. (p. 181)

In these passages the "untransmuted shapes," the "forests unapproachable by death," the "woods decaying, never to be decayed," refer to what the Germans call *Dauer im Wechsel*: endurance within a pattern of change.

De Man's conclusions, at least as far as they pertain to a description of a central principle of romanticism, seem unassailable. He could have quoted countless examples in which a limited, human mortality is seen against the ceaseless, cyclic repetitions of nature. William Butler Yeats's "Wild Swans at Coole" comes to mind. Romantic literature is filled with such laments for someone's tragic separation from nature's unconscious rolling on. The laments are often directed strictly at the fact of consciousness itself, yearnings for the fullness and immediacy of being while deploring, in Evelyn Waugh's words, this "vile becoming." But although this discovery is the source of a good deal of Romantic agony, it is also—even in the harshest, coldest recognitions of our separation from nature's immortality—a subtle source of some comfort as well. The frequent repetition of the separation constitutes a convention, and the convention, although it states a tragic separation between humans' mortality and nature's immortality— nevertheless preserves the image of immortality. In the soft underbelly of the Romantic tradition—poets like Dylan Thomas—is revealed the lyrical sentimentality implicit in that seeming eternity. Although humans are not immortal something other than humans is. Although we lament that we are not that something (nature) we take a degree of solace in nature's capacity to repeat itself forever. It is this conventional Romantic relationship of humans to nature that Wells, in the penultimate chapter of *Time Machine*, manipulates and finally transforms with startling effectiveness.

The first alteration of the expected pattern of experience is the "palpitating greyness," a peculiar sensory dislocation caused by the special circumstances of time travel, the whirring succession of day and night. But profounder alterations in patterns begin to occur, alterations in those very patterns from which humans have traditionally borrowed the notion of eternity. The "sun had ceased to set—it simply rose and fell in the west." The moon, a traditional inspirational source, has disappeared. The universe's stately saraband, that apparently timeless dance, "the circling of the stars," grows slower and slower. Finally, the Time Traveller recognizes that Earth has come to rest (and there is a special charge to that idiomatic expression) with one face to the sun.

When the Time Traveller finally brings his machine to a halt, there are nearly hallucinatory alterations or intensifications of the "natural" color scheme (and we must begin to put quotation marks around that term). But despite these transformations, life persists, although at first it seems to be only richly green moss that we usually associate with familiar crepuscular Romantic settings that lead to reflections on human mortality. But here it is Earth that has ceased its ceaseless roll and has gathered moss, has become its own tombstone. We might also note how alert the Time Traveller is for signs of life, for those conventional signals of life's eternal renewal. He thus acknowledges the pressure of the conventional expectations and at the same time the formal necessity of the imaginative need to carry the convention to its breaking point. Bearing witness to the strength of the illusions implicit in Romantic convention and its supporting diction, the sea is still referred to as the "eternal sea . . . still moving and living."[6] But now the Romantic diction is very nearly in an ironic relationship to the experience it records. No longer does this familiar Romantic phrasing convey the unending, life-giving, and life-renewing power of the sea, but instead, because of the extravagant context, it questions the premise of the convention.

There is soon another subtle modification of a standard Romantic relationship. In the early phase of the Romantic dialectic De Man has described, there is a moment at which the mystified self through the intensity of the subjective experience seems to absorb nature into itself and makes the landscape yield meanings and moods congruent with the interior landscape of the self. We find, as the Time Traveller stares out at the black sea, what may seem at first a standard desolate Romantic landscape defined by the dismal cry of some "thing like a huge white butterfly" that goes fluttering into the distance and finally disappears (p. 103). But there is a difference. Here the mournful mood is not a projection of a sense of self onto a landscape, not a congruency of subject and object that is the special product of the intense subjectivity of the perceiver, but a mood appropriate to external nature. This is not an instance of a self demanding sympathy for its own mood by construing images that forge an intimacy between its mood and nature. Instead, here a self extends sympathy to nature's mortality. The mood of "abominable isolation" hangs over the world, and in a fundamental way the observer merely shares it and does not impose it.

In the beginning of the journey into the extreme future the use of Romantic devices had been tentatively ironic. But in the final stage the tentative irony has become explicit parody of Romantic conventions and the devices that constitute those conventions. The Time Traveller pushes 30 million years into Earth's cold future, and when he stops his device, he has arrived at the edge of time. Again his first response is to check for signs of life, apparently present only as green slime. It is clear by now that what has driven him to this ultimate extremity is the need to see "old earth's . . . fate," to stand alone and unencumbered at its demise (p. 104). The culminating scene of his adventure is a weird parodic catalog of Romantic devices of death and renewal. An eclipse of the dull, nearly lifeless sun causes what seems to be a final darkness. There is a final silence— all of the background stir of our lives is absent. As the eclipse's darkness sweeps Earth into its void, a moaning wind sings an accompanying dirge to Earth's dark night. Finally, there is the traditional emergence from the dark despairing death. But now the conventions of renewal are purely parodic. First, the fraudulent dawn as the "red hot bow" of the sun appears in the sky. This dawn illuminates only desolation. Then life itself emerges from the sea. But the macabre hopping blob with its grotesquely comic parody of the dance of life is, in its mad persistence, not a promise of continuing life but a statement of its end. We need only compare this scene with any of those mentioned by De Man—or countless other familiar Romantic scenes in which a demystified self stands apart from the archetypal symbols of eternity, aware of its mortal confinement—to understand Wells's radical transformation of a Romantic convention and to understand how, through that subversion of a traditional relationship of humans to nature, Wells created a new post-Romantic posture: a self, a human consciousness free from time, standing witness to the demise of Romantic nature.

Paul de Man said that the Romantic experience culminates in a discovery of the inauthenticity of the self, an inauthenticity from which there seems to be no escape and for which there seems to be no cure. Here is De Man's description of Romantic irony:

Irony divides the flow of temporal experience into a past that is pure mystification and a future that remains harassed forever by a relapse within the inauthentic. It can know this inauthenticity but can never overcome it. It can only restate and repeat it on an increasingly conscious level, but it remains endlessly caught in the impossibility of making this knowledge applicable to the empirical world. It dissolves in the narrowing spiral of a linguistic sign that becomes more and more remote from its meaning, and it can find no escape from this spiral. (p. 203)

After such knowledge, what forgiveness? What way out of such an impasse? What remains for post-Romantic literature other than the spiral of endless restatement and repetition of this dilemma or a regression into the old mystified modes (and De Man's statement does serve as both a fairly accurate description and definition of *modernity*). The conclusion of the Time Traveller's adventure points to the way out. Only the replacement of the older forms takes place. Science fiction allowed Wells in the *Time Machine* to create what I am sure De Man would call a new version of the mystified self, a self unencumbered by contingency, by time, superior to and detached from the nature from which, traditionally, humanity had to borrow the notion of immortality. Science fiction, then, at least in this example of Wells, facilitated the emergence of new forms at the moment when the emergence of new forms seemed impossibly circumscribed by the understanding of the universe, at the moment when older forms and conventions, deadened by familiarity, seemed the only devices compatible with the understood principles that govern existence. (This is possibly a hypothesis we might extrapolate to explain the emergence of fantasy or science fiction at other critical moments in literary history.)

Wells's science fictions, like all art, were generated by formal requirements and solved formal problems. They appeared in order to repeat old conventions in new contexts or, in the case of *The Time Machine*, to invert the central convention through which the Romantic consciousness had expressed itself. But in the process enormous facts—the mortality of our species and even of our universe, facts blurred and obscured by conventions that had become familiar—were pried loose. We, along with the Time Traveller, have gazed upon them.

NOTES

1. Richard Sherwood, "Viktor Shklovsky and the Development of Early Formalist Theory on Prose Literature," in *Russian Formalism,* ed. Stephen Bann and John E. Bowlt (Edinburgh: Scottish Academic Press, 1973), 26–40.

2. Viktor Shklovsky, "The Connection between Devices of *Syuzhet* Construction and General Stylistic Devices," in *Russian Formalism*, ed. Stephen Bann and John E. Bowlt (Edinburgh: Scottish Academic Press, 1973), 53.

3. Darko Suvin, *Metamorphoses of Science Fiction* (New Haven and London: Yale University Press, 1979), 13.

4. H. G. Wells, *The First Men in the Moon* (New York: Berkley, 1967), 131. Further references appear in parentheses in the text.

5. Paul de Man, "The Rhetoric of Temporality," in *Interpretation: Theory and Practice*, ed. Charles S. Singleton (Baltimore: Johns Hopkins University Press, 1969), 173–209. Further references appear in parentheses in the text.

6. H. G. Wells, *The Time Machine* (New York: Bantam Books, 1968), 102.

Poe's "Berenice": Philosophical Fantasy and Its Pitfalls

Jules Zanger

"Berenice" is a seriously conceived and carefully composed work that directs an equally serious criticism at the optimism of the age. It represents Edgar Allan Poe's attempt to transform the sensational, gothic fiction of the period that preceded it into a genuine fantasy of ideas.

Edgar Allan Poe's "Berenice" is frequently anthologized and fairly well known ("that awful story about the teeth!") but has received relatively little critical attention. A survey of the major critical commentaries on Poe's fiction reveals that although the story is frequently cited, it is rarely given more than a few summary sentences. Much of this neglect stems from the story's horrific details, which are probably something of an embarrassment to Poe scholars, who include in even their most cursory comments critical evaluations such as "gruesome," "horrible," "offensive," "hideous," and "repulsive."[1]

Certainly, in Poe's own lifetime the story evoked a similar response, and in a famous letter to its first publisher, Thomas Willis White, editor of *The Southern Literary Messenger*, Poe wrote on April 30, 1835:

A word or two in relation to Berenice. Your opinion of it is very just. The subject is by far too horrible, and I confess that I hesitated in sending it to you especially as a specimen of my capability. The Tale originated in a bet that I could produce nothing effective on a subject so singular, provided I treated it seriously. But what I wish to say relates to the character of your Magazine more than to any articles I may offer, and I beg you to believe that I have no intention of giving you *advice*, being fully confident that, upon consideration you will agree with me. The history of all Magazines shows plainly that those which have attained celebrity were indebted for it to articles *similar in nature to Berenice*—although, I grant you, far superior in style and execution. I say similar in *nature*. You ask me in what does this nature consist? In the ludicrous heightened into

the grotesque: the fearful coloured into the horrible: the witty exaggerated into the burlesque: the singular wrought out into the strange and mystical. You may say all this is
bad taste. I have my doubts about it. . . . In respect to Berenice individually I allow that
it approaches the very verge of bad taste—but I will not sin quite so egregiously again.[2]

"Berenice" is clearly one of Poe's least succcessful stories, and most of the
horrified responses to it are justified. However, I reject the easy assumption that
it fails because of the reasons Poe offered: that it was either trivially inspired
(by a bet) or cynically contrived to win attention through its cheap sensation-
alism.[3] The frequency with which he reprinted the story and with which he
returned to and reworked more deftly a number of themes that this story first
introduced reveals that it was much more important to him than his demurrer to
White suggests. The letter to White represents the embarrassed response of a
young author who has attempted an ambitious literary experiment that has patently failed. But "Berenice" is an important and serious failure that represents
an early attempt at creating the type of fantasy that would distinguish Poe's most
mature and successful tales: a surface narrative that embodies, conceals, and
implies an undercurrent, however indefinite, of meaning. That undercurrent of
meaning is usually communicated to the careful reader of Poe's fictions by a
series of clues, allusions, suggestions, image clusters, that recur from story to
story—all of those devices that organically link the surface narrative to an implied
meaning that gives the details of that surface narrative, no matter how improbable
or inexplicable, a coherence, significance, and seriousness. Most contemporary
scholarship would agree that this structure is precisely what careful reading
reveals in Poe's mature fiction; it has failed to discover it in "Berenice."

The failure of "Berenice" results not from the absence of a serious and
coherent substructure of meaning or from the absence in the narrative envelope
of a system of details sufficient to imply that substructure but from an unsuc-
cessfully realized relationship between the two. Henry James, criticizing some
short stories of Nathaniel Hawthorne, wrote, "We are struck with something
stiff and mechanical, something incongruous, *as if the kernel had not assimilated
the envelope*" (italics mine).[4] Both James's analysis and his terminology are
useful if we apply them to "Berenice." First, beneath its sensational envelope
Poe's story contains a serious kernel of meaning; and second, the two, instead
of being mutually assimilated, merely parallel each other where one does not
overwhelm the other.

The kernel of meaning suggested by the narrative details of the tale begins to
emerge almost immediately, since Egeus, the narrator, quickly establishes an
intensely schematized world that opposes sunshine and shadow, male and female,
interior and exterior, experience and abstraction. It is a world the center of which
is the dim library in which Egeus was born, the library from which he tells his
story and from which we never see him emerge but from whose windows we
are permitted glimpses of shrubberies, fountains, and sunlit hillsides. He reveals
a world in which are opposed madness and sanity, and illness and health, but

it is important to notice that he makes these distinctions from the vantage point of reason and health. The clearly defined opposites of *illness* and *health, reason* and *insanity* in Egeus's world are described in language that accepts the commonsense application of those terms. Unlike those narrators of "The Tell Tale Heart" and "The Black Cat," who protest their sanity in language that convinces us of their madness, Egeus is a sane man describing a period of madness in his past, a rational man making a comprehensible statement of his own lapse from rationality. In this tale, as in so many of his others, Poe is denying that optimistic vision of humankind so popular in the eighteenth and early nineteenth centuries that saw humans as self-consciously reasonable creatures free to choose among the options of the world. Instead, Poe offered us as the informing insight of the tale a vision of human freedom limited by the vulnerability of human reason.

Egeus describes for us such a lapse in his account of the library:

In that chamber was I born. Thus awaking from the long night of what seemed, but was not, non-entity, at once into the very regions of fairy-land—into a palace of the imagination—into the wild dominions of monastic thought and erudition—[this listing suggests the progressive maturing of the speaker] it is not singular that I gazed around me with a startled and ardent eye—that I loitered away my boyhood in books, and dissipated my youth in revery: but it is singular, that as years rolled away, and the noon of manhood found me still in the mansions of my fathers—it is wonderful what stagnation there fell upon the springs of my life—wonderful how total an inversion took place in the character of my commonest thought. *The realities of the world affected me as visions, and as visions only, while the wild ideas of the land of dreams became, in turn, not the material of my everyday existence, but in very deed that existence utterly and solely in itself.* [Italics mine][5]

It is important to notice that his use of the terms *reality* and *dreams* is intended to correspond to the readers' conventional understanding of those terms, that the "inversion" he describes is clearly no longer operative.

This passage concludes the first section of the story (carefully separated from the rest of the text by a string of asterisks) and serves to warn us of how we are to read the subsequent narrative sequence—to see it as a product of what the narrator himself *now* regards as an aberration due to a "stagnation" of the mind resulting from lingering too long in fairyland, in the palace of imagination, in dreams, like an earlier Thomas Rymer or like Eliot's Prufrock to come.

The schematic polarization of the narrator's world that opens the story is further objectified in the two main characters of the tale, Egeus and Berenice, each of whom represents one of the opposing ideas that dominate the story.

Egeus is presented to us always in the dimness of the cloistered library and always physically inactive. The one passage in the original version of the story that showed him leaving his library to visit the bier upon which Berenice was lying was later excised by Poe, in part because its details were too gruesome for his readers but also, certainly, to preserve the physical immobility, the "bodily quiescence" of Egeus. Egeus's physical stillness is only the external aspect of the habit of mind that, even after the experience he will recount, dominates his perception of reality. His first act in the story is to transform felt experience into a metaphor and that metaphor into an object for contemplation. The story begins, "Misery is manifold. The wretchedness of earth is multiform. Overreaching the wide horizon as the rainbow, its hues are as various as the hues of that arch—as distinct too, yet as intimately blended. Overreaching the wide horizon as the rainbow! How is it that from beauty I have derived a type of unloveliness?" (pp. 145-46)

His recollected perception of Berenice was similar: "I had seen her—not as the living and breathing Berenice, but as the Berenice of a dream; not as a being of the earth, earthy, but as the abstraction of such a being; not as a thing to admire, but to analyze; not as an object to love, but as the theme of the most abstruse although desultory speculation" (p. 149). His time otherwise he spent, he tells us, in the fixed contemplation of "the most ordinary objects" about him to the point where he would lose "all sense of motion or physical existence, by means of bodily quiescence long and obstinately persevered in" (p. 147). Those objects, however, are remarkable if only in that they represent aspects of experience that are precisely opposed to the condition he aspires to: "a quaint shadow falling aslant upon the tapestry," "the steady flame of a lamp or the embers of a fire," "the perfume of a flower" (p. 147). What they possess in common is their vulnerability to change, to time: the moving shadow, the flickering flame, the dimming ember, the fading perfume. His attention is "riveted" on physical, transitory objects in order to rivet them, to fix motion and physical existence, not merely in himself, but in the enclosed world he inhabits.

Berenice, unlike Egeus, is always recollected in physical motion: "she, agile, graceful and overflowing with energy; hers, the ramble on the hillside—mine, the studies of the cloister; I living within my own heart and addicted, body and soul, to the most intense and painful meditation—she, roaming carelessly through life" (p. 146). When he perceives her, it is her image as it "flitted by his eyes." Even in that moment when he tells us she appeared directly before him in his study, she retained a "vacillating" outline. The disease that falls upon her Egeus likens to "the simoon," the destructive wind, and under its influence she is altered to the degree that he can no longer recognize her. She represents change to the degree of losing her identity, changing not merely physically but morally. Her disease, as he himself names it, is nothing more than change itself: "the spirit of change swept over her, pervading her mind, her habits, and her character, and, in a manner the most subtle and terrible, disturbing even the identity of her person" (p. 147).

Berenice's disease and Egeus's response to it anticipate the changes that overtake Morella's daughter and the response of the narrator to them in "Morella," which Poe published one month after "Berenice." "Strange indeed was her rapid increase in bodily size—but terrible, oh! terrible were the tumultuous thoughts which crowded upon one while watching the development of her mental being. Could it be otherwise, when I daily discovered in the conceptions of the child the adult powers and faculties of the woman?"[6] The cause of change in both cases is time itself. Berenice belongs to the evanescent, sensible world of time and history; Egeus aspires to the world of changeless and eternal objects of contemplation. It is in the conflict of these two worlds that the disaster of the tale is generated.

Confronted by the radically altered Berenice, Egeus becomes obsessed by the vision of her teeth:

The teeth!—the teeth—they were here and there and everywhere, and visibly and palpably before me; long, narrow, and excessively white, with the pale lips writhing about them, as in the very moment of their first terrible development. . . . I shuddered as I assigned to them in imagination a sensitive and sentient power, and even when unassisted by the lips, a capability of moral expression. Of Mad'selle Sallé it has been well said, "que tous ses pas étaient des sentiments," and of Berenice I more seriously believe que toutes ses dents étaient des idées. Des idées! ah here was the idiotic thought that destroyed me! Des idées—ah therefore it was that I coveted them so madly!" (p. 150)

Shortly afterward, Berenice suffers an epileptic stroke and apparently dies. Egeus digs up her coffin and pulls the teeth from the still-living Berenice. The story ends leaving a physically ravaged and mutilated Berenice and an Egeus, sane again, but trapped in an emotional cul-de-sac of self-revulsion and misery.

Why specifically does Egeus become obsessed with Berenice's teeth? It is because they represent to him the one relatively unchanging aspect of a Berenice who otherwise changes in every conceivable way: "her mind, her habits, and her character, and, in a manner the most subtle and terrible, disturbing even the identity of her person" (p. 146). They represent the external aspect of the skull beneath the skin, that which will be left when all the living changes have come to an end. In the changed Berenice of whom "not one vestige of the former being lurked in any single line," only the teeth remain "as in the very moment of their first terrible development" (p. 150). Her teeth become for him "des idées," that is, they are transformed into metaphysical essences in the Platonic sense.

Beneath the gruesome surface of the tale a coherent, significant, and serious structure of ideas is discoverable but only if we can get past the shock of those narrative details that overwhelm both that structure and the reader.

The source for this structure of ideas appears to be found in a classic philosophical opposition: Heraclitus's vision of the world as constant flux; Parmenides's vision of a world that is indestructible, eternal, and unchangeable. Plato was to reconcile these differences in postulating a dual world: a world of sense perception that is in constant flux and a world of *ideai* that is nonphysical, nonspatial, and nontemporal. These *ideai*, ideas or forms, are perceived not through the senses but through an intellectual act in which we ascend from the contemplation of Heraclitan particulars to the recognition of the Parmenidean (or, more properly, Platonic) ideas. According to T. O. Mabbott, Poe was reading in Plato with a specific emphasis on the Platonic doctrine of forms in the period between 1833 and 1835;[7] "Morella," published a month after "Berenice," in 1835, begins with an epigraph from Diotima's speech in the *Symposium* referring specifically to the idea of beauty: "subsisting of itself and by itself in an eternal oneness" that "however much the parts may wax and wane, it will be . . . the same inviolable whole."[8]

It seems clear that Poe objectified and dramatized the Platonic duality of change and permanence, of the temporal and the timeless, in his characterizations of Berenice and Egeus. Each represents a human extreme of these philosophical conceptions. The tragedy that occurs is, however, not implicit in the Platonic formulation, but results from the frailty of human reason. In Plato's *Symposium* Diotima describes the recognition of the ideal as resulting from an ascent from particulars to universals: "Starting from individual beauties, the quest for universal beauty must find him ever mounting the heavenly ladder, from rung to rung—that is, from one to two and from two to every lovely body, from bodily beauty to the beauty of institutions, from institutions to learning and from learning in general to the special lore that pertains to nothing but the beautiful itself— until he comes at last to know what beauty is." Egeus, in his illness, however, cannot ascend the ladder and remains fixed on its lowest rung—the particulars of sense perception: "In my case, the primary object was invariably frivolous, although assuming, *through the medium of my distempered vision*, a refracted and unreal importance [italics mine]. Few deductions, if any, were made; and those few pertinaciously returning in upon the original object as a center. The meditations were *never* pleasurable; and, at the termination of the revery, the first cause, so far from being out of sight, had attained the supernaturally exaggerated interest which was the prevailing feature of the disease" (Poe, "Berenice," p. 148). His "idiotic" confusion of her teeth with "des idées" leads him to remove her teeth from the wooden coffin of her grave and, "returning upon the original object as a center," to place them in the box ("of ebony" in the first three printings) upon his table (p. 152).

An even more specific allusion to the Platonic doctrine of ideas occurs in the opening of the tale, where Egeus remarks, "But it is mere idleness to say that I had not lived before—that the soul has no previous existence. You deny it? Let us not argue the matter. Convinced myself, I seek not to convince" (p. 146). This curious interpolation into the tale appears to have no particular relationship to the narrative and is never referred to again. Its relevance emerges only when we recall that Plato linked his doctrine of ideas to his theory of the previous existence of the soul, contending that we are born with our knowledge of the *ideai*:

Then if we obtained it before our birth, and possessed it when we were born, we had knowledge, both before and at the moment of birth, not only of equality and relative magnitudes, but of all absolute standards. Our present argument applies no more to equality than it does to absolute beauty, goodness, uprightness, holiness, and, as I maintain, all those characteristics which we designate in our discussions by the term "absolute." So we must have obtained knowledge of all these characteristics before our birth.[9]

Egeus retains, he tells us, the prenatal "memory of aerial forms—of spiritual and meaning eyes—of sounds musical yet sad; a remembrance that will not be excluded; a memory like a shadow—vague, variable, indefinite, unsteady (Poe, "Berenice," p. 146). When he directly encounters Berenice, the parallels to his prenatal memory are striking: "Was it my own excited imagination—or the misty influence of the atmosphere—or the uncertain twilight of the chamber— or the gray draperies which fell around her figure—that caused it so vacillating and indistinct an outline?" (p. 149) The "vacillating and indistinct" outline echoes and becomes confused with the "vague, variable, indefinite, unsteady" prenatal memory that he shall retain, he tells us, "while the sunlight of my reason exists" (p. 146). However, in his confrontation with Berenice the time is twilight, and it is not reason but "monomania" that leads him to commit the terrible act that concludes the tale. The object of Poe's irony in "Berenice" is not Platonic idealism but irrational human ability to pursue it successfully.

Given these elaborately worked out correspondences among the details of the surface narrative and the underlying structure of ideas, why does the story fail? In part, certainly, some of the narrative details, although Senecan in their presentation, remain sufficiently shocking as to abort the sensitive reader's pursuit of the clues so liberally sprinkled about. Also, Poe's pedantically detailed working out of his structure of ideas in the narrative's detail leads him to construct a tale that violates his own principles of composition, especially in regard to the singleness of emotional effect. How, for example, is the reader expected to respond to the grotesque inconclusiveness of the newly alive (as if faithful to her mutability) but toothless Berenice? To the heavy-handed underlining of "some instruments of dental surgery, intermingled with thirty-two [not "some" or "a number of"] small, white, and ivory-looking substances"? The envelope of narrative and the kernel of meaning not only do not absorb each other, they subvert each other, destroying that unity of effect that will mark his more successful fiction.

In spite of its flaws, however, "Berenice" marks a significant achievement for a young author. It is a seriously conceived and carefully composed work that directs an equally serious criticism at the optimism of the age. It represents Poe's attempt to transform the sensational, gothic fiction of the period that preceded it into a genuine fantasy of ideas. It contains all of the elements necessary to create such a fantasy and is marred only by the inability of a journeyman artist to fuse them into a coherent whole. That mastery would come later.

NOTES

1. See, respectively, Patrick F. Quinn, *The French Face of Edgar Poe* (Carbondale: Southern Illinois University Press, 1957), 216; Daniel Hoffman, *Poe Poe Poe Poe Poe*

Poe Poe (New York: Doubleday, 1972), 110; Charles Sanford, "Edgar Allan Poe," *Rives*, no. 18 (Spring 1962): 3; T. O. Mabbott, ed., *Collected Works of Edgar Allan Poe* (Cambridge: Harvard University Press, 1978), 2:207. David Halliburton's discussion of "Berenice" in his *Edgar Allan Poe: A Phenomenological View* (Princeton, N.J.: Princeton University Press, 1973), 199-206, is an important exception to my generalization.

2. In J. W. Ostrom, ed., *Letters of Edgar Allan Poe* (New York: Gordian Press, 1966), 1:578.

3. Sanford, "Edgar Allan Poe," 3.

4. Quoted in E. W. Carlson, ed., *The Recognition of Edgar Allan Poe* (Ann Arbor: University of Michigan Press, 1966), 67.

5. Edgar Allan Poe, "Berenice," in *Complete Poems and Stories of Edgar Allan Poe*, ed. Arthur Hobson Quinn and Edward H. O'Neill (New York: Knopf, 1946), 1:146. Further references appear in parentheses in the text.

6. Edgar Allan Poe, "Morella," in *Complete Poems and Stories of Edgar Allan Poe*, ed. Arthur Hobson Quinn and Edward H. O'Neill (New York: Knopf, 1946), 154.

7. Mabbott, *Collected Works*, 2:236.

8. Plato *Symposium* 211b Hamilton-Cairns.

9. Plato *Phaedo* 75c-d Hamilton-Cairns.

Compatibility of the Fantastic and Allegory: Potocki's *Saragossa Manuscript*

Will L. McLendon

Extended examination of the fictional elements and characters of the *mise en abyme* technique exploited by Jan Potocki would demonstrate Alphonse's encounters with the Persona, the Shadow, the Anima, and other such archetypes.

It has been more than twenty years since the late Roger Caillois resurrected and revealed to the Western reading public Jan Potocki's ill-fated *Manuscrit trouvé à Saragosse* by publishing a series of tales excerpted from a thoroughly mutilated whole.[1] Yet today very few members of the academic community on this side of the Atlantic seem to be aware of this seminal work.[2] But it has provided source material and inspiration of varying sorts to much better known writers than the Polish nobleman, archeologist, ethnologist, and globetrotter Count Jan Potocki (1761-1815), who wrote preferably in French and left publication of his fantastic masterpiece to the whims of friends and colleagues in Saint Petersburg and Paris between 1805 and 1814. Certain contemporaries of Count Potocki, however, were quick to realize the literary merits and other potentials of this incredibly haphazard and quasi-anonymous publication, among them Charles Nodier, Washington Irving, and the Comte de Courchamps, all three long since proven guilty of the most flagrant plagiarism.[3]

In our own time a handful of scholars, particularly Potocki enthusiasts such as Caillois, Tzvetan Todorov, Jean Decottignies, Daniel Beauvois, and Maria-Evelina Zoltowska, have been striving to call attention to Potocki's genius, as evidenced in his major contribution to French letters in general and to the literature of the fantastic in particular. Thanks to the still fragmented texts now available—an English translation, *The Saragossa Manuscript*, appeared between 1960 and 1967—readers are in a reasonably good position to judge Potocki's overall design and appreciate the orchestration of his complex narrative far better than his contemporaries did. The fact that Charles Nodier, Washington Irving, and the Comte de Courchamps successfully lifted individual episodes from Potocki's novel and passed them off as their own—only Courchamps was caught red-handed in his lifetime—bears witness not only to the rampant plagiarism of the early 1800s but to the deceptive structural design conceived and promulgated by Potocki so as to make an organic whole appear to be little more than disconnected fragments. It was this same lack of perception of the general structure that led most nineteenth-century readers of the incomplete French original to take it for a kind of decameron, a collection of fantastic tales somewhat in the manner of E. T. A. Hoffmann, although the first episodes of Potocki's *Manuscrit trouvé à Saragosse*, under other names, were in print in French many years before François-Ad. Loève-Weimars's translations of Hoffmann appeared in France.[4]

With the exception of those people who have been able to read Potocki's complete novel in the midnineteenth-century Polish translation, only in recent years has it become possible for most of us to study the extended text of this novel and find in it a brilliant and sustained example of the elements that Todorov proposed as basic requirements of any truly fantastic narrative. It is important to recall Todorov's definitions before attempting to demonstrate that an archetypal or allegorical reading of Potocki's novel is not incompatible with appreciation of the fantastic atmosphere, despite Todorov's categorical contention that the fantastic and allegory are mutually exclusive. I do not propose to question the validity or logic of Todorov's other tenets about the fantastic as repeatedly set forth in his *Introduction à la littérature fantastique*.[5]

The first basic principle extolled by Todorov is scarcely new, namely, that the fantastic can occur only "in a world which is indeed our own," a world without devils, sylphides, or vampires, "a world in which, nevertheless, there occurs some event which cannot be explained by our generally accepted laws." This event triggers the mechanism that most specifically engenders the eerie feeling we attempt to pinpoint when we use the term *fantastic*: that is, "the person who perceives or witnesses the event must choose between one of two possible solutions: 1) either there has been illusion of the senses . . . and therefore the laws of our known world remain intact; 2) or else the event actually *did* take place and has become an integral part of reality, but in that case what we have been designating all along as reality must be governed by laws still unknown to us" (p. 29).

So far so good, almost all of Todorov's predecessors would agree. This generally recognized principle then leads to what I consider Todorov's most original contribution in this realm of definition: his insistence upon the precariousness of the fantastic moment that can last only so long as the hero's or the reader's hesitation does. The fantastic is a fragile, evanescent state of our reactions when we are faced with an event in appearance supernatural. If the author opts for the easy solution of explaining away the disturbing event through revelations such as those dear to Ann Radcliffe, we are thrown straightway out of the fantastic realm into what Todorov and indeed most French critics label simply *l'étrange*, or the highly unlikely, the extraordinary coincidence. On the other hand, to opt for acceptance of the disturbing event as being the machination of supernatural creatures throws us headlong into the opposite realm of fairyland and the marvelous (*le merveilleux*), and once again the fantastic ceases to be. Todorov represented this graphically as three boxes:

The fantastic of necessity is in the center, with considerable fringe area separating each category. I would prefer to modify the diagram slightly to the "see-saw" structure, emphasizing the pivotal, evanescent nature of the fantastic:

There is, in any case, very little leeway; a step to the right or to the left may be enough to tilt the scale and make the fantastic disappear into an adjacent realm. But can a genre disappear so easily? This very sobering realization of the instability of the fantastic moment leads Todorov to bring into question the whole concept of the fantastic as a genre of its own and to reach challenging conclusions that cannot be taken into consideration here.[6]

To sum up Todorov's first point in defining the fantastic, "The text must force the reader to consider the world of the fictional characters as a world of living people and further force him to hesitate between a natural explanation and a supernatural explanation of the events presented" (Todorov, *Introduction*, p. 37).

The second basic point of the definition is that this same hesitation experienced by a theoretical reader can also be experienced by one of the characters in the narrative. If this is the case—and Todorov hastened to add that this second element is not absolutely necessary to the true fantastic—we can say that the hesitation (itself indispensable) is represented literally in the text; and, in the case of a "naive" reading, the reader identifies with the character. His third and final point, with which I take issue, constitutes, along with the first, his minimal definition of the fantastic: "the reader must adopt a certain attitude towards the text, must reject any allegorical or poetic interpretation" (p. 38). To be sure, the reader must resist any inclination to interpret the words of the text as signifying in the events of the narrative something other than what they normally indicate in "real" life. To do so and give these words immediate allegorical or poetic meanings would be at once to rob the text of any possibility of satisfying the first of Todorov's points (intrusion upon the stability of the "real" world). But a reading does not take place in so absolute and so one-dimensional a fashion. Todorov separated textual and interpretative levels to the point of declaring that allegory depends on "the existence of at least two meanings for the same words" and, furthermore, that "this double meaning is indicated in the text explicitly" (p. 68). Why thus limit textual expression of allegory to that low if not lowest common denominator the word? The syntagm and, *a fortiori*, the sentence, the paragraph, and the situation can also be the vehicles of allegory and subtler ones at that. We may indeed refrain from interpreting the words of the text in any untoward manner insofar as their surface meanings are concerned: when the word *lamp* occurs, for example, we will refrain from reading it as "truth" or "justice"; for the word *knife* we must not substitute "phallus" or "sex"; and so on. Such restraint on the lexical level, however, need not preclude our seeing in the events and objects described—both while we read and in retrospect—any number of analogies, symbols, allegories, and so forth on levels other than the literal, textual one. The reader is not yet, let us hope, a programmed machine.

It is Todorov's contention that Potocki's *Manuscrit trouvé à Saragosse*—in the incomplete version known to date—constitutes a powerful illustration of his definition of the fantastic, and I would agree that for this reason alone it deserves to receive far more critical attention. Yet, for all of its qualifications as a fantastic narrative by Todorov's yardstick, the novel is not limited to that realm or classification, nor did its author Count Potocki intend it to be, as Zoltowska's forthcoming critical edition should make abundantly clear. He has told his extraordinarily complex tale of the adventures of young Alphonse van Worden by making constant use of a structural principle that, by definition, involves the allegorical: the *mise en abyme* technique. Parallels, analogies, and near mirror images of a given situation or event abound in the *Saragossa Manuscript*. The proof that each story within a larger episode is to be understood as a *mise en abyme* and not as a gratuitous narrative is underscored by the author's regular and carefully devised return to his original first-person narrator, however many other first-person narrators may have intervened in the apparent digression. The number can be extreme, since Potocki has intercalated or inlaid an episode to the *sixth* degree in certain instances. Thus the reader of Alphonse's adventures experiences, along with him, something of the anguish with which one feels his way in the dark back through a series of labyrinthine passages to a relatively secure and familiar refuge. Furthermore, the reader is literally duplicated in the text, since Alphonse on several occasions reads analogs of his own situation in stories "accidentally" placed before his eyes. The episode where Alphonse is left alone in the Cabalist's library is a prime example of this duplication of the reader.

The disquieting events of the hero's first night alone in an abandoned hostel deep within the Sierra Morena may certainly be read to a point as an unusually effective fantastic narrative. The spunky young Flemish officer Alphonse van Worden, abandoned by his frightened and superstitious Spanish guides, is obliged

(p. 216). In this context it is significant that Emina and Zibeddé from the outset exhort Alphonse to accept on faith what they tell him, and others throughout his odyssey echo this exhortation.

Jung underscored other aspects of the spirit's nature that we find in Potocki's couples and twins: he is "many-sided, changeable, and deceitful . . . and 'enjoys equally the company of the good and the wicked' " (p. 217). His body may at times be masculine and his soul feminine, at other times the reverse. The apparent transformations of the alluring bodies of Emina and Zibeddé into the cadavers of the hanged brothers finds this further explanatory parallel in Jung's Mercurius: "As *vulgaris* he is the dead masculine body, but as 'our' Mercurius he is feminine, spiritual, alive and life-giving" (p. 219).

Lest such interpretations lead us too far afield, it should be noted that this identification of the two sisters as embodiments of the Mercurius figure does eventually lead us back, through allegory, to *individuation*, which, by definition, is a process culminating in the in–dividual, that is, a separate and indivisible whole.[11] For Mercurius is in the final analysis a symbol of the integration of diverse forces, a spirit of triadic nature, said Jung, whose affinities with the Holy Trinity are only apparent, not historical.[12] One may also invoke the unconscious concept of quaternity, another archetype, according to Charles Baudouin, and its unending variants, such as four objects or four personages, three of whom form a block while the other remains detached; or three present and the fourth conspicuous by his absence; or three encompassed by the fourth, whence the "three in one."[13] The third possibility is one of universal symbolism, according to Baudouin, and points to the concept of redemption and wholeness. Thus the couple Emina-Zibeddé and all of their avatars spring from Alphonse van Worden, become autonomous, and are at last one with him through the transformative and alchemical action of Mercurius. They and he form the three sides of the triangle inscribed within the greater circle of his individuality.

NOTES

1. Jan Potocki, *Manuscrit trouvé à Saragosse*, ed. Roger Caillois (Paris: Gallimard, 1958).

2. A first attempt to remedy this situation was made at the Colloquium in Nineteenth-Century French Studies held at the University of Houston Central Campus, 23-25 October 1980. In a session devoted entirely to Potocki the following papers were read: Maria-Evelina Zoltowska, "L'Edition critique du *Manuscrit trouvé à Saragosse*"; Daniel Beauvois, "Les Voyages de Jean Potocki, de l'Orient mythique à l'Orient conquis"; Daniel C. Gerould, "Potocki's *Parades*."

3. For the detailed histories of these cases, see Will L. McLendon, *Une Ténébreuse carrière sous l'Empire et la Restauration: Le Comte de Courchamps* (Paris: Lettres Modernes, 1981); idem, "A Problem in Plagiarism: Washington Irving and Cousen de Courchamps," *Comparative Literature* 20 (1968): 157-69; idem, "Le Rôle de Charles Nodier dans le plagiat de Courchamps," *Studi francesi* 50 (1973): 292-300.

4. M.L.C.J.P. [Monsieur le Comte Jan Potocki], *Avadoro, histoire espagnole* (Paris:

Gide fils, 1813); idem, *Les Dix Journées de la vie d'Alphonse van Worden* (Paris: Gide fils, 1814).

5. Tzvetan Todorov, *Introduction à la littérature fantastique* (Paris: Seuil, 1970). Further references are given in my own paraphrases, and page numbers appear in parentheses in the text.

6. One of the most convincing of his arguments against considering the fantastic as a genre concerns his criticism of H. P. Lovecraft, Peter Penzoldt, and even Caillois, who make the fantastic dependent on the generation of fear in the reader: "Can the genre of a literary work depend on the *sang-froid* of its reader?" (Todorov, *Introduction*, p. 40).

7. Zygmunt Markiewicz, "L'Aspect préromantique du *Manuscrit trouvé à Saragosse*," *Revue de Littérature Comparée*, 50 (1975): 69-76.

8. Jan Potocki, *Manuscrit trouvé à Saragosse* (Paris: Gallimard, 1958), 148.

9. Will L. McLendon, "The Incantation of a Name: from *mal armé* to *mâle armé*," *Mosaic* 12 (1979): 21-28.

10. C. G. Jung, *Alchemical Studies*, in *The Collected Works of C. G. Jung*, vol. 13, Bollingen Series 20 (Princeton, N.J.: Princeton University Press, 1967). Further references appear in parentheses in the text.

11. C. G. Jung, *The Archetypes and the Collective Unconscious*, in *Collected Works* 9, no. 1 (1959): 275, sec. 490.

12. Jung, *Alchemical Studies*, 221.

13. Charles Baudouin, *L'Oeuvre de Jung et la psychologie complexe* (Paris: Payot, 1963), 190-92.

H. G. Wells Upside Down: Fantasy as Allegory in William Golding's *Inheritors*

L. L. Dickson

The irony in *The Inheritors* affects each of its four levels of meaning: moral, psychological, mythic, and sociological. As a moral allegory the novel reverses the Wellsian concept of the superior race subduing the Neanderthal subhumans.

The Inheritors (1955), William Golding's second novel, is a highly imaginative fantasy of prehistory and a dark re-creation of the Garden of Eden-Genesis myth. It is also a reaction to the idea of evolutionary progress represented in some of H. G. Wells's science fiction stories and his *Outline of History*.[1]

Although there is often talk about Golding's "allegorical novels," I know of no critic who has ever specifically explained *how* such allegory applies to Golding's work. I discussed this matter with Golding and concluded that he modestly thought the term *allegory* was too grand for his brand of symbolism, but he seemed sympathetic to my particular approach. Using some of the critical theories of Edwin Honig, I can clarify the symbolism of the novel by analyzing four techniques that contribute to allegorical personifications in *The Inheritors*: (1) analogy through the use of names; (2) the correlation of a state of nature with a state of mind; (3) the implied comparison of an action with an extrafictional event, outside the novel itself; and (4) the correspondence of a state of mind with an action depicted in the narrative.[2]

The Inheritors has much in common with Golding's first and most widely known novel *Lord of the Flies* (1954). Both novels explore the nature of evil, and both dramatize the close relationship between intelligence and evil. Just as presumably intelligent British schoolboys opt for savagery and human destruction, so the innocent Neanderthals, from whose point of view *The Inheritors* is told, are annihilated by the "superior" race of *Homo sapiens*, whose increased intelligence only makes them more proficient murderers. Both novels also contain isolated settings as part of their allegorical method. Much of the action in *The Inheritors* occurs on an island bordered on one side by a raging waterfall. But Golding has isolated his characters in time as well as space. His second novel is set in prehistory, at the very dawn of humankind, as the Neanderthals first encounter modern humans. The story is told from the severely limited point of view of Lok, a subhuman primitive who is unable to rationalize and whose crude attempts at thinking are announced by "I have a picture." Because of Golding's brilliant technical achievement in manipulating point of view and language, *The Inheritors* may well be his finest novel, although some critics over the years have called it muddled, overly abstract, and even deliberately baffling.[3]

In the manner that *Lord of the Flies* reacted to the idealistic adventure book by R. M. Ballantyne called *The Coral Island,* so *The Inheritors* offers a contrasting version of H. G. Wells's *Outline of History.*[4] The epigraph to Golding's novel is taken directly from *The Outline*, in which Wells characterized Neanderthals with the words *ugliness, repulsive strangeness,* and *inferior stature* and then quoted from Sir Harry Johnston: "The dim racial remembrance of such *gorilla-like monsters*, with cunning brains, shambling gait, hairy bodies, strong teeth, and possibly *cannibalistic tendencies*, may be the germ of the *ogre* [italics mine] in folklore."[5] In a passage preceding the one quoted by Golding, Wells had discussed the way *Homo sapiens,* or "the true men," as he called them, had dispossessed *Homo Neanderthalensis*, driving them out of their caverns and quarries. Wells optimistically proclaimed that "The appearance of [*Homo sapiens*] was certainly an enormous leap forward in the history of mankind."[6] Golding objected to this tidy rationalistic philosophy of progress and evolutional superiority. He stated that *The Outline* "played a great part in my life because my father was a rationalist, and the *Outline* . . . was something he took neat."[7] But Golding was not content with Wells's pat optimism: *The Outline* "seemed to me to be too neat and slick. And when I re-read it as an adult I came across his picture of Neanderthal man, our immediate predecessors, as being the gross brutal creatures who were possibly the basis of the mythological bad man, whatever he may be, the ogre. I thought to myself that this is just absurd. What we're doing is externalising our own inside."[8] The Beast in *Lord of the Flies* is clearly one such externalization of "our own inside."

In an interview in which Golding talked about *The Inheritors* in relation to science fiction, he reiterated that his novel presents an ironic view of H. G. Wells: "I went back to Wells's book [*The Outline*] and looked at the premises that he was using and decided I didn't agree with them. So I stood them on their heads."[9] Hence the title of this chapter is "H. G. Wells Upside Down."

The Inheritors provides a more complicated view of humans than Wells's *Outline* and suggests that humans' potential for evil accompanies whatever social, moral, or intellectual progress they might achieve. Unfortunately, human capacity for self-destruction, or the destruction of others, partially defines what it is to be human. As Golding observed, "It's an odd thing—as far back as we can go in history we find that the two signs of Man are a capacity to kill and a belief in God."[10] *The Inheritors*, as do all of Golding's novels, offers the reader much more, however, than dark pessimism.

The first of the four patterns by which allegorical personifications are developed is analogy through nomenclature. This process establishes an attributive name of a character or place, and "as it constantly designates an event, person, idea, or quality existing outside the story, builds up a sense of like identity in the fiction."[11] In traditional allegory naming characters after vices or virtues is one manifestation of this process; in modern literature the use of names to suggest an extrafictional frame of reference is usually less obvious. The proper names in *The Inheritors* not only reflect abstract qualities of the characters but also reemphasize the Wellsian precedents for Golding's novel. Besides using *The Outline of History* as a background source that expands his meaning, Golding drew on short stories by Wells. In "The Grisly Folk," "The Monkey People," and "A Story of the Stone Age"—all sources for Golding—*Homo sapiens* emerge as victorious, superior creatures, and by contrast Neanderthal men are portrayed as subhuman gorillas.[12] The simple proper names used in *The Inheritors*—some names evolving from natural, physical features that the character possesses—point to an earlier work by Wells. The names in "A Story of the Stone Age" (Wau, Uya, Cat's-skin, One-eye, Snail-eater, Snake) are similar to Golding's character names (Lok, Liku, Pine-tree, Chestnut-head, Bush, Tuft).[13] The simplicity of the names is consistent with the crudeness of the characters' language and mentality. Golding's epigraph from *The Outline*, his admitted knowledge of Wells's short stories, and even the similarities in the names for his primitive characters suggest that Golding is fashioning a new version of Wells's thesis. The references, both direct and indirect, to Wells contribute to Golding's irony.

Besides recalling similarities to "A Story of the Stone Age," the names of Golding's fictional cavemen imply specific qualities of characterization. Since Golding's allegory offers what has been called "an anthropological version of the Fall of Man," the contrast between the innocent Neanderthals and the more corrupt *Homo sapiens* is reflected even in their names.[14] For example, Liku, the name for the happy little girl stolen by the new men, suggests "like you," and Liku's counterpart in the *Homo sapiens* group is Tanakil, the ideal of "kill" built into the last syllable. Some connotations, however, do not always involve neat contrasts between good and evil. Mal, the Neanderthals' old leader, is physically sick, as his name implies, and his death early in the novel signals the beginning of the end for the old order. Fa suggests "fall," which is the literal (and symbolic) fate of that character. Lok's limited mental powers "lock" his mind in ignorance throughout most of the narrative. The name Marlan, given to the leader of the new men, "sounds like a combination of 'Mal' with Merlin, and this leader proves in fact to be an evil magician."[15] Although Tuami— "your friend"—is used ironically, it also sounds like "You are me," an idea appropriate to the end of the novel, when Tuami is shown to be not only an

updated version of Lok (they both look into darkness and chaos) but a representation of all modern humans and consequently a character with whom the
reader must sympathize.[16]

Second, the analogy between a state of nature and a state of mind is developed
in Golding's novel in three ways. First, the primitive forest corresponds with
the innocent, Edenlike existence of the Neanderthals. The forest, until the time
at which the novel begins, has been kind to the primitives. They all remember
"when it was summer all year round and the flowers and fruit hung on the same
branch."[17] Second, the unknown territory of the island, inhabited by the new
men, is equated with fear and foreboding. The very atmosphere seems to threaten
the Neanderthals (and, when they finally encounter *Homo sapiens*, their fears
are confirmed). The swirling waters, separating the island from the Neanderthals,
are tempestuous, dangerous, evil (p. 41). The hidden eyes of the island cliffs
haunt Lok's mind (p. 41). When Lok and Fa, his mate, return from the island
territory without finding Ha (the first Neanderthal who is killed by the new men),
they feel as if some unseen evil is pursuing them: "As if the terror of the [forest]
sanctuary was pursuing them the two people broke into a run" (p. 86). To Lok
the water by the falls is a manifestation of evil and destruction, "a wilderness"
of foaming power that shakes the very earth (p. 126). Third, the Neanderthals
have come upon hard times (they have come too early to the spring camping
grounds; past forest fires have reduced their numbers and their food supply; and
they, unknowingly, are dangerously close to extermination at the hands of an
unseen enemy). Just as they live on the brink of extinction and disaster, so the
great forest fire that they discuss in fearful tones becomes a symbol of their
impending fate (p. 45). At one point, after the Neanderthals have discovered
that there are "others" on the island, the old woman, who has replaced the
deceased Mal as leader of the group, says that the fear they are experiencing
"is like when the fire flew away and ate up all the trees" (p. 93). At this moment
even the forest birds communicate the general uneasiness: "Birds began to cry
and the sparrows dropped down" (p. 92). Still later Fa uses the same symbol
to characterize the new people who bring destruction: "They are like a fire in
the forest" (p. 197).

A third process by which figures in the story take on allegorical significance
is the correspondence of an action with an extrafictional event. Such a correspondence enlarges the meaning of the literal action by suggesting an analog
that is either appropriate or inappropriate, the latter especially suited to the more
sarcastic views of twentieth-century fiction. An extrafictional event emerges when
particulars of the narrative suggest a parallel with, for example, classical mythology or with the passion and sacrifice of Christ. In *The Inheritors* extrafictional
events are contained primarily in biblical analog, through which Golding created
new versions of old myths. Golding imaginatively reworked the Genesis motif,
establishing an Edenlike setting in which the Neanderthals, as well as the *Homo
sapiens*, reenact the Fall of humankind. The tree from which Lok and Fa observe
the corrupt practices of the new people becomes a symbolic Tree of Knowledge,

particularly for Fa, who witnesses the cannibalistic destruction of Liku. Fa shudders in disbelief, "as though the moonlight that fell on the tree were wintry" (p. 175); she feels the cold chill of a bitter knowledge. The scene in which Lok and Fa sample the new men's liquor and subsequently become as brutal, selfish, and sadistic as their enemies reaffirms the idea of their Fall from innocence (pp. 199-204).

The waterfall is itself a symbol of the Fall. Its roaring waters—"monstrous," "unending," "profound"—make human voices sound "puny and without resonance" (p. 28). The *Homo sapiens* are called "people of the fall," and when Fa, with her newfound knowledge, is swept over the falls to her death, the action is enlarged symbolically (p. 195). Knowledge of evil is associated with the water. When Lok says that the water is "a terrible thing," Fa sorrowfully adds, "The water is better than the new people" (p. 197). The dramatic fall of Chestnut-head over the cliff to his death, "leaving not even a scream behind him," reiterates the Fall motif (p. 211).

Finally, the manifestation in an action of a state of mind, the fourth method of establishing allegorical agents, is embodied in the systematic destruction of the Neanderthals by *Homo sapiens*. As each member of the small group of Neanderthals disappears or is murdered, the terrifying depravity of the new men is revealed. Also with each death Lok becomes slightly more aware of the true nature of the new men. As the murders proliferate Lok's innocence diminishes, until finally he is left alone in the darkness, crying over the bones of Liku. The sequence of the seven Neanderthal deaths accounts for part of the suspense and narrative interest. First, Ha disappears in the vicinity of the island and is never heard of again (pp. 65-68). The death of Mal, the last of the Neanderthal leaders, implies that the old, innocent order cannot survive much longer (p. 91). The new men are even indirectly to blame for Mal's death, in that they have removed a log from across the water, and Mal falls into the river. As Fa says, "the log that wasn't there" killed Mal (p. 98). Lok discovers the old woman's dead body floating in the dark waters (pp. 108–9). Then young Liku and a baby simply called "the new one" are kidnapped (p. 105), and Nil is killed and thrown into the water (p. 114). Eventually, Liku is killed and eaten by the cannibalistic *Homo sapiens*, an effective point of irony in the light of the Wells epigraph about the Neanderthal monsters with "cannibalistic tendencies" (p. 169). Fa, trying to escape the new men, is swept over the waterfalls to her death (p. 216). When the *Homo sapiens* depart with the "new one," Lok becomes the last Neanderthal, curls into a fetal position and awaits death. The moment that Lok finally gains knowlege of humankind's evil (his discovery of Liku's bones) coincides with the extinction of his race.

The irony in *The Inheritors* affects each of its four "levels" of meaning— moral, psychological, mythic, and sociological. As a moral allegory, the novel reverses the Wellsian concept of the "superior" race subduing the Neanderthal subhumans: "Golding's Neanderthals, in their naive innocence, represent a morality preferable to that of the *Homo Sapiens* who overcome them."[18] However, the dichotomy is not so uniformly neat, for considerable sympathy is created for the new men, whose struggle to understand themselves is dramatized in the last chapter. On a psychological level the novel similarly reverses any notion of an Ego-Id conflict, and the stereotyping of the Neanderthals as a representation of the dark, uncontrolled forces of the Id. Although Lok's people technically qualify as "irrational," their human warmth and sensitivity preclude the category of "ogres" from the Id. The new men are much more capable of wholesale destruction or undirected passion. On the archetypal level Golding created new myths (his own fantastical version of prehistory) that contain the timeless patterns of quest, initiation, the scapegoat, and primitive ritual. However, the new men's rituals strike the reader as ironically more "primitive" than those of Lok's people. The *Homo sapiens* have not only resorted to violence and human sacrifice, they have superstitiously assumed that evil is external to themselves. Consequently, their world of symbolic stagrobes and primitive totems to ward off the Neanderthal devils (whom the new men have unknowingly just exterminated) is fashioned merely by their own ignorance.

Finally, *The Inheritors* presents the sociological conflict between a tightly knit Neanderthal group, whose priority is unselfish human cooperation, and a *Homo sapiens* group, whose increased rationality has only produced debilitating self-interests and social disintegration. The dissension among the latter group is particularly evident in the last chapter, as Tuami plots Marlan's murder. The small band of new men had been disenfranchised from a larger group when Marlan decided to steal Vivani, the wife of another. Now Tuami plans to steal Vivani from Marlan. The *Homo sapiens* have even stolen a Neanderthal baby from an alien society. In contrast, Lok's people cherish their social bonds. Their belief in human community and love expresses the ideals that Golding thought were still vital to the human condition. Lok recognizes what the presence of the "other" is doing to his group: "The other had tugged at the strings that bound him to Fa and Mal and Liku and the rest of the people. The strings were not the ornament of life but its substance. If they broke, a man would die" (p. 78). Later in the novel Lok has the same picture: "And because he was one of the people, tied to them with a thousand invisible strings, his fear was for the people" (p. 104). His joy at seeing Fa again, after she has been separated from him, is genuine: "It is bad to be alone. It is very bad to be alone" (p. 196). Ironically, the *Homo sapiens* will not admit to themselves that uncontrolled selfishness leads to their own alienation.

The ironies implicit in the title of the novel are significant. The meek Neanderthals will *not* inherit the earth, but the *Homo sapiens will* inherit (as do all people) knowledge and, with it, the discovery of their devastating capacities for evil. Not only does Golding's novel turn H. G. Wells "upside down," but it also combines the fantastic with the allegorical, a modern allegory in which Golding continues to explore the themes common to all of his work: that human innocence is ultimately an illusion, that human compassion and love are a powerful counterbalance to moral blindness and selfishness, and that humans cannot transcend their condition until they see themselves without deception.

NOTES

1. However distanced and unusual his subject, Golding never used the term *science fiction* to characterize his novel, for somehow he equated that term with a literature that is removed from the responsibilities of the real world and less reflective of the serious concerns of good fiction. See Jack I. Biles, *Talk: Conversations with William Golding* (New York: Harcourt Brace Jovanovich, 1970), 4-5.

2. Edwin Honig, *Dark Conceit: The Making of Allegory* (Evanston, Ill.: Northwestern University Press, 1959), 118.

3. See George Plimpton, "Without the Evil to Endure," *New York Times Book Review*, 29 July 1962, 21; William James Smith, "A Hopeless Struggle against Homo Sapiens," *Commonweal* 77 (28 September 1962): 19; Diana Neill, *A Short History of the English Novel*, rev. ed. (New York: Collier Books, 1964), 387; Frank MacShane, "The Novels of William Golding," *Dalhousie Review* 42 (Summer 1962): 174.

4. See particularly, H. G. Wells, "The Making of Man," book 2 in *The Outline of History*, rev. ed. (Garden City, N.Y.: Garden City Books, 1961), 50-104.

5. Ibid., 69-70.

6. Ibid., 69.

7. William Golding and Frank Kermode, "The Meaning of It All," *Books and Bookmen* 5 (October 1959):10.

8. Ibid., 10.

9. Biles, *Talk*, 4.

10. Maurice Dolbier, "Running J. D. Salinger a Close Second," *New York Herald Tribune Books* 38 (20 May 1962):6.

11. Honig, *Dark Conceit*, 118.

12. See, respectively, Peter Green, "The World of William Golding," *Transactions and Proceedings of the Royal Society of Literature* 32 (1963): 45-46; Biles, *Talk*, 107; and Brian W. Aldiss, *Billion Year Spree: The True History of Science Fiction* (Garden City, N.Y.: Doubleday, 1973), 117. See also Bernard S. Oldsey and Stanley Weintraub, *The Art of William Golding* (1965; reprint, Bloomington: Indiana University Press, 1968), 53.

13. H. G. Wells, *Twenty-Eight Science Fiction Stories* (New York: Dover, 1952), 360-417.

14. Samuel Hynes, *William Golding*, 2nd ed. (New York: Columbia University Press, 1968), 18.

15. Howard S. Babb, *The Novels of William Golding* (Columbus: Ohio State University Press, 1970), 40.

16. Ibid., 40.

17. William Golding, *The Inheritors* (1955; reprint, New York: Harcourt, Brace and World, 1962), 35. Further references appear in parentheses in the text.

18. Kirby Duncan, "William Golding and Vardis Fisher: A Study in Parallels and Extensions," *College English* 27 (December 1965): 233.

The Structure of the Fantastic in Cortázar's "Cambio de luces"

Amaryll B. Chanady

> This is the paradox of the fantastic—we have to be aware of the reader's codes in order to forget them and play the game created by the author.

Because of its great diversity of application, the term *fantastic* has never been adequately defined. In fact, such a task may seem arbitrary and of little value, because there would not be any general agreement. However, there do exist well-defined concepts such as *fantasy*, the *marvelous*, the *supernatural*, the *gothic, terror*, and *science fiction*. Since the fantastic has been variously equated with one or more of these terms, it would be useful to situate it with respect to them and establish tentative guidelines for a structural concept. This would provide us with a reading code rather than with prescriptive norms.

Tzvetan Todorov, in his *The Fantastic: A Structural Approach to a Literary Genre* (1973), attempted to establish a generic concept; the "fantastic is that hesitation experienced by a person who knows only the laws of nature, confronting an apparently supernatural event. . . . Once we choose one answer or the other, we leave the fantastic for a neighboring genre, the uncanny or the marvelous."[1] Although it is true that uncertainty in the face of an unusual event is often present in the fantastic, this definition is too restricted. Louis Vax's definition of the *fantastic* as the sudden intrusion of the inexplicable in a real world is more acceptable.[2] However, Todorov justly excluded the marvelous, in which supernatural events are accepted without any surprise, because they occur in a world totally removed from ours. An example of this is the fairy tale. But if the supernatural occurs in the real world, we think the story should be considered fantastic even if there is no hesitation, only surprise, disorientation, and maybe fear.

The other problem with Todorov's definition is that the "hesitation" occurs in the mind of the reader and not necessarily in that of the protagonist. Readers, however, never seriously consider whether or not ghosts exist. They peruse a story for pleasure and not to speculate on the existence of supernatural beings. As Louix Vax justly remarked in his *La Séduction de l'étrange* (1965), readers consent to play a game and to be carried away by the atmosphere of the fantastic.[3]

The most useful study on this subject has been Irène Bessière's *Le Récit fantastique, la poétique de l'incertain* (1974), in which she wrote (as did Todorov) that the fantastic is characterized by uncertainty, but that this hesitation is between several antinomic codes, or possibilities of interpretation, on the part of the protagonist.[4] Victim-subjects are constantly trying to understand their relation to the external world. The fantastic is always based on a realistic background, since, according to Bessière, it re-creates the human integrity that modern culture destroys and is therefore a liberating and salutary function. This brings us very close to Luis Leal's conception of magical realism, according to which the magico-realist tries to capture the mystery of life in its entirety. Bessière saw the fantastic as an ideological and logical examination of life. Although this may well have given the impetus to the genre, it does not help us to analyze the fantastic story in its structure. Her concept of antinomic codes is much more valuable if we leave aside ideological considerations and concentrate entirely on parallel antinomic structures, as she herself did in the last part of her book, where she discussed J. L. Borges and Julio Cortázar.

In Cortázar's "Cambio de luces" the obvious antinomic structure is that between the protagonist's everyday working life as an actor in radio plays and his acquaintance with a female admirer and the apparently supernatural appearance of his double at the end of the story. This fact in itself does not suffice to constitute the fantastic, since the reader has been informed by the protagonist (Tito Balcárcel) of his vivid power of imagination and may interpret the apparition as an hallucination. This would be especially plausible, since the protagonist spends his life acting out other roles and may well imagine himself as one of them in a situation outside work. In this case the story would be neither fantastic nor supernatural but realistic and symbolic, since the actor has lost his identity to such an extent by impersonating other characters that he finally sees himself as one of his possible fictitious images.

The ending, however, does not have this effect on the implied reader. The syntactic code of the whole story cannot be discarded at the end, since that would cause a narratological discrepancy. The implied reader's expectation is prepared by the various parallel structures in the story. First, the protagonist Tito spends his professional life impersonating others in soap operas, thus duplicating his real self. Then when he agrees to meet Luciana, an admirer of the "true" personality behind his roles, he construes an ideal image of her. In his imagination she has chestnut hair and light colored eyes and is sitting in a covered gallery with plants in a grayish twilight on a wicker chair. When he finally meets her, he finds that she is already thirty, more robust than he had imagined, and has long black hair and dark eyes. Instead of living in a large house she resides with an old aunt in a basement.

This is the second appearance of two parallel structures—the ideal and the real. The third immediately follows. Luciana confides to Tito that she had imagined him as being taller and having curly hair and grey eyes. So again we have the discrepancy between the real and ideal. Or maybe we should call it *el otro* ("the other"), since the ideal may be taken in the sense of an imaginary projection of the self, as in another one of Cortázar's stories, "La lejana," where the protagonist Alina Reyes identifies herself with a tattered beggar in Budapest. This theme is common in Cortázar, but it is usually easy to distinguish between the real and the ideal, as in *Rayuela*, and to disqualify it from the fantastic.

"Cambio de luces" becomes more interesting when the two parallel structures with regard to Luciana approach each other and ultimately fuse. After Luciana and Tito have been seeing each other for some time, Tito asks her to dye her hair to conform to his ideal. For the first time in his life he brings home recordings of his work, just to see Luciana sitting in the twilight and listening to his voice. Tito imagines her in the covered gallery and feels that the wicker chair is missing in this otherwise ideal picture. Finally, he gives her a wicker chair and table and changes the light bulb for a weaker one to reproduce the twilight of his fantasy. She has almost been transformed into his ideal, and he cannot imagine her any more as she was when he first met her. But her real self still exists in the morning when she walks about the house and plays with the cat.

Until this point the events could have a perfectly logical explanation. In fact, it could not even be called *étrange* ("uncanny"), in Todorov's terminology. All of the changes that Luciana undergoes are physical and superficial. Almost at the end of the story, however, Luciana changes psychologically. She becomes distracted, sad, and distant. Again this could be explained logically if the structure of the story had not prepared us for that moment, which corresponds exactly to Tito's ideal image of her, and follows a process of change in her, in accordance with his fantasy. The real and the ideal seem to have merged completely. This in itself is not necessarily fantastic, but her psychological change is perceived as uncanny and gives us a premonition of the ending.

When Tito meets Luciana at the end of the story in the company of a tall man with curly hair, we realize that her escort incarnates the ideal picture that Luciana had formed of Tito. This time the fusion of the real and the ideal is logically impossible. The different physical characteristics such as height cannot ensue from an explicable change in external appearance, as in the case of Luciana's transformation. Luciana and her double were only perceived by Tito, but at the end he sees his own double, which is logically impossible.

As mentioned previously, this ending may be interpreted as a hallucination. We have enough information to doubt the reliability of the narrator. His life as an actor, his fantasies, and the fact that Luciana described her ideal image of him contribute to this. A reliable third-person narrator would produce an entirely different effect. The apparition would then be clearly supernatural. But in this case the text does not remove all doubt from the interpretation. This would fit in with Todorov's theory and also with Bessière's concept of uncertainty.

The narrator, however, is silent about his surprise, if there is any. The apparently supernatural event is described laconically and objectively. The protagonist's hesitation with respect to the interpretation of the event is not described. Bessière's emphasis on the importance of the distinction between the protagonist, who knows that something improbable has happened, and the narrator, who tries to rationalize it, is certainly not applicable in this case. Do readers experience this uncertainty? They do only if they remain within the game of fiction. They must accept several codes, with which they will understand the infinite possibilities of meaning of the text. To appreciate a pastoral novel, for example, one must temporarily discard the codes of realism. The same occurs with the fantastic, which must not be read as a treatise on demonology, the double, or anything else of that nature.

If "Cambio de luces" were a document, readers would analyze Tito's character and arrive at a logical conclusion. His hallucination may be accounted for by an obsession with Luciana's ideal image of him and her dissatisfaction and sadness at the end. We are reading fiction, however, and the protagonists are not people we can speculate about but ensembles of actions, indices, and information given to us by the author. One could argue that there is enough information in the text to justify a logical explanation of the end. We do not discard this interpretation, since it is one of the possibilities of meaning of the text. A symbolic reading would also be justified. But in every text there is a hierarchy of meanings. In "Cambio de luces" we believe the structure of the story justifies our placing the code of the fantastic in the foreground and considering it as the most important stratum of meaning.

What then is the code of the fantastic? Although this poses many problems, there are some provisional guidelines. The most important prerequisite is that there are two or more antinomic logical codes. They may be the real and the supernatural, in which case Roger Caillois's definition would be adequate: the *fantastic* is the sudden appearance of a rupture in the laws of our everyday world.[5] However, the fantastic can be created by the sequential juxtaposition of two narrative syntagmata, which are in themselves logical and normal but mutually antinomic. This creates a logically impossible situation, without the presence of supernatural beings. Cortázar's story "La isla a mediodía," in which the narrator's idyllic life on a Greek island is juxtaposed with his simultaneous presence on an airplane, would be a good example of this.

The second criterion is that the fantastic must occur in an everyday situation, not in a world of fantasy. This would exclude all science fiction, fairy tales, and obviously supernatural stories. These neighboring genres are what Max Lüthi in his various books on the fairy tale would call "unidimensional." The real world is not threatened by one that is totally removed from ours. That is why the local legend, which is set in a more realistic location than the fairy tale, produced an effect of fear and awe in the listener. We may consider the folk legend as a precursor of the fantastic because of its two-dimensionality (the real world and the supernatural). But there are no antinomic codes, since the supernatural was accepted at that time and not seen as a mystery that defies logic.

This brings us to the third criterion. The depiction of the real world in the fantastic facilitates readers' identification with the narrator or protagonist and enables them to vicariously experience fear or disorientation. The fantastic story must be structured so that readers can accept the world presented as plausible; identify with the narrator, who must therefore be reliable; and be imperceptibly emotionally involved in a series of events that finally lead to the supernatural. Without a tightly coherent structure the first two criteria would not suffice to constitute the fantastic.

"Cambio de luces" fulfills these three criteria. There is antinomy of the natural and supernatural, and the events occur in a normal world. However, without the carefully structured sequence of events the story would not be perceived as fantastic. The implied reader is almost deceived by the author's *telaraña* ("spider's web"), a term that Tito himself used to describe his transformation of Luciana. The rapid ending is purposefully designed to prevent the reader from thinking logically about the supernatural event. The *fait accompli* seems almost natural after the previous events and only produces a shock when the reader realizes the impossibility of such a situation. The horizon of expectation has been set from the beginning.

The theme of the double is present at the start and develops from the most logical and banal situation toward the supernatural. Tito's two identities (professional and normal) are on one ontological level. His ideal picture of Luciana and hers of him are on another plane—the imaginary. When the real and the ideal merge, the reader hardly notices it in the case of Luciana, because the transformation is brought about by logical means. The same merging of two ontological levels with respect to Tito produces the supernatural, because his transformation is logically impossible. But it continues the structure of the double and is thus perceived within that particular code.

It is important to realize that there are no fantastic themes. There are supernatural ones, but the fantastic depends entirely on the context, as Louis Vax aptly remarked in his *La Séduction de l'étrange*. Oscar Wilde's story "The Canterville Ghost," in which the apparition is scoffed at, is not fantastic, even though a supernatural being is present. The destruction of the fantastic through irony occurs in many of Washington Irving's tales, where the victim of the supernatural is rendered ludicrous. Readers must identify with the narrator if the effect of the fantastic is to be achieved.

This brings us to another problem, especially with regard to Cortázar. That is the distinction between the fantastic, hallucination, symbolism, and the absurd. The demarcation is sometimes impossible. In "Ómnibus," one of his earlier stories, a young girl boards a bus and notices that everyone is staring indignantly at her, because she has no flowers, as everyone else has. This might be intepreted as an obsession on her part, but when another passenger without flowers experiences the same persecution, that interpretation is less plausible. Finally, when the driver and the ticket collector attempt to attack them physically, the story seems to become fantastic. However, we might also interpret it allegorically and see the aggressiveness of the other passengers as a condemnation of the rupture of a social norm, in which case it would not be fantastic. In "Carta a una señorita en Paris" the narration is in the first person, and the events are so absurd that we lose confidence in the victim as a reliable narrator and ascribe his incredible account of vomiting rabbits to insanity and hallucination. There readers cannot identify with the narrator, and this destroys his "rhetoric" of persuasion. The narrator must be reliable for the fantastic to exist.

"Cambio de luces," however, is definitely fantastic. We do not consider the fantastic as a genre because of its great diversity (for example, it can occur in a long novel, a short story, or prose poem). Neither do we consider it as an effect, since that is merely the possible result of a certain type of narration. We see it as a particular reader's code or as a series of codes arranged in a certain structure. It is thus not limited thematically, but it must contain the three main criteria mentioned earlier: logical antinomy, a realistic setting and identification with a reliable narrator, and a tightly knit narrative structure. All of these codes must be arranged so that readers can be oblivious to the fact that they are reading a most carefully structured narrative by a highly self-conscious artist. This is the paradox of the fantastic—we have to be aware of the reader's codes to forget them and play the game created by the author.

NOTES

1. Tzvetan Todorov, *The Fantastic: A Structural Approach to a Literary Genre* (Cleveland: Case Western Reserve University Press, 1973), 25.

2. Louis Vax, *L'Art et la littérature fantastique* (Paris: Presses Universitaires de France, 1960).

3. Louis Vax, *La Séduction de l'étrange* (Paris: Presses Universitaires de France, 1965).

4. Irène Bessière, *Le Récit fantastique, la poétique de l'incertain* (Paris: Larousse, 1974).

5. Roger Caillois, *Anthologie du fantastique*, 2 vols. (Paris: Gallimard, 1966), 9.

Martín Gaite, Todorov, and the Fantastic

Kathleen M. Glenn

Of particular relevance to *El cuarto de atrás* are Todorov's discussion of the use of figurative discourse and a dramatized narrator and his analysis of certain "themes of the self," such as the multiplication of personality and the transformation of time and space.

Before the twentieth century fantastic elements were relatively infrequent in Hispanic literature. An occasional work dealt with the world of dreams and the supernatural or treated the theme of metamorphosis, but it was not until this century that a number of writers assiduously cultivated the fantastic. The names of Jorge Luis Borges, Julio Cortázar, and Gabriel García Márquez are now familiar to many aficionados of fantastic fiction. Less familiar is the name of Carmen Martín Gaite, a contemporary Spanish author whose most recent novel, *El cuarto de atrás (The Back Room)*, was in part inspired by Tzvetan Todorov's *Introduction à la littérature fantastique*.

El cuarto de atrás, which was awarded the National Prize for Literature in 1978, is an intriguing blend of personal history, theories about fiction, and observations of time, memory, and dreams, all set within the framework of a fantastic text. Also included in the novel are comments about its own origin and development. Martín Gaite related how in 1975, while watching Franco's burial on television, she first thought of writing about what it was like to grow up in Spain during the 1930s and 1940s. The difficulty of finding an interesting and original way of presenting her recollections led her to shelve the project temporarily. Months later, having in the meantime read Todorov's book and having vowed to write a fantastic novel, the idea of combining the two projects in one provided the solution to the problem of how to interest the reader in yet another book about life during the Franco era. *El cuarto de atrás* is discussed here as an example of fantastic literature.

At the beginning of the novel the narrator-protagonist, who is specifically identified as Martín Gaite, is lying in bed trying to recapture the sense of expectation from her childhood. Her words "I would give anything to relive that sensation; I would even give my soul to the devil" constitute the first step toward the realm of the supernatural.[1] Unable to sleep, she gets up, looks at a print that portrays Luther and the devil deep in conversation, and then stumbles over a copy of Todorov's book, which literally and figuratively makes her lose her footing and fall into another world. From this point on the distinction between the real and the imaginary is suspended, as are the normal notions of time and space. Images of past and present are superimposed as the narrator confronts former versions of herself. The arrival of a mysterious visitor, the man in black, initiates a conversation that lasts until dawn and permits the narrator to reconstruct her personal past and that of Spain. The novel's end finds her back in bed, starting to read the manuscript *El cuarto de atrás*, which has been written during the night.

As Martín Gaite has acknowledged, the influence of Todorov's book on her own is considerable. This does not imply that she has used his analysis of the properties of the fantastic narrative as a pattern or formula to be followed slavishly. Rather, his book has served as a catalyst, firing her imagination, alerting her to the possibilities of the fantastic, and suggesting means of resolving the structural and formal problems that initially stymied her. It should be noted that her interest in the fantastic is of long standing, as demonstrated by her short novel *El balneario (The Spa)*, published in 1954. Of particular relevance to *El cuarto de atrás* are Todorov's definition of the fantastic, his discussion of the use of figurative discourse and a dramatized narrator, and his analysis of certain "themes of the self," such as the multiplication of the personality and the transformation of time and space.

Todorov maintained that the fantastic text must force the reader to hesitate between a natural and a supernatural explanation of the events described. " '*I nearly reached the point of believing*': that is the formula which sums up the spirit of the fantastic. Either total faith or total incredulity would lead us beyond the fantastic: it is hesitation which sustains its life."[2] *El cuarto de atrás* meets this requirement of hesitation or ambiguity, since we never know whether what is recounted is a dream experience or an actual conversation with a visitor who may well be the devil. His arrival at 12:30 A.M. and his affirmation that this is the time the protagonist had designated for his interview with her are decidedly odd not only because of the hour but because the protagonist has no recollection of having made such an appointment. The interview proceeds along highly unconventional lines. The interviewer asks none of the stock questions, nor does he take notes or use a tape recorder. Moreover, he demonstrates an uncanny insight into the protagonist's mind and appears to be able to perceive her unspoken thoughts. During the night there are a number of strange occurrences, such as shifts in the location of objects. The print entitled *Luther's Conversation with the Devil*, seen hanging in the protagonist's bedroom in chapter 1, turns up in the living room during chapter 4. Even more disconcerting is the steady increase in the number of pages of the manuscript—*El cuarto de atrás*—that the protagonist does not remember having written.

These events can, nevertheless, be accounted for by the laws of reason. The protagonist's allusions to her recent lapses of memory could explain the shift in location of the print, which she might have carried from one room to another without being consciously aware of doing so. Her partial deafness may have contributed to her feeling of disorientation and may have resulted in an inability to distinguish between her spoken and her unspoken thoughts. The entire visit may have been a dream provoked by the sight of the print and Todorov's book. There is, however, one crucial detail that appears to argue against this possibility. During the visit the interviewer takes from his pocket a small gold box filled with tiny pills that have the power to affect the memory, both stimulating it and throwing it into disorder. Even after he has departed, the pillbox remains. In the final chapter of the novel the protagonist's daughter returns home from a party, notices the pillbox, and asks where it came from. The protagonist stalls for time while she gropes for an answer. The credibility of the one she eventually comes up with—that the box was given to her long ago by a friend—is undermined by her reaction to the sight of the box and her delay in responding to the question regarding its origin. Thus Martín Gaite deftly keeps us off balance, obliging us to vacillate between belief and disbelief.

Todorov noted that the reader's hesitation, which is essential to the fantastic, may also be represented within the text, that is, experienced by a character. This is the situation in Martín Gaite's *El cuarto de atrás*. Repeated use of words such as "odd," "strange," "incredible," "incomprehensible," "fear," "shock," "anxiety," and the protagonist's description of herself as "upset," "frightened," and "paralyzed" underscore her uncertainty and feeling that the ground is giving way beneath her feet. The accumulation of extraordinary incidents causes her to remark that "entirely too many peculiar things are happening" (p. 102).

Two of the key structural properties of the fantastic narrative, as defined by Todorov, are the use of figurative discourse and a dramatized narrator. He pointed out that the appearance of the fantastic element is often preceded by figurative or simply idiomatic expressions that are common in ordinary speech but that, if taken literally, designate a supernatural event.[3] These expressions "condition" the reader to accept the supernatural. The most important single example of this use of figurative discourse in *El cuarto de atrás* is the narrator-protagonist's "I would give anything to relive that sensation; I would even give my soul to the devil." Martín Gaite here plays on the reader's acquaintance with traditional tales involving either the utterance of a wish that is subsequently fulfilled by supernatural means or the idea of a diabolic pact. The words "I would even give my soul to the devil," in conjunction with references to the print depicting

Luther's conversation with that personage, intimate who the visitor may be without excluding alternative possibilities. Although the mystery about his identity is never solved, there are numerous indications that there is more to this urbane, charming, and cultured gentleman than meets the eye, and the phrase "the man in black" is itself highly suggestive. His appearance does not immediately follow upon the uttering of the "invocation," nor does he reek of fire and brimstone—that would have been far too obvious—but there is about him a strange, sulfurous odor. The protagonist for no apparent reason trembles after shaking hands with him, and she finds several of his questions, particularly his point-blank "Do you believe in the devil?" decidedly unnerving (p. 99). Additional examples of rhetorical figures involving the word "devil" are spaced throughout the text, and the torrential rain and gusts of wind that rattle the windows of the apartment lead the visitor to exlaim, "What a hellish night!" (p. 199).

The use of a dramatized narrator in fantastic texts serves to authenticate what is narrated and encourages the reader to identify with the character. Todorov added that "in order to facilitate the identification, the narrator will be an 'average man,' in whom (almost) every reader can recognize himself."[4] The narrator's "normality" or "one-of-us" quality inspires confidence and inclines us to accept his or her testimony. In the case of *El cuarto de atrás* our knowledge of the existence of a historical, extraliterary Martín Gaite bestows a special credibility upon the words of the narrator who bears the same name, and the former's unquestionable reality helps substantiate that of the character. Critics have long cautioned us against failure to distinguish between the real and the implied author, but Martín Gaite deliberately invited a "naive" reading of her novel and a fusion or confusion in our minds of the real-life author and the fictional narrator-protagonist. The discussion within the novel of Martín Gaite's previous works and the inclusion of accurate details about her life and family foster such confusion. The historicity of so much of the narrative, which contains repeated references to Spanish politicians and writers and to American and English film stars, has the effect of lending an air of verisimilitude to those elements that might otherwise provoke total incredulity.

El cuarto de atrás is, in large part, a remembrance of things past. The title alludes both to the playroom of the narrator's childhood home in Salamanca and to a back room of the mind, filled with blurred memories that on occasion emerge from behind the curtain that normally conceals them. During her conversation with the man in black the narrator recalls experiences that cover a period of almost fifty years, and thus the spatial and temporal horizons of the book extend far beyond the confines of a Madrid apartment and a five-hour time span. The act of recounting her recollections is important in two respects. First, it enables her to salvage what might otherwise have been irretrievably lost. For Martín Gaite it is by narrating something in oral or in written form that we preserve it from destruction. The verbs *recover, recapture, rescue,* and *save* appear over and over on the pages of this novel. At one point the narrator leafs through old newspaper clippings stored in a folder labeled "Phantoms of the Past." Those phantoms are restored to life once she begins to speak or write of them. Second, in the process of recounting her recollections the narrator attains greater self-knowledge. The man in black is crucial to this growth in understanding, for his probing questions and comments stimulate the narrator's memory and compel her to examine the premises that have governed her approach to life and to literature.

Todorov distinguished two thematic networks in the literature of the fantastic: "themes of the self" and "themes of the other." The first network is the one that concerned Martín Gaite. The principle underlying it is the fragility of the limit between matter and mind. This principle engenders several fundamental themes, two of which are fully developed in *El cuarto de atrás*: multiplication of the personality and the transformation of time and space.[5] Todorov noted that because of the importance that the sense of sight and perception in general assume in the first network, its themes may also be designated as "themes of vision" and that eyeglasses and mirrors frequently figure in works linked to this network. In *El cuarto de atrás* the narrator not only sees but also converses with earlier versions of herself. Mirrors often serve as the medium for these encounters.[6]

Glancing into a mirror that hangs in the kitchen of her apartment, the narrator sees a series of images. The first is that of herself as she now is, a middle-aged woman who is holding a dishrag in her hands. Seconds later, from the depths of the mirror the images of a child of eight and a girl of eighteen emerge. The adult laughingly reassures both that she has not turned into one of those supposedly "model" housewives who make a fetish of cleanliness and orderliness. On the contrary, she has remained faithful to her childhood belief that dust and disarray are of no consequence whatsoever.

Subsequently, there occurs a more complex encounter that graphically illustrates the multileveled nature of reality and the interplay of past and present. The key image here is that of the world as stage and man or woman as player. Gazing into the mirror above the dressing table in her bedroom, the narrator sees reflected a wrinkled, time-worn visage. As she studies it the crow's-feet and circles under the eyes disappear. The face becomes that of herself as a second-year university student seated before a small oval mirror in the dressing room of a theater in Salamanca, moments before she is to step out onto the stage and perform her role in one of Cervantes's *entremeses*. The narrator, now existing simultaneoulsy on two different spatiotemporal planes, stares at the chipped wall of the dressing room and hears the rumblings of the public, which is impatient for the performance to begin. The "I" of the past is suffering from an acute attack of stage fright, and one of her fellow actresses advises her to put on a bit more eye shadow, because knowing that you look attractive builds self-confidence. The "I" of the present, nervous about returning to the living room where *her* audience is waiting, promptly picks up an eyebrow pencil and carefully touches up her makeup. Before pulling aside the curtain at the entrance to the living room, she takes a deep breath and then resolutely steps onto the stage.

She is somewhat surprised that her dramatic entry does not elicit a round of applause.

One of the pictures in the narrator's apartment is entitled *A Topsy-turvy World*. It depicts a sheep shepherding several farm hands, fish flying over a sea in which horses and lions swim, and a sky filled with buildings that look down on the sun and the moon, set in the earth. These scenes involve a reversal of the laws of nature as we know them. The detailed description of the picture indicates that in the narrative world, as in the pictorial, the ground rules of the extratextual world do not apply.[7] It therefore becomes possible for the narrator, once again split into two selves, to soar over the rooftops of Madrid in the company of a long dead childhood friend and to comment on the conversation of her adult self and the man in black. Because of the roaring of the wind the two girls have to shout at one another. This leads the narrator-as-child to worry that their remarks will be audible to the adults. Her friend reassures her: "Nonsense; how could they hear us above all this wind? Besides, she has said that she is hard of hearing" (Martín Gaite, *El cuarto de atrás*, p. 184). This episode is reminiscent of the scene in *Through the Looking-Glass* where Alice and the Red Queen skim through the air with the wind whistling in their ears. *El cuarto de atrás* is, significantly, dedicated to Lewis Carroll.

Todorov concluded that, because of the hesitation it engenders, the fantastic questions the existence of an irreducible opposition between real and unreal. In Martín Gaite's novel we find expressed a relativistic metaphysic according to which reality and imagination, fact and fiction, are not mutually exclusive.[8] The narrator insists upon the power of the imagination and the reality of its creations. During the Civil War she and one of her schoolmates invented the island of Bergai as a place of refuge from fear and cold. To emphasize the indubitable actuality of that island the narrator says that "it was much more real than the things we saw around us; it had the force and consistency of dreams" (Martín Gaite, *El cuarto de atrás*, p. 195). Dreams are one of the topics she and her visitor discuss. He maintains that there is no point in attempting to find logical explanations for them, because they are governed by their own special laws. The narrator concurs. She also acknowledges that whereas her waking experiences often strike her as problematical, she accepts with certainty what she sees in dreams.

The interplay of fiction and reality is constant in *El cuarto de atrás*. In the first chapter the narrator remembers the sentimental novels she read as a young girl. She used to pore over the illustrations that portrayed melancholy, sleepless heroines reclining on elegant divans and thinking of their absent lovers. The décor of the narrator's own bedroom was loosely patterned after one of these illustrations, and she used to sprawl on the day bed and fantasize about the time when she, too, would receive poetic love letters. Shortly after recalling those adolescent yearnings and the books that nourished them, the adult narrator comes upon a letter that corresponds exactly to the missives she used to dream about. In effect, she now finds herself living a role she had often played in her imagination.

El cuarto de atrás is an excellent example of the self-conscious or self-reflexive novel. It is filled with comments on the narrative process and the problems of literary creations, with allusions to or quotations from other texts, many of which contain fantastic elements. The narrator mentions Charles Perrault's "Bluebeard," "Puss-in-Boots," and "Tom Thumb," as well as Aesop's fable of the ant and the grasshopper. (Her sympathies clearly lie with the latter creature.) References to Daniel Defoe's *Robinson Crusoe* focus upon the inventiveness of its protagonist and relate to the island of Bergai. A descriptive phrase from the frontispiece of Dashiell Hammett's *Thin Man* is particularly important, because the words "contradictory evidence, false clues, and a surprise ending" also apply to Martín Gaite's own novel. Allusions to Todorov and Lewis Carroll are frequent. Franz Kafka is not mentioned by name, but the large cockroach that scuttles about the narrator's apartment during the night calls to mind the metamorphosis of Gregor Samsa. Martín Gaite has read Kafka's works, and his influence is evident in *El balneario*.

References to another broad category of texts help portray for us the early postwar period in Spain. During that era of asphyxiating grayness, sentimental novels, popular songs, and films offered an escape from the official propaganda. The narrator stresses the impact that these art forms had upon the members of her generation, coloring their view of the world and their expectations.

Most interesting are the comments on Martín Gaite's own previously published works. The man in black insists that "literature is a challenge to logic . . . not a refuge from uncertainty," and he criticizes the Martín Gaite with whom he is speaking for being too rational and concerned with understanding things, too cautious (p. 55). He asserts that her short novel *El balneario* was a faint-hearted venture into the fantastic and that it was ruined by the failure to maintain the ambiguity that predominated in its first part. The narrator recalls experiences or settings that served as inspiration for *El balneario* and the novel *Ritmo lento (Adagio)*. She does not discuss *Retahílas (A String of Words)*, although in several respects it resembles *El cuarto de atrás*: in both novels the art of speaking, reading, and writing is a major topic, and in both the protagonists resurrect long forgotten memories and take stock of their lives in all-night conversations.

In *Entre visillos (Behind the Window Curtains)*, which was published in 1958, Martín Gaite portrayed the dreary, circumscribed existence of a group of girls growing up in a provincial city. In *El cuarto de atrás*, published exactly two decades later, she again wrote of her early life in Salamanca, but the two novels differ greatly. The passing of twenty years has produced significant changes. A degree of nostalgia has softened what were once harsh memories. Martín Gaite has matured as a person. As a writer she has abandoned the limiting social realism of her first full-length novel, thrown caution to the winds, and plunged wholeheartedly into the realm of the fantastic.

NOTES

1. Carmen Martín Gaite, *El cuarto de atrás* (Barcelona: Destino, 1978), 10. Further references appear in parentheses in the text. All translations are mine.

2. Tzvetan Todorov, *The Fantastic: A Structural Approach to a Literary Genre*, trans. Richard Howard (Ithaca, N.Y.: Cornell University Press, 1975), 31.

3. With regard to the importance of figurative discourse to the fantastic, Todorov wrote: "If the fantastic constantly makes use of rhetorical figures, it is because it originates in them. The supernatural is born of language, it is both its consequence and its proof: not only do the devil and vampires exist only in words, but language alone enables us to conceive what is always absent: the supernatural." Ibid., 82.

4. Ibid., 84.

5. On two occasions the narrator of *El cuarto de atrás* quotes Todorov's observation that "the time and space of the supernatural world . . . are not the time and space of everyday life." Ibid., 118; Martín Gaite, *El cuarto de atrás*, 144, 160.

6. On the symbolism of the mirror, see J. E. Cirlot, *A Dictionary of Symbols*, 2nd ed., trans. Jack Sage (New York: Philosophical Library, 1971), 211-12.

7. For Rabkin the fantastic depends on a diametric reversal of the ground rules of a narrative world. See, in particular, chapter 1 of Eric S. Rabkin, *The Fantastic in Literature* (Princeton, N.J.: Princeton University Press, 1976).

8. For a discussion of this metaphysic, see Leon Livingstone, "Interior Duplication and the Problem of Form in the Modern Spanish Novel," *PMLA* 73 (1958): 393-406.

Words and Worlds: The Creation of a Fantasy Universe in Zelazny, Lee, and Anthony

Michael R. Collings

> If the wording, sentence structures, or the denotations and connotations of key words were altered, the fantasy universe would collapse into the mundane.

Fantasy writers manipulate language to create a universe in which the laws of our objective universe are suspended. Writers may achieve this effect by assertion; they may merely incorporate into the fantasy world references to beings and situations alien to our experience. In the *Deryni Chronicles*, for example, Katherine Kurtz defined an alternate universe peopled with both humans and Deryni, human-appearing beings who wield particular powers that we as readers must define as magical. Magic occurs in the *Chronicles* largely because Kurtz defined Gwynnedd as a place in which magic is viable.[1]

Yet language is forceful and capable of multiform effects. In fantasies the style of the prose itself may lend credence to the fantasy universe. Or alternatively, the writer may use a style consonant with the reader's expectations but, by giving common words new meanings, create a fantasy universe. In either case if the wording, the sentence structures, or the denotations and connotations of key words were altered, the fantasy universe would collapse into the mundane.

Several recent fantasies seem particularly effective as illustrations of the use of language and style in defining a fantasy universe. Roger Zelazny's *Chronicles of Amber* are an ideal starting point for discussion, since the language in the nine novels alters in form and structure as Zelazny fills in the outlines of his universe, moving from our objective reality to the alternate universe of Amber. In Tanith Lee's *Death's Master* language is, from the opening paragraph, consciously elevated and antiquated, creating the emotional effect in the reader of suddenly being immersed in an unfamiliar world. In Piers Anthony's trilogy—

A Spell for Chameleon, The Source of Magic, and *Castle Roogna*—language is inverted and redefined; the words are common and familiar, but their referents are rarely so. In each instance the language of the work becomes a primary method of creating a viable fantasy universe.

In the *Chronicles of Amber* the style and construction of the language define the universe of Zelazny's sword and sorcery hero Prince Corwin of Amber. *Nine Princes in Amber* (the first of the series) begins peculiarly for a fantasy. The as-yet-unnamed hero wakes up in a perfectly normal hospital bed. Nothing suggests that patient, hospital, or world are in any way unusual. The tone and style of the first paragraphs bear out this initial impression: "I was sprawled there in a hospital bed and my legs were done up in plaster casts, but they were still mine. I squeezed my eyes shut, and opened them, three times. The room grew steady. Where the hell was I?"[2] The language is colloquial—"sprawled," "legs done up," and "squeezed"—and the sentence structures are as uncomplicated as speech, even to the run-together sentences and the cliché of the final question.

Later, this impression of a plot line intimately connected to our world is enhanced as the hero (still largely amnesiac) speaks in tones reminiscent of the stereotyped "private eye" of popular literature: "The guy was sitting there in a garish bathrobe, at a big shiny desk, going over some sort of ledger. . . . He opened a drawer, put his hand inside, and I was wary. I knocked it down before he had the safety catch off: a .32 automatic, very neat; Colt" (pp. 6-8).

Traditional literary devices recur throughout the passage: the "tough guy" stance; staccato, fragmentary prose; the pose of self-assurance defined by the speaker's vocal patterns; and the replacement of key nouns by pronouns of unstated but obvious reference—"I knocked *it* down." The effect of the first chapter is to place the action convincingly within our world. We are introduced to kidnapping, amnesia, and possibly attempted murder; but there is nothing in the prose to suggest that the hero derives from a fantasy universe.

Into this normal-seeming world Zelazny gradually introduced anomalies: Corwin's visit to a woman claiming to be his sister; his discovery in her library desk of a secret drawer and an odd tarot deck, with his own picture on one of the cards; the sudden recognition of his own name and of the magical name "Amber"; and, finally, an unexpected call and subsequent visit from his brother Random. Random arrives, pursued by six men, humanoid but definitely alien, with "uniformly bloodshot eyes . . . an extra joint to each finger and thumb, and sharp, forward-curving spurs on the backs of their hands. . . . Their flesh was greyish and hard and shiny" (p. 35). These beings are from another Shadow, an alternate universe impinging upon our own only through the mediation of Amber; both their world and ours depend upon the primal pattern in Amber for existence.

After disposing of the intruders, Corwin and Random journey to Amber. Random alters details of the surrounding landscape, until he has imagined an approximation of Amber. As Corwin approaches Amber the settings become

increasingly fantastical, the language less stereotyped, and the hero less a reflection of the 1940s "private eye." Corwin gradually emerges as Prince of
Amber and a magician capable of manipulating countless Shadows at will. He
invades Amber to counter his brother Eric's pretensions to the throne, now empty
after the mysterious disappearance of their father, King Oberon. Corwin is
defeated and captured and ultimately forced to participate in Eric's coronation.
At this point the language Zelazny used approximates the rhythms and vocabulary
of heroic sagas, transporting us beyond the mundane world in which *Nine Princes
in Amber* began. A feudal prince-magician replaces the egalitarian, twentieth
century man.

Corwin is commanded to tender the crown to Eric. Instead, he hurls it at Eric,
who catches it and announces: "I assume the crown and throne this day. I take
into my hand the scepter of the kingdom of Amber. . . . I crown mysef Eric
the First, King of Amber. . . . Guards! Take Corwin to the Stithy, and let his
eyes be burnt from out his head! Then cast him into the darkness of the deepest
dungeon beneath Amber, and let his name be forgotten!'' (p. 129). The archaisms
in form and vocabulary ("let his eyes be burnt from out his head" and "stithy"),
as well as the almost ritual importance of the hero's name and reputation,
emphasize the other-worldliness of the coronation, just as the ceremonial stag-
ing—the crowning of an unjust king and the punishment of the hero as traitor—
elevates the characters beyond the common mortals Zelazny had first introduced
us to. In this other universe, the universe of Amber, we are willing (if not forced)
to suspend our disbelief and accept instant teleportation through the Tarot cards,
the existence of unnumbered Shadow worlds, and the creation of the Dark Road
from the Courts of Chaos through all Shadows and into Amber itself. Everything
that happens in the *Chronicles* accords with natural laws operant in Amber.

The language of the *Chronicles* does not alter continuously, however. On
occasion, Corwin lapses into the structures and forms of the earlier chapters. In
his least heroic state, imprisoned and blinded (but awaiting regeneration of his
eyes), he contemplates escape, again in terms borrowed from the colloquial,
"tough guy" stereotype: "I'd heard these stories of guys digging their way out
of cells with the damnedest things—belt buckles (which I didn't have)—etc."
(p. 141). Throughout the series Corwin and his brothers continually refer to
King Oberon as "Dad," a breach in the heroic decorum that is otherwise allowed
to build incrementally.

For the most part, however, the further we read in the *Chronicles*, the less
the language resembles that of Shadow Earth, where the series began. With the
final discovery that Amber is itself a secondary shadow, a reflection of an ultimate
pattern, the language elevates even further, until in the final volume, *The Courts
of Chaos*, we lose entirely the comfortable familiarity of Shadow Earth and find
ourselves immersed in an epic universe: "Led by the pale trumpeters came a
mass of horsemen mounted on white steeds, bearing banners, some of which I
did not recognize, behind a man-thing who bore the Unicorn standard of Amber.
. . . A deep noise came to us then—slow, rhythmic, rolling beneath the noise

of the trumpets and the sounds of the musicians—and I realized that the foot soldiers were singing'' (p. 412). The passage continues thus for two pages: long, convoluted sentences, replete with rhythmical repetitions that create a sense of austerity and solemnity at the passing of the old order and the inception of the new. The brash, self-confident, predictable human narrator of the opening chapters of *Nine Princes in Amber* has disappeared, replaced by a magician-prince mature enough to relinquish his unwarranted pretensions to the throne of Amber.

Throughout the series the tone, vocabulary, and construction of the language draw us as readers out of our familiar environment and insinuate us into the fantasy universe of Amber, where Earth is but a reflection, and true reality entails much more than we might initially be willing to accept. Beginning with sentences familiar and common to this Earth, Zelazny concludes the series in a style that accommodates the elevation, the sense of *outré* characters and actions into which his fantasy has grown.

In Tanith Lee's *Death's Master* language functions even more consistently in transporting us from conventionality to the fantastic. The stylistic differences between the language of *Death's Master* and our everyday patterns of speech and thought are apparent in the opening lines of the book: "Lady Plague wore her yellow robe, for the sickness was a yellowish fever, yellow as the dust that swirled up from the plains and cloaked the city of Merh and choked it, yellow as the sinking mud to which the wide river of Merh had turned. . . . The bedchamber of the queen of Merh was this way: Burnished weapons of hunting and war hung upon the walls which were painted with scenes of hunting and war.''[3] The sentences are elevated in style and structure, with a formulaic repetition of words and phrases (particularly the conjunctive *for*) and a strong sense of the archaic and the exotic, as, for example, in the highly evocative word *Burnished*.

In addition, the language of *Death's Master* distances us from the conventional by aligning itself with traditional epic devices. *Death's Master* uses figurative language and epithets and similes that reflect the epic impulse; phrasing is woven largely from familiar words but is nonetheless compatible with a world inhabited by demons, demiurges, and heroes. Throughout the novel, for example, Lee employed the Homeric device of allowing the coming of dusk or dawn to signal transitions between scenes, and she was rarely content merely to say that the sun came up or went down. Instead, she formalized her descriptions, creating formulaic communications within the image and establishing implicitly the relationship between the passage and the context. Chapter 5 of part 1 begins: "The sun had risen above the forest of petrified cedars. Its arrows had not pierced the black spreading canopy; the sun had gone away, and the blue dusk had followed. And the dusk permeated the forest as the sun had not been able to'' (p. 34). This passage provides an ideal fulcrum between Narasen's conjuring of the witch of the House of the Blue Dog and the queen's subsequent sexual coupling with a magically animated corpse. The birth of her child is described, and her own death adumbrated, in the next description of time: "The third day came. It rushed on slippers of silk, this gentle day, in at the palace gates. And just behind the day rushed another, less gentle, and through another door" (p. 40). In subsequent passages Lee continued to blend image and plot through a subtle evocation of the epic sense, for example: "It was the moment of the sun's death, and the whole camp bloody with it. In the red glow, the three brothers hastened to find their father the king, and they threw the child smelling of lions before him" (p. 62).

Even more overtly, Lee built her novel on episodes that, through their evocation of the mythological universe of classical epic, succeed in pulling us farther from our world and into one in which Death, Night, and multiple divisions and subdivisions of subservient demons interact with the realms of humans (who are themselves both terrestrial and submarine). Achilles's invulnerability provides an analog to Zhirem's through the agonies of the well of fire; Simmu's quest for the Garden of the Golden Daughters closely parallels Gilgamesh's quest for immortality; and the wanderings of Simmu and Kassefeh, culminating with their arrival at the immortal city of Simmurad, suggest the wanderings of Odysseus.

To emphasize the other-worldliness of the epic impulse (and thereby to distance us as readers from the fantasy universe in which *Death's Master* takes place), Lee employed linguistic patterns to capitalize on the epic characteristics of the plot; the vocabulary and sentence structure parallel plot development. For example, Simmu is described in a passage that suggests strongly the epic simile, both in being an explicit comparison and in being complex, formed of several levels of comparison: "For Simmu there began then a time of near humanness, a time of near forgetting. As the tree was dormant in the winter, empty of fruit and leaves, so was Simmu. Spring woke the tree; a spring would come also to wake Simmu, but Simmu's spring was yet far off" (p. 51).

The language of the novel is archaic, exotic, and elevated; words such as *burnished* (in the opening paragraphs) further emphasize the sense of antiquity Lee was weaving while suggesting the formulaic language of traditional military epics and sagas. Words interweave to create scenes evocative of the landscapes of epics: "Here grew exotic malformed trees with fruits that shone like brass, and here, on the wide, melanotic shores of the lake, unicorns had been known to dance, to fight, and to couple. And this night the unicorns came, as if they were the sigils of a man's terror and craving" (p. 104). Lee defined a landscape in which the sudden intrusion of the unicorns is not only possible but eminently fitting, while limning a counter-Eden, a garden of darkness and fear particularly appropriate to the plot at this point. Perhaps not coincidentally, Lee's garden strongly suggests John Milton's Paradise, including a meandering fog and fruits that "shone like brass."[4]

In *Death's Master* diction parallels from the first the language Zelazny developed more gradually in the *Chronicles of Amber*. Both Zelazny and Lee manipulated the language of their fantasies to create and support the alternative universe, distancing us from our accepted reality by weaving the plot out of words exotic, elevated in style, and inappropriate to the mundane, objective universe of the twentieth-century reader. Both authors suggestively re-created the worldview of the epic: Zelazny gradually, over the course of several volumes; Lee immediately and intimately, with the first sentences of *Death's Master*. By doing so both established the viability of the fantasy universe they were defining.

Piers Anthony approached the problem of creating an acceptable, believable fantasy universe from the opposite direction. He did not use vocabulary and style to "elevate" his novel; indeed, most of the diction in the Xanth trilogy is straightforward, almost colloquial, and certainly only rarely different from daily language. In Xanth words do not suggest a world separate from ours; instead, they are given the power to *create* a new reality. Like many (if not most) fantasy writers Anthony used words to actualize myth, to define a universe, for example, in which monsters have tangible existences. Unlike many writers, however, he inverted the traditional metaphorical function of language to create beings through the literalization of metaphor. Magic is treated as a matter of course and aids in reducing words to elements in a cosmic game substantially beyond the perceptions of mere humans.

On one level the Xanth trilogy shares much with more traditional fantasies. Almost immediately, we enter a world inhabited by basilisks, manticora, unicorns, harpies, assorted dragons, magic rings, and sorcerers, both good and evil. At this level the language merely asserts that creatures such as the ouroborous can exist in Xanth because Xanth is, in fact, a magical land. The fantasy universe is presented as reality, with monsters playing essential roles in the plot.

Quickly, however, we discover that Anthony was not content with asserting the existence of mythical monsters. Phenomena associated with the natural world, with the "scientific world," as it is viewed in Xanth, are defined in terms of actualized mythology. For instance, the hero Bink speaks of eclipses in the following terms: "There had been what the centaurs called an eclipse: the sun had banged into the moon and knocked a big chunk out of it, and a great wad of cheese had fallen to the ground. The whole North Village had gorged on it before it spoiled."[5] In addition to making humorous puns on clichés, Anthony was here allowing us to perceive a natural phenomenon from a new direction; he was fabricating in essence a *mooreeffoc* vision.[6] It is one thing to explain an eclipse mythologically or to speculate on the probable composition of the moon's surface (witness the concern among NASA personnel that the first lunar landing modules could conceivably disappear into a layer of eons-thick dust); it is another thing to provide the reader with evidence—Bink's consumption of the green cheese—that the mythological explanation is in fact the true one.

In Xanth words do not simply label things or ideas within an accepted, objective universe; they are not merely symbols standing (often for no good reason) for things. In Xanth they, like all other elements of the land, are imbued with magic totally their own. Words can perform magic; they can become the things represented. When Bink and his friends are attacked by curse burrs, the narrator explains that "There was only one way to get rid of such a burr; it had to be banished by a curse" (Anthony, *Source*, p. 91). In our reality we might curse at burrs, or at other inconveniences, primarily as a means of emotional adjustment. In Xanth the curse is the *only* way to eliminate the inconvenience. Words not only symbolize power, they *are* power.

Additionally, Anthony visualized the language of fantasy as one in which the metaphor-making, symbol-forming function of language is largely reversed. The magic of Xanth literalizes language; to call a thing by name is to define the nature of the thing, not merely its relationship to another thing or its meaning as defined by tradition and convention. Clichés thus cease to be hackneyed, stereotyped images and become instead living statements of truth. To be "nickeled to death" represents for us a trite way of speaking about the frustrations of petty bills; in Xanth it refers to a particularly painful way of dying: "in complete darkness, the nickelpedes [a form of vicious centipede, five times normal size] would be upon them in a mass, and gobble every part of their bodies in disk-chunks called nickels. What a horrible fate, to be nickeled to death!" (p. 63) Throughout the trilogy, common sayings are punned upon, creating new realities from dead metaphors: "get the lead out," "sowing wild oats," "pulling a shade," "crooked shops," and "rat races" are among the many phrases that become newly—and literally—meaningful in the context of Xanth's magic.[7] Even Murphy's law ("If anything can go wrong, it will") is transformed into a particular magical talent associated with the magician Murphy.[8]

In the same way words are often treated not as metaphors but as literal definitions. The name of a thing defines its function, shape, and purpose in Xanth. Words that suggest to us comparisons between things named and the normal referents are, in Xanth, hilariously literal. While on their quest for the source of magic Bink and his party stumble into a clump of hell's bells. "The vines of the plants reared up, their bells ringing stridently. The tintinnabulation became deafening—and disconcerting" (Anthony, *Source*, p. 50). Bink lives in a fine example of a "cottage cheese," a huge, hollowed-out cheese, dried and suitable for inhabiting (Anthony noted offhandedly that, as a home, it was "one of the most tasteful cottages extant" [p. 2]). Elsewhere in the *Source of Magic*, as the Good Magician Humphrey prepares to leave his castle to join the quest, he "mothballs" his castle. Smoke becomes a creature that flies up and drops a ball, which explodes and produces streamers that "shot out in a huge sphere, drifting down to touch every part of the castle. Then they drew in tight, and suddenly the whole edifice was sheathed in a silky net, and looked like a giant tent. A cold, bitter odor emanated from it, smelling vaguely disinfectant" (p. 87). Throughout the series we are introduced to strange, new meanings for common, everyday words: a *tiger lily* is a carnivorous, feline plant; a *jellyfish* smells suspiciously of lime jelly; *shoe-trees* and *lady slippers* produce footwear-fruit in varying sizes (and are notoriously difficult to grow in one place); a *picklepuss* pickles its victims with one whisk of its catlike paws; *snapdragons* are beautiful plants but vicious and hard to grow in pots; and a *sunflower* can blind anyone who looks directly into its light.

At the next level Anthony moved beyond the literalization of common terms and inverted our expectations. Writing to an audience familiar with, if not immersed in, the vocabulary of science and technology, Anthony treated scientific facts as the most blatant of magic, incomprehensible to Xanthians. In Xanth all occurrences are explainable, and the most obvious explanation—the magical one—is usually correct. Only when confronted with true science is Bink at a loss for an explanation, and even then he attempts to couch his explanations in terms of magic.

In two separate episodes he sees snow on the tops of mountains. Since mountain tops are demonstrably nearer the sun than are flatlands, and must consequently be hotter, the snow can only exist as a manifestation of powerful magic. Later, Chester the Centaur mentions *triangulation*, and Bink reminds himself that the word refers to "magical" indirection taken in "locating something." Although an ouroborous is fully acceptable and "natural" to Bink, the concept of the mobius strip as a scientific, abstract principle is treated as simply specialized magic.

In *The Source of Magic* Anthony took the inversion of literal and metaphorical meanings a final step, to suggest that even Xanth, which is defined principally through a literalization of metaphorical words, is in turn symbolic of a more abstract level of existence. When Bink finally enters the presence of the captive demon Xanth, he inadvertently steps into a thought pattern projected by the demon: "He saw stars. . . . They were so far apart that a dragon could not have flown from one to another in its lifetime, and so numerous that a man could not count them all in *his* lifetime, yet all were visible at once" (pp. 256-57). For the first time Bink is allowed to see the natural universe as *we* understand it, in all of its complexity and immensity and totally devoid of magic. For him the realities of our universe are startling and apparently impossible to comprehend; the things for which his word—*stars*—had stood are revealed as infinitely greater than the Xanthian conceptions of the word had suggested.

Bink had, in addition, continually conceived of the demon Xanth as a physical being, on a par with himself, sharing human experiences and existence. The Good Magician Humphrey shows him, however, that the demon is primarily a mathematical formula, with no external physical presence. The name is a metaphorical identification of an entity defined as a "scoring formula—three variables and a class exponent, as near as we can understand it" (p. 258). Xanth, that exotic name that had throughout the trilogy identified a particular land in a magical, fantastical universe, is stripped of this literal meaning to become essentially abstract. $X (A/N)^{th}$ is merely one of many celestial (or perhaps infernal) players in a cosmic game. His relationship with the land and inhabitants of Xanth is entirely coincidental; what awareness he has of Bink and the others is distant, as if they were but ants crawling along a shoelace.

There is some suggestion in *The Source of Magic* that Anthony intended the demon Xanth to represent a deity, either heavenly or hellish. The demon is "bound for a thousand years" deep below the surface of Xanth, as part of a game in which he is engaged; yet his binding is enforced only by his inherent sense of honor. Xanth seeks quietude: "All I want from your society," he informs Bink, "is that it not intrude on my private demesne" (p. 314); if he does not receive it he threatens to "cauterize the entire surface of the planet with a single sheet of fire." He is omnipotent, yet admittedly not omniscient. Since even the demon Xanth is not all-knowing, the possibility endures that he or it is in turn merely a literalization of a larger, more symbolical universe, a mathematical formula in a game that is, on an infinite scale, just a minuscule part of an even larger universe as Bink's Xanth is part of the demon's—and, not incidentally, provides a link between the fantasy universe of Xanth and our own.

In the Xanth trilogy Anthony manipulated language to create, first, a fantasy universe and then a universe beyond the fantasy in which both our mundane universe and Xanth's magical ones play roles. He began by literalizing, by reversing clichés and dead metaphors, breathing into them new life by treating them in terms of their surface meanings. He forced common words to divest themselves of metaphorical meaning and instead to represent literally what their constituent linguistic elements define. Then, after we had become used to that process he inverted it again, defining Xanth first as a land in which magic flows freely and naturally, then as a demon source of that magic, and finally as a merely metaphorical tag for a spirit essence engaged in a game of cosmic one-upmanship.

These two approaches roughly define the alternatives available to the writer of fantasy; in each, language is manipulated to create the fantasy universe. For Zelazny and Lee language is external, imposed upon plot and character, and consciously elevates the world of the novel beyond our own, while still retaining its essential credibility. We accept the fantasy universe precisely because it is *not* defined in familiar terms, because the words do *not* fit together as we might expect. The language functions in ways foreign to our expectations; we are thus more amenable to the vision of a universe that similarly functions in ways foreign to our expectations.

Anthony illustrates the opposite approach. He used common words and a common, conversational style. But in doing so he inverted the words themselves, forcing common words to represent new, unusual things or ideas. Ultimately, his inversions suggest a layering of reality that incorporates a constant shifting between the literal and the metaphorical, between the actual and the symbolic. Familiar words come to represent alien, unimaginable things, and we are led to accept the universe in which such things exist. In either case, with either technique, the author used language to create a universe distanced sufficiently from our own to allow us to embrace it as fantastic.

NOTES

1. Katherine Kurtz, personal interview, 28 August 1979.

2. Roger Zelazny, *Nine Princes in Amber*, in *The Chronicles of Amber*, 2 vols. (New York: Doubleday, n.d.), 1:3. Further references appear in parentheses in the text.

3. Tanith Lee, *Death's Master* (New York: DAW Books, 1979), 9. Further references appear in parentheses in the text.

4. Lee's "brass" is a debasement of Milton's "Ambrosial Fruit / of Vegetable Gold" that adorned the "Tree of Life" (Milton, *Paradise Lost*, bk. 4 [Hughes], lines 217-19). Similarly, the "meandering fogs" suggest both the meandering rivers of Paradise (bk.4, lines 237-40) and the mists with which Satan disguised himself to enter Eden (bk. 9, lines 69-76). As the fogs of Paradise suggest humankind's Fall, Lee's images prefigure the disruption of Simmu's idyllic existence.

5. Piers Anthony, *The Source of Magic* (New York: Ballantine, 1979), 64. Further references appear in parentheses in the text.

6. "Coffeeroom" inverted. See J. R. R. Tolkien, "On Fairy Stories," *Tree and Leaf* (Boston: Houghton Mifflin, 1965), reprinted in *The Tolkien Reader* (New York: Ballantine, 1966), 58.

7. Piers Anthony, *A Spell for a Chameleon* (New York: Ballantine, 1977), 43, 16, 69, 201.

8. Piers Anthony, *Castle Roogna* (New York: Ballantine, 1977), 134.

A Fantastic Pairing: Edward Taylor and Donald Barthelme

Carter Martin

> Such locutions I want to treat as a form of linguistic fantasy, that is, that language (as opposed to events) is the milieu or the ground upon which the protagonist (reader/experiencer) walks.

Fantasy is an abstraction capable of bringing together artists one expected never to compare, and so it is with Edward Taylor and Donald Barthelme. This is not a matter of influence but of method, in that both men expressed themselves through a form of fantasy that is one of language rather than events. Both attempted to convey the ineffable and in their individual ways confounded language and rationality in order to do so. Nevertheless, both are almost devoutly literary and return to the work in an almost apocalyptic sense after excursions into apparent absurdity.

Tzvetan Todorov defined the fantastic as the condition of "hesitation experienced by a person who knows only the laws of nature, confronting an apparently supernatural event."[1] Todorov went on to contend that the hesitation comes from an "ambiguous vision," that it can occur before the conflict of the real and the illusory, and that it can be effected by *locutions* that keep the reader or hero in two worlds at once, uncertain, puzzled, hesitating.[2]

Such locutions I want to treat as a form of linguistic fantasy, that is, that language (as opposed to events) is the milieu or the ground upon which the protagonist (reader/experiencer) walks. The opposition is between language in the conventional, grammatical, predictable, normal, syntactical sense, and the nonsense of disjunction, neologism, chaos, and mystery—words that cannot be understood to mean anything.

Edward Taylor's poem "The Almighty" (Meditation 48, 2nd series) develops a verbal conceit upon the homophone *might-mite*, capitalizing on the contradictory nature of the words.[3] It may be useful to recall that this poem was written as a meditation in preparation for the sacrament of Holy Communion. All such poems by Taylor cite a biblical text, but it is not quoted. For "The Almighty" it is Revelations 1:8: "I am Alpha and Omega, the beginning and the ending, saith the Lord, which is, and which was, and which is to come, the Almighty." In it the specifically linguistic conception of God (Alpha and Omega) is accompanied by conceptions of time and energy. Only the last word does not express a circularity, a tautological inclusiveness embracing opposites. Taylor provided those characteristics for the conception of God as energy (the Almighty) by his play on words and by his specific hope that his own powerlessness would be married to God's limitless power so that the concept of all power would include powerlessness. Taylor declared the inadequacy of language before this mystery by claiming that his word *mite* is a "solicism" and that his linguistic attempt to say here what he wanted to say is a rash adventure "t'dress Almighty up" (line 15). He even asked forgiveness for his erroneous, presumptuous, and mistaken words ("Stutting Stamring"), which he described as coming from his quill as a form of excrement befouling God's power: "Then spare my Stutting Stamring, inky Quill, / If it its bowells on thy Power distill" (lines 17-18). The Quill is involved differently at the end of the poem, when Taylor said, "My Quill makes thine Almightiness a String / of Pearls to grace the tune my Mite doth sing" (lines 41-42). This complex synesthesia mixes sight and sound imagery, but it also diminishes power by visualizing it as pearls and permits greatness to subserve insignificance (power decorates powerlessness). This extraordinary mystical irrationality is acceptable only in the context of *tune* and *sing*, that is, the absurdity is overcome by the poetry of an intuited truth (wrong though its semantics may be) concerning humankind's relationship to God.

The lyrical motion of this poem achieves itself through linguistic fantasy inasmuch as the meaning comes from reader/perceivers' hesitation not only before the startling metaphysical statement but before the dense and opaque sentences of the poem. The words here conform better than Barthelme's, but they are nevertheless a considerable syntactic challenge, leaving reader/perceivers knowing the point well enough but not the argument for it. For example, here is the opening of the poem: "O! What a thing is Might right mannag'd? Twill / That Proverb brain, whose face doth ware this paint" (lines 1-2). Which proverb? Which face? What paint? We can guess about these things, but like the character in fantasy, we are puzzled, we hesitate before the choices, which may be between proverbial truth and the falseness of the mask of dissembling. This confusing sentence is followed by another, "Might ore goe's right," which seems at first to make sense but on second glance brings one to a dilemma concerning the relationship of power and justice (line 3); logically, we cannot accept the notion that these are self-cancelling attributes of God or that God's attributes exist in some mysterious hierarchy. The poem continues to perplex, although there are windows of lucidity that call us on, confident that the title at least is still intact in spite of the locutions. Therefore, when we come to the following sentence we may try to analyze its syntax and semantics: "My Mite . . . would spend its mitie strength for Thee / Of Mightless Might, of feeble stronge delight. / Its little ALL Thy Sacrifice should bee" (lines 19-22). These words are locutions more subject to resolving analysis than the proverb-paint passage, but reader/perceivers must again feel themselves to have been led into linguistic fantasy, not knowing whether to turn and reject syntax and sense in favor of their intuition that they understand what is happening or to immerse themselves in the rational and conventional language world that they suspect informs the words. Either way, in this ingeniously constructed fantasy of Taylor's the result is miraculously the same, that *mite* and *might*, although opposite, are part of the same truth—which is the object of a "Preparatory Meditation," to become one with God in communion.

Barthelme's "Bone Bubbles" is also a linguistically based fantasy somewhat similar in its technique to Taylor's poem.[4] Moving through it readers are constantly faced with the hesitation or uncertainty about the ground they occupy, which Todorov contended is the essence of fantasy. Specifically, readers are drawn between two responses to the word structure before them: (1) that it is a flight of total absurdity beckoning to them like an evil spirit to enter and relish the objectification of nihilism, or (2) that it is an accurate representation of personal experience that, although confusing, follows a pattern so highly unique, because it is completely private and individual, that one must discover a key to its puzzle to respond to its essentially holistic structuring of reality. The story is a remarkably effective linguistic fantasy, because of all of the pieces in Barthelme's *City Life* it is the most successful one in resisting the resolution of this tension, hesitation, or ambiguity.

Looking at the story objectively one finds it to be an almost unbroken affront to rationality. Its title is apparently not related to anything in the subsequent words. Orthographics are almost totally absent, and when they do occur, they are of no help in making clear the ordinary, expected junctures of language. Some words are not to be found in any dictionary, and syntax is engaged only by its absence. Barthelme seems to have succeeded in putting most of his words in sequences that defy connection even in very short phrases, although the exceptions to this are crucial.

The story superficially appears to be a series of random blocks of words. After our first access to its sense through isolated phrases we may come to a structural access if we count lines and discover that there are sixteen in each of the fifteen blocks, which come out exactly two to each of seven pages plus one on the first page. Like a protagonist in a fantasy of events, readers attach to this clue hoping that it will lead them to a solution. Perhaps they reason from mechanical poetic forms such as the sonnet or large but confusing literary architectonics such as those of Edmund Spenser's *Faerie Queene* and James Joyce's *Ulysses*. Like Brockden Brown's Edgar Huntley finding himself in a cave with no light and a savage beast snarling somewhere near him, readers now know only the extremity of their dilemma and must grope in the dark for further clues.

The clues come in the form of occasional syntactic units of four or five words and in a few instances fifteen or sixteen words. For example, these disparate passages occur in Block 9: "intense activity / it would be better if we just piled all the stones on the floor / wheels out of alignment / prints rescued from the inferno / writing my article / streaked with raisins / something stuck in the gum / a humanizing influence / didn't they tell you / list of objects which have their own saucy life" (Barthelme, "Bone Bubbles," p. 121). Some of them are contiguous and some are not, but isolated this way the phrases are only minimally suggestive, and readers remain puzzled—that is, they remain enmeshed in the linguistic fantasy until they arrive at another sign that draws them on with renewed hope.

In the most lucid pastiche, the first block of the seventh page, readers discover a strongly felt conclusion to a section—words that are not a confusing allusion but a familiar, very humanly moving quotation from Psalm 137: "We sat down and wept." Here, finally, is a locution sufficient to constitute the firm ground of a knowable situation being experienced by people we generally can identify, and furthermore it comes down to us through many ages unchanged in a traditional text, the Bible. The great complexity of its meanings, if we can keep them intact, is the most promising key to Barthelme's story. Most obviously, it is a song (psalm) that sings the statement that singing is not possible. The speakers say that they have hung up their lyres: "How shall we sing the Lord's song in a strange land?" (Psalms 137:4) Instead of standing and singing they sit down and weep. Perceiver/experiencers in "Bone Bubbles" are like the Israelites, strangers in a strange land, that is, they are typical modern protagonists, despairing of a voice for themselves in the face of a fractured, discontinuous, threatening world.

This easy sort of modern typological criticism, however, is not all there is to the brief passage from Psalm 137. The more particular conditions calling forth the lament and antisong are: (1) The Babylonian captivity, which posits the opulence and decadence of that culture as a parallel to the present of the story; (2) the whore of Babylon (here called the "daughter of Babylon" but dealt with extensively in the highly symbolic Book of Revelation); and (3) by linguistic quirk or deliberate mythical association, the Tower of Babel. This third association fits into the "Bone Bubbles" response by inferring a golden time when all people understood one another and the time since the Tower when people have been separated from each other linguistically, confounded by myriad languages, the demonic extension of which is one language for one person.

The speaker/perceiver of "Bone Bubbles" may be understood to have constructed an antistory/antisong as an outcry for freedom from his oppressors, whom he does not want to understand and whom he wishes to confound in revenge for his captivity. In the words of the psalm, "Happy shall he be, that rewardeth thee as thou hast served us." Thus the words are a puzzle to the enemy or the uninitiate but a solace to those who, like the psalmist, have not forgotten Jerusalem and are willing to suffer to remember and preserve it: "Let my right hand forget her cunning. . . . Let my tongue cleave to the roof of my mouth; if I prefer not Jerusalem above my chief joy,'' which so far as the story goes is as much as to say that language may be almost totally lost (the loss of one's writing hand and the loss of clear verbal sounds) if one is separated from the truth (Psalms 137:5-6, 8). Put another way, this refers in the present of the story to the modern degeneration of language into the very token of deception and falsehood, the kind of expression Jonathan Swift's Houyhnhnms did not have a term for: the lie, which they called saying "the thing which was not."[5] Through the device of this biblical allusion, Barthelme proclaimed the breakdown of language and carried out a new language that uses words but not logic, rationality, or sequentiality. Words are the only signs, and the connections between them occur at a nonrational level. Therefore, readers conclude "Bone Bubbles" knowing what it means but not knowing how they know.

Although to analyze the story is to become a victim of Barthelme's trap for abstracters, legalists, sentimentalists, and traditional grammarians, we can venture to explain the situation and meaning of "Bone Bubbles" as an academic approach to a nonacademic and mystical communication.

Readers who have given themselves up to Barthelme enter a realm of language in which they cannot be sure of anything on the basis of the language itself, and this is the exciting element of fantasy, but at the same time they know, although not without a doubt, the significance of the irrational jumble. In "Bone Bubbles" that meaning is the simple affirmation of life, love, beauty, and art in the midst of a universal perceptual-abstractive situation constituted of mechanisms, war, destruction, discontinuity, and the various horrors of obscurity and confusion.

The situation/setting of the story is so unavailable that it must be described by an extravagant and erroneous claim that is akin to a metaphor for the story as story—a leap necessitated by trying to describe an antistory with inadequate critical apparatus (a defect I concede as a personal one). The word structure "Bone Bubbles" is the result of a microscopically small electronic brain probe yielding through a fantastic computer the multiple overlays of stored impressions available at that brain point. Since its complexity will submit only to the fantastic universal genius capable of commanding and organizing all knowledge, it will yield only part of its significance even to a committee of scholars and wise men, to say nothing of the ordinary reader. Only a fool would presume to begin with the author's intent. So we have the epitome of objective art, as hyperrealistic as a googol. Therefore, even though everything in the story conforms in some ideal realm to Edgar Allan Poe's requirement that all words function to achieve a single effect, no one can know enough to know everything about the essential unity of the words. We must take that on faith, on intuition—but more practically, on the basis of what sense we can make of portions of the word structure "Bone Bubbles."

Working back through the story to confirm what they feel and what they have been led to by the allusion to Psalm 137, readers may survey the patterns of words in the fifteen sections and find not only many references to music but a musical pattern of recurrence, although these thrusts toward meaning are part of the fantasy's very nature in that they cause hesitation and ambiguity. For example, at the juncture (indicated by blank space) between Blocks 12 and 13 one observes a link between them since number 12 ends with the "we sat down and wept" passage and number 13 begins with the words "poet's slurs." Aside from the poet-psalmist connection, the word *slurs* refers in the musical context to the almost indiscernible movement from one note to an adjoining one; as a deliberate technique it is the most subtle of shifts in which one thing becomes another, in which two become as one, in which the poet/composer/performer lets us see that notes as such are all one, as if the harmony of the spheres were one eternal sustained dominant chord made of an infinite number of notes that together sound like only one. This is indeed a positive and extravagant image and a taxing interpretation on the basis of slight evidence. So it should be in fantasy, especially a linguistic one concerned with the remaking of communication with words. Besides, there is the possibility that *slur* means a slight or an insult, an activity not at all uncharacteristic of poets, especially in times of despair and pessimism. Thus readers must entertain a doubt and remain suspended, in hesitation. As they look further, however, they may subject themselves to an exercise in extreme rationality, charting the recurrence of words and associations and actually quantifying them. For example, in Block 1 there are 11 words or word-units having to do with a broad positive category that I call "love-marriage-sex-society," for which no pejorative associations would count; there are 53 words in this category out of a total of 152 words in the block. The most outstanding locution in this category and in this block is a complete sentence, "I am glad to be here and intend to do what I can to remain." The others are: "grand and exciting world / fussy at times / misrecognitions of the ego / Hiltons and Ritzes / active enthusiasm / which gives me rest / the semi-private parts of their lives / a number of very attractive young girls / breasts like / social eminence." These units are, of course, separated by other words. The next most numerous category is music and art, which has 14 units and 26 words: "pings / rehearsal / world of his fabrication / surface irregularities / fragilization / gut / most mature artist / bases and pedestals / cellos / wailing / photographed / ballrooms / orchestras / destroyed many of these works." In spite of the fact that some of these words seem arbitrarily categorized, the subject/perceiver can stand by them as confidently as they can be questioned. "Gut," for example, refers to the strings of a musical instrument. "Wailing" is what good jazz musicians do when they play well. "Surface irregularities" are the signs of an especially achieved texture of a piece of sculpture. Other categories in this section are religion, vegetation, time, discovery, and miscellaneous abstract words. In subsequent blocks we will find further categories, some of them important, such as war, violence, and conflict. Without charting them here we can still isolate certain lucid and almost complete locutions scattered throughout that help to establish a pattern suggestive enough to be a reliable guide to the meaning conveyed by intuition. Some of them (from

Block 5) are as follows: "perverse cults which have replaced Christianity," "at the moment I was perfectly happy," "worn-out debauchees who had drained the cup of sensuality to its dregs," "other examples could be substituted for the examples which they give us," "happily the people dance about," "let's slip over to the foot of that tree to avoid getting crushed," "if there were no such affinity between atoms it would be impossible for love to appear 'higher up.' " In this last passage, if we have been aware of the counterpoint between love/society and war/mechanism, we find a conjoining of opposites in which the scientific analysis of the intimacies of atomic structures is a key to a typological sign of love/marriage/happiness/harmony among people. Thus suspecting now that the "poet's slurs" are confirmed to be reference to the harmony of the spheres, since we have found another different image of harmony (also from ancient philosophy as well as modern science) to confirm our first suspicion of meaning, we may come back to the block (number 13) beginning with "poet's slurs" and by adding junctures, lines, and punctuation read it as itself a phonic hymn, making its music of sounds, phrasings, rhythms, harmonies, and counterpoints:

> Poet's slurs, extra rations, business on 96th Street,
> Blueprints of uncompleted projects, drunk and naked too,
> Malphony,
> Down at the old boathouse dark little birds
> Astonishing propositions drummed out of the circle.
> I'll insult him.
> Scotch, student rags and bones, sunspots spoiled the hash.
> Keen satisfaction, honors and gifts fit to burst the blue,
> The white hoarse glee caught her knee in her hands with a click.
> Tonic night, favorite wine, well-known bumbler,
> Look at his head.
> The bomb is here.
> Gulls, twins rinse the seven of them,
> Appealing tot of rum, she rises, looks at him mysteriously, fades into the closet,
>   fades out of the closet again,
> Double meaning arms tighten weak with relief,
> Silence throwing down the letters,
> Her "wedding hat lackey" slakes thirst nervously, puts mask to face,
> Back door of the morgue-new raincoat, and draws away laughing,
> "Bit of dogfish" seated on a green stone bench, baked this meat loaf.

With the concrete banality of a bride baking meat loaf, this fantastic voyage of discovery returns to the beginning, the title "Bone Bubbles," and permits us to interpret it as another affirmation of the essentially holistic nature of the word structure it precedes, for bone bubbles are the atoms, figuratively, of human life, the red blood cells being manufactured by the soft interior of a person's bones, the marrow, filled with infinitely complex and mysterious channels of life and movement and creation, surrounded by the protective, stonelike substance of the skeleton. The image itself is so rich, so profound, and so easy to comprehend that it needs no explanation. Like Edward Taylor's title ''The Almighty,'' it is a concept of affirmation, mystery, and belief that requires no exegesis except an irrational one. Trying to explain either of them one becomes trapped in the inadequacy of language and disoriented in the linguistic fantasy of a rationalism insufficient to raise reader/perceivers above the hesitation, the ambiguity, and the awe they must feel when confronting mystery.

NOTES

1. Tzvetan Todorov, *The Fantastic: A Structural Approach to a Literary Genre*, trans. Richard Howard (Cleveland: Case Western Reserve University Press, 1973), 25 and *passim*.

2. Ibid., 38 and *passim*.

3. Edward Taylor, ''The Almighty,'' in *The Poems of Edward Taylor*, ed. Donald E. Stanford (New Haven: Yale University Press, 1960). Further references appear in parentheses in the text.

4. Donald Barthelme, ''Bone Bubbles,'' in *City Life* (New York: Farrar, Straus and Giroux, 1970), 115–24. Further references appear in parentheses in the text.

5. Jonathan Swift, *Gulliver's Travels* (New York: Rinehart & Co., 1948), fourth voyage, chap. 7, p. 252.

AUTHOR STUDIES

The chapters in this section treat a single author, and in some cases a single work, with a variety of approaches. They range from Mark Bernheim's analysis of the supernatural in I. B. Singer to David Ketterer's revolutionary reading of a science fiction classic, Jules Verne's *Twenty Thousand Leagues under the Sea*. Hans Ternes tries to locate the shift toward the fantastic in the early works of Franz Kafka, Laurie Edson explores the narrative tricks of Henri Michaux, and Stanton Hager traces the mirror mazes through which J. L. Borges "deconstructs" Western philosophy. In each case, the chapters isolate what is most characteristic in the authors' approaches to the fantastic.

I. B. Singer's *Yenne Velt*

Mark Bernheim

> Singer's ability to reawaken support for the irrational testifies to the
> necessity of that pole of cognition in human life. To use one of the
> author's repeated devices, it is "as if" irrationality could compensate for
> the bitterest blows the rational twentieth century has inflicted on
> humankind's image of itself.

In a recent two-volume collection of great works of Jewish fantasy and occult,
appropriately entitled *Yenne Velt* ("the world beyond" or "the other world"),
editor Joachim Neugroschel carefully established the validity of the fantastic
tradition in the Yiddish literature of Eastern Europe:

It would seem as if what we call "fantasy" is often an attempt at understanding what
rational and daily experience fails to grasp: forces, notions, possibilities frequent in our
everyday life, often at remote points in our coordinates of infinity and eternity. . . . The
Cabbalah . . . may have brought mythology into the Jewish religion and into Jewish
history. But the "fantasies," the "fairytales," the "fables" in the Bible and in . . . the
Talmud and what came after were not really regarded as fantasy by the Jews themselves,
until perhaps the Haskalah—the rational movement in nineteenth-century Judaism. . . .
The polarity of the rational and the irrational . . . does not historically exist for Jews, at
least not in the way we regard existence as rational and practical on the one hand and
fantastic and irrational on the other: a clean split, which literature and the occult movements try to bridge and turn into a dialectic. . . . Such fantasies and fairytales, such
mystical stories, actually preserve the unity of human life. They show that divine and
supernatural forces are quite human and natural; or vice versa; that the human and natural
are really integrated in a cosmos that allows for anything in the human or divine imagination.[1]

Neugroschel identified this essential unity in the Jewish imagination as fore-
shadowing the coming of a messianic age, an ultimate synthesis of both ration-

alism and irrationalism that would erase artificial distinctions and banish the dialectic that maintains the distance. He saw the two traditions—rational and fantastic—as inextricably linked, "so intergrown as to point out a recurrent theme: the attempt to reintegrate mysticism and messianism into religion and practical experience."[2]

I. B. Singer, conspicuously absent from the collection, stands in a curious position regarding this tenuous relationship. In numerous interviews and statements made over the past several years he has clarified what was apparent in a story as early as "Why the Geese Shrieked," from *In My Father's Court*. There, the impressionable young observer suffers conflicting emotional pangs over the battle of rationalism taking place between his mother and father. When the former produces bloody evidence and dismisses his father's ready acceptance of mystical possibilities, it is as if an autopsy has been performed upon the spirit of faith itself. One must recall the Orthodox repugnance toward autopsy and the ready acceptance of mystery in the Divine to grasp fully the conflicting desires of the young disbeliever, faced with proofs of validity in both faith and skepticism. Vacillation between these poles of cognition is a major theme in the majority of Singer's works. It is a mistake to view his efforts as directed toward a new synthesis, however, for the two elements do not join to create a new, third factor but retain their individual significance. Singer's protagonists often undergo crises of faith or belief; yet the result is not a new form of cognition but an apparent "resolution," usually ambiguous.

As a cultural voice closely tied to the Eastern European tradition of peasant superstitions and folklore, Singer has by necessity opposed the Haskalah emphasis on enlightened rational inquiry that Neugroschel saw as a major antagonist to unified cognition. In numerous Singer characters the tendency toward assimilationist views, antithetical to the tradition of divinely inspired faith, functions as a sure sign of confusion. If Neugroschel is correct in locating the source of tension between rationalism and irrationalism in relatively recent developments, which overemphasized Enlightenment values and banished instinctive elements of faith to the periphery of the tradition, Singer clearly belongs to an "earlier" time. Although he has now lived longer in this country than in Poland and has frequently set his stories in Brooklyn, Manhattan's West Side, and Miami Beach, much of what remains strongest in Singer harkens back to the life and customs of a relatively "unenlightened" culture. The persistence of an indefinable urge to faith, which reaffirms identity in isolation, moves many of Singer's most memorable characters and provides them with the opportunity to demonstrate their free will. Rejecting the limitations of consistently rational or irrational cognition, Singer sought throughout his works to expand rather than contract the limits of experience and redress, in the case of Jewish cultural prejudice against the mystical, overreliance upon the natural at the expense of the mysteries of the supernatural.

In a series of interviews published in the *New York Times* following his nomination for the Nobel Prize in 1978, Singer explained the "fantastic" elements of his work to interviewer Richard Burgin:

I don't really believe that there are two things: the natural and the supernatural. I will not say that gravity is natural and telepathy is supernatural. If telepathy exists, it has as much right to call itself a part of nature as gravitation. We call supernatural the things which we don't know, for which we have no evidence. For example, there is no real evidence that there is a soul or free will. The same applies to ghosts or spirits or to other entities whose existence we cannot prove (because we cannot take them into a laboratory and show evidence that they really exist). So we call them supernatural. . . . If these other things which we call supernatural really exist, they too are part of nature—although, for the time being, unprovable. Or perhaps they are unprovable by their very essence as is, for example, the existence of absolute ethics or other such higher matters. But in my view, ghosts, spirits, premonitions, telepathy, clairvoyance are actually part of nature. . . . Actually, our knowledge is a little island in a great ocean of non-knowledge. The supernatural is like the ocean, while the so-called natural is only a little island on it. And even this little island is a great riddle. . . . I try to call attention to the things which we cannot prove, but in whose existence I believe, nonetheless.[3]

Critics have called this reliance upon the "unknown" a "compositional shorthand" or "spiritual stenography" approaching the nature of a personal language. But even if one accepts the fantastic elements in Singer's works as serving his conviction that a writer's duty is to entertain with original tales and to avoid the boredom of the obvious and apparent, we are left with the question of the role of faith in his characters' lives, the reading of the "shorthand." Almost all of his stories present readers with protagonists who doubt the most essential tenets of established faith, and who have often devised their own credos, frequently in response to urgings from unknown sources, mysterious coincidences, or unexplained epiphanies. Figures who have completely rejected the possibility of faith, including even ritual practices of organized religion, are never comforted in their absolute skepticism but are tortured anew by doubts that reassert the primitive need to persist in believing *something*.

Singer has often said that he believes in the existence of God but rejects the notion that this mysterious being is in any way responsible or accountable to humans. On the contrary, Singer sees him as remote and coldly silent, "unfair to life," since he has failed to reveal his purposes or to clarify the meaning of existence. Because Singer is not devout in the sense of practicing a faith or maintaining formal religious affiliations, the significance of messianic belief in his works is diminished: whatever bleak optimism appears is more likely to attach itself to the human potential for survival or cultural persistence. Singer's works, for example, can be seen to validate the tenacity of Yiddish language and culture, through his continued affiliation with *Forward* as well as through his portraits of the vanished world of East European Jewry. Indeed, Singer's career itself would be unthinkable without the validity of the "other world" mirrored there.

Singer's ability to reawaken support for the irrational testifies to the necessity of that pole of cognition in human life. To use one of the author's repeated devices, it is "as if" irrationality could compensate for the bitterest blows the rational twentieth century has inflicted upon humankind's image of itself. In 1966 Irving Howe asked Singer: "Do you agree that at the heart of your attitude there is an illusion which is consciously sustained?" Singer replied, "Yes. . . . We all behave 'as if.' The 'as if' is so much a part of our life that it really isn't artificial."[4] This deliberately irrational self-deception that sustains the modern individual's existence includes the exploration of psychic possibilities, grotesque phenomena, occult and telepathic suggestions—anything, in short, corresponding to the interior drama of souls asking questions that they know are without answers, yet must be posed. Behind appearances, each claiming its own particular enlightenment, Singer's cynics find a mistakenly dogmatic human system. As Morris Fcitclzohn in *Shosha* speculated, "One day, all people will realize that there is not a single idea that can really be called *true*—that everything is a game—nationalism, internationalism, religion, atheism, spiritualism, materialism, even suicide. . . . Since we are sure of nothing . . . play is the very essence of human endeavor. . . . God is a player, the cosmos a playground."[5]

In this light we may note that Singer's success in dealing with irrationality and other-worldliness represents no small achievement. When Saul Bellow, another exile from the Jewish-American literary tradition, sought to write his most surreal and, in a sense, most Jewish novel, *Mr. Sammler's Planet* strongly divided critical reception. Between Bellow and Singer certain parallels, as well as wide distances, exist, and no place except in his own translation of *Gimpel the Fool* does Bellow approach Singer's other world more closely than in his portrayal of Sammler, the one-eyed biographer of H. G. Wells. Yet the uncertainty of theme and exaggeration of mood, often bordering on caricature, make Bellow's novel at times difficult to interpret. Mr. Sammler himself lacks the vitality and individuality that carries the best of Singer's protagonists beyond social polemics.

The importance of other-worldliness in Singer's traditional stories of faith and doubt may be illustrated by the title story of a collection issued in 1973, "A Crown of Feathers." Its protagonist, Akhsa, is a metaphysical seeker after truth who discovers multiple answers to every question relating to her position and destiny. From the start Akhsa is ambiguously placed. Her grandfather, Reb Naftali Holishitzer, is the community leader but has no suitable descendants to whom he may bequeath his glory. Already victimized by Divine indifference to human suffering, for each of his children has died painfully before him, Reb Naftali and his enlightened wife, Pesha, struggle over the shadowy destiny of their granddaughter. In the tradition of many of Singer's female seekers, Akhsa is painfully aware of the limitations forced upon her by her sex. In her attempt to achieve fulfillment she must cross traditional boundaries separating the sexes in social and religious functions but, once the initial barriers are crossed, must journey further into ambiguity.

Initially, Akhsa breaks with traditional ways by embarking upon a worldly education that mixes biblical studies with dancing, music, and French. After Pesha dies, unexpectedly, Akhsa moves to assume a role that is even further from normalcy and becomes surrogate consort to Reb Naftali. Completely alienated from her contemporaries, educated above the level of her society, she finds "her grandfather . . . her only companion. . . . Sometimes Akhsa would cry out, 'I wish you were my fiancé, not my grandfather!' and kiss his eyes and his white beard."[6] At this point the first of Akhsa's deadly questions is posed: when Reb Naftali assures her that he is not the only man in Poland, "there are plenty like me," she asks, "Where, Grandfather? Where?" (p. 5)

Indeed, Akhsa has already moved to distance herself from established beliefs and customs, and it is consistent that there can be no answer to this question in absolute terms, for there is no one exactly "like" Reb Naftali in Poland or elsewhere. Since Akhsa is shown lacking in the ability to discriminate between what is given to humankind for human comprehension and what may be but guessed at intuitively, readers can accept her later misreading of other vital indicators. Whenever she is faced with a necessary choice of actions, she will ask what is in a sense the wrong question and, rather than move according to her own will, affirming the validity of her own existence, retreat into criteria belonging to others—Reb Naftali and Pesha. Thus each suitor is judged by them, not by her, and the voices of other worlds displace her own. Akhsa has entered a part of the other world where she can no longer recognize a familiar landscape, and for a guide she will have her physical opposite, the "Z" to her "A": Zemach, a fanatical believer.

In every way Zemach is Akhsa's opposite: dark, small, and crude, where she is proudly refined and lofty; he believes in upholding faith by the letter of the commandments. Spiritually, he is all that she is not, for she has dabbled in a Polish version of the New Testament and is without the strength of will to choose between the versions of faith or reject them entirely. Instead, she again wills her grandparents' guidance by asking questions. The ancient Greek dramatists knew how to build drama upon ironies: Oedipus goes to Delphi supposedly to ask if he is his parents' son but flees before the oracle can finish pronouncing the unexpected reply. Akhsa's questions similarly drive this story toward, but never fully to, a discovery of self. Singer provides an other-worldly phenomenon, the crown hidden in the pillow, as the sign Akhsa never actually requests ("If you don't believe me, ask for a sign." "What sign?" "Unbutton your pillowcase, rip open the seams of the pillow, and there you will find a crown of feathers" [p. 10.]), but which arises in a sense unbidden from the multiple possibilities of faith.

In the years following her conversion and unhappy assumption of a Polish identity, Akhsa continues to attempt to find Divine guidance in others' wills, calling up devils and saints both, violating the principle that Judaism is not a religion that provides ready answers through miracles and Divine appearances. Yet there *is* a force that drives her to rediscover Zemach "the Teacher," the agent through which she will eventually complete an act of perfect faith, symbolized by the strength of the crown, eternally evanescent like her "salvation," which is also apparently her eternal punishment. Zemach, for all of his repulsiveness, is the counterweight to compromised faith and human usurpation of Divine prerogatives. (The rabbi opposes Zemach's harsh sentence upon Akhsa weakly: "Nowadays people do not have the strength for such rigors," the rabbi said after some hesitation. Zemach replied, "If they have the strength to sin, they should have the strength to expiate" [p. 22]). As in many other Singer stories, the most unlikely combinations of spiritual needs (here, Akhsa's and Zemach's), although often seen by others as incompatible, are most likely to lead to whatever fragment of truth humans may find.

When Akhsa approaches her end, she has one final vision of her grandfather, but when she persists, asking one last question, "When, Grandfather?" the image dissolves, providing no more answers than any previous spirit. On the next day, her last, she continues to wrestle with doubts and clings to her "one desire—that a sign should be given, the pure truth revealed. She lay and prayed for a miracle" (pp. 27, 29).

At this point the real miracle may occur, for without "guidance" from the god surrogate, the grandfather, "she opened her eyes and knew what to do. With her last strength she got up and found a knife. She took off the pillowcase and . . . from the down stuffing she pulled out a crown of feathers" (p. 29). Akhsa has now arrived, against all odds, at the border of the truth, but she cannot communicate it to others: Zemach has vanished, for her destiny has been fulfilled, and the others will never understand the one thing that "remained a riddle, [the] bits of down between her fingers. . . . What has she been searching for?" (p. 30) Although readers may for a moment smugly feel they can answer this question, they would be wise to bear in mind the challenge posed by the narrator in the final word of the story. Whereas Akhsa's invited satanic visitor had told her, "The truth is that there is no truth," the narrator clearly refines this solipsism: "if there is such a thing as truth it is as intricate and hidden as a crown of feathers" (pp. 15, 30). But we have been told at least twice before that it was an other-worldly "master" who had produced such a miracle, one clearly belonging to the other world that Singer posits and, at the high points of his work, allows us to glimpse.

Singer's children's stories reveal their other-worldliness with far more ease. As the author has noted, "In my writing there is no basic difference between tales for adults and for young people. The same spirit, the same interest in the supernatural, is in all of them. . . . In our time, when literature is losing its address . . . children are the best readers."[7] For these readers a tale such as "Zlateh the Goat" moves easily between natural and supernatural worlds. The young adventurer Aaron is sent with a sacrificial goat to the butcher's to help tide the family through economically difficult times. Although Aaron is against the loss of the faithful pet, he obeys until a force of supernatural intervention—in this case a gigantic Hanukkah blizzard that ends an unprecedentedly mild winter—intercedes to first trap and then save both Aaron and Zlateh.

When it appears that both of the innocents will perish as the price for adult expediency, Aaron discovers a haystack sufficiently large to shelter them both. Once inside, the two help each other to survive by supplying all the basic necessities—food, warmth, trust, and love. When Aaron's food supply is exhausted, he nourishes himself on Zlateh's milk, for "she seemed eager to reward Aaron for bringing her to a shelter whose very walls, floor, and ceiling were made of food." Their mutual needs ensure their mutual survival, and all else fades from view: "Sometimes Aaron felt there could never have been a summer, that the snow had always fallen. . . . He, Aaron, never had a father or mother or sisters. He was a snow child, born of the snow, and so was Zlateh."[8] Predictably, they are rescued, and Zlateh is reprieved by the grateful family, so that she may resume her role at the literal hearth. "Nature," human and animal souls, all communicate, at least in the other world where understanding is differently defined.

Singer wrote a number of stories more apparently fantastic in terms of their distance from the human. In "Shiddah and Kuziba" from *The Spinoza of Market Street*, Singer presented an ironic view of humanity from the viewpoint of a pair of devils whose underground home is invaded by human excavations. The devil mother, Shiddah, is tending her "schoolboy" son Kuziba, who has dreamt of the actual breakthrough into the human world that ends the tale. All of the fears and superstitions humans have of the underworld are reversed in the story, as when Kuziba asks for a definition of this creature he has been taught to loathe:

"Man!" Shiddah spat. . . . "Man is the mistake of God. . . . He has a white skin but inside he is red. . . . Throw a stone and he breaks; use a thong and he bleeds. In heat he melts. In cold he freezes. There is a bellows in his chest which has to contract and expand constantly. . . . He depends upon a thousand accidents, and that's why he is so nasty and angry. . . . Why some of them even deny our existence. They think that life can only breed on the surface of the earth. Like all fools they consider themselves clever."[9]

When such "monsters" eventually extend their explorations into the "home" of the devils, they create at the same time a passageway for the residents of the underworld in *their* journey upward. In all events, the "liberated" forces of darkness need not fear loneliness, for above there are "caves, marshes, graves, dark rocky crevices . . . dense forests and empty deserts . . . demons, imps, shades, hobgoblins" (p. 95). The faithfulness with which the same relationships and attitudes are shown to prevail on both sides of the "frontier" suggests strongly the closeness of the essences of both natural and supernatural.

Similarly, "Jachid and Jechidah" from *Short Friday* portrays a pair of fallen angels whose punishment for lustful impiety is banishment below to "that cemetery called Earth . . . where a dead soul immediately began to rot and was soon covered with a slimy stuff called semen. Then a grave digger put it into a womb where it turned into some sort of fungus and was henceforth known as a child.''[10] These living corpses are doomed to repeat on Earth their transgressions above, affirming the sense of predestined connections between kindred spirits, Cabalistic influences revealing the hand of the supernatural in seemingly mechanical existence.

Whether Singer localized his characters' strivings in the recognizable world of earthly doubts or occasionally ventured more fully into allegories of supernatural forces, his *Yenne Velt* appears in virtually every story and novel. As Neugroschel pointed out, a refusal to accept a ''clean split'' between the rational and the irrational ''preserve[s] the unity of human life'' by allowing ''anything in the human or divine imagination'' its possibility for expression as part of cosmic potentiality (Neugroschel, *Yenne Velt*, ix-x). Yet Singer did not ''synthesize'' these polarities of cognition; he explored, and sometimes ambiguously resolved, the apparent conflicts.

NOTES

1. Joachim Neugroschel, ed., *Yenne Velt: The Great Works of Jewish Fantasy & Occult* (New York: Stonehill, 1976), ix-x.

2. Ibid.

3. *The New York Times Magazine*, 3 December 1978, 46, 50.

4. Irving Howe, ''I. B. Singer, Storyteller,'' *Encounter* 26 (March 1966): 60.

5. Morris Feitelzohn, *Shosha* (New York: Farrar, Straus & Giroux, 1978), 134.

6. I. B. Singer, ''A Crown of Feathers,'' in *A Crown of Feathers* (New York: Farrar, Straus & Giroux, 1973), 4. Further references appear in parentheses in the text.

7. I. B. Singer, Preface to *When Shlemiel Went to Warsaw and Other Stories* (New York: Farrar, Straus & Giroux, 1969), n.p.

8. I. B. Singer, ''Zlateh the Goat,'' in *Zlateh the Goat and Other Stories* (New York: Harper & Row, 1966), 89.

9. I. B. Singer, ''Shiddah and Kuziba,'' in *The Spinoza of Market Street* (New York: Farrar, Straus & Giroux, 1979), 90-91. Further references appear in parentheses in the text.

10. I. B. Singer, ''Jachid and Jechidah,'' in *Short Friday* (New York: Farrar, Straus & Giroux, 1964), 82.

The Fantastic Pastoral of Thomas Burnett Swann

S. Casey Fredericks

Swann has produced a unique kind of imaginative narrative related to the older, conventional fantasy but one that requires us to turn our expectations in unusual directions: to an aesthetic appreciation of delicacy, peace, harmony, beauty, nature, and the erotic. His underlying feelings and concerns are a subtle inversion of the ideology of heroic fantasy.

The exotic tales of Thomas Burnett Swann may be connected with several genre categories of fantastic literature ("fantastic" referring to the introjection of an unmistakable impossibility, or "irreality," into the fictionalized world of the story). First and most broadly, Swann's narratives may be classed as "fantasy" fiction, because from beginning to end they are taken up with characters and events impossible by any known empirical standard. However, this technical irreality does not prevent his imaginary worlds and characters from being *emotionally* true to life, and often they are more desirable and attractive than so-called real life (Swann is certainly a fantasy writer in the erotic and emotive sense that we conventionally associate with the word *fantasy*). Still another dimension of fantasy, according to critics Eric Rabkin and W. R. Irwin, is its capacity for inversions and reversals of expected norms.[1] That is, the fantasy worlds of Swann present readers with "antinorms" and "counterrealities." This notion of Swann's worlds presenting fantastic counterstructures is central to the view I develop throughout this chapter and in particular should be closely associated with two other special categories, heroic fantasy and the pastoral.

There is a marked tendency to classify all fantasy that appears from science fiction presses or in science fiction magazines as heroic fantasy or, as it is sometimes named by its most enthusiastic fans and its most hostile critics, "sword and sorcery.'' Swann presented some odd problems for this classification. Although violence is a regular part of Swann's universes, and genocidal wars are never farther away than the horizon, his heroes and heroines are lovers, and the primary focus is on their feelings; although usually of the ''beast'' stock in origin, they are more humane than their ''human'' warrior opponents. These works are, properly, antiwar novels.

But look how Lin Carter, a sword and sorcery writer and editor, came up mainly with negatives about the author, because he expected him to be writing heroic fantasy:

There is a sort of parochial narrowness of scope in his mythological novels: the gods seldom enter into them, and there is seldom any note of cosmic grandeur or epic conflict. They are, however, unfailingly pleasant to read and consistently entertaining, demonstrating a considerable talent for imaginative invention, especially in picturing the personality and life-style of alien creatures who inhabit a prehuman civilization far closer to nature than that of man. Despite the cloying sweetness that obtrudes at times into these stories, and the lack of scope and grandeur in his plots, I have long been convinced that Swann has it in him to produce a truly first-rate work of fantasy, that he has yet to tap his full potential.[2]

In Swann's defense the overall chronological schema into which his major narratives fit, albeit with inconsistencies, has a scope of some five thousand years and presupposes a grandeur of vision that is not incommensurate with some of the best-known fantasists.[3]

Affinities with the very broad literary genre of pastoral is an even more unusual feature of Swann. Thomas Rosenmeyer, an important recent critic of the pastoral genre (*The Green Cabinet*), isolated several themes that pastoral has in common with Swann: an Arcadian natural realm, removed from human culture (especially from urban civilization); a heightened appreciation of peace and love and an utter rejection of aggression and warfare; a sensitivity to animal life, accompanied by a communal and fraternal attitude toward the nonhuman—an attitude nonexploitative and nonpaternalistic but always esthetic and often even erotic.[4] A primitivistic desire for simplicity (the basic, the direct) in life and feelings is an equally characteristic point of comparison.

The environmental emphasis in Swann's pastoral attitude toward nature is something special. Everywhere he showed a concern for plant, animal, and insect life; he showed the need to protect their apartness from human exploitation; he referred to a broad variety of flowers, trees, spiders, insect species, and birds in appropriate environmental conditions and connections; the forest is the central image of the natural world in a great number of the tales. Swann was particularly unusual in his appreciation of the rare beauty and ephemerality of insects. This is typified in the title of one novella, ''Love Is a Dragonfly,'' as well as in his Thriae (beautiful but cold-blooded bee-folk), Telchines (giant antlike creatures, not quite intelligent), and in the story of ''The Murex,'' where a group of ant-boys (recalling Ovid's Myrmidons) contract a polyandrous marriage with a female not of their species.

In the case of so allusive and erudite a writer as Swann it only makes sense for the literary interrelationships to get complicated and subtle here: in ancient literature the pastoral was self-styledly a contrasting response to heroic epic; in turn, heroic epic has served as the archaic model, and authority, for modern heroic fantasy—perhaps intuitively Swann gravitated toward pastoral in conjuring up an equal but opposite response to "sword and sorcery."

In ancient literature the archetypal pastoral theme of peace versus war is typified in Vergil's first eclogue, where the shepherd Meliboeus has lost his tiny estate in Arcadia (an imaginary landscape) due to the influences of war, while his fellow Tityrus is allowed by the victorious ruler to remain. Whether or not this fictive event corresponds historically to Vergil's supposed loss of his own ancestral lands due to Octavian's resettlement of his soldiers there, later pastoral writers follow the Roman, because a central fictional concept of the genre is a peaceful, natural, nonurban setting momentarily free from the immediate consequences of war—although its indirect and long-term influences are evident everywhere. Nor is the pastoral universe free from human frailty and mortality: its denizens are hurt by failed love, by friendship gone wrong, by death. Indeed, other ancient pastoralists, like the Greek Theocritus or the Roman elegist Tibullus, also considered their verses on low-key topics as a counterstructure to epic, a genre that they rejected as much for its content of war as for its overserious mood and its overambitious muse.

In Swann's works the Remus of *Where Is the Bird of Fire?* is a delicate, lovely boy with telepathic powers and sensitivities that represent a mystic ability to commune with nature; his twin brother Romulus is the typical warrior, bloody and cruel, fit to found an empire; Remus's dearest friend is a gentle faun. The hero in the *Day of the Minotaur* is a gentle, somewhat shy and retiring creature, a poet and a gardener; as a lover he is affectionate and brotherly, in contrast to the nasty Mycenean warrior Ajax, ruthless in war and lovemaking alike. Aeneas remains a likable hero in *Green Phoenix*, but it is because we see his touching, sensitive love for a dryad and their half-dryad child, half sister to Ascanius. She is the Green Phoenix of the title—a new Green child for the ever-dwindling world of the forest. She is a symbol of possible rebirth (the Phoenix is a very traditional Graeco-Roman symbol of rebirth and renewal) that is reaffirmed by Aeneas's preference for the wild forest world of the Beastfolk over the war-haunted world of the Italic Iron Age. The Old Testament Jonathan, son of the violent Hebrew king Saul, turns out in *How Are the Mighty Fallen* as a delicate, winged homoerotic alien in a prehistoric world darkened by the nearness of genocidal battles.

Swann's Remus and Jonathan and Aeneas are the opposites of their originals in ancient myth and legend. Hence Swann's "mythology" is typically a countermythology to the expected classical motifs, characters, and tales: the original human heroes are Swann's villains, and the ancient monsters turn out more human and loving and modern than their heroic counterparts. Swann also mixes his mythologies freely for effect: Old Testament themes and figures blend freely with the fauns, dryads, and centaurs of Graeco-Roman legend, but Rome and Northern Europe are not neglected: also, there is a mixed Near Eastern/Arabian Nights fantasy ("Vashti") and the make-believe Etruscan mythology of *The Weirwoods* (that is, it's really a blend of Greek, Roman and Celtic mythlore). Although Swann always grounded his tales in scholarly allusions and apparatus—and he is well read in prehistory and archeology—his vision of prehistory (for example, the fall of Jericho or the founding of Rome) and a prehuman civilization is completely fantastic.

As the Minotaur narrator of *Day of the Minotaur* insists, the Beasts are not animals; they are another kind of people. Indeed, there is a strong case for saying that they and we belong to the same species, because matings between Beasts and normative Humans in the story come out fertile and true. In still a deeper, psychosexual sense they and we together comprise an enlarged definition of "humanity" since the Beasts in Swann's fantastic mythology are equally the progenitors of modern humans as normative people. For example, Remus (*Where Is the Bird of Fire?*) is a Human with the special sensitivities of the Beasts as well as a possessor of a special sensitivity *to* them; thus he is described as a "mutant," a kind of "throwback" to the primordial Beast heritage; there are also many examples of hybrid Human/Beast offspring, like Thea and Icarus in *Day of the Minotaur*.

Earlier phases in Swann's fictive prehistory are set closest—both emotionally and geographically—to ruined, fallen, or decadent civilizations: the Minoans, Palestinians at the time of the Hebrew conquest (*Moondust*), Etruscans; beliefs and customs of ancient pagans are treated with more sympathy than Judeo-Christian mores, which are regarded as too narrow and repressive ("dehumanizing"). In this version of the ancient world peaceful civilizations were going extinct, although they had long antedated the harsh war and conquest cult that came to dominate the Western world. (As one respondent to the oral delivery of this chapter commented, Swann related the history of Western civilization from the losers' point of view.)

Later phases of the fictive history (*Bear, The Not-World, The Gods Abide*) are set in a northern landscape and deal with the remnants of a long-lost pagan sensibility. In this phase of the countermythology the death of the old gods comes as a loss, and there is a plaintive note to these stories as though written as an elegy on an extinct realm of the imagination. Yet as one title intimates, "the gods abide," lurking in secret nooks and crannies around the edges of our destructive civilization. In another way they abide in the hidden fantasy realms of our minds, as the heritage of the powerful love the Beasts felt for some of our human ancestors. Either way, these remnants are always furtive, elusive, and very vulnerable.

This new "mutant" hybrid mythology, along with the pastoral emphasis, indicates how Swann has produced a unique kind of imaginative narrative related to conventional science fiction and fantasy but one that requires us to turn our expectations in other, unusual directions: to an aesthetic appreciation of delicacy, peace, harmony, beauty, nature, and the erotic. His underlying feelings and concerns are a subtle inversion of the ideology of heroic fantasy. Loving—and falling in love—are everywhere, and almost all of Swann's tales may be taken, straight, as love stories. In response to a questionnaire Swann insisted upon this aspect of his work: "I think of myself as writing domestic rather than epic fantasy—stories in which the focus is on the daily lives of a very small group of people or humanized beasts. Someone once called my stories too bland. I prefer to call them microcosmic."[5]

Thomas Burnett Swann commanded a regard for literary, esthetic, and didactic dimensions to his work. He is a writer's writer and will continue to be appreciated by those with a taste for fabulatory classics like Ovid's *Metamorphoses* and Ariosto's *Orlando Furioso*. Yet Swann's fantasies also discuss morality and are informed with an authentic altruism, a concern for the feelings and needs of others, including our fellow nonhumans. Undeniably, too, Swann espoused a *carpe diem* philosophy: his morality is not puritanical, and although he showed an understanding of a whole range of human love relationships, pleasure and passion are not denied. Swann's environmentalism, and his exotic sensuality and androgynous sexuality, make him a liberal fantasist as distinct from a conservative one like, say, C. S. Lewis. Finally, as with so many other fantasies, Swann's worlds mirror the same polarized possibilities that face our own "real" world: the possibility for all-out violence and destruction of human and nonhuman alike, balanced against the beautiful, delicate, ephemeral Green Cabinet, where living freely and loving may well satisfy "the Beast in us."

NOTES

1. Eric S. Rabkin, *The Fantastic in Literature* (Princeton, N.J.: Princeton University Press, 1976), 12; W. R. Irwin, *The Game of the Impossible: A Rhetoric of Fantasy* (Urbana: University of Illinois Press, 1976), 8-9. A full discussion of critics and theories of the fantastic appears in S. Casey Fredericks, "Problems of Fantasy," *Science Fiction Studies* 5 (1978): 33-44. A similar review is Elinor Winsor Leach, "Parthenian Caverns: Remapping of an Imaginary Topography," *Journal of the History of Ideas* 39 (1978): 539-60.

2. Lin Carter, *Imaginary Worlds: The Art of Fantasy* (New York: Ballantine, 1973), 169.

3. Robert A. Collins, *Thomas Burnett Swann: A Brief Critical Biography* (Boca Raton, Fla.: The Swann Fund, 1979), 12-16.

4. Thomas Rosenmeyer, *The Green Cabinet: Theocritus and the European Pastoral Lyric* (Berkeley and Los Angeles: University of California Press, 1969), 6-18 and *passim*.

5. R. Reginald [Mike Burgess], ed., *Contemporary Science Fiction Authors*, vol. 2 of *Science Fiction and Fantasy Literature* (Detroit: Gale Research, 1979), 1096.

Arthur Schnitzler and the Fantastic

Frederick J. Beharriell

Although the generally accepted picture of Schnitzler is that of a
"scientist in literature," he has employed extraordinary measures to make
the apparently magical genuinely believable in three genuinely
preternatural, mysterious, and uncanny works.

For a decade around the turn of the century the reigning triumvirate in the theater
of the German-speaking world consisted of Henrik Ibsen, Gerhart Hauptmann,
and Arthur Schnitzler. Schnitzler also enjoyed for some decades an unsurpassed
reputation as a writer of fiction. After a twenty-year eclipse during the Nazi era
(although he remained a much-studied master of the one-act play in American
drama schools) a Schnitzler renaissance began about 1950 and is still flourishing.
It is now clear that Schnitzler is and will remain one of the most important
German-language authors of this century. Corrections in the generally accepted
view of his work and his worldview are therefore not without importance.

Until the decade of the 1970s the generally accepted picture of Schnitzler was
that of a "scientist in literature," a rational thinker calmly contriving plots and
blueprinting characters to illustrate abstract ethical puzzles. Sigmund Freud referred to Schnitzler as a "psychologist in literature," and Schnitzler described
himself as "more a scientist than an artist." Schnitzler's *Weltanschauung* is
usually characterized as a Voltaire-like skeptical, ironic, naturalistic rationalism.
His themes, plots, and characters were thought to have been purely imaginary,
"invented" to illustrate and work out preconceived moral problems. In a study
on "reality and invention" in his novella *Fräulein Else* I recently corrected this
view by demonstrating that in his works Schnitzler incorporated an important
and previously unsuspected component of personal experience, confession, and
portrayal of actual persons and occurrences.[1] I was able to establish this fact

from evidence in his autobiography, in various correspondences, and in materials from his posthumous papers, which had been unavailable to scholarship until the last ten years.

An element in his work of what had at first seemed a strangely incongruous irrationality, mysticism, or fairy tale-like mystery has long been identified as a highly sophisticated use of psychological insights and theories closely paralleling those of Freud. Schnitzler was, after all, a Viennese medical doctor, a contemporary of Freud, who had received the same psychiatric training and had, like the master, used hypnosis in the treatment of the neuroses. My study ''Schnitzler's Anticipation of Freud's Dream Theory'' pioneered in this work as early as 1953.[2] As recently as 1977 I demonstrated that the many apparent mysteries and enigmas of his best novella, *Fräulein Else*, can all be rationally understood as deliberate and conscious use by Schnitzler of depth-psychology concepts. Other critics have likewise demonstrated that the seemingly surreal or magical in Schnitzler's works is in fact a highly realistic exploitation of psychological ideas so close to Freud's that Freud in fact avoided Schnitzler for many decades because, as he said, of an uncanny ''fear of my own double.'' A typical example of this important achievement of Schnitzler criticism is the case of his mysterious ''Dream Novella,'' long considered a work of pure fantasy but now explained in terms of depth-psychology concepts by Hans-Joachim Schrimpf.[3] In the same way the once mysterious ''Threefold Warning'' has been psychoanalytically explained.[4] Nor was Schnitzler, incidentally, merely an exploiter of ideas borrowed from Freud: several studies have shown that Schnitzler had ''discovered'' some of these ideas before he could possibly have acquired them from Freud.[5]

Having attained this state of understanding, the Schnitzler literature now largely ignores or overlooks the fact that there is a small but very significant residue of works and portions of works where examples of the supernatural, of pure magic, of mysticism, of the ''fantastic,'' do indeed defy rational-psychological explanation. An analysis of this element in Schnitzler's *oeuvre* reveals the following components of what must be called the ''fantastic.'' There are a number of short works that obviously partake of the atmosphere, the style, and the content of the fairy-tale genre or the fable. These little works are meant to convey a message or lesson about human nature or about life, and the ''magic'' in them is certainly not intended to be taken seriously. Freud said in his essay ''The Uncanny'' that he ''cannot think of any genuine fairy story which has anything uncanny about it,'' because readers understand that they are expected to suspend their disbelief only briefly and playfully and that the magic in the fairy tale is not seriously intended.[6] Thus Schnitzler's story ''The Three Elixirs'' about three magic potions of a sort readers know can never have existed may be dismissed as an exercise in the fairy-tale genre that tells us nothing about the deeper problems of the fantastic. The same is true of the story ''Legend,'' whose very title betrays that this tale of religious miracles in the prehistoric Orient is not meant to be read as fact; it is true of the brief work ''For One Hour,'' where the ''angel of death'' makes an unconvincing appearance. These frank uses by Schnitzler of the device of fairy-tale magic symbolism as a kind of shorthand in parables and legends can be dismissed as not serious examples of the fantastic.

Different are the cases of three genuinely preternatural, mysterious, and uncanny works, where true enigmas of metaphysics and explorations of the nature of reality play a central role. These works are the strange and for Schnitzler highly uncharacteristic stories "The Fate of Baron Leisenbogh," "The Diary of Redegonda," and "The Prophecy." Unlike his fairy tales these stories have contemporary modern and realistic settings, and in each case Schnitzler has employed extraordinary measures to make the apparently magical genuinely believable and thus to create in the reader what Freud called a sense of the "uncanny." Strenuous critical efforts have been made to "explain away" the apparently surreal. Admirers of Schnitzler the master psychologist and scientist do not want to acknowledge any element of what must be called credulity, superstition, or naiveté in his work. "The Fate of Baron Leisenbogh," for example, involves a mysterious curse that does, in fact, kill the hero, and the work deals quite seriously with questions of superstition, magic ritual, foretelling of the future, spiritualism, and omnipotence of thought. Barbara Eger, however, was able to demonstrate that all of the seemingly fantastic elements in this work permit (although they do not require) alternative, natural explanations, if such is the reader's preference.[7]

The truly fantastic novella "The Diary of Redegonda" tells a dizzying tale of a process of mental telepathy lasting over a year, involving a fantasy love affair imagined so vividly by both partners that, although the lovers never meet, the woman is able to record all of the details in her diary just as the man has imagined them. The man accepts death in a duel as though his wishes have made him just as guilty as if the adulterous affair had actually taken place. This whole incredible tale is told to the narrator by the ghost of the man concerned, after his death. Yet the well-known Schnitzler scholar Richard Lawson has argued that all of this can be naturalistically explained through the application of Freudian concepts, the whole weird business being seen as an occurrence of telepathy within a dream within another dream.[8] Several weighty considerations speak against this interpretation. The most obvious objection is the completely realistic narrative mode and the fact that the alleged "dream figures" express themselves in carefully polished, often long and complicated, and always elegant sentences of a completely undreamlike kind. Schnitzler was a careful student of dreams, and in other works (like "Dream Novella," "Spring Night in the Dissection Room," and later *Fräulein Else*) he showed a consummate ability to recreate the true dream atmosphere. Nils Ekfelt's study "The Narration of Dreams in the Prose Works of Thomas Mann and Arthur Schnitzler" shows that "Schnitzler's day dreams and visions show no discernible relationship [in prose style] to his nocturnal dreams."[9] Thus if this story were intended as a true nocturnal dream, its style would have to be very different. "The Diary of Redegonda," the tale of a lengthy but imaginary telepathy-romance, is far too cerebral a structure for the narrator to have produced in a dream, not to mention that

Freudian theory, to which Schnitzler's psychology was very similar, would call for this dream to represent an unconscious love of the narrator for Redegonda, which is impossible since the narrator had never seen this woman. I am simply not persuaded that, as Lawson argued, the fantastic in this story can be explained by psychoanalysis as completely, as he said, as can Schnitzler's story *Fräulein Else*. His *Fräulein Else* is a thoroughly consistent piece of psychological realism without a hint of the unnatural; "Redegonda" is of a very different order, an excursion so deep into the strange realm where illusion and reality blend, with admixtures of telepathy and magic, as to defy all naturalistic explanation.

To solve this problem let us adduce in evidence another work. By demonstrating unequivocally the presence of the fantastic and the supernatural in Schnitzler's novella "The Prophecy," our conclusions will reflect back on and dispel the doubts about its presence in "Redegonda" and in "Baron Leisenbogh." This examination, which might be unnecessary in the case of a writer who is an acknowledged practitioner of the fantastic, is useful and necessary in the case of Schnitzler precisely because of those studies that argue that he would not and could not leave the world of science and the natural.

Our concern is one that was raised by the author himself. Toward the end of "The Prophecy" Schnitzler wrote, "Could not this whole business . . . be explained in a *natural* way?"[10] In contrast to Schnitzler's other works of fantasy, here the answer to this question must be an unequivocal negative. The hero Franz von Umprecht asks a magician to show him a scene from his own life ten years in the future. Instantly, and for a brief moment, Umprecht does have a vividly detailed vision in which he himself, now bearded, looking ten years older, and with a scar on his forehead, lies obviously dying on a litter in a forest clearing. There are other figures: a red-headed woman kneeling by the litter, a boy and a girl—evidently his future wife and children. Nearby stand two hunters with torches and a bald old man with a green scarf and upraised hands. For the next ten years Umprecht, like Oedipus, does his best to avoid situations that could permit this prophesied death scene to come to pass. Yet inexorably, and one by one, the details materialize in his life. He is struck by a stone thrown at someone else and acquires the scar. He marries a woman who eight years later dyes her hair red. He has a son and is forced to adopt a niece, and the children gradually grow to look like those in the vision. He becomes increasingly alarmed at the relentless pursuit by this mysterious power and at last is infinitely relieved to be asked to play the hero in a newly written drama whose final scene inexplicably duplicates—with the exception of the bald old man—the scene in the vision. He feels certain that this is the way Fate can make the prophecy come true while he himself merely *portrays* a dying man. For the first time he feels safe from the curse. But during the performance, as he lies on the litter in the final scene, the bald man unexpectedly appears, and the hero does in fact inexplicably die. At that very moment there is a tremendous gust of wind that almost extinguishes all of the garden lighting. A sketch of his vision made ten years before by Umprecht is found mysteriously to have gone blank.

"The Prophecy" is Schnitzler's most unequivocal foray into the realm of the preternatural. The original "prophecy," which could as easily have been cast in the form of the traditional verbal prophecy, is instead a vivid vision in which the hero Umprecht sees with photographic clarity and detail a scene from his own life ten years in the future. Had Schnitzler wanted to follow his frequent practice of leaving open the possibility of a "natural" explanation, he could have made this prophecy of death verbal. Then its fulfillment ten years later could be interpreted as coincidence or as a self-fulfilling psychological compulsion. But a *visual* tableau replete with numerous unlikely details, which then actually duplicates itself in *reality* ten years later, must be seen as a deliberate decision by the author to make any "natural" interpretation impossible.

It is difficult to avoid the conclusion that Schnitzler added several more really unnecessary supernatural elements to emphasize the inexplicable nature of the whole series of events. One would think that the realization of the vision is itself sufficiently wondrous. The whole additional motif of the sudden appearance of the prophesied bald man with upraised hands adds little to the story aesthetically but does make even more impossible a psychological interpretation. As if to drive an additional nail in the coffin of rationality, Schnitzler added the gratuitous disappearance of this man who, although he is a well-known local personality, is never seen or heard from again, alive or dead. When the envelope signed and sealed by the notary ten years before is opened, it depicts perfectly the final scene of the play that the playwright has just composed with no knowledge of either the vision or the sealed sketch. There is no conceivable psychological explanation of this correspondence. Nor must we forget additional elements of the fantastic surrounding the figure of the running bald man. This figure appeared in the vision and in the sealed sketch. The hero was vastly relieved to find him missing in the final scene of the play. But to his consternation he learns that the playwright had actually contemplated having just such a figure in that scene, old, clean shaven, bald, wearing glasses and a green scarf; but he had finally decided against including this character. When precisely such a figure unexpectedly runs across the stage we have a raising of the fantastic to the third power: first, the original prophetic vision is preternatural; second, the playwright's conceiving this figure ten years later is preternatural; and third, the materializing of precisely such a figure during the performance of the play is—although possibly a natural event—obviously contrived by that same supernatural power that caused the original vision and later guided the playwright's thoughts. All of the proponents of psychoanalysis and the defenders of Schnitzler's rationality will not be able to explain away this chain of magical events.

When the playwright, to prove the truth of the whole strange tale, goes to show the notarized sketch to his host, the sheet of paper has inexplicably gone blank. The previous day the ten-year-old sketch was perfectly preserved. This incident, again, adds little to the basic tale of the realization of an old vision. It does contribute powerfully to the atmosphere of the uncanny, since no amount of mental effort can cause a vivid ten-year-old picture suddenly to vanish. No character in the story, furthermore, has any motive for wanting the sketch to disappear.

Finally, we have the ultimate mystery of the death, precisely according to the prophesied timetable, of the hero Umprecht, lying on a litter, at the conclusion of the performance. Efforts have been made to explain this death as heart failure caused by the sudden fear and shock at the appearance of the bald man, who supplies the one still missing detail of the original vision. Such a death from shock and heart failure would not, it is true, be unusual in a Schnitzler work. The hero of "Baron Leisenbogh" dies unexpectedly in just this way. As Barbara Eger shrewdly pointed out, however, those who explain the death this way are ignoring the fact that Umprecht cannot have been greatly surprised: he was already expecting such a character to appear, in view of the long list of elements of the vision that had already come true in spite of his efforts to thwart their materializing. He had already prepared himself mentally by thinking of harmless explanations for such an apparition. In answer to the playwright's question regarding the bald man, Umprecht had answered, "I assume that one or another of the onlookers . . . or one of the local farmers might get unduly excited at the end of the play and rush onto our stage . . . but perhaps Fate will have it that, through one of those turns of chance that no longer surprise me, an escapee from a mental institution will run across the stage just while I'm lying on the litter."[11]

Lawson, in his Freudian study, made the main key to the story the hero's deathwish for himself. It is then necessary to assume a deathwish on the part of the playwright directed against the hero.[12] But there is really no evidence for these two deathwishes, and this interpretation leaves unexplained a whole series of preternatural events and coincidences such as the sketch turning blank, the appearance of the running bald man, Umprecht's being struck by a stone thrown at someone else and thus producing the prophesied scar, and many others. On the other hand, the psychoanalyst Theodor Reik, who early devoted a book to the psychology in Schnitzler's work, called this story an example of the Freudian concept of the "omnipotence of thought."[13] But again, this concept leaves unexplained many, indeed most, of the elements of magic and fate in the story.

It is relevant to these psychoanalytic attempts at explaining away the supernatural that Freud himself, who was a faithful reader of Schnitzler, knew this story well and discussed it in his essay "The Uncanny." Far from seeing it as an exercise in depth psychology, Freud actually criticized the story for depicting events "far beyond what could happen in reality."[14] With this fairly authoritative opinion that it is a story not of psychoanalysis but of the preternatural, we may perhaps conclude our demonstration that "The Prophecy" clearly proves that Schnitzler the ironic skeptic was occasionally drawn irresistibly to the world of the fantastic. It is a world, as Oskar Seidlin once said, where "everything has become uncertain, where there is nothing left to hold fast to, a world ruled by magic . . . a world of primitives."[15]

"The Prophecy" concludes with a so-called final comment by the editor (*Nachwort des Herausgebers*). It reveals that a medical doctor and a literary man sometimes "discussed all sorts of dark questions, especially second sight (seeing ghosts), parapsychology, and foretelling the future."[16] As Schnitzler was himself both a doctor and a literary man, this rather gratuitous piece of information sounds much like a shy admission by him of an interest in the preternatural.[17] It is much easier to find in Schnitzler scornful references to the preternatural such as this: "Do *all* souls transmigrate? Or are there some which after their first earthly existence, or after their thousandth, get tired of migrating, and live on as pure souls with nothing more to do than rap tables for curious spiritualists, giving silly answers—probably ironic—to silly questions?"[18] But the real ambivalence of this scientific-superstitious scientist-doctor-writer is perhaps best summed up in the following passage found when his *Aphorisms and Observations* was belatedly published in 1967:

Admission to the realm of metaphysical problems should perhaps be granted only to those who have proved themselves worthy by their decent conduct in the realm of reality known to everyone. Anyone who has not demonstrated a good mastery of the relatively obvious should be denied any activity in the occult. And no one should be permitted to enter the realm of the unconscious who has not conscientiously explored the realm of the conscious to its very limits. But naturally it is precisely those little-known areas of metaphysics, occultism, and the unconscious, so difficult to define, where the adventurers, the mental speculators, and the philosophical swindlers feel most at home. They can bring back from their ventures into these areas the most confused or untrue reports and there will always be fools and dullards who will listen to them with more credulity than to the scholars who are predestined by vocation, responsibility, and courage for such voyages of discovery.[19]

NOTES

1. Frederick J. Beharriell, "Schnitzler's *Fräulein Else*: 'Reality' and Invention," *Modern Austrian Literature* 10, nos. 3-4 (1977): 247-64.

2. Frederick J. Beharriell, "Schnitzler's Anticipation of Freud's Dream Theory," *Monatshefte für deutschen Unterricht* 45, no. 2 (February 1953): 81–89.

3. Hans-Joachim Schrimpf, "Arthur Schnitzler's 'Traumnovelle,' " *Zeitschrift für deutsche Philologie* 82 (1963): 172-92.

4. Theodor Reik, *Arthur Schnitzler als Psycholog* (Minden, Westfalen: Verlag J. C. C. Bruns, 1913), 28-31.

5. Frederick J. Beharriell, "Freud's 'Double': Arthur Schnitzler," *Journal of the American Psychoanalytic Association* 10, no. 4 (1962): 722-30; idem, "Schnitzler's Anticipation of Freud's Dream Theory," 81-89.

6. Sigmund Freud, *On Creativity and the Unconscious* (New York: Harper, 1958), 154.

7. Barbara Frame Eger, "Supernatural and Apparently Supernatural Elements in the Works of Arthur Schnitzler" (Ph.D. diss., Indiana University, 1971), 11-25.

8. Richard Lawson, "Schnitzler's 'Das Tagebuch der Redegonda,' " *Germanic Review* 35 (1960): 202-13.

9. Nils E. Ekfelt, "The Narration of Dreams in the Prose Works of Thomas Mann and Arthur Schnitzler" (Ph.D. diss., Indiana University, 1973).

10. Arthur Schnitzler, *Die Erzählenden Schriften* (Frankfurt: S. Fischer, 1961), 1:611.

11. Ibid., 614; translations by Frederick J. Beharriell.

12. Richard Lawson, "An Interpretation of 'Die Weissagung,' " in *Studies in Arthur Schnitzler*, ed. Herbert W. Reichert and Herman Salinger, University of North Carolina Studies in Germanic Languages and Literatures, no. 42 (Chapel Hill: University of North Carolina Press, 1963), 71-78.

13. Reik, *Arthur Schnitzler*, 20.

14. Freud, *On Creativity*, 159.

15. Oskar Seidlin, ed., *Der Briefwechsel Arthur Schnitzler-Otto Brahm* (Berlin: Selbstverlag der Gesellschaft für Theatergeschichte, 1953), 27.

16. Schnitzler, *Die Erzählenden Schriften*, 619.

17. As Eger, "Supernatural," pointed out (p. 218).

18. Arthur Schnitzler, *Aphorismen und Betrachtungen*, ed. Robert O. Weiss (Frankfurt: S. Fischer Verlag, 1967), 179.

19. Ibid., 71.

The Fantastic Travel Adventures of Henri Michaux

Laurie Edson

Henri Michaux has led us gradually into a Kafkaesque universe, where
the fantastic becomes the rule, and we soon habituate as the new order
becomes familiar. All of Michaux's works point to the subjectivity
inherent in reality.

Henri Michaux, one of France's most prominent contemporary poets, has ex-
perimented with a variety of genres, styles, and art forms since his first major
work of 1927, *Qui je fus*. Although he is usually categorized as a poet, Michaux's
oeuvre contains essays on dreams and on his poetics, meditations on Chinese
calligraphy and on René Magritte's paintings, five texts exploring his experiences
with the hallucinogenic drug mescaline, one film about mescaline, a book describing his evolution as a painter, several volumes of prose poems and poems
in verse, and five travel adventures. His recent expositions at the Centre Georges
Pompidou in Paris and the Guggenheim Museum in New York (1978) attest to
his importance as a painter.

Michaux's five travel adventures include *Ecuador* (1929), *Un Barbare en Asie*
(1933), *Voyage en Grande Garabagne* (1936), *Au pays de la magie* (1941), and
Ici, Poddema (1946) (the last three were grouped together in 1948 to form
Ailleurs). Most critics of Michaux's work distinguish between his real and imaginary travelogs, although some wonder which of the two groups is more
"real."[1] The works contained in *Ailleurs* are generally categorized as "imaginary," but critics immediately qualify their categorization by admitting that the
adventures defy definition and often bear an uncomfortable resemblance to events
in our own world. These works have been labeled parody or ironic commentary
by some, whimsical fantasy by others; some critics have spoken of a utopian
vision. Maurice Blanchot has even suggested that the meaning of these works

lies in their resistance to categorization and explanation.[2] This study shows that such resistance to classification stems, to a large extent, from the readers' inability to make up their minds concerning the nature of Grand Garabagne, the Land of Magic, and Poddema.

Voyage en Grande Garabagne relates the attitudes and customs of the inhabitants of Great Garabagne: the Omobuls, the Halalas, the Nonais, the Hivinisikis, to name a few. Although the names are clearly fictional, their descriptions seem real or at least plausible. The Emanglons, for example, thrive best near rivers, where their attitude toward others becomes mysteriously more welcoming; yet they will readily strangle a fellow Emanglon with breathing problems because of their great sympathy, which makes them cry at the sight of trembling leaves. Passing their fingers continuously through their hair reveals their fear of decaying ceilings. The Emanglon leaders prefer to give speeches from behind wooden statues of great men of the past, pretending to adhere to their principles. All Emanglons prefer not to cohabit with flies. Michaux acutely perceived events in our own world, yet poetically raised the habitual to the level of humorous fantasy. At the same time, his perceptions contain biting irony.

Many sections of *Voyage en Grande Garabagne* relate too closely to customs and habits of our own world to be construed as anything but ironic commentary. Fights between relatives, especially between brothers, are interesting to crowds. Crowds also enjoy watching fires. The rich fear the starving masses, who might destroy their neighborhood. Too much work prevents the Emanglons from sleeping. When a criminal is condemned, he is imprisoned and forgotten, but thieves are treated differently: they must be driven insane by administrative red tape so that justice can be satisfied. Eventually, Michaux posed the question of how the Emanglons have resisted the influence of other cultures and replied with sharp irony: "It's because, like a lot of small-minded natures, they are, by their very weakness, more rigid about being faithful to their petty habits and manias."[3] Readers feel uneasy in this playfully fantastic yet uncomfortably familiar world.

In representing the narrator as a traveler Michaux established an analogy between the narrating I, having just arrived, and the naive reader, unaccustomed to the world of the text. Both initially approach Great Garabagne cautiously, experiencing the strangeness, yet unwilling to pass judgment. In the land of the Hacs the narrator attends Spectacle 24, where two men in heavy wooden shoes attempt to kick each other to death. " 'So,' my neighbor asked me, 'what do you think of that?' 'And you?,' I asked, for one must be prudent in these countries."[4] Like the narrator, readers must suspend judgment until they can determine what kind of world they have entered. Since the narrator is "one of us," readers identify with him and willingly make him a center of orientation.

But Michaux soon withdrew this support. Surprisingly, the narrator adapts quickly to Great Garabagne, accepts its customs and rules, and becomes an interpreter for readers. Our adaptation, however, is less rapid: we hesitate, hoping to assemble enough empirical evidence to justify a choice between reality and fantasy. Yet our expectations are disappointed, for Michaux deliberately maintained the tension between the two.

The situation is further complicated by the tone of the narrating voice. As in Michaux's first two travel adventures, *Ecuador* and *Un Barbare en Asie*, the narrator relates the manners and lives of these strange people with scientific precision and an air of authority, as if he had carefully gathered the empirical evidence that we so desperately seek. Each section of *Voyage en Grande Garabagne* begins with a generalization that is developed and supported by example: "The Emanglons do not tolerate bachelors." "The Emanglons of the Avord peninsula have many troubles because of their houses." "The religion of the Mazanites displeases the Hulabures and revolts them."[5] These descriptions of the inhabitants of Great Garabagne are as believable as those of *Un Barbare en Asie*: "Indians do not now have a preoccupation with beauty. Beauty doesn't count." "The romantic Chinese is not yet born. He always wants to *seem* reasonable." "Malays like correctness. Batik is very correct. Their hair styles, even more so."[6] In both works the narrator speaks in a tone of authority that compels readers to accept his statements. The referential language serves to reinforce our belief in some reality that exists independently and precedes the act of relating. Clearly, however, Ecuador and Asia exist in the "real" world; Great Garabagne apparently does not. Since Michaux actually did travel through South America (1927) and Asia (1930-31), readers tend to accept these two works as "real" travel journals. Yet we question the reality of the third travel adventure, because the names seem fictional and the social injustices unlikely.

Readers seek entry into the world of Great Garabagne through their own experiences, of societal pressure toward marriage, religious persecution, deterioration of housing, or whatever is being narrated. The events themselves are not so far removed from their own experiences. But as the text continues readers find themselves becoming confused, for the narrated descriptions and explanations often depart significantly from what is normally construed as real. Yet the narrator continues to relate his experiences with the same self-assured tone that characterizes *Un Barbare en Asie*. Even when the material becomes patently unrealistic, as when fog transports a worm that then destroys the Emanglons' homes, the narrator continues *as if* nothing were out of place. He is still apparently concerned with presenting an objective portrayal of his experiences in Great Garabagne, and his careful attention to detail serves to deceive readers. Yet readers hesitate: the events do not conform to habitual expectations concerning the real, but the line separating reality from the fabulous is not that clear. It is not easy to dismiss these descriptions as imaginary, but it is difficult to accept them as real.

It is this hesitation on the part of readers that characterizes the genre of the fantastic, according to Tzvetan Todorov; as readers progress such hesitation tends to disappear. Readers may discover a rational explanation for the strange events, thus reducing them to "the uncanny," or decide that the events are genuinely supernatural and thus examples of "the marvelous."[7] However, in most of Todorov's examples the hesitation that defines response to the fantastic is felt by both the narrator and the readers. As in Gérard de Nerval's *Aurelia* and Prosper Mérimée's *La Venus d'Ille*, the readers' acceptance of a strange world depends upon the narrator's acceptance of it, since we tend not to question his reliability as long as he seems "one of us." Michaux's narrator no longer serves that function, however. If he were "one of us," we feel, he would hesitate when confronted with the events he reports; he would at least express shock when recording the torturing of children, the murdering of officials, the strangling of the ill. Yet he remains detached, cool, ironic. Our unease results both from the events narrated and from the way the narrator relates these events. Our last support in the strange lands of Great Garabagne, the narrator, is on the verge of crumbling.

Exasperated and confused, we wander alone through Great Garabagne, seeking explanation. We come to the Court of the Kivni, where so many rules of etiquette must be observed that uninitiated strangers rarely visit. The narrator relates the total disorder that resulted one year when the absence of rules was the latest mode: "Alas, the interpretation of rules that year, although perhaps not really difficult, was so exceptionally reduced that most of the people, for fear of making mistakes or appearing to make mistakes, would no longer leave their houses, or, seeing one another, would flee in haste, not knowing how to behave."[8] With this example Michaux pointed to our own confusion as uninitiated strangers in this bizarre text, where everything familiar has disappeared. Finally, the breakdown of communication intensifies as Michaux introduces neologisms and nonsense words into his descriptions.

Michaux has led us, gradually, into a Kafkaesque universe, where the fantastic becomes the rule rather than the exception. Inevitably, we soon habituate to our disorientation and discomfort. The new order thus becomes familiar and monotonous; the fantastic becomes the accepted "reality" of the text, as Michaux warned in his preface: "Certain readers have found these countries a little strange. That will not last. This impression is already passing. . . . These countries, one will notice, are in short perfectly natural."[9] Michaux is showing us that a large part of our acceptance of something as "real" depends on our habituation to it. Since our experience falls short of all possible experiences (as science is progressively revealing to us), our concept of "reality" is partial and subjective at best. All of Michaux's works point to the subjectivity inherent in "reality," and he often spoke of various ways he enlarged or modified his own reality through drugs, travels, imagination, meditation, painting, and writing. We are wrong to consider *Ecuador* and *Un Barbare en Asie* "real" travel adventures and to dismiss *Voyage en Grande Garabagne* as fantasy, for one of the functions of the fantastic is precisely to force us to reevaluate the distinction we normally make between the two.

Au pays de la magie is Michaux's fourth travel adventure. In this fantasy land, suggestive of *Alice in Wonderland* and the paintings of Magritte, waves roll along the streets, water remains contained after its container has been broken, and magic clearly dominates: "On a large road, it is not rare to see a wave, a wave all alone, a wave separate from the ocean. It has no use, does not constitute a game. It's a case of magic spontaneity."[10] Again the narrator relates his experiences with a calm detachment, showing no signs of surprise at such magical phenomena; on the contrary, his phrase "it is not rare" suggests an ordinary, banal occurrence. As we do in reading *Voyage en Grande Garabagne*, we hesitate: our own experience of reality differs greatly from the one portrayed in *Au pays de la magie*; yet the forces bear just enough resemblance to phenomena in our own reality (gravity, magnetism, radio waves, laser beams, tides) that we, like the narrator, cannot dismiss them as pure invention. Many of the magical forces are attributed to the influence of the Mages, a superior people with seemingly unlimited psychic powers. Because the existence of these people is never questioned, their capacity for magic is also taken for granted. The magic becomes the norm around which other phenomena and customs are explained: "No laughter before noon. Severe prohibition, followed without too much trouble, for one laughs little there, laughter. . . being accused of emptying the reservoir of magical forces."[11] This world is not chaotic. The narrator, himself convinced of its underlying order, attempts to introduce us to the rules that govern the society. In this work the fantastic functions by showing us that our ideas about reality are partial and inadequate, and mystery assumes a valid place in the world.

Michaux's fantastic universe frees us from the constraints to which we have grown accustomed. P. G. Castex, in *Le Conte fantastique en France*, spoke of our liberation from constraints imposed by reason, ordinary experience, custom, and rules of art.[12] Roger Caillois, in *Images, Images*, pointed to the characteristic break from the fundamental laws of the physical sciences.[13] Todorov noted the refusal of "realistic" time and space.[14] Since the fantastic deliberately confuses us by depriving us of traditional points of support, readers are plunged into a refreshingly new order. Thanks to the fantastic, disoriented readers enjoy the privileged position of flirting with chaos without running the risk of being destroyed by it, thus satisfying conflicting desires for order and disorder.

NOTES

1. See, for example, René Bertelé, *Henri Michaux* (Paris: Seghers, 1975), 7.

2. Maurice Blanchot, *Faux pas* (Paris: Gallimard, 1943).

3. "C'est que, comme beaucoup de petites natures, ils sont, par leur faiblesse même, plus tenus d'être fidèles à leurs petites habitudes et manies." Henri Michaux, *Ailleurs* (Paris: Gallimard, 1948), 59. Translations in the text are my own.

4. "Alors, me demanda mon voisin, que pensez-vous de cela?—Et vous? dis-je, car il faut être prudent en ces pays." Ibid., 12.

5. "Les Emanglons ne tolèrent pas les célibataires." Ibid., 31. "Les Emanglons de la presqu'île d'Avord ont bien des ennuis à cause de leurs maisons." Ibid., 33. "La religion des Mazanites déplaît aux Hulabures et les révolte." Ibid., 92.

6. "Les Indiens n'ont pas actuellement la préoccupation de la beauté. La beauté ne

compte pas.'' Henri Michaux, *Un Barbare en Asie* (Paris: Gallimard, 1933), 44. ''Le Chinois romantique n'est pas encore né. Il veut toujours *avoir l'air* raisonnable.'' Ibid., 174. ''Le Malais aime la correction. Le *batik* est très correct. Leur coiffure, encore davantage.'' Ibid., 219.

7. Tzvetan Todorov, *Introduction à la littérature fantastique* (Paris: Editions du Seuil, 1970), 25.

8. ''Hélas, l'interprétation des règles cette année, quoique peut-être pas vraiment difficile, était si exceptionnellement réduite que la plupart des gens, par peur de se tromper ou de paraître se tromper, ne sortaient plus de chez eux, ou, se voyant, fuyaient en hâte, ne sachant comment se comporter.'' Michaux, *Ailleurs*, 76.

9. ''Certains lecteurs ont trouvé ces pays un peu étranges. Cela ne durera pas. Cette impression passe déjà. . . . Ces pays, on le constatera, sont en somme parfaitement na-turels.'' Ibid., 7.

10. ''Sur une grande route, il n'est pas rare de voir une vague, une vague toute seule, une vague à part de l'océan. Elle n'a aucune utilité, ne constitue pas un jeu. C'est un cas de spontanéité magique.'' Ibid., 167.

11. ''Pas de rire avant midi. Interdiction sévère, suivie sans beaucoup de mal car on y rit peu, le rire. . .étant accusé de décharger le réservoir de forces magiques.'' Ibid., 195.

12. P. G. Castex, *Le Conte fantastique en France* (Paris: José Corti, 1951), 64-65.

13. Roger Caillois, *Images, Images* (Paris: José Corti, 1966), 42.

14. Todorov, *Introduction*, 124.

The Fantastic in the Works of Franz Kafka

Hans Ternes

In most of Franz Kafka's narratives the realms of the real and the supernatural are no longer separated or distinguished, and the protagonist/narrator shows no or very little hesitation vis-à-vis the extraordinary. What surprises readers is the ease with which the so-called normal reality is displaced and called into question.

An essential feature of most attempts to define the *fantastic* is the view that supernatural or abnormal events constitute temporary transgressions of reality or normalcy. *Reality*, as Eric Rabkin defined it, is "that collection of perspectives and expectations that we learn in order to survive in the here and now," and the *fantastic* involves a temporary "reversal" of those perspectives.[1] In Tzvetan Todorov's structuralist approach the *fantastic* is defined as that "hesitation experienced by a person who knows only the laws of nature, confronting an apparently supernatural event." If such hesitation is resolved by rational explanation, we have the *uncanny*, and a judgment of the event as purely fanciful produces the *marvelous*.[2] For C. N. Manlove the *fantastic* "is a fiction evoking wonder and containing a substantial and irreducible element of the supernatural with which the mortal characters in the story or the readers become on at least partly familiar terms."[3] The main difference between Todorov and Manlove lies in the reaction of the characters to the supernatural: for Manlove "wonder" or "astonishment" is enough; for Todorov "hesitation" or "insecurity" is essential.

Todorov's approach, although useful when applied to traditional literature, proves less fruitful in the case of Franz Kafka, for in most of Kafka's narratives the realms of the real and the supernatural are no longer separated or distinguished, and the protagonist/narrator shows no or very little hesitation vis-à-vis the extraordinary (hesitation and insecurity are not rare in Kafka, but they pertain to an inherent inability of the characters to take a decisive step, to react or respond out of conviction). What surprises readers, for example in "The Metamorphosis," is the ease with which so-called normal reality is displaced and called into question. The world of Gregor Samsa, the giant bug, appears with the same, if not greater, "reality" and intensity as the "normal" states at the beginning and the end of the story. Thus the extraordinarily different and abnormal drowns out conventional reality, the standard norm. The hesitation that Todorov considered the essential element of the traditional fantastic is shifted in Kafka from the narrator/protagonist to the actual reader. Although in the traditional fantastic the characters are thrown into a state of confusion about the extraordinary, in Kafka it is the reader alone whose conception of reality is constantly being challenged or at least called into question. If the concept of the fantastic can be extended to include the ambivalent reaction of the reader, the definitions of Todorov and Manlove—with this important modification—become applicable to Kafka.

An essay by Jean-Paul Sartre, entitled "Aminadab ou du fantastique considéré comme un langage," dealing with the fantastic in the works of Maurice Blanchot and Franz Kafka, will help us—it is hoped—refine and develop the concept of the fantastic as it pertains to Kafka.[4]

Sartre regarded the fantastic as a language all its own and as such as a particular category of perceiving and representing humans and their world. In Sartre's opinion Kafka saw the world as fantastic, that is, as an upside down, inverted image of the "normal" world, as a realm with its own categories (p. 125). Our "notion of means and ends" (an extension of the notion of cause and effect) is no longer valid in this world (p. 129). The "means" more often than not lack their appropriate "ends." As examples, readers of Kafka can cite messages without content or goal, windows and doors that open unto walls, signs that lead nowhere, and objects whose function is unknown or drastically altered. Thus things appear, in terms of language, as signifiers without reference to the signified, as "signs" devoid of meaning and purpose, as useless implements and tools. Humans are not excluded from this "rule." Sartre claimed that Kafka had inverted the Kantian imperative: "Agis toujours de telle sorte . . . que tu traites l'humain en toi-même et dans la personne des autres comme un moyen et jamais comme une fin" [Always act in such a way . . . that you treat the human in yourself and in others as a means and never as an end] (p. 132). It follows that humans too, are viewed as a means without ends, as beings whose purpose remains on the whole unknown. This is the reality, the fantastic reality of modern humankind and of the human condition within the world.

Representation of the human condition posed a difficult technical problem for Kafka. Sartre led us to an understanding of the difficulty by resorting to an analogy. To angels looking at us from the outside we must appear like ants or bees involved in seemingly senseless activity. But to show the world from their viewpoint would free readers from the basic fact of the human condition, namely, the imprisonment in a world of meaningless hustle and bustle. The trick for the writer is to present the "stifling immanence" of the world without offering any chance for escape. Presenting an entirely inverted world with everyone and everything in it upside down would, however, not grant readers a foothold in it; they would condemn it as totally chaotic and nonsensical and reject it altogether (pp. 135-36). Sartre put it this way: "ils [Kafka and Blanchot] ont supprimé le regard des anges, ils ont plongé le lecteur dans le monde, avec K., avec Thomas; mais, au sein de cette immanence, ils ont laissé flotter comme un fantôme de transcendence" [they have suppressed the glance, that is, the point-of-view, of the angels, they have plunged the reader into the world with K., with Thomas, but at the bottom of this immanence, they float a phantom of transcendence] (p. 137). The task, in other words, is to indicate vaguely a superior perspective without ever letting it become manifest, to show the state of being caught up within as seen from the outside. In his article Sartre identified the realm of the fantastic, the law that pervades it, and the method Kafka used to convey this world to readers. The last point, that is, Kafka's method of presentation that aims at infusing the "stifling immanence" with a sense of transcendence, leads back to an essential part of our definition, namely, to the ambivalent reaction of readers. Sartre's explication makes it clear that the fantastic world is not to be perceived from the perspective of angels or that of the insane asylum. It is an ambivalent perspective that issues, on the one hand, from the constrained condition of the fantastic realm and, on the other hand, from an unattainable superior outlook.

An analysis of the entire *oeuvre* of Kafka on the basis of the results we have arrived at would go beyond the format and the exploratory nature of this chapter. Such a detailed undertaking may perhaps not even be warranted. Our reading of Kafka's fiction has turned up three stages concerning the development of the fantastic: the first shows the formation and the emergence of the phenomenon, the second its fullest manifestation, the last its decline. By discussing exemplary works from each period we can convey, in a condensed fashion, what a more thorough approach would produce. The novels, particularly, despite their obvious relevance (which seems to be especially true for *The Castle*), cannot be handled justly within the bounds of this chapter and deserve separate treatment.

One of Kafka's earliest stories, "The Description of a Battle," written about 1904-5 and not published until after his death (in *Sämtliche Erzählungen*), offers pertinent information about the initial formation and development of the fantastic in his fiction. The story deals with various approaches and attitudes to life, all condemned to fail from the very beginning, because the author is out to prove that it is impossible to live life (one would have to add: without pain, guilt, despair, and so on). Two characters, among a cast of three, are very similar, if not identical, and are therefore discussed together. Both are extreme egocentrics. On the one hand, they are imprisoned in their own egos so that they are really unable to communicate with each other or anybody else; on the other hand, they are extremely weak and insecure and constantly in need of other people's support and approval. They are emotionally very unstable and unbalanced individuals of a highly sensitive and easily aroused imagination. Many of the extraordinary events that take place in the story can be seen as projections of an irritated or excited imagination. However, at this point we are not so much interested in these imaginary feats as in a central experience that both characters share.

The protagonist complains: "it takes enough effort to keep a hold on oneself during the day, but if you don't get enough sleep then fortuitous [literally "purposeless"] things will happen to you."[5] The supplicant utters at one point: "Sir, I have always such a craving desire to view things the way they may exist before they show themselves to me. I assume they're beautiful and calm in that state. It must be so, for I often hear people talk about them that way" (p. 218). The first statement implies that it takes conscious and untiring effort to keep the world together in a "normal" state; any relaxation or diminution of conscious control will unleash a kind of behavior in things that is contrary to our expected notions of reality. The second statement goes one step farther: the character asserts that the world appears to him in a way that deviates from the "norm," or from what the "average" person perceives. The fat man, the third member of the group, diagnoses this lapse into a different kind of perception as a condition of seasickness on dry land, that is, as a condition of disorientation and amnesia. As a result, the familiar world begins to show a strange face, the most natural incidents become incomprehensible, and the true names of things retreat into oblivion. The experiences of the two suggest that their perception of reality has been shattered, that they have come to see so-called normal reality as fantastic (in Sartre's sense), and that that encounter has drastically changed their lives as well as the world around them.

The following examples illustrate the effect of this experience: For no apparent reason the supplicant's thighbone is dislocated and his kneecap comes loose; the protagonist's hands dangle independently of his will as if they were strange objects. The most natural and familiar turns into incomprehensible jumble, a point that is made by the reaction of the two to a very naive dialog between two women in the garden scene. But the most conspicuous manifestation of the fantastic realm must be the mysterious, all-pervasive cry that disquiets and unsettles the exuberant attitude of the protagonist. Is it an expression of the pain and sorrow of humans' captive immanence, their true, that is, their fantastic, condition? These manifestations of the fantastic have to be separated from the primarily imaginary feats performed by the protagonist: he swims through the air; like a demiurge he fashions and manipulates the landscape according to his whims, and he can expand and extend his body over wide stretches of land. These impossible deeds seem to be clearly the product of a willfully manipulated imagination that is called up during moments of wanton exuberance or oppressive despair. In Freudian terms the willful manipulation of natural phenomena and the projection of the self may be viewed as compensatory actions of a weak and insecure personality, actions that may grant a temporary elation of power, however delusory that feeling may be.[6]

The two states we have described, one involuntary and the other voluntary, are not always separable, especially in one instance: As the world around the protagonist begins to fall apart he conjures up a fictitious love affair with a beautiful girl. The reason for that might be that he would rather attribute the disorder to an act of his own doing, that is, by willing it, than have to deal with it face to face. Toward the end of the story Kafka made use of an analogy that has direct bearing on an important point made by Sartre. He compared human beings to tree trunks lying in the snow: "We are, to be sure, like tree trunks in the snow. They apparently lie smoothly on the ground, and it should be easy to move them. But no, that is not possible, for they are firmly bound to the ground. But look, even that is only seemingly so" (Kafka, *Sämtliche Erzählungen*, p. 227). The analogy implies that humans are only seemingly bound to this world, an idea that calls to mind Sartre's definition of the *fantastic realm* as a world of "stifling immanence" above which floats the phantom of transcendence.

The story just examined is not entirely fantastic; most of the supernatural events can be explained rationally as imaginative projections of a psychologically insecure and unbalanced self. However, there are key scenes in which the fantastic becomes visible and is experienced as a strange and incomprehensible phenomenon; it is depicted as something mysterious, as an unshakable undercurrent of pain, as a power that shatters the world of coherent logic and order and that thoroughly disorients the individual who is in its grip.

"The Description of a Battle" plays an important, almost paradigmatic, role in our discussion of the fantastic in Kafka. The story is significant not only for its characterization of the fantastic but for the distinction it makes between two kinds of extraordinary events, namely, those that are the product of a hyperactive imagination and those that defy explanation. Kafka's early stories, collected as a group he called "Meditation," follow primarily the former pattern. The impossible event in "Children on a Country Road" is clearly recognized as an escape into the mythical realm of fantasyland, where children no longer have to go to sleep. The transition between ordinary reality and the supernatural is still marked. In "The Tradesman" the highly unusual episode in the lift can be seen as the compensatory expression of the protagonist's lack of real life experiences; his vital life impulses find an outlet in wild flights of fancy. The impossible in "Unhappiness" is not as fanciful as in the previous stories. Readers may hesitate in his explanation of the apparition of the child ghost, but the introductory section of the text indicates that this appearance is the result of a wish at least to momentarily overcome an emotional state of extreme isolation and despair. The unusual in all three stories is seen through the subjective perspective of the narrator, a perspective that at the same time supplies the key to an understanding of the events. Perhaps a distinction is in order: although the extraordinary incidents in the first story are purely fanciful rather than fantastic, they fall into the category of the uncanny in the last two stories; the laws of psychology, especially Freudian psychology, can provide rational answers to the mysterious phenomena.

The miraculous, imaginary feats that characterize the first phase begin to disappear about 1912 and with them definite hints that alluded to their sources, certain subjective states of the psyche; they reappear in several stories later, for example, in "The Country Doctor" and in "The Bucket Rider" but never again with the corresponding indications of the subjective states of mind. In "The Judgment," a transitional work that leads from the first to the second stage, the imaginary flights of fancy are totally absent, but there are still some psychological, motivational factors given that ultimately help explain the characters' actions. Among the fantastic traits that become apparent, especially after the father's "resurrection," are, for instance, the stifling captivity that emanates from the inexorable law connected with the father figure, the insecurity of the son vis-à-vis this power, and the readers' reaction of baffled incredulity concerning the son's almost serene state of mind during the execution of the sentence— as if he could escape, transcend his guilty existence. The contextual frame, within which "informed readers" read this story nowadays, will provide a rational explanation for the seemingly abnormal behavior of the characters. The readers' knowledge of Freudian psychology (one can assume that most readers possess that knowledge today) will make the text accessible on a rational level. Thus we hesitate to call this short work fantastic; it comes closer to the uncanny.

"The Metamorphosis" (1912) represents the purest example of what we have defined as *fantastic* in Kafka's fiction. The narrative deals with three phases in the life of Gregor Samsa: his professional life before the transformation (reported in Gregor's reflections on his former life), his life as an insect after the transformation, and his death and the ensuing return to the "normal" world, presented in a slightly different light in the end. The author concentrates on the second stage, a nightmarish state, not as removed and therefore made harmless as in the fairy tale and not as distantly perceived as in the horror story, but uncompromisingly real and immediate. Gregor's reaction to the transformation is extremely incongruous. To be sure, he is somewhat startled but not overly so: "And for a little while he lay quiet, breathing lightly, as if perhaps expecting complete repose to restore all things to their real and normal condition."[7] He does not accept the change as permanent at first, but hopes that it will somehow go away. The family members react just as incongruously if not more so. They treat the insect as if it were Gregor and thus come to accept the monstrosity as reality. The narrative direction of the text as a whole moves toward acclimatization and adaptation to the incredible.[8] Although there is practically no hesitation on the part of the characters, readers, torn between identification and rejection, are called upon to accept the impossible as a given fact of reality, knowing full well, at the same time, that such an acknowledgment is really inadmissible. Their reaction during the course of the events can be described in the following terms: in the beginning, incredulity, a skeptical stance mixed with aversion; then, slow and reluctant acclimatization to the monstrous and a certain sympathy for Gregor (at the same time there is a countermovement in the readers' emotional reaction to the family's behavior: from a degree of commiseration to near dislike); finally, a compassionate form of relief over Gregor's fate (coupled simultaneously with severe dislike for the family's lack of compassion). Hence readers are constantly torn between compassion and aversion. Their overall reaction remains ambiguous and ambivalent throughout. They feel compelled to accept the abnormal, because it is presented with even greater intensity and authority of truth than "normal" reality; yet they never quite acquiesce to the inadmissible, for that would make their own stance fantastic.[9]

The elements that constitute the fantastic in "The Metamorphosis" are the hesitation and ambivalence of the reader vis-à-vis the monstrous and the characters' reactions to it; the oppressive atmosphere of Gregor's captive condition; the loss of orientation and the disintegration of human consciousness; and finally, the sense of transcendence that surfaces in a paradoxical counterdevelopment: as Gregor loses his human nature and as the instinctual demands of the animal grow, he begins intuitively to comprehend spiritual matters, such as music, as he never did before. Despite the relentless determination of a gruesome fate that crushes Gregor, his departure from this world has an air of dreamy lightness and serene spirituality about it. Like Georg Bendemann he leaves willingly and without rancor: "He thought of his family with tenderness and love. The decision that he must disappear was one that he held to even more strongly than his sister, if that were possible. In this state of vacant and peaceful meditation he remained until the tower clock struck three in the morning.... Then his head sank to the floor of its own accord and from his nostrils came the last flicker of his breath."[10]

Beginning already with *The Trial* (1914), but especially since "The Country Doctor" (1916-17), the tendency toward abstraction, parabolic reflection, and generalization that were always present in Kafka's fiction to a degree increase to an extent that threatens the nature of the fantastic.[11] To be sure, Kafka's parables and metaphors are not to be equated with the traditional devices; they often remain paradoxical and unfathomable. Nevertheless, they hold out the promise of revelation, and some of them do indeed point to experiential knowledge of general validity based on Kafka's own subjective experience but projected onto a universal level.

Kafka wrote in a letter to Milena that he was constantly trying to convey something unexplainable, something that was in his bones and that he associated with a general fear of practically all things.[12] Within the context of our analysis this fear was connected with the impending invasion of the inverted world and the dissolution of "normal" reality. As Kafka continued to explore this perplexing experience he succeeded in representing the enigma in a parabolic form that retains the paradox and, moreover, fixes the configuration of the situation. The parable "Before the Law" illustrates the point: The man from the country follows a calling that freezes him in a state of self-delusion. His condition of "frozen ambivalence" is the prison that Sartre spoke of, and his hope to enter the law is the phantom, the illusory delusion of transcending it. The parable "Before the Law" is, in other words, a parabolic embodiment of the human condition of captivity coupled with the illusion of transcendence. The later novel *The Castle* (1922) is in essence an elaborate parabolic reflection of this basic pattern. The parabolic-metaphorical method—besides holding out the promise of solving the problem—tends to steer readers onto a level of reflection and philosophical consideration that grants them distance from the fictional world. The method we have just described, even though it seems to affect most of the works after *The Trial*, has not been applied to all works with the same consistency. "A Country Doctor" and "The Bucket Rider" (1917) seem to defy the general pattern. Both stories are of a metaphorical quality that is inexhaustible. In the case of "A Country Doctor" readers are caught in a web of puzzled ambivalence. The symbolic imagery of the pigsty, the horses, the name "Rose," and the wound will guide them toward a psychological reading; however, only up to a point, for too many unanswered questions remain. The metaphorical reading also turns out unsatisfactory, for the metaphors that fit the text are too numerous and often too general to be meaningful. The situation is not much different in "The Bucket Rider": one is tempted to seek answers to the incredible events in the psychological makeup of the protagonist but cannot really fit all pieces together and turns to a metaphorical reading with little or only partial success. Without too much difficulty one can recognize the fundamental pattern of the fantastic condition. The "normal" life of the characters in the two stories has been shattered; in the attempt to overcome, that is, transcend, an untenable situation, they are caught in a frozen realm that allows them no way out. Depending on the readers' perspectives, approaching the texts on a psychological, metaphorical, parabolical, or allegorical level, the two narratives fall somewhere between the marvelous-fantastic and the uncanny-fantastic. Most of the works after 1914 are, however, because of overt metaphorical intentions, not fantastic.

This study has attempted to show that the fantastic is connected with Kafka's basic vision of the world. The vision was termed "fantastic" when readers were at a loss to explain the extraordinary in rational or other ways and yet thought that there was meaning in the inexplicable. The progressively clearer elaboration of Kafka's vision on the more reflective level, by the metaphorical-parabolic method, tended to diminish the ambivalence, the hesitating insecurity, of readers by increasing their distance to the fictional world and by allowing them to perceive a certain pattern in the chaotic disorder. Wherever and whenever the fantastic does appear, its function is one of unsettling and shattering the readers' complacent view of the world by confronting them with a reality that is presented both as absolutely true as well as unbearably oppressive.

NOTES

1. Eric S. Rabkin, *The Fantastic in Literature* (Princeton, N.J.: Princeton University Press, 1976), 12, 227.

2. Tzvetan Todorov, *The Fantastic: A Structural Approach to a Literary Genre*, trans. Richard Howard (Cleveland: Case Western Reserve University Press, 1973), 25, 33.

3. C. N. Manlove, *Modern Fantasy: Five Studies* (Cambridge: Cambridge University Press, 1975), 1.

4. Jean-Paul Sartre, "Aminadab ou du fantastique considéré comme un langage," *Situations* 1 (1947): 124-39. Further references appear in parentheses in the text; translations are mine.

5. Franz Kafka, "The Description of a Battle," in *Sämtliche Erzählungen* (Frankfurt: Fischer Taschenbuch Verlag, 1972), 204. Further references appear in parentheses in the text.

6. Freud associated such powers of the mind ("the narcissistic over-estimation of one's own psychic processes...the omnipotence of thought") with the animistic phase, still present in every individual's early development. Sigmund Freud, *Das Unheimliche* (Frankfurt: Fischer Doppelpunkt, 1963), 69.

7. Franz Kafka, *The Penal Colony* (New York: Schocken, 1972), 73.

8. F. D. Luke, "The Metamorphosis," in *Franz Kafka Today*, ed. Angel Flores and Homer Swander (Madison: University of Wisconsin Press, 1964), 28-36; Todorov, *The Fantastic*, 171.

9. Todorov, *The Fantastic*, 172.

10. Kafka, *Penal Colony*, 127.

11. Peter U. Beicken, *Franz Kafka: Eine kritische Einführung in die Forschung* (Frankfurt: Athenaüm Fischer Taschenbuch Verlag, 1974), 294.

12. Franz Kafka, *Briefe an Milena*, Ed. Willy Haas (Frankfurt: Fischer, 1952), 249.

Palaces of the Looking Glass: Borges's Deconstruction of Metaphysics

Stanton Hager

> Like the Tlönists J. L. Borges thought that "metaphysics is a branch of fantastic literature." Because this is not readily apparent to the metaphysicians and their believers Borges's fictional strategy was to invent and deconstruct metaphors of metaphysical systems.

> Confound this crystal palace! One sees everything too many times. It's like a dream.
> —G. K. Chesterton, "The Sins of Prince Saradine"

In the preface to Ronald Christ's *Narrow Act: Borges' Art of Allusion*, J. L. Borges wrote: "I am neither a thinker nor a moralist, but simply a man of letters who turns his own perplexities and that respected system of perplexities we call philosophy into the forms of literature."[1] More often than not, the forms that Borges's fictions take in their investigations of philosophical perplexities are fantastic. Like the Tlönists in his story "Tlön, Uqbar, and Orbis Tertius," Borges thought that "metaphysics is a branch of fantastic literature."[2] In recalling his *Anthology of Fantastic Literature*, coedited with Silvina Ocampo and Adolfo Bioy Casares, Borges noted the "culpable omission of the unsuspected and greatest masters of the genre: Parmenides, Plato, John Scotus Erigena, Albertus Magnus, Spinoza, Leibnitz, Kant, Frances Bradley."[3] However, what he was forced to leave out as editor he made the persistent source and subject of his own writing.[4]

To achieve the fantastic Borges did not resort to griffins, trolls, and unicorns (he confined his interest in these creatures to his bestiary *Book of Imaginary Beings*) but turned to topoi of metaphysics such as life is a dream, the many and the One, and the world as Text. Because the fantastic nature of such topoi is not readily apparent to the metaphysicians and their believers who make them the cornerstones of rational, systematic edifices of ontological explanation, Borges's fictional strategy, to borrow Martin Heidegger's metaphor, was to "deconstruct" those edifices;[5] or, more precisely, it was to invent and deconstruct *metaphors* of metaphysical systems. He did so for no mean or pedantic reasons— to ridicule metaphysics, to demonstrate the fallacies of particular systems, or to reconstruct his own system, for he had none—but to admire it more, to reveal philosophy's and theology's kinship with poetry, music, painting, and other constructing/deconstructing activities of the human imagination in its attempts to mirror or explain the unexplainable universe.

In a much-quoted passage from his essay "The Wall and the Books," Borges wrote: "Music, states of happiness, mythology, faces molded by time, certain twilights and certain places—all these are trying to tell us something, or have told us something we should not have missed, or are about to tell us something; that imminence of a revelation that is not yet produced is, perhaps, the aesthetic reality."[6] To feel imminently near a revelation that is never quite produced was not only the aesthetic reality for Borges, it was the central human experience. If, as Heidegger defined it, the distinguishing characteristic of humankind's *being* is its ability and need to inquire into the nature of Being, Borges would only add that it is also a part of humankind's being ultimately to recognize and reject the illusion of its "answers" to its inquiries, to return continually to a state of teasing and unsatisfied "imminence." Time and again in Borges's fictions the illusion of satisfaction is created and dissolved; closed, rational systems of explanation are elaborately constructed and as elaborately deconstructed.

The mirror and the labyrinth are Borges's chief tools of deconstruction. Borges traced his lifelong fascination with mirrors to a childhood fear. He related this fear in a number of places, including a conversation with Richard Burgin:[7]

Burgin: I wonder how and when you began to use another of your favorite images, the image of the mirror.

Borges: Well, that, that also goes with the earliest fears of my childhood, being afraid of mirrors, being afraid of mahogany, being afraid of being repeated.[8]

In the same conversation Borges recounted another early fear: "I don't know why, but when I first read *The Republic*, when I first read about the types, I felt a kind of fear.... I felt that the whole world of Plato, the world of eternal beings, was somehow uncanny and frightening."[9] As with mirrors, Platonism and other forms of philosophical idealism became lifelong fascinations. One can easily guess that the initial fright at Platonism was the same as that caused by the reflecting surfaces of mahogany, ivory, water, and polished metal, for in Platonism reality and identity are made illusory: by duplication all substance becomes shadow. Frederick Goldin, in his book *The Mirror of Narcissus and the Courtly Love Lyric*, wrote:

One reason for the frequency of the mirror figure is that the medieval world view was essentially Platonic: the objects of actual experience were known and judged by their

drives to the remote scene of the second crime, the Rue de Toulon, readers are told that "to the left and right of the automobile, the city disintegrated" (p. 132); and the Rue de Toulon itself is described as "that dirty street where cheek by jowl are the peepshow and the milk store, the bordello and the women selling Bibles" (p. 133). Reality is manifestly not ordered and intelligible. Moreover, and perhaps most significant, it is carnival time in the city—a time of the abandonment of reason. The reality through which "Lönnrot the reasoner" moves is a chaos, a dream, an intoxication. The carnival metaphor is reinforced by a fever metaphor that Scharlach provides at the end of the story in relating that he had received his own vision of reality as a labyrinth of mirrors during a feverish delirium and that he had decided then that it would be by means of such a labyrinth that he would entrap and kill Lönnrot.

However, although it is Treviranus the empiricist, and not Lönnrot the idealist, who is vindicated by the story's plot, and although Lönnrot suffers a fatal defeat not often suffered by the sleuths of the genre, he is by no means ridiculed by the story. His rabbinical solution, although "wrong," *remains* more interesting than the Inspector's; for Borges being interesting is more important than being correct. Besides, even though the series of crimes began accidentally, upon that accident Scharlach *did* construct a secret design to which the Inspector, but not Lönnrot, was oblivious. The import is that reality is neither pure accident nor pure design but a combination of both and that a worldview that is either wholly empirical or wholly metaphysical is not just inadequate; it is fantastic. As the empiricist is at all times vulnerable to a dumbfounding recognition of a secret order or realm beyond his scheme (the gothic is full of such moments of fantastic revelation), so the metaphysician is vulnerable to a recognition of the limits of his scheme—of the corporeal limits of time, space, and human reason.

Borges employed construction and deconstruction not only in his fictions but in his essays. Most elaborately constructed and deconstructed of all of his essays is "A New Refutation of Time." The essay consists of three parts: Prologue, part A—which, as Borges explained in the Prologue, is the original article published in 1944—and part B, which is the revised article published in 1946. The argument of both articles is that time is annihilated by duplication: "[W]e can postulate two identical moments. Having postulated that identity, we must ask: Are those identical moments the same? Are the enthusiasts who devote a lifetime to a line by Shakespeare not literally Shakespeare?"[13]

The argument is constructed upon the idealist principles of David Hume and Berkeley; or, rather, it is a deconstruction of those principles: in Borges's words at the outset of the essay, "it is the anachronous *reductio ad absurdum* of an obsolete system (Idealism) or, what is worse, the feeble machination of an Argentine adrift on the sea of metaphysics" (p. 180)—a wry sentence in which Borges not only announces his intention to deconstruct the idealists but also deconstructs, or undermines, his deconstruction with the word *anachronous* and the whole demurring last clause—not that it is unusual to find in Borges's essays a thesis that does not believe in itself, that argues against itself while asserting itself. Deconstructing his deconstruction further, he drew attention to the "subtle joke" of the essay's title, which is a "*contradictio in adjecto*, because to say that a refutation is new (or old) is to attribute to it a predicate of a temporal nature, which restores the notion that the subject attempts to destroy" (p. 181). As a final stroke, Borges ended this brief five-hundred-word Prologue—dense with the rubble of a demolished argument he has not even begun to construct— with an echo of the opening. He dedicated the essay to Juan Cristósmo Lafinur, who "like all men. . .was born at the wrong time" (p. 181). That is, Lafinur's life, like that of all humans, is anachronous. Thus Borges was writing an anachronous argument dedicated to the anachronous lives lived by all people— anachronicity undermining both the achronicity of the idealist argument that he set forth in parts A and B *and* the sequentiality that saturates language, as that which is out of place in time is neither atemporal nor sequential.

Borges constructed his refutation of time first in part A and then again in its mirror duplication in part B. He did not choose to collapse the two articles into one, as he explained, because reading the pair of texts would make understanding the "indocile subject" easier (pp. 180-81). More wryly, more obviously, he intended the presentation of two mirrored moments—himself refuting time—in articles that must be read one after the other as both proof and disproof of his argument. But although there is a constant wryness of proof and confutation, avowal and disavowal, construction and deconstruction, that makes this essay his deftest and wittiest, poignancy is also present. Borges made metaphysics the source and subject of his writing because he was haunted by it: throughout his life he "sensed a refutation of time, which. . .comes to visit me at nights and in the weary dawns with the illusory force of an axiom" (p. 181). His refutation of time, although disbelieved and playfully mocked by his logical being, is deeply felt, is axiomatic for another part of his being—the being that moves through the haunting landscape of the story fragment that closes part A. In the midst of his witty "*reductio ad absurdum* of an obsolete system" is a poignant and persuasive avowal of that system, providing a temporary resolution of the essay's antinomies. Although time can be easily refuted at the level of the senses, its refutation is not so easy at the intellectual level, because the idea of succession is inseparable from the intellect. Temporality and atemporality have their separate and legitimate spheres. But having launched the argument a second time, in part B, guided it carefully with repetition and variation, persuasively drawing upon Hume, Berkeley, and Chuang Tzu, he brought part B and the essay as a whole not to another resolution but to an almost despairing disavowal:

And yet, and yet—To deny temporal succession, to deny the ego, to deny the astronomical universe, are apparent desperations and secret assuagements.... Time is the substance I am made of. Time is a river that carries me away, but I am the river; it is a tiger that mangles me, but I am the tiger; it is a fire that consumes me, but I am the fire. The world, alas, is real; I, alas, am Borges. (p. 197)

Thus the essayist ends with a revelation suffered by so many of the characters of his fictions: having come to the limits of reason, of imagination, of metaphysical construction, he must admit the "and yet" that demolishes and makes fantastic all of his schemes. Although Borges found the blithe, fantastic denials of reality of Plato, Berkeley, Hume, and others compelling, unlike his idealist predecessors he could not escape waking from his dreams of mirrors, tigers, and labyrinths to sequential time, to Scharlach's gun, to the seeker's "fall, which is infinite."

NOTES

1. Ronald Christ, *The Narrow Act: Borges' Art of Allusion* (New York: New York University Press, 1969), ix.

2. Jorge Luis Borges, *Ficciones*, trans. Anthony Kerrigan et al. (New York: Grove Press, 1962), 25. Further references appear in parentheses in the text.

3. Jorge Luis Borges, *Discusión*, in vol. 1 of *Obras Completas* (Buenos Aires: Emecé, 1969), 172.

4. Borges himself commented repeatedly that he appropriated metaphysics for esthetic uses and that he regarded it as fantastic. My contribution is to examine the "vertiginous dialectic" of construction and deconstruction as a strategy for revealing the fantastic in metaphysics. Critics who discussed Borges's antinomic style in other terms include J. Alazraki, "Oxymoronic Structure in Borges' Essays," *Books Abroad* 45 (1971): 421-27; and F. Weber, "Borges' Stories: Fiction and Philosophy," *Hispanic Review* 36 (1968): 124-41. D. P. Gallagher [*Modern Latin American Literature* (New York and London: Oxford University Press, 1973), 118] hit on my thesis in a passing remark: "Characteristically, Borges has erected a grandly metaphysical design in this story ["Guayaquil"] only self-mockingly to demolish it."

5. As Martin Heidegger ["Introduction to *Being and Time*," in *Basic Writings*, ed. and trans. David Krell (New York: Harper & Row, 1977), 67-78] sought not to destroy the philosophic tradition to which he applied the technique of deconstruction (*Destruktion*) but to reveal its limitations, so Borges deconstructed not nihilistically to convince us of the chaos of being but to reveal the interstices of chaos in the fabric of design; the sense of design is no less compelling than the sense of chaos. His implicit theory of the fantastic does not concern utter improbabilities or total invention but the strangeness of the real, familiar, and intelligible. The technique of deconstruction lays bare this strangeness.

6. Jorge Luis Borges, "The Wall and the Books," in *Other Inquisitions*, trans. Ruth Simms (New York: Washington Square Press, 1966), 3-4. Further references appear in parentheses in the text.

7. Cf. Borges's poem "Mirrors" and the fictional sketch "The Draped Mirrors," in *Dreamtigers*, trans. Mildred Boyer and Harold Morland (Austin: University of Texas Press, 1964), 27-28, 60-61.

8. Richard Burgin, *Conversations with Jorge Luis Borges* (New York: Avon, 1970), 31.

9. Ibid., 27.

10. Frederick Goldin, *The Mirror of Narcissus in the Courtly Love Lyric* (New York: Cornell University Press, 1967), 4.

11. The "rabbinical solution" is ostensibly a Cabalistic, numerical one. See John Sturrock, *Paper Tigers: The Ideal Fictions of Jorge Luis Borges* (London: Clarendon Press, 1977), 129-31. But it may also be seen as a mirror that reverses right and left. Treviranus the Christian reads reality from left to right, but the rabbinical "key" reads it from right to left.

12. Jorge Luis Borges, "Death and the Compass," in *The Aleph and Other Stories* (New York: Dutton, 1978), 268-69.

13. J. L. Borges, "A New Refutation of Time," in *Other Inquisitions*, trans. Ruth Simms (New York: Washington Square Press, 1966), 187. Further references appear in parentheses in the text.

"Warp and Weft": Patterns of Artistry in Nabokov's *Pale Fire*

Margaret Peller Feeley

It is *Pale Fire*'s achievement to show us both sides of the fabric at once.
Opposing threads of fantasy and reality, madness and rationality,
creativity and sterility, interlace.

The two seemingly separate works that comprise the splendid comedy *Pale Fire* have disturbed a number of critics who seek to subsume either John Shade's poem or Kinbote's prose under a "primary" author. In one reading Shade, Kinbote, and Gradus are three aspects of one person; in another reading Kinbote has invented Shade and written the poem himself; in still another reading Shade has created Kinbote.[1] The problem with these interpretations is that they clash with the spirit of pluralism in the book and Vladimir Nabokov's world generally. Kinbote reports Shade—who in many ways represents the author's values—as observing: "Resemblances are the shadows of difference. Different people see different similarities, and similar differences."[2] This observation about the relativity of truth or reality is the key to the thematic relation between the two genres. In a rare moment of lucidity Kinbote declares that "it is the underside of the weave that entrances the beholder," and it is *Pale Fire*'s achievement to show us both sides of the fabric at once (p. 17). Opposing threads of fantasy and reality, madness and rationality, creativity and sterility, interlace, unfurling a metaphor for the mind of the artist.

Jolting readers' expectations by the inversion of opposites is a typical strategy of *Pale Fire*. At the very outset Nabokov tricked innocent readers who assume a text to be fiction and the notes "real"; instead, they find a perfectly level-headed poem annotated by a paranoid Russian refugee who imagines himself the exiled king of "a distant northern land" called Zembla, a king who is being pursued by a regicide named Gradus.[3] Egocentric Kinbote fantasizes that Shade is writing "Solus Rex," a work about him. An obvious parody of scholarly editing, his commentary takes off on the least excuse—such as the word *often*, which hardly needs annotation—to tell his own tale of the romantic and improbable adventures that he is sure Shade's wife—his enemy—"repressed" from the draft.

Kinbote's fantasy that Shade's poem "has no human reality at all" without his commentary is silly (Nabokov, *Pale Fire*, p. 28). It can certainly do without a lunatic reading into its adamantly sublunary concerns—mortality, nature, married love, domestic habits—echoes of a lost kingdom. Yet Kinbote's comments do have an uncanny truth or reality in relation to the poem. For instance, Shade calls a snowscape "that crystal land" (p. 33); Kinbote pounces on the words as "perhaps an allusion to Zembla, my dear country"(p. 74). He's wrong but also right, insofar as he describes Zembla as "a land of reflections, of 'resemblers,' " and nature and experience seem to yield the same meaning to Shade (p. 265). Thus poem and commentary, rather than simply standing for rationality and madness, respectively, as it might first appear, interact with and complete each other by continually qualifying and expanding the ways in which a thing may be considered real.

Kinbote's fantasy of kingship can be seen as wish fulfillment, a means of attaining self-importance and immortality. Shade also employs his artistic imagination to create a meaningful life and transcend mortality. A fantasy of immortality begins the first canto of Shade's poem: "I was the shadow of the waxwing slain / By the false azure in the windowpane; / I was the smudge of ashen fluff—and I / Lived on, flew on, in the reflected sky" (p. 33). The imagination of the poet can penetrate the mirror world—like Alice in Wonderland—and emerge unharmed. But the illusion of continued space killed the bird, and the illusion of continued hope killed the poet's daughter, who "always nursed a small mad hope" of love, was disillusioned, and committed suicide (p. 46). Hazel's death is especially sad, because it occurs just as winter breaks, heralding the rebirth of nature:

> It was a night of thaw, a night of blow,
> With great excitement in the air. Black spring
> Stood just around the corner, shivering
> In a wet starlight and on the wet ground.
> The lake lay in the mist, its ice half drowned.
> A blurry shape stepped off the reedy bank
> Into a crackling, gulping swamp, and sank. (p. 51)

Hazel's death at the springtime of her life suggests the seasonal myth of death and rebirth that is often celebrated by comedy. Death or disappearance and resurrection or return usually involve a female figure who has obvious affinities with fertility ("Old Pan would call from every painted hill, / And still the demons of our pity spoke: / No lips would share the lipstick of her smoke" [p. 44]).

Denied romance and marriage, Hazel, like Kinbote, sublimates her fertility into other creative outlets.

Although the girl's prominent place in her father's poem makes Kinbote jealous, because she rivals his Zemblan fantasies, he rather grudgingly notes "that Hazel Shade resembled me in certain respects," and indeed she does (p. 193). The male parallel to the female fertility figure is the scapegoat king, who in ancient rites was crucified to banish winter or death.[4] Kinbote fantasizes that he is a king marked for murder. He translates his name from Zemblan to mean "regicide," "a king's destroyer," explaining that a king who "sinks his identity in the mirror of exile is in a sense just that" (Nabokov, *Pale Fire*, p. 267). So Kinbote commits figurative suicide; Hazel, literal suicide.

Both Hazel and Kinbote share the fantasy of omnipotence, one of the deepest of human obsessions. While Kinbote dreams of kingship Hazel tries to create and control her world despite terrific limitations. Hazel, with her witchy name, is a teenage poltergeist. Kinbote describes her psychokinetic activities as an "outward extension or expulsion of insanity" (p. 166). They are also the dark underside of the creative impulse (there is a wound behind every bow in *Pale Fire*). While the worried father creates poetry out of the reflection of furniture upon the snow (p. 33), his disturbed daughter demonically causes "the little table from his study" to stand "in a state of shock outdoors" (p. 166). Socially outcast, Hazel becomes an amateur parapsychologist, finding her sympathetic spiritual world in a local deserted barn, where she observes and takes notes on mysterious "roundlets" of light (pale fires). Kinbote's Zembla fabrication, the pale fire reflected from Shade's poem, serves exactly the same exorcist and creative function as Hazel's magic; he writes to banish his demons, focus his lucidity, and control his shaky inner world.

Madness, rationality, and creativity wreathe together intricately. *Pale Fire* resonates with echoes of the eighteenth century, an age of controversy about madness, reason, fantasy, and the proper role of the artist. The novel begins with an epigraph by James Boswell from the *Life of Samuel Johnson*. Shade writes his poem in pentameter couplets, a form used by Johnson and Alexander Pope, defenders of reason who thought of themselves as craftsmen. Shade shares this view: his muse wears overalls (p. 64). Shade has also written a book on Pope, and so did Johnson, whom Shade is said to resemble physically. Kinbote, whose Zembla appears in Pope's *Essay on Man* (Epistle 2, V), evokes Johnson's mad acquaintance, Christopher Smart, visionary poet and religious ecstatic. Kinbote, furthermore, notices "a whiff of Swift" in himself. He too is "a desponder . . . an uneasy, peevish, and suspicious man," and he is certainly a misogynist like Swift (p. 173). Generally, Kinbote is associated with ideas that were anathema to Augustan rationalism and deism: fancy, imagination, enthusiasm unrestrained by good judgment. He is afflicted with Pope's *bête noire*, the "ruling passion," the blindness to anything but private illusion that violated Swift's standard of "right reason" and Johnson's good sense. Shade's "web of sense" (p. 63) and "all is right" (p. 42) recall Pope's view of design in nature and dictum that "whatever is, is RIGHT." Kinbote's religious orthodoxy, on the other hand, his propensity to get carried away with spiritual mysteries, predisposes him to take a leap of faith from our shared world to one of his own design.

But the opposing worldviews, which in the eighteenth century often came into conflict, in *Pale Fire* circle round each other in a kind of ether of goodwill. At first we see Shade's tight little world progressively invaded and disrupted by Kinbote's rambling digressions, until it seems as if his nuttiness is about to take over. The commentary is, in one sense, a parasitic growth upon the poem: Kinbote himself translates Botkin, his real name, to mean Kingbot or maggot, and Shade's indignant wife calls him "an elephantine tick, a king-sized botfly; a macao worm; the monstrous parasite of a genius" (pp. 171-72). But the poem manages to retain its integrity in spite of Kinbote's attempt to work it to his will. Shade accepts Kinbote as "a fellow poet," gently chiding the community of New Wye for calling Kinbote "insane," or "a loony": "That is the wrong word.... One should not apply it to a person who deliberately peels off a drab and unhappy past and replaces it with a brilliant invention. That's merely turning a new leaf with the left hand (p. 238). Both men share the same definition of the artistic imagination: Shade writes in quest of "some kind of correlated pattern in the game" (lines 806-15), while Kinbote fantasizes "to wean [himself] abruptly from the habit of things, [to] see the web of the world, and the warp and weft of that web" (p. 289).

What is the difference between what Kinbote calls the "magical madness" of art and clinical insanity (p. 296)? *Pale Fire* poses and answers this question. "Gradus" is Kinbote's imaginative embroidering of Grey, the "real" criminal, who shoots Shade, mistaking him for the judge who sentenced him. Gradus means degree in Russian, and Gradus, who advances by degrees to New Wye, also measures the distance between creative fantasy and destructive psychosis. Like Kinbote, Gradus is another character motivated by an *idée fixe* who takes life from Kinbote's very "ruling passion" or humor. Like the miser who is always counting his money or the hypochondriac who rattles on about his ill health, Kinbote is obsessed with his Zembla, and it is this constant repetition of a theme that we find so funny, his inane search for allusions that do not exist. Gradus represents the same character type with all of the comedy drained out. There is nothing but loathing and disgust in Nabokov's portrait of a mindless, political terrorist who carves his identity out of an important assignment and an ideology he doesn't understand. Gradus commits the only two sins in which Shade believes: "murder, and the deliberate infliction of pain" (p. 225). He is a "clockwork man," a petty hedonist who gets the same satisfaction from pulling a trigger as squeezing a pimple. He also tries to castrate himself. As a foil to Kinbote, Gradus/Grey exemplify the sterility of true insanity.

Sterility and creativity are key motifs in *Pale Fire*: Gradus is physically, emotionally, and intellectually sterile, and Kinbote, like Hazel, is physically sterile, although by choice rather than misfortune; he rejects women. A heroine often brings about a comic resolution (love, marriage) dressed as a boy, like Viola in *Twelfth Night*. In a fantasy about Zembla, Kinbote remembers first meeting his queen Disa, Duchess of Great Payn and Mone (read "pain and moan") at a ball, where she comes "in male dress, as a Tirolese boy" (p. 173). The ironic reversal is prefigured by Disa's companions: male guards "disguised as flowergirls" (p. 173). Kinbote, a pedophile, desires only boys. He marries Disa because he is under pressure to produce an heir, but the marriage is never consummated, and Disa is eventually exiled to Villa Paradisa, later abbreviated to Villa Disa. Disa derives from *Dis*, Dante's name for hell. The gods who guard the sites of Kinbote's sterile homosexual affairs are "Mercury, conductor of souls to the Lower World" (p. 133) and Libitina, "the Roman goddess of corpses and tombs" (pp. 198-99).

Hell, a barren wasteland, replaces the romantic paradise we expect in comedy, which Northrop Frye called "the green world."[5] In fact, as Mary McCarthy pointed out, green is the color of death in *Pale Fire*; red is associated with the king and his loyalists and green with the king's enemies. (At the end it is Gerald Emerald who gives Gradus—Death—a lift to Kinbote's house, where he shoots Shade). Green is the color nature wears in spring and summer, and comedy traditionally celebrates the victory of summer over winter. In *Pale Fire*, however, winter has ascendency over summer; Shade, a craggy Appalachian poet, is supposed to suggest Robert Frost; like Jack Frost he fashions dazzling winter imagery. Kinbote's Zembla, too, is full of winter sports and scenery. The title "Pale Fire" has a plurality of meanings, but surely one is winter light. Toward the end of the novel, in spring and summer, Kinbote increases his half-mocking references to New Wye, Appalachia as green Arcadia. By contrast, Kinbote's Zembla is a comic Saturnalia, a winter festival of unrestrained license and revelry that he imposes upon the stable, pastoral New Wye.

Just as Zembla contrasts with New Wye, Kinbote's pederastic promiscuity contrasts with Shade's long and staid marriage. "Pale Fire" refers to a homosexual in Russian.[6] This suggests that the homosexual Kinbote is less than a man—King Charles lost his Crown Jewels as well as his throne—but in a way he is more than a man. His homosexual fantasies let him transcend conventional sexuality just as his royal fantasies let him transcend ordinary life. While Shade turns to poetry for self-knowledge Kinbote turns to sex for "underground" knowledge of himself. His image for this is an underground tunnel discovered during an adolescent tryst with a Zemblan schoolmate: "he stood on the threshold of a secret passage" (Nabokov, *Pale Fire*, p. 125). The language he uses to describe the passageway is unabashedly sexual: he observes "here and there magic apertures and penetrations, so narrow and deep as to drive one insane," as he follows the "shapely buttocks" and "erect radiance" of his companion (p. 126). The secret passage leads to the green room of the Onhava National Theatre and eventually to New Wye (Arcady): green, as I have noted, is the color of death and sterility in *Pale Fire*. The underground tunnel leads Kinbote to freedom—full expression of his sexual desires—but also to exile, loneliness, exclusion—and finally, the death of his only friend. Guilty Kinbote eagerly seizes upon John Shade's paean to his wife as a more apt description of the beauties of his rejected Disa. Actually, it is not Sybil whom Disa resembles so much as Hazel: both Hazel and Disa smile when they are in pain, and both are in pain when they are abandoned by men. Kinbote's nonrelationship to Disa is the dark underside of the weave in which the Shades are happily entwined. The passages about his "dream-love" for Disa (an actual deserted wife or just a phantom of his lovelessness?) express his deepest feelings in the book, and its theme that the most profound experiences come to us in terms of contradiction:

> The gist, rather than the actual plot of the dream, was a constant refutation of his not loving her. His dream-love for her exceeded in emotional tone, in spiritual passion and depth, anything he had experienced in his surface existence. This love was like an endless wringing of hands, like a blundering of the soul through an infinite maze of hopelessness and remorse. (p. 210)

The emotional squalor of the life he has chosen for his "surface existence" oozes out again and again in images of filth. When he imagines revisiting the secret passageway, he notes that "the pool of opalescent ditch water had grown in length; along its edge walked a sick bat like a cripple with a broken umbrella" (p. 133). This murky pool appears later as "the shallow diaphanous filth" of the lake shore at which Kinbote tells Disa that he does not love her (p. 210). Disa is the "sunken treasure" of a slimy lake at whose surface his lovers float like "sexual scum" (p. 210). He begs God's forgiveness for burrowing "in filth every day" (p. 222), begs Shade's forgiveness for the "intrigues and the dirt" (p. 99), and cries out from "the frozen mud and horror in my heart" (p. 258).

"Pity" is John Shade's "password." Is it meant to be ours? At first the reader—along with Sybil Shade, "bad Bob," and the entire Faculty Club— may be repelled by Kinbote. He acts irritatingly superior about being a vegetarian. An obvious imposter, he is no king but an eccentric Russian refugee. He passes himself off as a literary editor when he is the worst person for the job. Unintentionally, he destroys all of his credibility as Shade's intimate friend, "literary advisor," and responsible editor by his shameless confession that he lurked about in the bushes spying on the Shades. Finally, he admits that he practically pried away Shade's manuscript from the hands of the poet's shocked and grief-stricken widow. Gradually, however, we may become ambivalent about Kinbote and even find him rather endearing: both the windows at which he snoops and his vegetarianism are barriers that cut him off from other people, prison walls of his solipsism. He is at once a rascal and a sympathetic figure: because he suffers, because he cannot sleep, because he is a homeless wanderer. We respond to the refugee as to one lost, between two worlds, but also with the magic of the Old World about him. Indeed, Nabokov enhances Kinbote's shamanlike quality with the promise of special powers. At the end of the novel Kinbote insists, "I shall continue to exist. I may assume other disguises, other forms, but I shall try to exist" (p. 300), as if he is intended to be a mythical figure for the shifting forms of imagination, a sort of personified *élan vital*.[7] He even goes on to suggest that "I may turn up yet, on another campus, as an old, happy, healthy, heterosexual Russian, a writer in exile, sans fame, sans future, sans audience, sans anything but his art." In this final statement Nabokov identifies himself with Kinbote's spirit and ties the knot of reality and fantasy.

NOTES

1. Respectively: Carol T. Williams, " 'Web of Sense': *Pale Fire* in the Nabokov Canon," *Critique* 6, no. 3 (Winter 1963-64): 29-45; Page Stegner, *Escape into Aesthetics: The Art of Vladimir Nabokov* (New York: Dial, 1966), 116-35; Julia Bader, *Artifice in Nabokov's English Novels* (Berkeley: University of California Press, 1972), 31-57.

2. Vladimir Nabokov, *Pale Fire* (New York: G. P. Putnam's Sons, 1962), 265. Further references appear in parentheses in the text.

3. I take for my premise the Kinbote/Botkin-Gradus/Grey interpretation first elaborated by Mary McCarthy, "Vladimir Nabokov's 'Pale Fire,' " *Encounter* 19, no. 4 (October 1962): 71-84.

4. Northrop Frye, *Anatomy of Criticism* (Princeton, N.J.: Princeton University Press, 1957), 183.

5. Ibid., 182.

6. Williams, " 'Web of Sense,' " 39.

7. In an interview with Alfred Appel [*Nabokov: The Man and His Work*, ed. L. S. Dembo (Madison, Wisc.: University of Wisconsin Press, 1967), 29] Nabokov is reported as saying that Kinbote "committed suicide. . .after putting the last touches to his edition of the poem." But the novel as a whole militates against this. It is hard to know how seriously to take Nabokov's comments on his own work. At any rate, as Kinbote said at the end of his foreword: "for better or worse, it is the commentator who has the last word."

Hegelian Stratagems in Calvino's *Invisible Cities*

Kenneth Smith

Invisible Cities can be read as a declarative phenomenology of city life, fantastic, because the modernist dichotomy of subjective and objective is patently belied by the city: here inert and merely material elements are animated by the human purposes under which they have been subsumed. The city is the metabolism of human with subhuman necessities, no work of rational design but a natural kind like a species.

Between the writing of his whimsical short fiction, *Cosmicomics* and *t zero*, and a novel of combinatorial fortuity, *The Castle of Crossed Destinies*, Italo Calvino produced *Invisible Cities*, a novel in which his genius for serendipitous composition seems to have assumed a more serious, even a sublime, tone. His power of poetic evocation, likewise, seems subjugated here to philosophical themes. Certainly, the scale of his interests—if not of his composition—seems to have become more epic. His ability to insinuate conceptual issues into the narrative, at a level that is more logic than story, has always been pronounced. To describe the peculiar accentuation and integration of these traits in *Invisible Cities*, however, I want to propose that Calvino's previously innocuous flirtations with Hegelian concepts have coalesced into a persuasive organic architecture.

In spite of its labyrinthine devices of myth and trope, *Invisible Cities* can be read as a declarative phenomenology of city life. What is the status of the *urbs* as an object of individual experience, how is its presence declared to our consciousness? Many authors have required the services of a city as a backdrop— a matrix that does not itself rise into the consciousness of the actors, a public medium that somehow governs private moods—but no other authors in my recollection have set themselves the task of anatomizing the variety of possible forms in which the city tones (and tunes) our interactions with one another.

Such a task is indeed fantastic, a proper marvel, because the modernist dichotomy of subjective and objective (so self-evident that literature as well as criticism takes its bearings from it) is patently belied by the city: here inert and merely material elements are animated by the human purposes under which they have been subsumed; here the subtlest and most inward of human purposes can find a supple medium of expression, since the city—like our face or hands or voice—is in its own way an eminently responsive instrument, adequate to the nicest qualifications of our intentions. The city is human ecology, the metabolism of human with subhuman necessities, the interleaving of the works of humans with the works of nature. As such it seems to beg for a hermeneutics, a method for reading these enigmatic figurations of the intuitive mind: here is human soul writ large, extended and elaborated into a macrocosm with an integrity of its own. The Heraclitean harmonies in this musical Babel seem to argue cogently that individuals are not ultimately autonomous worlds unto themselves but are rooted somehow in a common soil. But how, then, are we to respect and to comprehend the organic molarity of the city, taken as an utterance of humankind's more subliminal self? How are we to read this pictograph in which concrete factors also stand as symbols and vice versa, in which the natural and the artificial are joined eerily together?

It is a task so grand we expect no one even to make the motion of rising to it. It has an order of complexity that reminds us of nothing so much as Georg Hegel's concept of objective spirit, spirit's objectification of itself, and its correlative incorporation of objectivity into the world of spiritual dynamics. This hermeneutics of the city has been incidentally struck upon by novelists or even by our own commonsense efforts to discriminate between the flavor of one city and that of another. *Invisible Cities*, a finely crafted congregation of vignettes, makes such a hermeneutics explicit and thematic throughout a caravanserai of fanciful and exotic realms, rendered up to the Great Khan in Marco Polo's accounts of his travels. With a freshet of startling turns of mind and phrase, the sprightly style of this work ably bears a weight of grave and profound issues that found little place in Calvino's previous writings: the Khan expects to hear from Marco Polo nothing less than "the invisible reasons which make cities live, through which perhaps, once dead, they will come to life again."[1] Calvino wrote that "Contemplating these essential landscapes, Kublai reflected on the invisible order that sustains cities, on the rules that decreed how they rise, take shape and prosper, adapting themselves to the seasons, and then how they sadden and fall in ruins" (p. 122). But Marco Polo's tales have a pointed ulterior motive, to induce the Khan to take the cities as they are, not to impose on them the errant rationality of conscious common sense. It is in these efforts to correct any misconceiving of the cities that we see recurrent themes of Hegelian social theory: these tactics are described in the following sections as *holism, obliquity, immanentalism, coincidentia oppositorum*, and *Aufhebung*.

HOLISM

Hegel's theory is one of the most imposing critical attacks on nominalism or positivism. Isolable individual existences are not, for it, the ultimate and irreducible realities; the relations and wholes into which these individuals are inserted are not mere epiphenomena or mechanical conglomerations of parts but have a mode of reality, a coherence or integrity, relatively independent of those atomic components. The perfect isolability and abstractability of individuals are only illusory. Calvino everywhere presumed such an overarching integrity, as he described the organic patterns that make the most haphazard of cities regular and organic. Describing a bridge, he said that it is not supported by individual stones, "but by the line of the arch that they form" (p. 82). Every vignette aims at the incorporation of apparently discrete phenomena into an organic totality: reciprocal definition among the parts and between the parts and the whole—the classical Aristotelian conception of organism—mark the peculiar way in which individuals, acts, things, and places are colored by that urban matrix. Not, like Khan's dreams, produced by mind or chance, the city is "made of desires and fears...the thread" of its "discourse is secret," its "rules...absurd...and everything conceals something else.... You take delight not in a city's seven or seventy wonders, but in the answers it gives to a question of yours" (pp. 43-44). Cities draw not just their order—the coordination of their parts—but their power, their morale and purpose, from forms that have more in common with subrational Jungian archetypes than they do with Platonic-intellectual *eidoi*. The city is "the inferno where we live every day, that we form by being together" (p. 165); its order is neither that of the conscious-rational individual mind nor that of inorganic accident, but it is like some great natural fatality, a necessity implicit in the cultural-animal cohesion of human beings with one another. The city is a kind of instinct played out in a spate of visible artifacts and actions but for reasons and necessities that are not so visible. The city is no work of rational design but is a natural unity, a natural *kind* like a species.[2]

OBLIQUITY

Since it is not a work of conscious reason—not the product of humankind's finite purposings—the city's coherence is not a fit object accessible to humans' conscious ego. Like Hegel, Calvino seems to have argued for the indirect or merely implicit phenomenality of higher social structures vis-à-vis the lower, individual ones: like Hegel's concept of customary morality (*Sittlichkeit*) the city affects the individual by subliminal or unobjectifiable forms of evidence and influence. The characters out of which the language of the city is formed are not humanly formulatable: when he talks about the city, Polo has to rely on "gestures, grimaces, glances." Khan's hands begin to speak the same language. "As an understanding grew between them, their hands began to assume fixed attitudes" (Calvino, *Invisible Cities*, p. 39). About these subliminal strata there is not only reticence to speak but great apprehensiveness about their very volatility in the hostile medium of language. Polo fears that speaking about Venice will cause him to lose it: "Or perhaps, speaking of other cities, I have already lost it, little by little" (pp. 86-87). Cities—like the roots of everything that possesses, obsesses, the minds of humans, be it holiness, beauty, sex, or whatever—have a chthonic authority, an ineffable or inarticulable primordiality by which they betray their priority over individuals, as the power that brought them into existence (and not vice versa, as they may from time to time flatter themselves).

But Calvino's craft obliged him to subvert this ineffability, to conduct it into roughly appropriate Apollonian forms. His methodology here was exactly Hegelian: what cannot be our direct object can be given indirectly, implicitly. Cities might "elude the gaze of all, except the man who catches them by surprise" (p. 91). This obliquity governs not just Calvino's style but the wholly objective traits of the cities: they betray their laws only *en passant*, by way of transitory phenomena. The laws of the cities are indeed Heraclitean laws, the harmonics of dissonant events, captured in evanescent patterns. The order or lawfulness of a city is perceptible but never more than *verging on* being intelligible: it is an order that *belongs* essentially in the background of conscious thought—it can only be addressed glancingly and can only be captured incidentally.[3] This peripheral relation to consciousness implies that the city is a presence that can only haunt human awareness, an elusive, viscous wraith behind the foreground-preoccupations of individuals. Kublai Khan thus accuses the merchant Marco Polo of trafficking in linguistic contraband: "confess what you are smuggling: moods, states of grace, elegies!" (Calvino, *Invisible Cities* p. 98) Mood is exactly the object of these vignettes, but it is by no means passive or static mood: mood here is opalescent with the supraconscious or infraconscious interplay of sense and surd, the ambiguous passage of the unintelligible into the intelligible. Poetic throughout, *Invisible Cities* is an intercourse in semiarticulable meanings, imperfectly resolvable even into metaphor or myth.

IMMANENTALISM

Hegel is probably most sharply divided from the Platonic-Kantian tradition by his efforts to demonstrate that organizing principles or essential structures are not abstractable, transcendent factors over against their phenomena but are concrete ingredients imbedded in the historical-empirical medium. The phenomena and their inner essence are not radically differentiable, not metaphysically heterogeneous. Recalling Marco Polo's illustration of the bridge and its stones in mutual support of one another, Kublai Khan continued with some impatience: " 'Then why do you speak to me of the stones? It is only the arch that matters to me.' " But Polo corrects him: " 'Without stones there is no arch' " (p. 82). Hypostasis and reification are mere intellectual presumption: abstractions have no independent or substantial status—true universals, on the contrary, are not abstract but inherent or ingredient in their instances. This immanentalist metaphysics makes a dialectical union with the holism previously discussed.[4]

Such a metaphysics has a certain analogy with animism; indeed, Hegel used the theological notion of *Parousia* to describe the copresence of the absolute within the relative and finite (or, alternatively, its self-identity in the midst of alienation—*Beisichsein-im-Anders*). For Calvino not only do the governing principles reveal themselves by phenomenal forces, but they are, like those phenomena, ephemeral and conditional. The principles of organization around which historical constellations revolve are themselves historical. Successive cities on a site, manifesting separateness, might as well be identical—the "voices' accent" of the inhabitants identical—yet "the gods who live beneath names and above places have gone off without a word" (Calvino, *Invisible Cities*, pp. 30-31). Part of the vertiginous pathos of the human condition—the dependence of human life upon an infinitude of factors not subject to human will—consists just in the necessity that even the most durable and most substantial city, already itself beyond the reach of human will, is a prey to forces and exigencies even more remote from the human world. Octavia, "the spider-web city," hangs above a void, suspended on a net, and its inhabitants know their lot more clearly than do those of other cities, because "they know the net will last only so long" (p. 75). If the people's presumption of independence from their environing city is an illusion, so also is it delusional for them to take their city for a true firmament: the little consciousness of humans arrogantly but systematically obscures the deeper pathos to which they are liable.

COINCIDENTIA OPPOSITORUM

One of the plainest traits common to Hegelianism and perhaps all fantastic literature is their modality of the grotesque, that is, the collapse of apparently distinct orders of phenomena into a continuum or a confusion.[5] Hegel meant to argue that radical discreteness, even between antinomian concepts, is not ultimately defensible: all oppositions presuppose derivation from a common base, and opposition is indeed the mark of finite *relata* that cannot be ultimate terms in an argument. The conflation of dream and waking life in surrealist art, the arrogation of divine status by modern Promethean humans, the artificial-mechanical duplication of acts of thinking ("intelligence" cybernetically reproduced as an electronic-physical event), the Freudian public science of interpreting the private dream world, the synthesis of organic and mechanical functions in bionics (in Lem's anthropomorphic robots or in Giger's "biomechanoid" nightmares)—all of these things are illustrations of this same grotesque modality. The grotesque is, by this standard, any experience or representation that transgresses supposedly inviolable normative boundaries between one fundamental kind of reality and another. The grotesque describes the extraordinary convergence or coincidence of opposites, which in premodern culture may have been unique to certain forms of mysticism with a pronounced need to confound human reason.

If it is little understood how exactly Hegel managed to execute this reconciliation of opposites, it is nonetheless notorious that he meant to vitiate any dualism of mind/body or subject/object. His syntheses of freedom/necessity, abstract/concrete, social/individual, and so on are equally well acknowledged. All of these things, but especially the first dualism (of subject and object), appear also to be pertinent contexts of the grotesque in fantastic literature. Calvino gave us repeated examples of this confusion of realms—cities in which the concepts living/dead (Calvino, *Invisible Cities*, p. 110), solid/empty (p. 126), and order/disorder (p. 97) appear to be reversed—but the prevalent form of *coincidentia oppositorum* seems to be that of subject/object.

One of the most prominent expressions of this confusion is an analogy Calvino shared with J. L. Borges, the world taken as book: the city's past is expressed not in words, but "contained" in it, as "scratches, indentations, scrolls" (p. 11). So convincingly does Marco Polo portray his cities as psychic landscapes that the Khan is overwhelmed by the notion that his rule may encompass nothing but projections of the soul, "nothing but a zodiac of the mind's phantasms" (p. 22). For certain, the power of the city to enmesh the mind in moods—to instate a primordial ground from which the mind takes its departure—signifies a momentous grotesquery, the invasion of the subjective by its environing reality. The mind is determined in a peculiar way—is oriented, biased, colored—by this concrete condition of being situated in time and place and with qualities like a "slight breeze." The city evoked by Polo's narrative will be seen "from such a vantage point" (p. 27).

The potency of the city is indeed seldom so mild. Some cities exercise a certain tyranny over the mind: fetishistically, like Borges's "Zahir," they dictate by their objective properties what we will remember and what we will forget. The quality of Zora remains in the memory as a catalog of unalterable particulars, "names" and "numbers," even "constellations" (p. 15). Another city, Pyrrha, has the power to expunge irretrievably all of one's anticipations of what it might turn out to be like. The real city, once seen, makes Polo forget all he had imagined of it, and he comes to think he had "always known" the streets as they appear, "always known that the sea is invisible from the city" (p. 92). This very fetishistic power is the key, perhaps, to the longevity of cities, their ability to survive however permutated: cities reproduce themselves from era to era through the form they regenerate perennially within our most intimate feelings. There are two kinds of cities, those that eliminate desire or are eliminated by it, and those "that through the years and the changes continue to give their form to desires" (p. 35). The very essence of the city lies in this paradoxical-grotesque power to transcend the single-minded, univocal simplicities of the individual mind: the reality of the city is its complexity, its plurality of purposes and perspectives, which Hegel once described as the "Briareus," the fifty-eyed and hundred-handed Leviathan, of moral community. Such a "model city" is constituted "only of exceptions, exclusions, incongruities, contradictions" (p. 69). As with Hesiod's god Eris and Heraclitus's all-fathering Polemos, Calvino's city, too, has a benign strife and war at its heart, the rich inconsistencies that it is the privilege of the city to be able to contain.

AUFHEBUNG

Hegel assumed it was the duty of philosophy by a circular path to recapitulate the familiar, to deduce ordinary reality as transfigured by entirely extraordinary sources of illumination.⁶ The test of a philosophy lies in its power concretely to synthesize what it once analyzed, to reproduce received experience out of some depth level of principles. The contribution of these principles lies just in their integrative power: that is, comprehension for Hegel is much like Bernard Lonergan's notion of *Insight*: a supervening, synoptic vision encompassing the field of problems and divulging a subtle unity coordinating them, to which they are keyed. This sublimation or subsumption of a finite element within a more comprehensive totality is termed by Hegel an *Aufhebung*, an ambiguous preserving-invalidating procedure that retains the inferior, finite ingredient but qualifies it as subordinate to a higher principle that has priority (or is the "truth" of that lesser component). The concrete particular is not sacrificed by this process but merely has its atomistic hubris curbed: since Hegel's arguments are designed to show that that self-abstraction is vicious—that no finite being as such can be self-sustaining—it is then not the self-assertion of the finite being but its comprehension within a superior principle that is the preservation of it. It is for this reason that the Scottish Hegelian Edward Caird suggested a profound affinity of Hegelianism with the Christian wisdom of self-sacrifice (for example, Luke 9:23-25).⁷

Calvino's art seems likewise to nurture such a concept of salvation and not merely in *Invisible Cities*. Like Borges's, his whimsical inventories of concrete particulars, or his apparently adventitious juxtapositions of chance elements, seem to evoke a world of unrelated, finite ingredients: but we are shown, by the subtlest manipulations of legerdemain, that the Many are really One, or the One is really the Other, or the Unforeseen and Accidental is really the Necessary, or the Familiar is really the Strange, or vice versa. By these reversals and transmutations the alienated world—like the dismembered Orpheus—is reunited; the opacity of particular-factual existence is imbued with an almost Plotinian translucency; what had suffered under the yoke of enslavement to Accident is redeemed and freed to its own proper nature. In virtually all of Calvino's work the dramatic acme is an intuitive climax, an epiphany of intense conceptual insight within which the awkward particles of experience become fused and fluid. By the very concept of it this subtle unity and transcendence over intellection mark Calvino's work as sublime, and nowhere does this very complex of concerns seem to be so well traced as in *Invisible Cities*.

NOTES

1. Italo Calvino, *Invisible Cities*, trans. William Weaver (New York: Harcourt Brace Jovanovich, 1974), 136. Further references appear in parentheses in the text.

2. H. B. Acton, Introduction to *Natural Law*, by G.W.F. Hegel (Philadelphia: University of Pennsylvania Press, 1975), 25, 27, 35, 37. Also germane to the topic of "natural kind" is Hannah Arendt's exposition of the Greek concept of species as superorganism in *Between Past and Future* (New York: Viking, 1968), 41-42.

3. Cf. Borges's overt exploitation of this ambiguity in "The God's Script," *Labyrinths* (New York: New Directions, 1964); also John Findlay, "The Perspicuous and the Poign-

ant," *Aesthetics in the Modern World*, ed. Harold Osborne (New York: Weybright & Talley, 1968), 142.

4. In spite of recalcitrant popularizations to the contrary, it remains evident that Hegel of all philosophers had the least use for transcendence. See John Findlay, *Hegel: A Re-Examination* (New York: Collier, 1962), 353-56.

5. Wolfgang Kayser, *The Grotesque in Art and Literature* (New York: McGraw-Hill, 1966), 24, 100-102, and *passim*. Hegel's criticism of the grotesque emphasizes its sub-spiritual, pictorial level and would not obviously apply to Calvino's modal or metaphysical grotesqueries or to Hegel's own concept of "abolition of differences."

6. Georg Hegel, *The Philosophy of Right* (London: Oxford University Press, 1962), 1; idem, *The Phenomenology of Mind* (London: Allen & Unwin, 1964), 92. The necessity for the recapitulation strictly precludes remaining with the simple and unqualified familiar.

7. Edward Caird, *Hegel* (Philadelphia: Lippincott, 1891), 212-13, 218.

Tolkien's Elvish Craft and Frodo's Mithril Coat

Douglas A. Burger

That so many of the major themes of the work become reflected in so slender a strand as the mithril coat demonstrates the consistency and thoroughness with which the moral-aesthetic "laws" of Middle Earth pervade the narrative.

More than with most other modes of fiction, the success of a fantasy depends upon the success of the storytelling itself. Anyone with the power of the adjective can invent fantastic images (like "green sun") as J. R. R. Tolkien said in "On Fairy-Stories."[1] Many fantasies have marvels rivaling those of *The Lord of the Rings*.[2] But to create a context where those images become believable, to give them "the inner consistency of reality" (Tolkien, "Fairy Stories," p. 42), a fantasist must have a "special skill" in storymaking, "a kind of elvish craft" (p. 49). In that high narrative art that Tolkien discussed in his essay, he was himself the master craftsman.

It is obviously with the One Ruling Ring that Tolkien most strikingly works his special skill. During the trilogy the image grows from the "least of Rings,"[3] Bilbo's handy bauble for conferring invisibility, to a symbol so complexly and profoundly significant that if I, like Gandalf, "were to tell you all that tale, we should still be sitting here when Spring had passed into Winter" (Tolkien, *Fellowship*, p. 81). Fortunately, there is no need, for the specialists in Ringlore, from Middle Earth's wizards to America's college professors, have laid bare its secret fascinations more fully and wisely than I could here. Yet despite the unique potency of the image and the craftsmanship lavished upon the narrative that develops it, Tolkien's storytelling genius is certainly not limited to the Ring. His high artistry in spinning story and meaning from image is manifest throughout the entire fabric of the work—in the seemingly peripheral as well as in the central: for example, the image of Frodo's mithril coat.

Even without the story generated from it the image would be effective, a marvel altogether worthy of a work seeking to evoke wonder. A gift from Bilbo, who earned it for his successful burglary of Smaug's treasure trove, it is an example of the best dwarvish work. Designed originally for a great elven warrior, the chain-mail corselet is studded with white gems, tied with a belt of pearl and crystal, and the rings are all of pure silver—and not just ordinary silver but the splendidly beautiful Moria silver, or mithril (as the elves call it), which has a hardness surpassing tempered steel, yet the lightness and flexibility of linen. It never tarnishes. In addition to having these properties, mithril has immense value (ten times the worth of gold, Gandalf surmises) because of its scarcity: it is no longer mined because of the terror that now lurks in the deeps of Moria, the only place where the metal is found. In Gandalf's words the coat alone is worth the whole Shire, and later Gimli says that Gandalf undervalued the coat.

With an image of something so precious Tolkien stirred deep-rooted human desires and struck a note that resonates with others from the realm of legend and romance—dragon hoards, leprechauns' pots of gold, the jewel-paved streets of golden cities. The image has a specially charged psychological energy and a basic, universal appeal, whether Tolkien here tapped into a Jungian archetype or merely activated an innate avarice. Yet in Tolkien's typical fashion Frodo's marvelous chain-mail not only evokes a fundamental human response but has a fresh particularity of its own. Such an ability to appeal to age-old, universal desires through his own vivid individual creations accounts for much of the aesthetic success of Middle Earth.

But as Tolkien insisted, invention of images is but one aspect of the operation of the imagination; for along with the "perception of the image" (Tolkien, "Fairy Stories," p. 46) he mentioned "the grasp of its implications, and the control, which are necessary to a successful expression" (pp. 46-47). The mithril coat, minor though it seems at first, provides a telling example of Tolkien's own sure grasp of the narrative potential in an image and of his own masterful control of the story that issues from it.

The strand of plot is introduced unobtrusively. The day before the Fellowship's departure from Rivendell, Frodo and Bilbo are alone in the old hobbit's room. Bilbo rummages through his things and finds the sword Sting, which he gives Frodo as a token of his love and concern. Then he says off-handedly, "Also there is this" (Tolkien, *Fellowship*, p. 363). Out of an old cloth he produces the beautiful mithril shirt, which, after some hesitation, Frodo accepts and puts on under his clothes. On a first reading Tolkien seems to have included the episode for no more reason than to reemphasize the bond of warm affection between the two hobbits and to provide Frodo's departure with a sense of oc- casion. We little guess at the coat's immense worth and its later importance in the plot. Not until the Company is deep in the mines of Khazad-dûm does the value—in both senses—become clear. There, Gandalf tells his companions (and

readers) of the stupendous value of mithril and of Bilbo's ringed mail, a speech
that Tolkien introduces naturally and appropriately in the only place where the
metal was mined. By postponing the full revelation of its astonishing worth until
this point in the story Tolkien achieved two interesting narrative effects. First,
there is dramatic irony arising from the fact that Frodo, unknown to the rest of
the Company, is wearing the coat at the very moment that Gandalf is speaking
of it. Second, such a technique of little-by-little exposition helps convey the
texture of reality. Just as in life we fill in our view of the world piece by piece,
so in *The Lord of the Rings*, the characters (and we) learn only gradually of the
value, history, and relationships of everything in Middle Earth.

That the coat is useful as well as precious is shown shortly afterward. A savage
chieftain of the orcs bursts into the Chamber of Marzibul and deals Frodo a
murderous and apparently mortal blow. But, incredibly, Frodo is not dead—or
even very badly injured. Tolkien deferred explanation with Gandalf's urgent,
"There is no time for wonder now," but after a moment's reflection we suspect
(as Gandalf does) that it is the mithril rings that have saved Frodo (p. 423).

The next episode in which the mithril coat plays a significant part in the plot
comes many hundreds of pages later, and so its reappearance at the end of Book
5 comes as an effective surprise. Before the troops assembled in front of the
Black Gates of Morannon, Sauron's foul Lieutenant shows Frodo's coat, along
with his sword and elven cloak, as proof that Frodo has been captured and
imprisoned in Mordor. The bold defiance with which Gandalf responds and
seizes Frodo's things masks the grief that the leaders of the West feel at this
sudden blow to their hopes. Unlike the earlier incident in the mines of Moria,
we do not at this point in the narrative have a knowledge much superior to the
characters'. The shock that they feel, in which "a blackness came before their
eyes" and "their hearts were dead," is a shock that we share.[4] As far as we
know Frodo is indeed in the dungeons of the Dark Tower, awaiting torments
that only so nice a malice as Sauron's can devise. Such a scenario is all too
plausible, since the last pages of Book 4 show the orcs carrying Frodo, captive
and unconscious, to the virtually impregnable watch tower of Cirith Ungol. As
in the earlier episode in Moria, here Tolkien employed the mithril coat to create
suspense. But here the uncertainty is more momentous, more fraught with anxiety, and longer lasting, since the first part of Book 6 takes place, in chronological
time, *before* the conclusion of Book 5. Given this overlap in time, Tolkien, for
many pages in Book 6, left open the possibility that what the Lieutenant says
is true. (Even if, at that point, we cannot envisage so disastrous an ending as
the ultimate failure of the Quest, another alarming possibility may occur to us:
that Frodo remains in torment, while Sam, who now has the Ring, continues to
Mount Doom.) Only when Sam enters Cirith Ungol to find a courtyard befouled
with the blood of dead orcs does the light begin to dawn on him and on us—
the orcs have savagely slaughtered one another, quarreling over what else but
Frodo's immensely valuable coat. Only when we see the wounded Shagrat
sloping off with his precious bundle, do we learn how Sauron actually got the

coat. Against all odds, hope remains. Once more the coat has saved Frodo, this time not from death but from a fate far worse.

When at last Mordor is cast down and Frodo is recovering in the glades of Ithilien, Gandalf goes off to bring the hobbits suitable clothes for the King's victory feast. To Frodo's delight and astonishment he returns with the mithril shirt. In the great celebration that follows Frodo wears it openly for the first time, and perhaps even the splendid mail, designed for the mightiest of elven warriors, is unworthy of the unpretentious hero that it clothes. Nevertheless, the coat has served him well; twice it has saved him. Little does Frodo suspect that it will do so again.

But when the hobbits return to the Shire, they discover that the War of the Rings is not over. A vengeful Saruman has corrupted and enslaved the once innocent land, and still another battle is needed to overthrow him and his henchmen. After the Shire is scoured Frodo, in a gesture of clemency, lets Saruman go free. But as the wizard leaves he flashes a knife, dives at Frodo, and stabs him. The hobbits are appalled and rush to save Frodo, but "The blade turned on the hidden mail-coat and snapped" (Tolkien, *Return*, p. 299). The coat has done Frodo one last, good service.

As revealed by such a survey of the episodes involving the mithril coat, Tolkien used this strain of plot primarily to bring about those sudden reversals that surprise, heighten suspense, and accelerate the breakneck pace of the trilogy. Twice—in Moria and in the Shire—the presence of the coat allows Tolkien to introduce hairbreadth escapes, exactly the sort of episode that creates the edge-of-the-chair excitement that many readers find a chief strength of the work. In addition to its inherent appeal, the taut suspense is a significant part of Tolkien's magic in enchanting us into a "secondary belief" in his world. Involvement in the plot leads to involvement in the whole fantasy world. If the action of the story has sufficiently excited our curiosity we do not care a whit if the action *could* happen; we just want to know what *does* happen. Thus plot excitement creates its own kind of plausibility by disarming our critical, judging faculties.

But the episodes with the coat *could* happen and are plausible per se. By slipping the coat into the narrative long before it plays a role in the action of the plot, Tolkien avoided any sense of gimmickry. The protection of the mithril rings is not brought in as one of those awkward, after-the-fact explanations that are all too typical of much fantasy writing. What is more likely than Frodo's being attacked in dangerous Moria and being saved by the mithril shirt? What could be more credible, given Tolkien's previous characterization of the orcs, than their self-destructive greed in Cirith Ungol? What could be more natural than Frodo's wearing the coat in the last battle in the Shire? Such plausibility of events, although desirable in any kind of narrative, has a special significance in fantasy. For with its relative strangeness and unlikeness to our primary world, a fantasy world depends for its success upon being believable in its own terms— and one of those terms is plot. If the action of the story itself is credible and consistent the writer has gone far toward achieving that "inner consistency of reality" that induces "secondary belief."

But it is not only in crafting a suspenseful, believable plot that Tolkien demonstrated his mastery of the art of storytelling. *The Lord of the Rings* fully demonstrates the natural and unforced way in which character and meaning arise from plot. In this respect, too, the mithril coat serves Tolkien well, for in his exploration of the narrative implications of that image he managed to add substantially to the characterization of Bilbo and Frodo and—without being arbitrarily symbolic and without editorializing—to touch upon the centrally important themes of the whole work.

In developing character and theme Tolkien used the coat in several ways, but among the most important is his use of the coat in his searching and profound examination of greed. (What could be more natural, given an object so valuable?) Indeed, the mithril coat becomes a significant building block in the moral construct of Tolkien's world, for it is one element in a number of parallels and contrasts that illuminates the nature of possessiveness. For example, the essential moral soundness of both Bilbo and Frodo is shown by the parallel of their strikingly similar attitudes toward the coat.

With the first appearance of the coat in *The Hobbit* Bilbo shows himself to be Frodo's spiritual predecessor in his remarkable freedom from possessiveness. When the mithril mail is first mentioned as being among Smaug's treasures, Tolkien said, "Bilbo kept his head more clear of the bewitchment of the hoard than the dwarves did."[5] With both the coat and the even more valuable treasure from the same hoard, the Arkenstone, Bilbo is impervious to the lures of wealth. His generosity in surrendering the stone in order to bring peace elicits an awe-struck tribute from the Elvenking: "Bilbo Baggins! you are more worthy to wear the armour of elf-princes than many that have looked more comely in it" (Tolkien, *The Hobbit*, p. 250).

In *The Lord of the Rings* Bilbo gives up the mithril coat with the same ingenuous openhandedness with which he relinquishes the Arkenstone. Without grand gesture or any feeling of loss he offers the coat in a simple act of love for Frodo and concern for his welfare. Bilbo just wants his beloved young cousin to have something "pretty"—and more important, something that will protect him. The immense value of the coat means nothing to Bilbo, except insofar as it is a worthy gift for Frodo. Frodo at first refuses it, saying, "I don't think I should look right in it" (Tolkien, *Fellowship*, p. 363). Just how much the hobbits are kin, in many senses, is shown by the similarity of Bilbo's first reaction to the armor: "I feel magnificent. . . but I expect I look rather absurd" (Tolkien, *The Hobbit*, p. 220). It is only after Bilbo says that the coat might turn even a Black Rider's knife that Frodo accepts the treasure, taking it in the same spirit in which Bilbo gives it. Much later, when Gandalf speaks of the coat's enormous value, Frodo cares nothing about the fact that he himself possesses the mail— what he thinks of is Bilbo's generosity and the happy days he shared with the old hobbit at Bag End: "He wished with all his heart that he was back there, and in those days, mowing the lawn, or pottering among the flowers, and that he had never heard of Moria, or *mithril*—or the Ring" (Tolkien, *Fellowship*, p. 414).

Significantly, Frodo thinks of the Ring along with the mithril coat—a natural association since both are precious legacies from Bilbo. The conjunction of the two suggests another way in which the coat contributes to the structure of similarities and differences that enriches characterization and generates moral viewpoint. Frodo's and Bilbo's similar attitude toward the coat serves as an analog to their attitude toward the Ring. With the coat both show themselves uncommonly free from the cravings of ownership, and the mithril mail has the function of providing an index to their normal behavior with the valuable. With the Ring, in contrast, their possessiveness becomes an obsession. That the Ring can corrupt even such naturally generous, unusually nonpossessive characters testifies to its immense and insidious power for evil. The extent of that power is made clearer by Tolkien's inclusion of the mithril coat.

Two of the later episodes with the coat serve to bring another moral contrast more sharply into focus—the hobbits' absence of greed as opposed to the cravings of the dwarves and the orcs. In Moria, at the same time that Frodo is thinking of Bilbo's generosity, Gandalf recounts the history of the dwarves of Khazad-dûm. Like their kinsmen in *The Hobbit* the dwarves fell disastrously under the "dragon-spell" of treasure. They sought the mithril with a desire so unquenchable and compulsive that they delved too far—and roused (or perhaps freed) the Balrog, which became their bane and drove them forever from Moria and from the mithril. As Gandalf says, "even as *mithril* was the foundation of their wealth, so also it was their destruction" (p. 413). Tolkien's thematic point of the moral dangers inherent in the desire for possessing wealth thus becomes fully reflected in the physical action of the story itself. The idea that avarice is self-destructive is even more directly conveyed by the vicious battle among the orcs, with each one trying to get Frodo's coat for himself. So brutish, selfish, and unmitigated is their greed that death is the only restraint on it. Greed, like all evil in Tolkien's view, is ultimately self-defeating, and that fact provides hope for the forces of goodness. As Sam says, when he arrives at the watchtower, "It looks as if Shagrat, Gorbag and company have done nearly all my job for me" (Tolkien, *Return*, p. 181). Without the orcs' crazed greed for the coat, there would have been no chance of escape for Frodo (who, interestingly, seems to have no regret about losing it).

As well as using the coat as one element in a number of comparisons and contrasts involving possessiveness, Tolkien created character and meaning from the image of the coat in another way: he made the hidden coat emblematic of Frodo. After the young hobbit has put his weather-worn clothing over the sparkling coat, Bilbo says, "Just a plain hobbit you look...but there is more about you now than appears on the surface" (Tolkien, *Fellowship*, p. 363). In Moria Gandalf makes a similar remark: "You take after Bilbo...there is more about you than meets the eye'' (pp. 425-26). Bilbo and Gandalf are thinking of the concealed coat—but not of it only. For what is true of Frodo's apparel is likewise true of him himself. Underneath his humble, commonplace exterior is a remarkable and precious strength of character. Boromir, Galadriel, Faramir, even Saruman—all are astonished at the courage and wisdom that this "plain" hobbit eventually reveals. Even Gandalf, who "goes in for hobbit lore" (p. 78), is often surprised at Frodo's determination and incorruptibility. Like the mithril Frodo's character resists tarnish, and the coat comes to be a natural emblem for him, a token of his hidden strengths and great inner worth.

Thus the hidden mithril mail makes an important contribution to another theme that looms large in the work as a whole: "All that is gold does not glitter" (p. 325). Although Frodo and his mithril coat exemplify the theme well, the line literally refers to Aragorn, and it is interesting that with him as well Tolkien used depiction of clothing as one method for conveying this theme: Aragorn, the mighty heir of Isildur, conceals his regality under the travel-stained garb of Strider the Ranger. Gandalf, too, has an initially unprepossessing look and hides the light of his power under a gray cloak. Thus it is not clothing or, by extension, any other superficial appearance by which we should judge the greatness of the people of Middle Earth. Only by dint of their deeds and their inherent worth is the essential nature of the protagonists gradually revealed. In the great culminating moment on the Field of Cormallen we see them as they truly are: Aragorn in his kingly robes, Gandalf in the white of the highest of the Istari, and Frodo in his resplendent mithril rings.

In the final episode with Saruman, as in the victory celebration, Frodo's armor becomes the sign of his innate heroism and his spiritual achievement. Defeated, Saruman hurls a curse so ghastly that most of the hobbits recoil in horror. But Frodo remains unmoved. He is as invulnerable to the dangerous onslaught of Saruman's words as he is to the physical danger of Saruman's dagger. Here, as before, the literal action of the narrative, the snapping of the blade against the mithril coat, becomes virtually a metaphor for Frodo's essential strength in resisting evil.

In summation, Tolkien's mastery of narrative is amply demonstrated by the skillfulness and variety of techniques by which he created meaning from the episodes with the coat. Still another technique remains, in which the very pattern of narrative movement becomes thematically significant. In the incidents with the coat the plot shows a sudden, unexpected "turn" from danger to comparative safety, from loss to recovery, from threatened death to life. In Moria Frodo is thought dead by the others, but he is alive; his apparently miraculous return from "death" foreshadows that other and greater death-resurrection that takes place in Moria—Gandalf's. Likewise at Cirith Ungol, Frodo seems dead from Shelob's sting, but (in the words of the button) he lives and escapes to renew the Quest. Death is cheated again when the armor stops Saruman's knife. In all of these "happy" incidents there is a "sudden joyous turn" (Tolkien, "Fairy Stories," p. 68), which mirrors in miniature the great Eucatastrophe, the final overthrow of Sauron's kingdom of fear and death. Such recurrent patterns in themselves convey a truth about the essential nature of Middle Earth. Even the few episodes with the mithril coat help to form the texture of a world in which, wondrously, evil is defeated, hope rises from despair, and life triumphs over death.

By examining the several ways whereby Tolkien created a rich significance from the few appearances of the coat, we not only see more clearly the nature of Tolkien's artistry, we understand something of his success in bewitching us into belief in his world. The fact that even these brief episodes bear so varied and manifold a relation to the work's principal themes is indicative of the complex interconnections between images, plot, characterization, and theme in the trilogy as a whole. The very extent and intricacy of those interrelationships suggest the complexity and fullness of a whole, real world—a world that, like ours, is filled with an astonishing variety of interrelated life.

The credibility of a fantasy world depends, as Randel Helms said, upon the extent to which the action, varied though it may be, conforms to the artist's "structural principles," to "the peculiar laws of the sub-created cosmos."[6] That so many of the major themes of the work become reflected in so slender a strand as the mithril coat demonstrates the consistency and thoroughness with which the moral-aesthetic "laws" of Middle Earth pervade the narrative. In the little as in the large, Tolkien conveyed a vision of such scope and unity that if *The Lord of the Rings* dealt with the primary world, literary critics would be likely to speak of a "worldview."

NOTES

1. J. R. R. Tolkien, "On Fairy-Stories," in *The Tolkien Reader* (New York: Ballantine Books, 1966), 48. Further references appear in parentheses in the text.

2. J. R. R. Tolkien, *The Lord of the Rings* (New York: Ballantine Books, 1965). Further references appear in parentheses in the text.

3. J. R. R. Tolkien, *The Fellowship of the Ring* (New York: Ballantine Books, 1965), 317. Further references appear in parentheses in the text.

4. J. R. R. Tolkien, *The Return of the King* (New York: Ballantine Books, 1965), 203. Further references appear in parentheses in the text.

5. J. R. R. Tolkien, *The Hobbit* (New York: Ballantine Books, 1966), 220. Further references appear in parentheses in the text.

6. Randel Helms, *Tolkien's World* (London: Thames and Hudson, 1974), 85-86.

Fathoming *Twenty Thousand Leagues under the Sea*

David Ketterer

If Jules Verne's view of the world as a cipher to be cracked is reflected in a fiction that is also coded, perhaps an archetypal key is required to open up Verne's most famous novel, and perhaps that archetype is the cross.

What's in a title? In the case of Jules Verne's *Twenty Thousand Leagues under the Sea*, it is more than meets the unreflective eye. What the title refers to is distance covered horizontally. But a reader's initial impression is almost certainly one of verticality, of depth. The element of verticality provided by the word *under* is placed in a syntactically ambiguous relationship to the preceding phrase, "twenty thousand leagues." It is, therefore, hard to resist the subliminal suggestion that "twenty thousand leagues" measures distance downwards. This misconception is corrected or obviated by the knowledge that vertical distance under the sea is measured in fathoms. The use of "leagues" must then indicate horizontal distance covered under water.

Whether or not a reader "misconceives" the title in the way I have hypothesized, it is undeniable that the words concerned point to directions or movements of a combined and possibly intersecting horizontal and vertical nature. The addition of the pun "Fathoming" in my own title is designed to encourage further this "double take." To use the language of the structuralists, if Verne's title is a sign, what is being signified covertly is the sign of the cross.

But what has this signification—presumably deliberate—to do with the story itself? Does the concept of a cross, formed by the intersection of horizontal and vertical movements (or, alternatively, of diagonal movements), in any way aid our understanding of what Verne's fiction is all about? Michel Butor and Marcel Moré have drawn our attention to various archetypal structures in Verne's work.[1] They argued that Verne's view of the world as a cipher to be cracked is reflected in a fiction that is also coded—hence the important role of the cryptogram and pervasive images of hidden depths in several of the novels. It follows that all that ever will be known is currently available, somehow within reach. Moré's and Butor's attempts to break Verne's code focus on the entire canvas of his writings. There is, in fact, throughout criticism of Verne, little sustained explication of individual novels, including, surprisingly, *Twenty Thousand Leagues under the Sea*. It is clearly time to apply the more general approaches to individual cases. Perhaps an archetypal key is required to open up Verne's most famous novel, and perhaps that archetype is the cross.

Butor has pointed to Verne's obsession with the four elements. Fire, which because of its heat is opposed to the coldness of death, appears to be the primary element. The spiritual quality of fire (which Verne characteristically linked with electricity) is suggested by the fact that it is always in ascension. With Butor's analysis in mind and noting that there are four major characters in *Twenty Thousand Leagues* and that one of them is called "Land," we would seem to have good reason to consider the four elements angle.

The four characters may be viewed as symbiotic pairs. Ned Land, the French Canadian, and Conseil, Professor Aronnax's manservant, are transparently complementary characters, the one practical, the other theoretical. Conseil, with his book knowledge of the classification of marine species, "was the opposite of the Canadian," who could identify the actual fish.[2] "Without a doubt," adds Aronnax, the narrator, "Ned and Conseil put together would have made one distinguished naturalist" (p. 131). Ned Land is a most peculiar name for a French Canadian. It can only be assumed that Ned Terre in the French original would have made an association with the element of earth all too obvious. As a character, he is very much down to earth. The head-in-the-clouds Conseil would appear to be identified with the element of air. Thus the French *ciel* for "sky" is contained anagrammatically in his name.

If earth and air are to be viewed as polarized but complementary elements, what of fire and water and Nemo and Aronnax? Aronnax does, in fact, admit "that having become a fanatic on the subject of the *Nautilus*, I was beginning to identify myself with its commander" (p. 283). As a marine biologist and the author of *The Mysteries of the Ocean Depths*, Aronnax can be linked easily enough with the element of water. Somewhat less obviously, a series of images noted by Walter James Miller may be interpreted as explaining Aronnax's interest in the sea in terms of a desire to return to the womb.[3] Aronnax's apparently incidental statement, in relation to a mysterious cry at sea, that "The times are long past since Jonahs take refuge in the bellies of whales" is the first of three progressive images of womblike enclosure (Verne, *Twenty Thousand Leagues*, p. 61). Subsequently, Aronnax reflects of life aboard the *Nautilus* that "Like snails, we were becoming attached to our shell and I declare, it is easy to become a perfect snail" (p. 226). The series culminates with an image of conflated enclosures. Asleep within an "enchanting" cave, Aronnax dreams—stressing in retrospect the involuntary nature of that activity, "one does not choose one's dreams—that my existence was slowly being transformed into the vegetative life of a simple mollusk" and "that this grotto was the bivalve of my shell" (p. 365). The subliminal temptation to misinterpret this situation as involving a double enclosure—that of a mollusc within its shell within a cave—is given impetus by what appear to be two inspiring circumstances: the occasion when Nemo leads Aronnax into a previous "grotto" containing "an oyster of extraordinary size" (p. 273) and the more recent sight of "gigantic crustaceans" lurking under rocks which form "a second shell" (p. 349).[4] If these images of containment reveal a desire to return to the womb and if the sea is regarded (as it is in traditional symbolism and in actuality) as the womb of life, Aronnax's unconscious interests no less than his conscious ones argue for his identification with the element of water. At the same time it should be emphasized that a desire to retreat to the womb expresses some kind of death wish. Thus Aronnax, asleep in the grotto, might well have drowned had not Conseil awakened him to the danger of the rising tide.

Nemo is also to be linked with water. He is referred to in one chapter title as "The Man of the Seas," a title that suggests the mythological figure of Proteus (Verne, *Twenty Thousand Leagues*, p. 10). Indeed, when the *Nautilus* approaches the island of Carpathos, Nemo recites a couple of lines from Virgil concerning Proteus: "Est in Carpathio Neptuni gurgite vates / Coeruleus Proteus" may be translated as: "The cerulean Proteus, prophet of Neptune, lives in the Carpathian abyss" (p. 310). But although in his symbiotic relationship with Aronnax Nemo does not share with him the element of water, that is not the only element with which he is associated. Because of his success in harnessing the power of electricity it seems reasonable to identify Nemo primarily with the remaining element of fire. The *Nautilus* works "All by Electricity," as the title of chapter 12 has it, or as Nemo puts it, "electricity gives the *Nautilus* heat, light, movement—in short, life" (p. 108). The title of chapter 22, "La Foudre du Captaine Nemo," the sense of which may be translated as "Lightning Action by Captain Nemo," again connects Nemo with electricity and thereby also with fire. Real fire depends upon air, and it might be observed that Nemo's electric fire, being derived from "let us say sea coal," is ambiguously associated with the elements of water and earth (p. 108). Symbolically, then, fire incorporates or impinges upon all of the elements.

The correlation between the four characters in *Twenty Thousand Leagues* and the four elements suggests the diagram on page 266. My arrows are intended to represent the fact that earth and air, fire and water, exist, like the corresponding characters, in somewhat antagonistic relationships. In a very loose allegorical fashion the interaction of the four central characters corresponds to the interaction of the elements that are conceived as being in a continual state of dynamic movement. Indeed, numerous passages in the book indicate that life involves a perpetual struggle of the elements.

The present condition of the world's surface is the result of a millennia-long contest: "The solid had wrested from the liquid thirty-seven million, six hundred

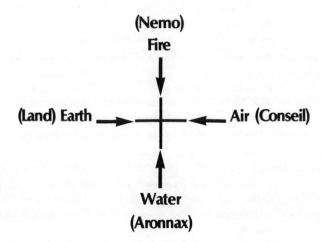

and fifty-seven square miles—more than thirty billion acres" (p. 122). But since fire or the processes of vulcanism *within* the earth is the central factor, the more significant struggle in *Twenty Thousand Leagues* often appears to be that between water and fire. In a description of the Mediterranean area the four elements are alluded to, but it is clear that especially beneficial is the antagonistic relationship between fire and water:

The Mediterranean, that incomparable blue sea. . .adorned with orange groves, cactus, aloes, and sea pine, scented with the fragrance of the myrtle, framed with rugged mountains, immersed in a pure, transparent atmosphere, yet incessantly stirred by volcanic eruptions—this sea is a veritable battlefield in which Neptune and Pluto are perpetually disputing the empire of the world. On its shores and on its waters, says Michelet, man is continuously rejuvenated in one of the most invigorating climates of the globe. (p. 319)

In the preceding chapter Aronnax has been treated to a close-up view of this conflict: "the spectacle of a submerged volcano." Nemo explains that "the earth is constantly being worked by subterranean fires" (p. 315). One sulphurous convulsion will cause the emergence of a new island, another its disappearance. But such instances of rise and fall are no longer very frequent. Aronnax subsequently points out that "Volcanoes. . .are slowly being extinguished" as the "lower strata of the globe" cool off, "much to the detriment of our globe, for heat is life." In time Earth will be like the moon, "a cold lifeless body" (p. 324).

It is soon revealed that the disappearance of Atlantis was caused by elemental turmoil in Earth's distant past. Amidst the eerie submarine ruins stands a still active volcano: "Fifty feet below the summit, in the midst of a deluge of stone and slag, a large crater vomited forth torrents of lava, which dissolved into a cascade of fire in the water all around" (p. 350). Aronnax recalls reports of "underwater volcanoes" in the area and "rumblings indicating a struggle of the elements going on below." "One day," he speculates, "perhaps, some eruptive phenomenon will bring these sunken ruins back to the surface!" (p. 352). The violent clash of the elements is both destructive and generative.

When the *Nautilus* docks, via a natural channel, inside its secret harbor, "the very heart of an extinguished volcano," further opportunity is provided to consider the spectacular action of the elements. After "some convulsion of the earth,... the waters of the Atlantic swept into the interior of the mountain. There must have been a terrific struggle between the two elements, a struggle which was won by Neptune" (pp. 361-62).

Toward the conclusion of the narrative the *Nautilus*, in the vicinity of Long Island, runs into a situation where "a struggle of the elements was imminent." In the midst of describing the "war of the elements during the ensuing hurricane," as "The *Nautilus*, sometimes lying on her side [horizontally], sometimes standing up [vertically] like a mast, rolled and pitched frightfully" (p. 476), Aronnax pauses to explain his sudden understanding of the relationship between air and water: "Now I realized the role of these waves that capture air in their flanks and force it down to the bottom of the sea, where its oxygen nurtures life" (p. 476). An imagistic exchange of air and water occurs, incidentally, every time the progress of the *Nautilus* is likened to that of "a balloon in the air" (p. 375). But to return to the coming storm, shortly, a third element comes into the picture: "By ten o'clock that night, the sky was on fire. The heavens were streaked with violent flashes of lightning." In imitation of Ahab confronting a similar tempest in *Moby Dick*, Nemo confronts the lightning "appearing to inhale the soul of the tempest" (p. 477). While Ahab uses his harpoon as a lightning rod the *Nautilus* itself "reared her steel spur like a lightning rod and I could see sparks dancing on it" (p. 477).[5]

At each different point in the story one of the four elements is of particular relevance. The sight of land always holds out the possibility of escape, something that Ned Land is particularly interested in. At the beginning of the chapter "A Few Days on Land," "Ned felt the ground with his foot, as if he were taking formal possession of it (Verne, *Twenty Thousand Leagues*, p. 193). In fact, this particular piece of land, "the island of Gueboroar," holds the likelihood of death, and Nemo's electric fire is required to repulse the attacking natives (p. 191). The different danger of asphyxiation is foreshadowed early in the narrative, when Aronnax considers "it was urgent that the air in our prison should be renewed, and also without doubt, all the air in our submarine craft" (p. 78). Much later, in the chapter "Lack of Air" (Verne's chapter titles often point directly to what is important), when the *Nautilus* is trapped by ice, this danger becomes very real.

But the outstanding element throughout is water. The state of dynamic movement that characterizes the interaction of the four elements is the sea's very nature. The sea exemplifies movement in all directions, the full potentiality of life. But in describing the sea's movement Verne repeatedly specified two directions, the horizontal and the vertical (among various other directions that may be conceived as interacting). There are the "horizontal" currents and counter-currents we all know about. In describing the ocean's "circulation" Nemo explains the relationship between temperature changes and these currents: "Evaporation, which is nil in the extreme north, but very high in equatorial regions, brings about a permanent exchange of the tropical and polar waters" (p. 163). "Moreover," as he goes on to remark, there are also less obvious "vertical" movements: "I have actually come across currents flowing top to bottom and bottom to top, which form the ocean's respiratory system. I have seen molecules of sea water, heated at the surface, dropped down into the depths, attain maximum density at two degrees below zero, then, cooling further, become lighter and rise again" (p. 163). Microscopic organisms play a part in this vertical exchange by absorbing salt from drops of water that, becoming lighter, rise to the surface, where, absorbing the salts resulting from evaporation, they become heavy again:

We have, then, a double current, ascending and descending—a continuous movement and continuous life! The life is more intense than life on land, more exuberant, more infinite [what seems to be bad grammar here is, as we shall see, indicative of the sea's double nature], spreading throughout the parts of the ocean. They say it is the element of death for man, but it is the element of life for myriads of animals—and for me. (p. 164)

Later in the narrative, as if to remind readers of what they have learned, Aronnax repeats that there "are vertical currents, caused by the differences in salinity and the densities of the water, that produce a movement which is sufficient to support the rudimentary life of the encrinidae and the starfish" (p. 374).

What is said of the movement of the sea, then, reaffirms the impression conveyed by the book's title, the impression of two contrary movements intersecting. The crosslike design that results is reflected in numerous ways throughout the novel and appears to be intended as a sign that, variously interpreted, may be said to account for everything in the novel if not, indeed, for everything in Verne's collected works. The title *Extraordinary Voyages*, which Verne used to cover his science fiction series, is followed by the subtitle *Travels to Known and Unknown Worlds*. It may be demonstrated that both the "known" and the "unknown" are comprehended by the sign of the cross.

As an image of the known the four points of the upright cross do suggest the four cardinal points of the compass: north and south, east and west. But so much importance is given by Verne to the "horizontal" and "vertical" lines of latitude and longitude in determining the matter of precise location that the criss-cross of coordinates might well be isolated as a particular symbol of the known. *Twenty Thousand Leagues* is full of references such as the following: "On the 18th of January, the *Nautilus* was at longitude 105°, latitude 125° south" (p. 226); "Our bearings showed our position to be latitude 45° 37' south and longitude 37° 53' west'' (p. 372). The chapter in which Nemo shows Aronnax the sunken wreck of the *Avenger* is titled after the coordinates of its location: ''At Latitude 47° 24' and Longitude 17° 38''' (p. 20). At one point Aronnax puts his finger ''on the very spot where our latitude and longitude crossed'' (p. 124). In two novels, *The Children of Captain Grant* (1868) and *The Barsac Mission* (1920), an appeal for help is received that states the latitude but omits the longitude. Precise knowledge clearly depends upon the availability of both vertical and horizontal coordinates.

If for a moment we tilt our intersecting horizontal and vertical lines to form a diagonal cross we have the standard symbol of the unknown. On one occasion Aronnax comes across Nemo ''immersed in what looked like a calculation, in which x and other algebraic signs were not lacking'' (p. 214). In fact, the diagonal cross is persistently associated with the mysterious and mysteriously named Nemo. In confronting the world or, more particularly, in confronting the unknown, Nemo characteristically adopts a gesture that Verne himself favored: he crosses his arms. There appear to be eight such occasions.[6] Here are three of them: ''Captain Nemo, arms crossed over his chest...knelt in prayer'' (Verne, *Twenty Thousand Leagues*, p. 238); ''He climbed up to a rock...and standing there with his arms crossed...he seemed to be claiming possession of these southern regions'' (p. 408); ''He came toward me, silent, with his arms folded, gliding like a specter rather than walking'' (p. 506). Ned Land is also observed ''crossing his arms'' before admitting that he is not altogether sorry that fate has thrown him ''in the hands of Captain Nemo'' (p. 307). Presumably, Land is grateful to have experienced the unknown.

The x (ax) in ''Aronnax'' bespeaks his symbiotic sympathy for Nemo. Just as Aaron acted as his brother Moses's mouthpiece in asking the Pharaoh for the release of the Israelites from Egypt, so Aronnax, as the narrator, speaks to the reader for Nemo, making the unknown known and voicing Nemo's love of freedom. What may be understood as another instance of x the unknown occurs during an underwater stroll. Glancing up, Aronnax observes that ''A light bower of marine plants...grew crisscross at the surface of the water''(p. 150).

For Verne the unknown includes both physical and metaphysical reality. Indeed, some kind of transcendent unknown is clearly the ultimate goal in *Twenty Thousand Leagues*. For a symbol of this transcendent unknown we must return to our upright cross, the Christian sign of redemption. However, a particular religious context should not be assumed. Aronnax observes that Nemo's dining table includes ''neither bread nor wine,'' the substance of Christian communion and salvation (p. 74).

At the end of part 1 and again toward the end of part 2 the reader is presented with an image of sacrifice. In the first case the scene is Nemo's underwater cemetery: ''In the middle of the clearing, on a pedestal of rocks thrown on top of each other, stood a cross of coral, whose long arms, one would have thought, were made of petrified blood'' (p. 238). This is the occasion, quoted above, when Nemo crosses his arms and prays. Hildibrand's engraving from Alphonse de Neuville's illustration of this episode in the original edition clearly shows both the coral cross and several characters, one standing and at least three kneeling, with crossed arms.[7] In the second case, after visiting the "tomb" of the *Avenger* (Verne, *Twenty Thousand Leagues*, p. 486), Nemo creates what the title of chapter 21 terms "A Hecatomb" by sinking an unidentified enemy ship. The image of the cross is suggested as "The *Nautilus*, propelled forward by her powerful momentum, plowed right through the body of the ship, just as the needle of a sailmaker goes through a canvas!" (p. 498)

As Butor suggested, the Poles, still points of the turning world, and the center of the Earth are used by Verne as symbols of transcendence. Thus when the *Nautilus* is at one of these privileged locations, the South Pole, the notation that "At the zenith the beautiful Southern Cross, the polar star of the Antarctic, glittered brilliantly" is hardly accidental (p. 421). If we superimpose x the unknown on the upright cross (which paradoxically signals both the known and transcendent redemption),

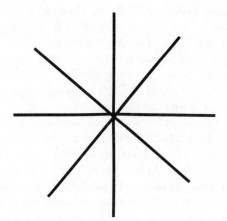

we have an image both of the pole itself, "that unknown point where all the meridians of the globe intersect," and of the sign of the cross as embracing all aspects of physical and metaphysical reality (p. 399).

Something of this sense of a mystical reconciliation of opposites is provided by the sea itself. Not only is it the epitome of movement and life—"continuous movement and continuous life!" as Nemo's key statement puts it—but it is also associated with death and transcendence (p. 164). In an earlier formulation Nemo touches on its mystical quality: "The sea is nothing but the means which permits man to lead an almost supernatural and wondrous existence; it is all movement

and love. It is the living infinite, as one of your poets [Victor Hugo] has said''
(p. 93). It offers an escape from Earth's gravity. Consequently, as we have
observed, Nemo describes the sea in terms both relative and absolute, both
comparative and superlative, as "more infinite" than the land (p. 164). Death,
we may presume, is a condition of stasis, of fixity.

It will be recalled that the arms of the coral cross in the midst of Nemo's
underwater graveyard appear to be "made of *petrified* blood" (p. 238; my italics).
Toward the conclusion of the narrative an episode occurs in which the dire
prospect of a final immobility is particularly threatening: for an extended period
Nemo and company find themselves trapped beneath the polar ice shell because
of an overturned iceberg. "Thus, all around the *Nautilus*, above and below, an
impenetrable wall of ice" (p. 431). On a more humorous level, in the chapter
that includes Conseil's nearly fatal accident with a sting ray, there is a strong
imagistic suggestion that what has narrowly been avoided is a Medusa-induced
state of petrification. The incident in which Conseil is "half paralysed" (p. 450)
is sandwiched between a reference to jellyfish with "an opulent blossoming head
of tentacles" (p. 449) and a reference to "octopi, medusae, and squids" (p.
451). As Nemo has said, the sea may be "the element of death for man" and,
indeed, for the world as a whole (p. 164): "It was through the sea that the earth,
so to speak, began, and who knows if it might not come to an end through the
sea!" (p. 93) We have already seen that, for Aronnax, the sea offers, if not
exactly death, at least a retreat from life. Subconsciously, Aronnax yearns for
a state of cosy enclosure, a return to the dreamy, surrealistic womb of the sea.

The *Nautilus* itself offers a self-enclosed, womblike, utopian existence. Named
for a mollusc it provides a protective shell for its occupants, including Aronnax,
who views life aboard the submarine in just such terms. At the same time, like
the sea the *Nautilus* gives the paradoxical impression of both a retreat and a
source of adventure, an encircling security and stability combined with the idea
of freedom and unimpeded movement—movement in all directions but usually
of a vertical or horizontal nature. It is driven by a four-vaned, that is, crosslike
propeller.

The motto of the *Nautilus* and the title of chapter 8, "Mobilis in Mobile,"
proclaim the vessel's ease of movement. Aronnax translates the Latin as "Mobile
within the mobile element!" and then pauses to reflect "What an apt motto for
the undersea craft—as long as the preposition 'in' is translated 'within' and not
'on' " (p. 74). What the motto "capsulizes" is the ideal of contained movement,
in other words, movement within a self-sufficient container in a direction that
is ultimately discovered to be circular, or movement that actually reveals a
condition of stasis—we are back within Aronnax's shell within a cave. The
dynamic movement of the elements occurs within an enclosed ecological system.
The movements that create the impression of cross-currents, of intersecting or
colliding horizontals and verticals, are, in their completion, circular. Related
circular movements in Verne's work may be found most obviously in *Around*

the World in Eighty Days (1872) but also in the moon dilogy (1865, 1880), which is concerned essentially with the round trip there and back—landing on the moon is irrelevant.

As for the actual shape of the *Nautilus*'s round-the-world voyage, it will come as no surprise to discover that it is roughly cruciform with its most easterly, southerly, westerly, and northerly points being somewhere in sight of the Marquesas Islands, the South Pole, off the coast of Newfoundland, and north of Norway, respectively.

Perhaps the clearest instance of the reconciliation of the image of the cross with circular movement (we might think of the ancient and auspicious image of the rotating cross or swastika) is provided by the tempest to which I have already drawn attention in relation to the role of the elements.[8] The hurricane turns into a counterclockwise cyclone.[9] This image of a horizontal movement is combined, it will be recalled, with Aronnax's appreciation, in an apparent aside, of the vertical cycle of the air captured and forced to the bottom of the sea by the waves only to rise again in the form of evaporation. One hundred fifty feet down, within the *Nautilus* all was "tranquil," "silent," and "peaceful" in contrast to the "frightful hurricane" "on the surface" (Verne, *Twenty Thousand Leagues*, p. 478).

This kind of combination of the static (with its connotations of death, womblike security, and an eternal transcendence) and the mobile (with its connotations of life, adventure, discovery, and restless change, including death and birth) may well go back to Verne's experience of growing up on the Ile Feydeau in the Loire River off Nantes. Every March when the Loire flooded, the young Jules expected this pointed, ship-shaped island to float away. As Walter James Miller noted, the title of chapter 1, "A Shifting Reef," referring to uncomprehended sightings of the *Nautilus*, and Ned's reference to the same as "a floating island" hark back to Verne's childhood fantasy of his secure, self-contained, island home floating away (p. 62).[10] This alarming but fascinating vision of movement, movement confined to and generated by the imagination of a gifted child, strongly suggests the situation of the author-to-be. Verne's concern with the relationship between movement and stasis has much to do with the fact that he was an author. Sitting at his desk, virtually immobile, his adventurous mind roamed far and wide. This situation is also compatible with the Vernean idea that, as previously observed, new knowledge is not so much located elsewhere but lies encoded in the world we know. At the same time, it is the nature of a work of fiction to combine movement and stasis in its marriage of content and form.

We have seen that in *Twenty Thousand Leagues* the spiral form of shells and presumably spirals in general, the *Nautilus*, the cyclone, the South Pole, and the sea itself provide images whereby the combination of the static and the mobile points to an area of reconciliation. Two other images associated with the sea and two other spiral forms—the Sargasso Sea and the maelstrom off the Norwegian coast—appear to polarize the possibilities. The Sargasso Sea (perhaps because it lacks the vital interaction of contrary currents) is an ocean graveyard, a circular image of the fundamentally inert. As Aronnax explains, quoting from Matthew Maury's *Physical Geography of the Sea*: "If one were to put pieces of cork or fragments of any floating material in a basin of water and a circular motion be given to the water, one will soon see the scattered fragments come together in the center of the liquid surface—*that is where there is the least motion*. In the phenomenon with which we are concerned, the basin is the Atlantic, the circular current is the Gulf Stream, and the center where all the floating fragments come together is the Sargasso Sea" (Verne, *Twenty Thousand Leagues*, p. 368; italics mine).[11] But this seemingly unpromising area, redolent of loss and decay, is teeming with life: "the fish, lovers of marine plants and crustacea, find abundant food" (Verne, *Twenty Thousand Leagues*, p. 369).

The importance of the Sargasso Sea and the later maelstrom is suggested by the fact that the reader is provided with a prefiguring image. In the vicinity of the Bay of Bengal is what is "known as a milk sea" owing to the presence of myriads of minute, luminous worms (p. 252). Aronnax observes that the *Nautilus* "glided through these frothy waves silently, as if it were floating in one of those frothy eddies that can be seen when two currents, flowing in opposite directions, converge" (p. 253). The lactic fertility of these "eddies" applies, as we have seen, to the Sargasso Sea and may also be applied to the maelstrom.

Indeed, the maelstrom, into which Nemo and the *Nautilus* disappear, however frightening it may be (heralded as it is imagistically by the cyclone three chapters earlier), suggests, by way of contrast with the Sargasso Sea and in the context of the value placed on interacting movements, an image of the dynamic potential of life. One may assume that what awaits Nemo, like the Norwegian in Verne's source, Edgar Allan Poe's "A Descent into the Maelström," is some form of transcendent rebirth, of deliverance. After all, this vortex is "rightly called the 'Navel of the Ocean' " (p. 507). No wonder that Nemo prepares for his transfiguration by creating at his organ "a musical ecstasy that was carrying him beyond the confines of this world" (p. 505). No wonder he reappears in *The Mysterious Island* (1875) as a godlike being.[12]

No doubt with the maelstrom in mind (and also perhaps some recollection of the Job epigraph to the epilogue of *Moby Dick*), Aronnax concludes his narrative with the question posed in the Book of Ecclesiastes: "Who has ever fathomed the depths of the abyss?" "Captain Nemo and I," is Aronnax's reply. Nemo certainly; his strange destiny "is also sublime" (Verne, *Twenty Thousand Leagues*, p. 510). But whatever Aronnax's understanding, it must derive in large part from the reflection involved in writing the book. It is now the reader's task to fathom the dynamic depths of that book.

NOTES

1. See Michel Butor, "Le Point suprême et l'âge d'or à travers quelques oeuvres de Jules Verne," *Repertoire* 1 (Paris, 1962): 130-62; and two books by Marcel Moré, *Le très curieux Jules Verne: Le Problème du père dans les Voyages Extraordinaire* (Paris:

274   Author Studies

Gallimard, 1960), and *Nouvelles explorations de Jules Verne* (Paris: Gallimard, 1963).

2. Because of the inadequacy of every English translation published to date all quo- tations from *Twenty Thousand Leagues under the Sea* have been freshly translated from *Vingt mille lieues sous les mers* (Paris: Lidis, 1960). I am grateful to Professor Marc Angenot for his assistance with these translations. Further references appear in parentheses in the text.

3. See Walter James Miller, *The Annotated Jules Verne: "20,000 Leagues under the Sea"* (New York: New American Library, 1976), 258, 359. In this volume Miller is concerned with exposing the appallingly botched nature of what until relatively recently was the standard translation of *Twenty Thousand Leagues under the Sea*, a translation perpetrated by Lewis Page Mercier (1820-75). Rather than provide the reader with a usable text, Miller reprinted the Mercier translation and incorporated corrections among his annotations. Can we assume that Miller believed he himself had previously produced a usable text? See what is billed as "A definitive modern translation by Walter James Miller," "assisted by Judith Ann Tirsch" (New York: Washington Square Press, 1966). Curiously, however, no mention is made of this translation in *The Annotated Jules Verne*. Perhaps this is because, although an improvement on Mercier's work, Miller's "defin- itive" English version is also far from reliable. Apart from numerous oddities in trans- lation, Miller's text is radically abridged in many important places.

4. I am indebted to Kirpal Singh and Michael Tolley for pointing out this detail.

5. Ray Bradbury provided an impressionistic comparison of *Moby Dick* and *Twenty Thousand Leagues under the Sea* in "The Ardent Blasphemers," his introduction to Anthony Bonner's translation (less imperfect than some) of Verne's masterpiece (London: Corgi Books, 1962), 1-12.

6. An ex-student of mine, Orin Mannitt, made the count.

7. The engraving is reproduced on page 184 and as the cover of Miller's *Annotated Jules Verne*.

8. At this point my analysis of *Twenty Thousand Leagues under the Sea* might usefully be related to the arguments presented in Michel Serres, *Jouvences sur Jules Verne* (Paris: Editions de Minuit, 1974). While revealing Verne's "mathematical onericism," Serres provided examples of what Angenot describes as "transpositions of the circle, the ellipse, the hyperbole, the eccentric circle, the loxodromic curve" chiefly drawn from the lesser known stories. See Marc Angenot, "Jules Verne and French Literary Criticism [II]," *Science Fiction Studies* 3 (March 1976): 48.

9. It should be recalled at this point that Aronnax earlier drew attention to the fact that "right-handedness is a law of nature" and hence his excitement at discovering an "olive shell" "curled from left to right." Generally, shells "form right-handed spirals, and when, by chance, one turns out to be left-handed, collectors will pay its weight in gold to possess it" (p. 213). Presumably, Aronnax's attachment to shells has something to do with this spiral interaction of the cross and the circle.

10. See Miller, *The Annotated Jules Verne*, 43 n. 6. Two of Verne's titles relate directly to the same floating island fantasy: *Une ville flottante* (1871; translated as *A Floating City*, 1876) and *L'Ile à helice* (1895; translated as *The Floating Island*, 1896), which is about the seagoing, futuristic, electrically powered Milliard City on Standard Island.

11. Miller claimed that because Verne is quoting from a book originally published in English, it behooves anyone producing an English version of *Twenty Thousand Leagues*

to quote Matthew Maury's original words rather than offer a translation of the French translation in Verne's novel. See Miller, *The Annotated Jules Verne*, 260 n. 8. However, Miller did not point out that the French translation of the passage from Maury is not Verne's. Verne simply transcribed it from the French version of Maury's book *Géographie physique de la mer*, trans. P. A. Terquem (Paris: J. Correard, 1858). Verne's English translator is thus presented with an insoluble problem. Should he translate the text used, as has usually been done, or substitute, as Miller insisted, Maury's original text? Miller left the reader to assume that only the English original of Maury was available to Verne, who attempted but failed to create an exact translation of the passage concerned. The purist solution, and the one I am here adopting, would be to provide the English reader with both a translation of the French translation and with Maury's original. The original words, as transcribed in Miller's "definitive" translation, are as follows: "Now, if bits of cork or chaff, or any floating substance, be put into a basin, and a circular motion be given to the water, all the light substances will be found crowding together near the center of the pool, where there is the least motion. Just such a basin is the Atlantic Ocean to the Gulf Stream; and the Sargasso Sea is the center of the whirl" (p. 271).

12. I am grateful to Michael Tolley for pointing out that the imagistic game of O's and X's in *Twenty Thousand Leagues* carries over into *The Mysterious Island* (1874-75). Considerable attention is paid to establishing coordinates of latitude and longitude. The importance of the arms crossed position to Nemo is borne out by this detail: "At length, shortly after midnight, Captain Nemo by a supreme effort succeeded in folding his arms across his breast, as if wishing in that attitude to compose himself for death" (p. 473). Nemo is enclosed within his *Nautilus*, which is permanently harbored in the center of a cavern inside the island; it is to be sunk to the bottom of the abyss therein, after Nemo's death. Since the island blows up, we cannot be certain that Nemo's wishes are carried out. However, it is noteworthy that the volcanic explosion that wrecks the island is the result of a titanic "battle between fire and water" and so announced in the contents heading for chapter 19 (p. 485), a chapter that contains a graphic account of a struggle between lava and water of a lake: "This time water would be vanquished by fire" (p. 491). The quotations above are taken from the Great Illustrated Classic edition (New York: Dodd, Mead, 1958).

Bibliography of Fantasy Scholarship: Theory and Aesthetics, Literary Techniques, Author Studies

Marshall B. Tymn

THEORY AND AESTHETICS

Apter, T. E. *Fantasy Literature: An Approach to Reality*. Bloomington: Indiana University Press, 1982. This work challenges the explanatory role of psychoanalysis and suggests that, in contrast, fantasy literature can elucidate and extend psychoanalytic notions, especially those involving the function and aim of fantasy. Fantasy themes are traced back to the realist tradition and are shown to have been developed by writers in the mainstream of fantasy literature, such as Franz Kafka, Vladimir Nabokov, and Jorge Luis Borges.

Boyer, Robert H., and Kenneth J. Zahorski, eds. *Fantasists on Fantasy: A Collection of Critical Reflections*. New York: Avon Books, 1984. This broad-based collection brings together eighteen recognized authors who explore the theory, technique, and aesthetics of fantasy literature, offering their insights to a broad spectrum of readers. The volume includes essays, reviews, published talks, prefaces, editorials, excerpts from texts, interviews, and letters. An informative and useful overview which serves a variety of needs.

Prickett, Stephen. *Victorian Fantasy*. Bloomington: Indiana University Press, 1979. Traces the evolution of the aesthetics of fantasy from its beginnings into the Victorian era, showing how the fantastic flourished in the popular and comic tradition of the period. Examines in detail the development and influence of six writers: Edward Lear, Lewis Carroll, Charles Kingsley, George MacDonald, Rudyard Kipling, and Edith Nesbit.

Rabkin, Eric S. *The Fantastic in Literature*. Princeton, N.J.: Princeton University Press, 1976. An exploration of the nature and uses of the fantastic following from the recognition that it is not the unreal by itself that is fantastic but the unreal in a particular context. Each chapter develops this view, using examples from other literary modes. By analyzing different works of literature, Rabkin shows that the fantastic depends on a reversal of the ground rules of a narrative world. This reversal signals most commonly a psychological escape to an unknown world secretly yearned for, whose order, although reversed, bears a precise relation to reality.

Schlobin, Roger C., ed. *The Aesthetics of Fantasy Literature and Art*. Notre Dame: University of Notre Dame Press, 1982. This critical anthology brings together a wide spectrum of approaches to the theories of fantasy literature and art. Its essays focus on the basic principles that distinguish fantasy from other literary types and make a strong argument for its place as a major approach to the understanding of the creative act in art and literature

Slusser, George E., Eric S. Rabkin, and Robert Scholes, eds. *Bridges to Fantasy*. Carbondale: Southern Illinois University Press, 1982. Thirteen essays presented at the Second Eaton Conference on Science Fiction and Fantasy (University of California, Riverside, 1980) discuss the structure, contexts, and themes of the genre and together outline various theoretical approaches to the study of fantasy.

Todorov, Tzvetan. *The Fantastic: A Structural Approach to a Literary Genre*. Trans. Richard Howard. Cleveland: Press of Case Western Reserve University, 1973; reprint ed., Ithaca, N.Y.: Cornell University Press, 1975. A discussion of certain verbal, syntactic, and thematic strategies that recur with frequency in the literature of the fantastic, and an examination of the precise response that a confrontation with the fantastic characteristically evokes in the reader. Speculating on the social and cultural function of the supernatural within the framework of the modern sensibility, Todorov draws upon such thinkers as Buber, Freud, and Sartre.

LITERARY TECHNIQUES

Irwin, W. R. *The Game of the Impossible: The Rhetoric of Fantasy*. Urbana: University of Illinois Press, 1976. Examines some of the common characteristics of fantasies written between 1880 and 1956, a period in which, according to Irwin, fantasy existed as a distinct literary mode. Selected works by major fantasists are analyzed for their intrinsic importance and illustrative value.

Kennard, Jean E. *Number and Nightmare: Forms of Fantasy in Contemporary Fiction*. Hamden, Conn.: Archon Books, 1975. A discussion of the techniques and devices used by Joseph Heller, John Barth, James Purdy, Kurt Vonnegut, Jr., Anthony Burgess, Iris Murdoch, and William Golding to deal with existentialism, absurdity, and myth.

AUTHOR STUDIES

De Campe, L. Sprague. *Literary Swordsmen and Sorcerers: The Makers of Heroic Fantasy*. Sauk City, Wis.: Arkham House, 1976. The evolution of sword-

and-sorcery fantasy through biographical sketches of its leading practitioners whose works were central to the evolution of the genre: William Morris, Lord Dunsany, H. P. Lovecraft, E. R. Eddison, Robert E. Howard, Fletcher Pratt, Clark Ashton Smith, J. R. R. Tolkien, and T. H. White.

Manlove, C. N. *Modern Fantasy: Five Studies*. New York and London: Cambridge University Press, 1975. A major literary analysis and evaluation of the achievement of five fantasy authors—Charles Kingsley, George MacDonald, C. S. Lewis, J. R. R. Tolkien, and Mervyn Peake—with an introduction discussing the nature and character of fantasy.

Index

About the Editors and Contributors

Frederick J. Beharriell is Professor of German and Comparative Literature at SUNY, Albany. The recipient of both Guggenheim and Fulbright fellowships, he has published numerous studies in modern German literature in *PMLA*, *The German Quarterly*, *Literatur und Kritik*, and elsewhere.

Mark Bernheim teaches English at Miami University, Oxford, Ohio, and spends his summers at Chautauqua. He has published articles about business communications, modern literature, and Jewish studies.

Douglas A. Burger is Associate Professor of English at the University of Colorado, where he also serves as Director of Undergraduate Studies. A teacher of Chaucer and fantasy literature, he has published in *Chaucer Review*.

Currently teaching at Dalton Junior College, Rebecca R. Butler has received a National Defense Education Act fellowship and an English-Speaking Union travel grant and has participated in a National Endowment for the Humanities seminar in southern literature. Her recent articles are studies of the fiction of Flannery O'Connor and Walker Percy.

Peter Cersowsky was a scholar of the German National Fellowship Foundation and has taught German literature at the University of Würzburg, where he is now a doctoral candidate. He has published an article about Kafka and has been working as a free-lance music critic.

Amaryll B. Chanady has taught at the University of Regina and the Lycée J.-B. Pocquelin in Paris, has held a Carleton fellowship, and was a Killam Scholar for three years. An editorial assistant for the *Canadian Journal of Comparative*

Literature, she has been awarded a doctoral grant by the Social Sciences and Humanities Research Council of Canada.

Michael R. Collings is Assistant Professor of English at Pepperdine University, where his courses include science fiction. He is the author of an article about C. S. Lewis and a volume of poetry and has recently had several science fiction short stories accepted for publication. He is now preparing the book *A Reader's Guide to Piers Anthony*.

Robert A. Collins is Associate Professor of English at Florida Atlantic University. He has published widely about science fiction literature and literature of the fantastic. He is the founder of the International Conference on the Fantastic in the Arts and is Editor of the *Fantasy Review*.

L. L. Dickson is Associate Professor of English at Northern Kentucky University. He has published poetry in the *Beloit Poetry Journal* and articles about William Golding. A book-length study of Golding's novels is forthcoming.

Laurie Edson is Assistant Professor of French at Harvard University and specializes in symbolist poetry and twentieth-century French literature. She has published articles about Henri Michaux and recently completed a book on his work.

Margaret Peller Feeley is Lecturer in English at the University of Wisconsin at Whitewater. She has published articles about Rudyard Kipling, Flannery O'Connor, and the novel as a creative process and is currently completing the book *Metamorphoses of Rudyard Kipling*.

S. Casey Fredericks is Associate Professor of Classical Studies at Indiana University, Bloomington. He is coauthor of *Roman Satirists and Their Satire* and *Atlantis: Fact or Fiction?* and has contributed numerous articles to *Science Fiction Studies* and *Helios*, journals for which he also serves as editorial consultant.

An Assistant Professor of German at Columbia University, Shelley L. Frisch has published articles about Middle-High German, Romantic literature, and the films of Wim Wenders.

Kathleen M. Glenn, Associate Professor of Spanish at Wake Forest University, is the author of *The Novelistic Technique of Azorín* and *Azorín* and has contributed to journals such as *Hispanófila*, *Modern Language Journal*, *Revista de Estudios Hispánicos*, and *Romance Notes*. She is an associate editor of *Anales de la literatura española contemporánea*.

Stanton Hager is a member of Phi Kappa Phi, winner of a Wurlitzer Foundation grant, a recent honors graduate (B.A., M.A.) of Florida Atlantic University, a poet, and a free-lance journalist.

Currently Associate Professor of Languages at Florida Atlantic University, Jan Hokenson completed the doctorate at the University of California in 1974. She has received research grants from the University of California, the Danforth Foundation, the American Association of University Women, and the Republic of France. Author of five major articles on modern European fiction, she has also published minor articles about British and American literature.

A Professor of Spanish and Classics at the University of California at Davis, Didier T. Jaén has published the books *Homage to Walt Whitman*, *José Vasconcelos: La raza cosmica / The Cosmic Race* (a bilingual edition), and *John II of Castile and the Grand Master Alvaro de Luna*. He has written articles about J. L. Borges, Juan Rulfo, Mariano Azuela, and others and is currently working on the book *Borges' Esoteric Library*.

David Ketterer is Professor of English at Concordia University, Montreal. He is the author of *New Worlds for Old*, *The Rationale of Deception in Poe*, and *Frankenstein's Creation: The Book, the Monster, and Human Reality*. His numerous articles and reviews have appeared in *PMLA*, *Mosaic*, *Criticism*, *Canadian Review of American Studies*, and various symposia volumes. His annotated edition of *The Science Fiction of Mark Twain* will be published in 1984.

Clarence Lindsay is an Associate Professor of English at the University of Toledo. He has published articles about Joseph Conrad and a monograph about Hart Crane.

John M. Lipski teaches Romance languages at Michigan State University. His areas of interest include Romance linguistics, literary semiotics, and formal theories of language. His publications on linguistics have appeared in journals such as *Lingua* and *Vox Romanica*; his papers on formal studies in journals such as *Semiotica* and *Poetica*; and his literary studies in *Revista de Estudies Hispánicos*, *Sprache*, and other publications.

Carter Martin is Professor of English and Chairman of the Department at the University of Alabama in Huntsville, a member of Phi Kappa Phi, and the recipient of a Carnegie Foundation grant. His publications include *The True Country: Themes in the Fiction of Flannery O'Connor*.

Will L. McLendon, Chairman of French at the University of Houston, is co-translator of Charles Mauron's *Introduction to the Psychoanalysis of Mallarmé*, author of *Une Ténébreuse Carriere...le Comte de Courchamps*, and author of more than twenty articles about Stéphane Mallarmé, Marcel Proust, André Gide,

Jean Giraudoux, W. R. Irving, and Charles Nodier in journals such as *PMLA*, *French Review*, and *Studi francesi*.

Howard D. Pearce is currently Chairman of the English Department at Florida Atlantic University. He has published articles about American writers of both fiction and poetry, but his major output concerns dramatic literature. His recent writing reveals a developing interest in phenomenological thought.

William G. Plank is Professor of French at Eastern Montana College. Author of numerous papers on philosophy in literature and the history of ideas, especially existentialism, structuralism, and the philosophy of technique, he has recently published *Sartre and Surrealism*.

Educated at Cambridge and Oxford and having taught in the United States, Stephen Prickett is now Chairman of English at the University of Sussex. Besides the detective story ''Do It Yourself Doom,'' his writings include *Coleridge and Wordsworth*, *Romanticism and Religion*, and *Victorian Fantasy*.

Eric S. Rabkin is Professor of English at the University of Michigan. His distinguished list of publications includes *The Fantastic in Literature*, *Science Fiction: History, Science, Vision* (with Robert Scholes), and *Fantastic Worlds: Myths, Tales, and Stories* as well as numerous monographs, articles, and reviews. His chapter in this volume is based on the text of his address as keynote speaker at the First International Conference on the Fantastic.

Richard Alan Schwartz pursued, for one year, computer programming and has been an Assistant Professor of English at Florida International University since 1979. His publications include articles about John Hawkes, Robert Coover, John Barth, and Thomas Pynchon as well as short stories of fantasy. Currently, he is pursuing interests in twentieth-century fiction and in the relationships between science and the humanities.

Kenneth Smith is the author of *Studies in Nihilism and Ideology* and articles about Friedrich Nietzsche and Karl Marx. His illustrations and stories in the fantastic vein have appeared in *Heavy Metal*, *Fantasy and Science Fiction*, *Galaxy*, *Phantasmagoria*, and elsewhere.

Hans Ternes, a native of Rumania, is Associate Professor of German at Lawrence University, Wisconsin. He has published a book-length study of the grotesque in Thomas Mann and articles about Franz Kafka and Friedrich Dürrenmatt in *Germanic Notes* and elsewhere. He has been awarded a fellowship in the School of Theory and Criticism at the University of California, Irvine.

Marshall B. Tymn is Associate Professor of English at Eastern Michigan University. A pioneer researcher in the fields of fantasy and science fiction, he coedits the annual "Year's Scholarship in Science Fiction and Fantasy" in *Extrapolation* and has produced numerous volumes of bibliographical materials, including *Fantasy Literature: A Core Collection*, *A Research Guide to Science Fiction*, and *The Science Fiction Reference Book*.

Ralph Yarrow teaches at the University of East Anglia, Norwich. His current interests include twentieth-century European literature, theories of consciousness, and teaching methods. He has published articles about Rainer Rilke and Paul Valéry and the article "Beetles, Butterflies, and the Metamorphosis of Language."

Jules Zanger is Professor of English at Southern Illinois University. His articles have appeared in a wide variety of journals, including *American Literature*, *American Quarterly*, *Landscape*, and *Educational Theater Journal*. He has been a Newberry Library Fellow, a Heermans Fellow, twice a Senior Fulbright Lecturer, and president of the Midcontinent American Studies Association.

An Associate Professor of history at Eastern Montana College, James D. Ziegler has taught at Eastern Washington State College and Augustana College. During the 1980-81 academic year he was Visiting Fellow, Harvard University, and House Scholar, Dunster House.